The Sustainability of the European Social Model

The Sustainability of the European Social Model

EU Governance, Social Protection and Employment Policies in Europe

Edited by

Jean-Claude Barbier

Emeritus Professor, CNRS, Université Paris 1 Panthéon-Sorbonne, France

Ralf Rogowski

Professor of Law, University of Warwick, UK

Fabrice Colomb

Associate Professor, Evry University, Centre Pierre Naville, France

EE Edward Elgar PUBLISHING

Cheltenham, UK • Northampton, MA, USA

Published by
Edward Elgar Publishing Limited
The Lypiatts
15 Lansdown Road
Cheltenham
Glos GL50 2JA
UK

Edward Elgar Publishing, Inc.
William Pratt House
9 Dewey Court
Northampton
Massachusetts 01060
USA

A catalogue record for this book
is available from the British Library

Library of Congress Control Number: 2014952159

This book is available electronically in the **Elgar**online
Social and Political Science subject collection
DOI 10.4337/9781781951767

MIX
Paper from responsible sources
FSC® C013056
FSC www.fsc.org

ISBN 978 1 78195 175 0 (cased)
ISBN 978 1 78195 176 7 (eBook)

Typeset by Columns Design XML Ltd, Reading
Printed and bound in Great Britain by T.J. International Ltd, Padstow

Contents

Figures

Tables

Contributors

Jean-Claude Barbier is sociologist (Centre national de la recherche scientifique) researcher at the Centre d'économie de la Sorbonne. He conducts extensive comparative research on systems of social protection, especially in Europe, and studies European integration in the domain of social policies, culture and language. His research interests also include epistemological and methodological issues of the very practice of comparison. His recent publications include: *La flessibilità del lavoro e dell'occupazione*, Donzelli, Roma (2003) (with Henri Nadel); *Le nouveau système français de protection sociale,* La Découverte, Repères, Paris (2010) (with Bruno Théret); and *Politiques sociales/Social Policies: Enjeux méthodologiques et épistémologiques des comparaisons internationales/Epistemological and Methodological Issues in Cross National Comparison,* Brussels, PIE Pieter Lang (2005) (ed. with Marie Thérèse Letablier). *La longue marche vers l'Europe sociale*, Paris, PUF (2008) was translated and adapted for Routledge, as *The Road to Social Europe, a Contemporary Approach to Diversity and Political Cultures in Europe*, 2013.

Iain Begg is a Professorial Research Fellow at the European Institute, London School of Economics and Political Science. His main research work is on the political economy of European integration and EU economic governance. Recent research and publications have included work on EU cohesion policy, the governance reforms associated with the euro crisis and labour market developments in the EU.

Fabrice Colomb is sociologist, Associate Professor at Centre Pierre Naville, Evry-Val-d'Essonne University. He conducts research on employment policies, systems of social protection and European integration. He is currently working on the interaction between social policies and state development. His recent publications include: *Les politiques de l'emploi (1960–2000). Sociologie d'une catégorie de politique publique*, Presses universitaires de Rennes, 2012; 'EU Law as *Janus bifrons*, a sociological approach to "Social Europe", *European Integration Online Papers*, Vol. 16 (2012) (with Jean-Claude Barbier); 'Le succès des incitations. La construction d'une nouvelle orientation des politiques de l'emploi en France', *Gouvernement et action publique*, no. 3 (2012); and 'Les nouveaux cadres normatifs de la protection sociale' (ed.), *Socio-Logos*, no. 9 (2014).

Christine Erhel is Associate Professor in Economics at University Paris 1 Panthéon-Sorbonne and a member of the Centre d'Economie de la Sorbonne. She is currently the Director of a research unit on public policies and employment (including European policies) at the Centre d'Etudes de l'Emploi (French Employment Research Centre). She is doing research in labour economics, especially on European labour markets comparison, labour market policy reforms and adjustments to the financial crisis. Over the last eight years, she has been leading several projects on job quality indicators and trends in Europe.

Jérôme Gautié is Professor of Economics at the University of Paris 1 Panthéon-Sorbonne. He has worked extensively on labour market policies, low wage work and job quality. His publications on these topics include *Low Wage Work in the Wealthy Countries* (Russell Sage Foundation, NY, 2010), edited with John Schmitt.

Bernard Gazier is Emeritus Professor at the University of Paris 1 Panthéon–Sorbonne. His research focuses on labour market policies and labour market reforms, and develops the 'Transitional Labour Markets' approach. His publications include Günther Schmid and Bernard Gazier (eds) *The New Dynamics of Full Employment: Social Integration Through Transitional Labour Markets*, Edward Elgar (2002).

Miriam Hartlapp is Professor for Multilevel Governance at Leipzig University. Before joining the University in 2014 she was doctoral and postdoctoral researcher at the Max Planck Institute for the Study of Societies in Cologne, worked at the ILO and the WZB Berlin Social Science Center, and was Professor for Governance and Organizational Studies at the University of Bremen. She is co-author of *Complying with Europe: The Impact of EU Minimum Harmonisation and Soft Law in the Member States* (CUP, 2005, winner of the EUSA Best Book in EU Studies Prize 2007) and *Which Policy for Europe? Power and Conflict inside the European Commission* (OUP, 2014). Her research focuses on the EU political system, particularly the European Commission, questions of implementation, (non-)compliance and enforcement, and regulation and governance in multilevel systems, as well as on international, European and comparative economic, employment and social policies.

Maarten Keune is Professor in Social Security and Labour Relations in the Law Department, University of Amsterdam and Co-Director of the

Amsterdam Institute for Advanced Labour Studies. His research deals mostly with the interface between the labour market, the welfare state and industrial relations. His most recent books are *Deconstructing Flexicurity and Constructing Alternative Approaches: Towards New Concepts and Approaches for Employment and Social Policy* (ed. with Amparo Serrano, 2014, Routledge) and *Economy and Society in Europe: A Relationship in Crisis* (ed. with Luigi Burroni and Guglielmo Meardi, 2012, Edward Elgar Publishing).

Aristea Koukiadaki is Lecturer in Law in the School of Law at the University of Manchester. Her research focuses on the empirical study of law and on applied legal and policy analysis, with particular emphasis on labour market regulation, EU social policy and corporate governance. She has published in a number of law (e.g. *Industrial Law Journal*) and social science (e.g. *Economic and Industrial Democracy*) journals as well as in edited book collections.

Paul Marginson is Emeritus Professor of Industrial Relations, University of Warwick, United Kingdom. His research interests are comparative and European industrial relations, including collective bargaining and social dialogue; and employment relations in multinational companies. He has published extensively on these topics, including (with K. Sisson) *European Integration and Industrial Relations*, Palgrave Macmillan, 2006.

Nuria Ramos Martín took her Degree of Law at the University of Salamanca (1992–1997). Afterwards she followed postgraduate legal studies at the Universities of Bristol and Salamanca. From 1999 to 2003, she worked as a researcher and lecturer at the Labour Law Department, University of Salamanca. In 2004, she visited the University of Amsterdam as a Marie Curie Fellow Researcher. In 2005, she successfully defended her PhD thesis (Cum Laude, European Doctorate Label and Extraordinary Doctorate Prize) on 'Equal Treatment in EU Social Law' at the University of Salamanca. Since 2005, she has been affiliated as Assistant Professor to the AIAS/HSI, Law Faculty, University of Amsterdam.

Ralf Rogowski has worked extensively on European labour law and labour market policy and regulations. His publications include *Reflexive Labour Law in the World Society* (2013), *Transforming European Employment Policy: Labour Market Transitions and the Promotion of Capability* (2011, with Robert Salais and Noel Whiteside), *The European Social Model and Transitional Labour Markets: Law and Policy* (2008), *The Shape of the New Europe* (2006, with Charles Turner), *Labour Market Efficiency in the European Union: Employment Protection and*

Fixed Term Contracts (1998, with Klaus Schömann and Thomas Kruppe), and *Reflexive Labour Law: Studies in Industrial Relations and Employment Regulation* (1994, with Ton Wilthagen).

Tomáš Sirovátka is Professor of Social Policy at the Faculty of Social Studies, Masaryk University, closely cooperating with the Research Institute of Labour and Social Affairs. He has carried out a number of national as well as international research projects on social policy and employment policy. He publishes regularly in international journals (including special issues).

Els Sol is sociologist and associate professor at the Faculty of Law, University of Amsterdam. Her main research work is on the evaluation of social policy and governance. Recent research and publications include theory and praxis of re-employment policies, governance reforms and the use of private instruments such as contracts and bonds in the context of public policies.

Mara van der Vos was a student-assistant at the University of Amsterdam, where she completed her Master's degrees in private law and employment law. Currently she is a lawyer in Amsterdam.

Introduction: The sustainability of the European Social Model

Jean-Claude Barbier, Ralf Rogowski and Fabrice Colomb

The sustainability of the European Social Model (ESM) is a topic of highest relevance in the current climate of European policy making. At least since the economic crisis of 2008 the focus of attention has shifted in the European Union to economic and fiscal policies, and the question is: what is the expense of social and employment policies? The future of the latter policies is unclear. In this situation an appraisal of their achievements seems a good basis for an assessment of times ahead.

Until recently the Commission was proud to view integrated economic, social and employment policies as representing an ESM. The concept was repeatedly invoked by Commissioners responsible for social and employment policies (for example, Diamantopoulou 2001). It seemed to characterise not only the special nature of European social policies but of responsible economic policies in general. However, enthusiasm has subsided gradually since about 2004 and we are now in a post-2008 economic crisis era. This certainly demands new perspectives but, at least in our view, does not require abandoning the utopias of the past.

The findings presented in this book are guided by concerns to discover new answers based on research carried out within the FP7 project GUSTO (Governance of Uncertainty: Meeting the challenges of economic uncertainty and sustainability through employment, industrial relations, social and environmental policies in European countries). The book is divided into three parts. The first part deals with general issues related to social and employment policies. It analyses interactions between EU law and national policies from a comparative perspective and discusses the role of the main institutions responsible for interpreting and enforcing EU law: the Court of Justice of the EU (CJEU) and the Commission. Chapters in this part contain analyses of key characteristics of EU governance, including underlying principles like sustainability and the use of alternative legal instruments to hard law in the form of soft law and the Social Dialogue.

The second and third parts are devoted to assessments of core social and employment policies and focus more specifically on governance issues. The second part evaluates the Working Time Directive and its implementation in four countries: France, the Czech Republic, the Netherlands and the UK. Analyses of EU policies regarding social services of general (economic) interest and their implementation in the same four countries are topics of the final third part.

1. THE MOBILISING EUROPEAN SOCIAL MODEL VERSUS THE EXISTING ESM

In the following we use the notion of the ESM as an analytical tool. We distinguish a normative and an analytical dimension. The normative aspect can be linked to a 'mobilising ESM' (Barbier 2008); that is, the ESM as a political resource for mobilisation of actors. The expression 'European Social Model' was first used while Jacques Delors was president of the Commission during an era when competition between the United States and Europe triggered debates among international and especially European elites (Jepsen and Serrano Pascual 2005). The steps leading to the introduction of the European Employment Strategy (EES) in 1997, the adoption of the 'Lisbon Strategy' in 2000, and the ensuing introduction of various open methods of co-ordination (OMCs) in other social policy fields, were influenced both by the debate over an ESM and by competition with the 'US model'.

A number of observations can be made about the ESM. First, the normative ESM bears similarities to the German concept of *soziale Marktwirtschaft* (social market economy), which was promoted as an economic doctrine by German economists such as Alfred Müller-Armack after the Second World War (Müller-Armack 1981). It became the ideological cornerstone of the political project of restructuring the German economy pursued by successive conservative German governments in the 1950s and 1960s and captures well the specific economic model of post-war West Germany. The influence of the concept of social market economy on the normative ESM dates back to the formative years of European integration. It was advocated by the first president of the European Commission, Walter Hallstein, in developing 'a workable model of European competition law' (Mestmäcker 2013). And in this context it should be emphasised that the draft Constitution of the EU contained a reference to the 'social market economy', in addition to the objective of achieving 'a high level of social protection' (article I-3), although it did not mention the ESM (Joerges and Rödl 2004).

Secondly, in order to be able to contrast the concept of an ESM analytically with other 'models', especially the US one, we have to identify the defining characteristics of an 'existing ESM'. For this purpose, we assume an ESM with two 'layers', consisting of an aggregate of the existing national systems of social protection in the 28 member states, plus an EU-level component. Social protection is thereby defined broadly, including traditional sets of institutions and policies pertaining to the national systems of industrial relations and to welfare systems such as health, pensions, education and training (Barbier and Théret 2009). These systems include various sets of actors, and their institutions comprise trade unions and employer associations, labour law and employment rights, as well as the various more or less informal norms governing employment relationships. The use of 'models' is common in the comparative literature on welfare states. This research operates with causal relations between, on the one hand, institutions and systems and, on the other, 'outcomes'. In accordance with such an approach, our two-layered ESM can be operationalised by indicators such as security of income, jobs, poverty, inequality, demographic patterns, employment and activity rates. In such a way it could be possible systematically to compare the US model with the ESM.

Thirdly, in order to understand social protection systems fully it is necessary to establish their structural links with economic policies. For the ESM, which is characterised by a mix of national systems and a quasi-federal layer of institutions and policies, this implies taking into account the complex interaction of four types of policy: (1) EU-level economic and monetary policies; (2) national economic policies; (3) EU-level social policies; and (4) national social policies. With respect to the comparison of the 'existing ESM' with the 'US model', this leads to the question: Does the set of empirical relationships that exist between the four types of policy have any similarity with the US model (Alber 2010, Alber 2006)? Such a question is of significant importance in light of the fact that a great deal of the comparative literature on social policies in Europe tends to support the idea that the very existence of the (normatively defined) ESM will in the long run have to succumb to a US-style free market and competition ('antitrust') policy.

2. THE FUNCTIONS OF THE ESM

It is obvious that the notion of the ESM pursued by the European Commission until recently combines a contradictory set of values. On the one hand, it is largely synonymous with the so-called 'social dimension' of European integration based on values such as security, inclusive society and adaptability that are guaranteed by rights introduced at the supranational level. On the other, the Commission also pursues under the heading of the ESM neo-liberal economic policies of reduced public expenditure for social services, financial sustainability, competitiveness, deregulation, flexibility, and privatisation and individual responsibility.

However, a proper assessment of the ESM needs to look not only at its contradictory content and value basis but at its function as well (Rogowski 2013, ch. 8). The ESM has a number of specific characteristics in this respect that delineate it from any national welfare model. Three functional aspects of the ESM can be highlighted: its multi-layered structure, its decentred and plural nature, and its reflexive style of policy making.

First, the ESM consists of a multi-layered structure, accompanied by multi-level governance. The European Union as such is not the main player in devising and carrying out economic, social and employment policies; the responsibility for carrying out and financing these policies rests with the member states, and they stay ultimately in control. Officially the European Union only assists the member states and acquires competences beyond coordination only in specific areas. Decision making and the provision of welfare and protection are inherently decentred in the European Union. Even the most sophisticated co-ordination efforts at the centre cannot change this fact and 'decentralisation' (or, more accurately, the absence of centralisation) is widely viewed as a positive feature, and indeed appreciated as a major virtue of the model. Coordination is not disguised harmonisation. It is deliberately designed to preserve the right of the member states to be the ultimate decision makers, captured by the subsidiarity principle.

Secondly, the ESM is plural. It does not consist of one but of several models. The plural nature of the ESM supports both homogeneity and diversity (Scharpf 2002). The ESM does not favour a European federal welfare state that replaces national welfare approaches but encourages instead 'competitive federalism' (Barnard 2000) in its coordination policies. Depending on the intensity of the role of state intervention, it is possible to distinguish four basic social security models that are in operation in a variety of combinations among the member states. In the statist model the state is responsible for providing welfare financed out of general taxes. In the solidarity-based social insurance model the role of the state is to provide general regulation under which employees are insured against social risks and employers and employees are obliged to pay contributions. In the corporatist model the state supports the regulation of welfare through collective agreements or company agreements between trade unions and, respectively, employee representatives and employer associations or companies. Finally, under the individualist solution, favoured by neo-liberal economic policies, protection against risks is left to the individual seeking it through private insurance, thereby reducing the role of the state to granting tax relief or other concessions.

The third functional aspect of the ESM is that it is at its very core characterised by reflexive policy making (see Luhmann 1990; Teubner 1993, ch. 5) and an increased use of soft law instruments, in particular the OMC. Reflexive in relation to the OMC means that the EU makes creative use of its limits, in particular limited legal competences. The OMC is policy making in the absence of hard legal competences. In fact, the EU takes advantage of lacking hard law in order to become innovative in introducing new soft law instruments. This self-awareness makes the European Union's understanding of the ESM particular and reflexive. It reflects on the needs for reform of the member states' economic and welfare policies and understands its role as being a facilitator. Reflexive modernisation of economic policies and welfare states is demanded in order to cope with the challenges that both the risk society and globalisation pose. The EU becomes reflexive by reducing its role to acting as the coordinator of self-transformation of the member states (Rogowski 2013, ch. 8).

3. IS THE ESM SUSTAINABLE?

In the following we link the discussion of the ESM to the social sustainability debate that has emerged at the international level and is fast becoming a central topic in EU policy development. The question of the sustainability of the ESM transcends the narrow concern with political conditions for pursuing social and economic policies. It looks at the broader context, including in particular global environmental conditions. In fact, sustainability is nowadays a separate policy discourse in the EU and beyond and includes a specific debate about social sustainability.

a) The Social Sustainability Discourse – General Remarks

The idea of social sustainability originated in the international debate over sustainable development. The paradigm of sustainable development emerged as a normative concept in discussions within the United Nations (United Nations 1993) and combines social, economic, environmental and institutional objectives (UNDSD 2009). It calls into question the orientation towards a global deregulated free trade economy without concern for social or environmental conditions (Thiele 2013).

Social sustainability at the international level and in the EU is closely linked to the Millennium Development Goals pursued by various UN bodies. There is a lively discussion over the right courses by which to pursue the goals, although the EU seems to favour a linkage to trade as the path to sustainable development (Lightfoot and Burchell 2005). The World Bank is particularly active in issuing *Social Indicators of Development* (http://www.ciesin.org/IC/wbank/sid-home.html) which contain data for more than 170 economies, assessing human welfare to provide a picture of the social effects of economic development.

There is a considerable debate over the meaning of 'social sustainability'. For our purposes the working definition offered by Jesse Dillard and his colleagues is useful. They define social sustainability as 'the processes that generate social health and well-being now and in the future, and those social institutions that facilitate environmental and economic sustainability now and for the future' (Dillard et al. 2009, p. 4). This definition captures both the linkage of policy processes and the institutional side needed to achieve the policies in the long run. These dimensions are relevant for an assessment of the ESM.

b) Three Discourses of Social Sustainability in the European Union

Within the debate over social sustainability in the European Union we can distinguish three distinct discourses of sustainability: The socio-ecological discourse, the socio-feminist discourse and the social systems theory discourse of a sustainable ESM.

i) Socio-ecological discourse of sustainability

The socio-ecological discourse dominates the policy discourse on social sustainability in the EU. It acknowledges that ecology has become a main concern of global politics and that economic and social policies have to be streamlined in order to achieve the global ecological goals.

Prominent in the socio-ecological discourse of sustainability is the three-pillar model of sustainability consisting of the ecological, the economic and the social pillar. Sustainability is achieved if these pillars are intelligently combined. There exist various so-called 'policy integration' concepts. Social sustainability is considered an integral part of sustainable development, and social sustainability criteria (in addition to economic and environmental criteria) provide the basis for strategies, initiatives and 'scenarios' (see Begg, in this volume).

The socio-ecological sustainability discourse challenges the 'European development model' for presupposing a trade-off of 'alienating working conditions for a compensation by high consumption levels', externalisation of social costs of production and an unsustainable labour-based social security system (Spangenberg and Omann 2006). The alternative is an integrated system that pays equal importance to each of the three pillars.

ii) Socio-feminist discourse of sustainability

The socio-feminist discourse of sustainability focuses on the link between paid and unpaid work, the latter most often carried out by women. This link should be of central concern in economic, social and employment policies in the EU. Feminists argue that social sustainability is intricately linked to social reproduction and requires in particular addressing the need for better redistribution of care giving between men and women. Achieving equality has to be seen to be integral to long-term social and economic sustainability (Dujon 2009).

If the EU wants to increase female labour market participation the problems of balancing family and work commitments must become central. There are a number of EU policies that indeed address this topic, for example working time regimes. To some extent these policies have been shaped by feminist demands for more flexible and varied working-time arrangements (Conaghan 2006). Although mainly promoted for reasons of economic efficiency, they are nevertheless supported by feminist authors in order to facilitate female employment opportunities and the opportunity for men to engage in care giving. 'In a context such as Poland, where the tensions between employment and social reproduction have been particularly evident since the country's political-economic transition, family- or employee-friendly working-time measures may be key to easing the burdens currently carried by women workers' (Zbyszewska 2012, p. 428).

Linking social sustainability to social reproduction transcends the traditional confines of social and employment policies and requests social sustainability policies that are able to achieve equal opportunities. Stephen McKenzie goes a step further. For him social reproduction is not an individual affair but linked to policies that aim at systemic guarantees of 'even gender structures'. These objectives can only be pursued collectively and should be built on notions of 'community ownership' (McKenzie 2004).

iii) System-theoretical discourse of a sustainable ESM

The focus of the system-theoretical discourse is on the sustainability of the field of European social policy as such. It analyses conditions at the supranational level and is concerned with sustaining the achievements of the ESM at this level. The thesis of the system-theoretical discourse is that successful sustainability of the ESM is linked to reflexive governance (Deakin and Rogowski 2012). The question of sustainability has to be applied to sustainable policies pursued by the ESM itself.

In linking sustainability to appropriate governance, the centre of attention becomes the use of new instruments to achieve sustainable policy goals pursued under the heading 'ESM'. In particular, the increased use of soft law is interpreted as self-aware policy making. In shifting the focus of the ESM from protection to promotion of employment and coordination of welfare reforms in member states, European regulation becomes reflexive insofar as it embarks on conscious regulation of self-regulation.

Furthermore, the system theory discourse analyses EU governance as reflexive in another sense. Social policy making is increasingly confronted with problems that arise from using different OMCs for different social policies. The EU has embarked on reforming this soft law instrument and calls these reforms 'simplification'. In a reflexive governance perspective these reforms can be interpreted as attempts to cope with self-created complexity and engage in 'coordination of coordination', a typical form of reflexivity using the very idea of OMC to reform the method itself (Zeitlin in Armstrong et al. 2008; Kjaer 2010; Dawson 2011; Rogowski 2013, Ch. 8).

4. GOVERNANCE OF THE EUROPEAN SOCIAL MODEL

A main thesis of this book is that the future and the sustainability of the ESM depend on the combination of various modes of governance. A good example of the governance approach adopted for EU social and employment policies is the concept of 'flexicurity'. The linguistically awkward combination of flexibility and security into flexicurity succinctly captures the essence of European social and economic policy making since its inception, a balancing of economic and social interests that understands social and employment policy as an integral part of economic policy (Rogowski 2007, 2008).

EU social policy includes in our definition the entire array of policies and programmes that constitute the systems of social protection and social services, as well as labour law. These areas are often treated separately and by different specialist scholars, predominantly in law, sociology and political science. Whether it is precisely defined or rather crafted in political terms by politicians, a specific ESM has de facto underpinned the entire array of social policies pursued by the European Commission, whereby member states have tended to prefer a 'consociational' mode of governance over more integration of the national systems of social protection.

There exists a substantial theoretical and empirical literature on EU governance. Governance can be differentiated according to the steering modes (more or less hierarchical), the instruments, the decision levels (transnational, regional and local) and the actors involved (public or private, experts or elected representatives ...). We envisage EU governance as the combined purposive intervention of relevant EU-level actors, forming a constellation in the coordination, steering and regulation of a great variety of policy areas.

EU governance is political in many ways, despite the 'non-partisan' appearance it always takes at the EU level (see Barbier and Colomb, in this volume). Because of this political dimension, EU governance can never be equated with the rational management of public choices about public goods: power relationships are always involved (see Smith 2006; Marginson and Keune, in this volume). The Commission makes political choices, for instance by promoting social housing as a safety net in contradiction with the Dutch universal conception of housing corporations (see Sol and Vos, in this volume). Furthermore, there exists a political bias in favour of economic freedoms over social collective entitlements in EU policies, supported by EU law and interpretations of it by the CJEU (see the chapters by Barbier and Colomb, Hartlapp and Rogowski, in this volume).

The main actors in promoting a de-politicised approach in EU policy making are the CJEU and the Commission. The CJEU's decision-making practice contributes to a surface de-politicisation, which is also visible in the discourse and lexicon used by the EU Commission. However, since distributional issues are always in the background, 'de-politicisation' cannot be taken as an empirical fact, as the handling of the economic crisis since 2008 has amply demonstrated (Barbier 2013).

Inspired by the literature on governance 'instruments' (Lascoumes and Le Galès 2007), and for the sake of simplifying the present analysis, we suggest that five main instruments constitute the core substance of EU governance in the area of social protection and social rights. These are:

1. Legislation and formal regulation in the form of EU law; regulative decisions (for instance, 'prudential' regulation) of the independent and autonomous European Central Bank form part of this first instrument.
2. The second instrument is money redistribution (at the EU level, the Structural Funds and the Common Agricultural Policy).
3. The third instrument acts by way of devising, promoting and disseminating common standards, strategies and ideas, and here the ideal-typical instrument is the OMC (Rogowski 2013, Ch. 8). The best known example among EU policies is macroeconomic and monetary coordination (using 'Broad Economic Policy Guidelines'). Other specific coordination policies can be found in the area of 'sustainable development' (see Begg, in this volume) and for employment policies in the form of the European Employment Strategy (see by Erhel, Gautié and Gazier, in this volume; and Rogowski et al. 2011).
4. A fourth instrument of governance is provided by negotiations between social partners at the EU or at sector level ('social dialogue'; see Marginson and Keune, in this volume).
5. A fifth instrument is also involved; that is, communication with the general public. To use Viviane Schmidt's typology, this latter mainly refers to a 'communicative discourse', as opposed to a 'coordinative' type of instrument (Schmidt 2006). This form of coordination is not addressed as such, but the reader will find that it is present in many of the chapters.

The use of these instruments is directly influenced by unequal power resources. Much social science literature has emphasised the 'newness' of the instruments used in EU policy making, and some social scientists have been fascinated by what they observe as promotion of a Habermassian discursive democracy by new soft law instruments (Goetschy 2003; Jacobsson and Vifell 2003; Zeitlin and Trubek 2003). Empirical work, however, has shown that this is at best a dream (or perhaps a nightmare) (Büchs 2007; Kröger 2007; de la Porte 2008). Even when scholars were able to precisely identify 'learning effects', they had to take into consideration that power relationships were involved in what was learned and by whom (Barbier 2013).

5. THE ESM IN THE LIGHT OF EMPIRICAL ANALYSES

Several contributions in this volume combine sociological accounts of EU policy making with legal analyses in evaluating modes of governance. Some focus on new methods of governance, like multi-level governance (Marginson and Keune, in relation to the Social Dialogue) and the OMC (Erhel, Gautié and Gazier), while others compare hard law making in the form of the 'community method' with new methods of governance (Hartlapp; Rogowski). Areas of European social and employment policies covered in these contributions are social inclusion, active ageing policies and job or employment quality. They provide sober accounts of achievements of the EES and the Lisbon Strategy and contain evidence that the idea of an ESM has often served as a fig leaf or Trojan horse for the relentless pursuit of neo-liberal free market policies at the EU level (Countouris and Freedland 2013).

Parts II and III of the volume contain comparative empirical assessments of governance and regulation in two policy areas: the regulation of working time and social services of general interest. The contributions in these two areas analyse the reality of implementation of EU law and political change as a result of European policies in four countries: the Czech Republic, France, the Netherlands and the United Kingdom. Social services, on the one hand and labour law, on the other serve here not as representative areas of governance of social policy but as highly significant areas of the play existing today between EU governance and the traditional national means of governance and government.

The case studies on the Working Time Directive confirm the diversity of worlds of compliance that has been found in previous research on enforcement of EU law (Falkner et al. 2005). Each of the countries studied adopts a specific way of implementing and coping with European demands. Implementation has been ambivalent in most countries, with improvements for some categories of employees combined with new uncertainties, due to opt-out policies and unclear reform attempts of the directive at the EU level. Moreover, research presented in this part reveals a number of ways in which member states have tried to influence European policies in order to convert their own policies into EU law.

In the case of social services the case studies reveal that implementation of EU law and policy is widely differentiated. In the Netherlands the threat to Dutch policy of social housing deriving from European law and policies on services led to a challenge to European law in front of the CJEU. In the UK, not only social housing but also social care and health care have been significantly transformed by EU law. In the Czech Republic, EU service provisions had a particular impact on labour law and employment services, leading to interesting interactions of EU law and Czech law. In France, finally, the areas of old-age care and child care, domains where associations are dominant, were negatively affected by the implementation of the Services Directive.

The findings show that the current ESM is under considerable strain as a result of uneven social and economic policies. In order to maintain its distinct character of balancing economic and social interests that understands social and employment policy as an integral part of economic policy and as an important factor of production in the European economy, the ESM has to face up to the new challenges. These derive nowadays also from global competition (Moreau 2011; Schiek 2013). Bold approaches to boost European social and employment policy through, for example, the introduction of European unemployment insurance (Chopin and Fabre 2013) and comprehensive social risk management (Schmid 2006, 2008) can be helpful to stem the neo-liberal tide. However, the analyses of policies and the case studies in this book show that in the medium term the sustainability of the ESM depends heavily on addressing governance failures and rethinking European governance.

The editors are well aware of the great transformation that was brought to 'Social Europe' as a consequence of the economic crisis since 2008. The neo-liberal redirection of EU policy making in addressing uncertainties and ambiguities regarding appropriate governance/government in the European Union increasingly irritates voters (citizens). Recent elections, conducted at the supranational and the national levels, have shown a growing concern with the European integration process, thereby reducing the margin of manoeuvre for technicians and non-partisan experts (Scharpf 2014). However, it is an open question if 'politicisation' will lead to 'resocialising Europe' (Countouris and Freedland 2013) or to further victories of the 'EU liberalisation machine' (Streeck 2014) that is flattening not only economic and fiscal but increasingly also social and employment policies in the European Union.

BIBLIOGRAPHY

Alber, J. (2006), 'The European Social Model and the United States', *European Union Politics*, **7** (3), 393–419.

Alber, J. (2010), 'What the European and American Welfare States Have in Common and Where They Differ. Facts and Fiction in Comparisons of the European Social Model and the United States', *Journal of European Social Policy*, **20** (2), 102–125.

Armstrong, K., I. Begg and J. Zeitlin (2008), 'The Open Method of Co-ordination and the Governance of the Lisbon Strategy', *Journal of Common Market Studies*, **46** (2), 436–50.

Barbier, J.-C. (2008), *La longue marche vers l'Europe sociale*. Paris: PUF.

Barbier, J.-C. (2013), *The Road to Social Europe: A Contemporary Approach to Political Cultures and Diversity in Europe*. Abingdon and New York: Routledge.

Barbier, J.-C. and B. Théret (2009), *Le système français de protection sociale*. Paris: La Découverte.

Barnard, C. (2000), 'Regulating Competitive Federalism in the European Union? The Case of EC Social Policy', in J. Shaw (ed.), *Social Law and Policy in an Evolving European Union*. Oxford: Hart, pp. 49–69.

Borrás, S. and K. Jacobsson (2004), 'The Open Method of Co-ordination and New Governance Patterns in the EU', *Journal of European Public Policy*, **11** (2), 185–208.

Büchs, M. (2007), *New Governance in European Social Policy: The Open Method of Coordination*. Basingstoke: Palgrave.

Chopin, T. and A. Fabre (2013), '"Social Europe", a Lever for Euro Zone Integration', Robert Schuman Foundation, European Issues Policy Papers no. 292. Available at: http://www.robert-schuman.eu/en/doc/questions-d-europe/qe-292-en.pdf. Last accessed 19 May 2014.

Conaghan, J. (2006), 'Time to Dream? Flexibility, Families and the Regulation of Working Time', in J. Fudge and R. Owens (eds), *Precarious Work, Women and the New Economy: The Challenges to Legal Norms*. Oxford and Portland, OR: Hart Publishing, pp. 101–30.

Countouris, N. and M. Freedland (eds) (2013), *Resocialising Europe in a Time of Crisis*. Cambridge: Cambridge University Press.

Dawson, M. (2011), *New Governance and the Transformation of European Law: Coordinating EU Social Law and Policy*. Cambridge: Cambridge University Press.

De la Porte, C. (2008), The European Level Development and National Level Influence of the Open Method of Coordination: The Cases of Employment and Social Inclusion. Thesis. Fiesole: European University Institute.

Deakin, S. and R. Rogowski (2012), 'Reflexive Labour Law, Capabilities and the Future of Social Europe', in R. Rogowski, R. Salais and N. Whiteside (eds), *Transforming European Employment Policy – Labour Market Transitions and the Promotion of Capability*. Cheltenham and Northampton, MA: Edward Elgar, pp. 229–54.

Diamantopoulou, A. (2001), The European Social Model: Promoting Economic and Social Progress. Speech of the Commissioner responsible for Employment and Social Affairs at the European Commission in Tallinn on 19 March 2001, address to the International Conference on Achieving Balanced Economic and Social Growth. Available at: http://europa.eu.int/comm/dgs/employment_social/speeches/010319ad.pdf. Last accessed 19 May 2014.

Dillard, J., V. Dujon and M.C. King (2009), 'Introduction', in J. Dillard, V. Dujon and M.C. King (eds), *Understanding the Social Dimension of Sustainability*. New York: Routledge, pp. 1–12.

Dujon, V. (2009), 'In the Absence of Affluence: The Struggle for Social Sustainability in the Third World', in J. Dillard, V. Dujon and M. King (eds), *Understanding the Social Dimension of Sustainability*. Abingdon and New York: Routledge, pp. 122–36.

Falkner, G., O. Treib, M. Hartlapp and S. Leiber (2005), *Complying with Europe – EU Harmonisation and Soft Law in the Member States*. Cambridge: Cambridge University Press.

Goetschy, J. (2003), 'The European Employment Strategy, Multi-level Governance, and Policy Coordination, Past, Present and Future', in J. Zeitlin and D. Trubek (eds), *Governing Work and Welfare in a New Economy: European and American Experiments*. Oxford: Oxford University Press, pp. 59–87.

Hall, P.A. and D. Soskice (eds) (2003), *Varieties of Capitalism: The Institutional Foundations of Comparative Advantage*. Oxford: Oxford University Press.

Jacobsson, K. and A. Vifell (2003), 'Integration by Deliberation? On the Role of Committees in the Open Method of Co-ordination', in E.O. Erikson, C. Joerges and J. Neyer (eds), *European Governance, Deliberation and the Quest for Democratisation*. Oslo: Arena Report no. 2/2003.

Jepsen, M. and A. Serrano Pascual (2005), 'The European Social Model: An Exercise in Deconstruction', *Journal of European Social Policy*, **15** (3), 231–45.

Joerges, C. and F. Rödl (2004), '"Social Market Economy" as Europe's Social Model?', EUI Working Paper LAW No. 2004/8. Fiesole: EUI.

Kjaer, P.F. (2010), *Between Governing and Governance: On the Emergence, Function and Form of Europe's Post-National Constellation*. Oxford and Portland, OR: Hart.

Kröger, S. (2007), 'The End of Democracy As We Know It? The Legitimacy Deficits of Bureaucratic Social Policy Governance', *Journal of European Integration*, **29** (5), 565–82.

Lascoumes, P. and P. Le Galès (2007), 'Understanding Public Policy through its Instruments', *Governance*, **20** (1), 1–21.

Lightfoot, S. and J. Burchell (2005), 'The European Union and the World Summit on Sustainable Development: Normative Power Europe in Action?', *Journal of Common Market Studies*, **43** (1), 75–95.

Luhmann, N. (1990), *Political Theory in the Welfare State*. Berlin: de Gruyter.

Majone, G. (1993), 'The European Community between Social Policy and Social Regulation', *Journal of Common Market Studies*, **31** (2), 153–69.

Majone, G. (2005), *Dilemmas of European Integration*. Oxford: Oxford University Press.

McKenzie, S. (2004), Social Sustainability – Towards some Definitions. Magill: Hawke Research Institute Working Paper Series No 27.

Mestmäcker, E.-J. (2013), 'Towards a Concept of a Workable European Competition Law – Revisiting the Formative Period', in K.K. Patel and H. Schweitzer (eds), *The Historical Foundations of EU Competition Law*. Oxford: Oxford University Press, pp. 191–206.

Moreau, M.-A. (ed.) (2011), *Before and After the Economic Crisis: What Implications for the 'European Social Model'?* Cheltenham and Northampton, MA: Edward Elgar.

Müller-Armack, A. (1981), *Genealogie der Sozialen Marktwirtschaft*. Second ed. Bern/Stuttgart: Haupt.

Rogowski, R. (2007), 'Flexicurity and Reflexive Coordination of European Social and Employment Policies', in H. Jørgensen and P.K. Madsen (eds), *Flexicurity and Beyond. Finding a New Agenda for the European Social Model*. Copenhagen: DJØF Publishing, pp. 131–53.

Rogowski, R. (ed.) (2008), *The European Social Model and Transitional Labour Markets – Law and Policy*. Aldershot: Ashgate.

Rogowski, R. (2013), *Reflexive Labour Law in the World Society*. Cheltenham and Northampton, MA: Edward Elgar.
Rogowski, R., R. Salais and N. Whiteside (eds) (2011), *Transforming European Employment Policy – Labour Market Transitions and the Promotion of Capability*. Cheltenham and Northampton, MA: Edward Elgar.
Scharpf, F.W. (2002), 'The European Social Model: Coping with the Challenges of Diversity', *Journal of Common Market Studies*, **40** (4), 645–70.
Scharpf, F. (2014), 'Legitimierung, oder das demokratische Dilemma der Euro-Rettungspolitik', *Wirtschaftsdienst*, Sonderheft, **94**, 35–41.
Schiek, D. (ed.) (2013), *The EU Economic and Social Model in the Global Crisis*. Farnham: Ashgate.
Schmid, G. (2006), 'Social Risk Management through Transitional Labour Markets', *Socioeconomic Review*, **4** (1), 1–33.
Schmid, G. (2008), *Full Employment in Europe: Managing Labour Market Transitions and Risks*. Cheltenham and Northampton, MA: Edward Elgar.
Schmidt, V.A. (2006), *Democracy in Europe – The EU and National Polities*. Oxford: Oxford University Press.
Smith, A. (2006), 'Le gouvernement de l'Union européenne et une France qui change', in P.D. Culpepper, P. Hall and B. Palier (eds), *La France en mutation, 1980–2005*. Paris: FNSP, pp. 343–72.
Spangenberg, J.H. and I. Omann (2006), 'Assessing Social Sustainability', *International Journal of Innovation and Sustainable Development*, **1** (4), 318–48.
Streeck, W. (2014), *Buying Time: The Delayed Crisis of Democratic Capitalism*. London: Verso.
Teubner, G. (1993), *Law as an Autopoietic System*. Oxford: Blackwell.
Thiele, L.P. (2013), *Sustainability*. Cambridge: Polity.
UNDSD Division for Sustainable Development, UN Department of Economic and Social Affairs (2009), *Indicators of Sustainable Development*. Third ed. New York: United Nations.
United Nations (ed.) (1993), *Earth Summit: Agenda 21. The United Nations Programme of Action from Rio*. New York: United Nations.
Zbyszewska, A. (2012), 'Regulating Working Time in Times of Crisis: Flexibility, Gender and the Case of Long Hours in Poland', *International Journal of Comparative Labour Law and Industrial Relations*, **28** (4), 421–42.
Zeitlin, J. and D.M. Trubek (eds) (2003), *Governing Work and Welfare in a New Economy: European and American Experiments*. Oxford: Oxford University Press.

PART I

EU law and governance of social and employment policies

1. The Janus face of EU law: A sociological perspective on European law making and its influence on social policy in the EU[1]

Jean-Claude Barbier and Fabrice Colomb

1.1 INTRODUCTION

In order to assess the influence exerted on 'social policy'[2] by the European Union as one actor in a 'multi-level' governance system, it is essential to focus on law. What was emerging 20 years ago (Leibfried and Pierson 1995) is all the more visible now. The consequences of the gradual Europeanisation[3] of law in the areas of social protection and social rights have been documented by political scientists (Falkner et al. 2005; Ferrera 2005; Falkner and Treib 2008; Martinsen 2009; Scharpf 2010; Höpner 2011) and by legal research (Davies et al. 2005; Rodière 2008; Bercusson 2009). However, sociological approaches analysing the

---

[1] A different and shorter version of this chapter was published in J.-C. Barbier and F. Colomb (2012), 'EU law as *Janus bifrons*, a sociological approach to "Social Europe"', in Jean-Claude Barbier (ed.), *EU Law, Governance and Social Policy*, European Integration online Papers (EIoP), Special Mini-Issue 1, Vol. 16, Article 2. Available at http://eiop.or.at/eiop/texte/2012-002a.htm. Accessed 22 May 2014.

[2] 'Social policy' is a shortcut, as is 'welfare policy' or 'the welfare state'. Empirically the scope of our research encompasses the entire systems of social protection, the systems of labour law and the provision of social (often public) services.

[3] The Europeanisation of law is the gradual transformation of national law through the incremental insertion into it of elements of EU law that merge with it. In a sociological view, Europeanisation includes the socialisation processes of actors engaged in law making.

phenomenon have remained rare (Vauchez 2008; Favell and Guiraudon 2011). This chapter is an attempt to bridge this gap. It focuses on the role of actors, both at the national and the EU level, as they are affected by the implementation of EU law, but also as they participate in EU law making in various ways. The central finding of our study lies in the ambivalent role of EU law and the variable support it commands among actors across the European Union. New social rights have been added over the years for individuals and new freedoms for firms. Yet, at the same time, threats to social protection and collective entitlements have appeared, because of the intrinsic asymmetry of EU law, and because of various spill-over effects. Actors are thus confronted with EU law as *Janus-faced*. One face promises opportunities, the other poses threats. Hence, there are two groups of actors, individuals or interest groups and organisations: those which are and feel threatened and those relishing and using the possibilities opened up for them by EU law. This opens up to a political bifurcation. What we found in meeting actors and in discussing with legal scholars is increased politicisation of EU law in the social domain: for this policy area, this is a new phenomenon.

The chapter proceeds in four steps. First, we describe our sociological approach and methods. We identify what we call the relevant 'social actors' (actors of social policy) in defined spaces, where EU law and governance are discussed. Following Bruno Jobert (1998, 2003), we call these spaces fora. In some cases, we are also able to situate them in 'arenas' where decisions are made. As no research is able to cover the whole area of social policy coordination at the EU level, we chose to focus on case studies that we considered highly significant. Secondly, we analyse the special institutional characteristics of EU law and contrast them with traditional social policy in the national context. Next, we deal with our central object, the ambivalence of EU law and explore it through themes that arose from the interviews and were 'triangulated' with views of legal scholars interviewed (and our review of the legal literature). Four aspects emerged as central: the subordinated status of social law at the EU level; the uncertain 'implementation' of EU law; the tension between economic and social rights, and, last but not least, the ambiguities of EU social citizenship. Finally, in an exploratory manner, we conclude by identifying coalitions of actors. This latter reflection leads to a broader theme – the comparative legitimacy of EU and national governments/ governance – which emerged as central in the evolution of the EU in 2014 after the completion of our sociological fieldwork.

1.2 A SOCIOLOGICAL VIEW OF RELEVANT ACTORS, OBSERVED IN THEIR FORA AND ARENAS

'Social actors', that is, actors involved in the implementation of social policy in the broad sense chosen here (see note 1), play two main roles with respect to EU law. They are first involved as the object/target of EU law application, which, after being transposed, is incorporated into national law. For actors in the social domain, EU law is a relatively new concern. They are foremost national actors accustomed to national law and it is only because the reach of EU law has gradually extended into more and more areas of social policy (Rodière 2008; Hartlapp 2012; Barbier, chapter 11 in this volume) that they have become aware of its importance. We observe increasingly a second relationship to EU law resulting as a consequence of greater involvement with EU law. Secondly, social actors have developed judgements and opinions about EU law and criticise or, alternatively, praise EU law; they actively comply with it and promote it, or, alternatively, resist its implementation (for instance by resorting to non-application or to litigation) and try to influence its making. This role is not only observable, however, in national 'spaces'. It mainly takes place at the EU level, and the most common form it takes is lobbying in the EU fora. Hence, as table 1A.1 (in the Appendix) shows, one should not assume a clear-cut separation between 'national' and 'EU level' actors. Apart from national administrations and the formal EU institutions, sociologically, all the actors concerned with the application of EU law are in practice at the same time national actors and potential participants in fora at the EU level (this is why table 1A.1 has a similar list of categories at both levels). All actors also have a link to a personal/national history in one or more countries, even when they have acquired the role of participants in the 'Brussels fora'. Legal experts and the legal community in general also act both at the EU and the national level.

Before describing in some detail how we draw the map of the actors we consider 'relevant' for the purpose of the present research, it is important to be specific about what we call 'fora' and 'arenas' – the places where we meet them. We rely on Bruno Jobert's essential distinctions (Jobert 1998: 133–37; 2003), for whom fora and arenas are sites that have a predominant cognitive and normative dimension and where the formation of policies takes place. What informs the policy is what he calls the '*référentiel*' (Jobert 2003), which can be translated as 'frame of reference', where ideas and interests are not strictly separable.[4] Actors participate in the formation of policies in three main types of fora: the 'fora of political communication', the 'fora of policy communities' and the 'scientific fora'. Jobert distinguishes fora, where debate about policies is conducted, from arenas, where a smaller number of actors participate, reach compromises and make decisions. How does this help the present research? We concentrate our observations on the 'fora of policy communities', where actors belonging to a particular area, or network of policy, meet. National 'policy communities fora' in the area of social services, for instance, are not insulated from EU-level social services fora. In these fora we identify the relevant actors for our interviews. Understanding the role of the 'scientific fora' in social policy is not a task with which we will deal in the present chapter. However, as researchers who have been involved in evaluation studies, in consultancy and in various scientific and dissemination activities over the last 20 years (Barbier 2008), we are aware that participation in these scientific fora provides highly informative long-term participatory observation from within. This position has many advantages for the identification of actors because policy communities fora and scientific fora overlap to some degree.

Our typology of actors (presented in table 1A.1) distinguishes five types. Types 1 and 2 group the social actors who manage social protection (unions have a special role and cannot be confused with nongovernmental organisations (NGOs)), which are providers of services (among them, commercial actors). Essentially we meet their representatives in professional organisations, but also some direct providers. Types 3 and 4 group together the formal institutions of the EU. Note that the Commission belongs to both types: in type 3, the Commission is considered both for its administrative and legislative roles (it shares the latter with the Council and the European Parliament). In type 4, alongside the Court of Justice of the European Union (CJEU, formerly ECJ), it is considered as the author of legal decisions. Four long (and essential) interviews were conducted with this type of actor, three with former *référendaires* in the Court and one with a legal specialist in the Commission administration. Finally, type 5, translators, although marginal for the present chapter, is nevertheless relevant for the whole interpretation because language is important for the very existence of law.

---

[4] For readers more accustomed to English-language literature, the closest approximation, from which however Jobert wants to distance himself, would be the notion of 'paradigm', in Peter Hall's terms.

What themes within social policy did we select? The themes were social services of general interest, labour law and social policy coordination. The interviews listed in table 1A.1 include two case studies conducted in France, but do not include three other case studies conducted by colleagues in the Netherlands (see Sol and Vos, chapter 12 in this volume), in the Czech Republic (Sirovátka, chapter 14 in this volume) and in the United Kingdom (see Koukiadaki, chapter 13 in this volume). The findings which are presented in the following sections are illustrated by quotations drawn from the interviews. The general interpretation of the corpus of interviews is the result of their comparison and 'triangulation' with views derived from discussions with legal scholars. Moreover, in the course of four years of research it was possible to meet some of our interviewees several times, and we were thus able to cross-check their answers with previous statements. As one of our interviewees in the DG Employment of the Commission noted in December 2010, fora are small worlds: 'it's a family, it's a club, and they are always the same, rotating among themselves'.

1.3 THE FOREIGNNESS OF EU LAW: SPECIAL CHARACTERISTICS

Law is part of the everyday life of citizens and meeting actors dealing professionally with EU law always brings to the fore a strong contrast with their idea of what law ordinarily is, namely 'national law'. The situation is different with EU law, because, we learn when talking to EU law makers, it has to be foreign in principle. Only a handful of our interviewees are conscious of this fact. European lawyer-linguists certainly know that it is part of their task. 'We try and avoid sticking too closely to national terms', report two lawyer-linguists interviewed in the Council's administration.[5] They are officially instructed to choose legal concepts that are different from any counterpart notion in national legal systems. Indeed, guidelines prescribe lawyer-linguists and reviser lawyer-linguists to avoid terms too closely linked to the national legal orders (Piris 2006).[6] It is more surprising that even experienced legal scholars

[5] Interview, March 2011, EU Council.

[6] '*En ce qui concerne la terminologie proprement juridique, il faut éviter les termes trop étroitement liés aux ordres juridiques nationaux*', Guideline 5.3.2, p. 19, of the *Guide pratique commun du Parlement européen, du Conseil et de la Commission à l'intention des personnes qui contribuent à la rédaction des textes législatifs au sein des institutions communautaires* (French version 2003).

are unaware of this fact.[7] Indeed, compared with national law, the possibility of a 'common legal culture' is much more improbable with regard to EU law, which in principle is not grounded in any of the legal systems of the member states (Kjaer and Adamo 2011). The very fact that EU law is formulated and translated into many languages – 95 per cent of texts are now originally drafted in English[8] – implies that it is written in a language cut from the ordinary legal consciousness, not only of the concerned actors, but also of citizens in general. A case in point here is the term 'workers', which is used in chapter 1 of Title IV of the Treaty (TFEU) (freedom of movement of workers), which means something different from the British legal term 'worker'.[9] From interviews with members of the Court,[10] we get the clear impression that this legal and linguistic strategy is part of the collective goal to build a *sui generis* legal order. No wonder then that, as we will see in the following section, a general puzzlement at the term 'social services of general economic interest' is constantly documented, and even more in the 'new' member states: in the Czech Republic, 'the concept is still studied'[11] (see also Sirovátka, chapter 14 in this volume). In a way, some form of common 'misfit' with the classic term (i.e. public services) is incorporated ex ante into the legal system.

Apart from these basic linguistic problems (Kjaer and Adamo 2011), certain characteristics of EU law immediately stand in contradiction with the principles generally taken for granted in national law. They can be summed up easily in the following way. First, from the initial negotiations with member states about introducing new EU legislation to the eventual adoption of Directives and Regulations by the Council, the creation of EU law takes significantly longer than national legislation (Falkner et al. 2005; Falkner and Treib 2008). In EU fora and arenas, the process generally starts with the Commission drafting EU legislation

[7] At a Copenhagen conference on social services (May 2011), a specialist of competition law confessed to the audience that he 'still had problems' with the term 'undertakings' used in EU law instead of the more common term 'firms' or 'companies'.

[8] Interview, EU Council, March 2011.

[9] Accordingly the French version '*les travailleurs*' is distinct from the mainstream French '*salariés*'; the German version, for its part, has '*die Arbeitskräfte*' instead of the German classic '*Arbeitnehmer*'.

[10] For reasons of confidentiality we cannot be more specific about the identification of the four persons interviewed in 2010 and 2011.

[11] Legal scholar, May 2011, Copenhagen conference on social services.

(Directives and Regulations) after lengthy rounds of consultations. Certainly not all the Directives take as long to adopt as the Working Time Directive – three years between the Commission's proposal and the final passing in 1993.

Secondly, at the national level, the discussion of law happens in public spaces (*nationale Öffentlichkeiten*) through the media, in parliaments, and so on, and the debate extensively relies on political communication. A special form of political communication – spin – is organised by politicians and consultants for the purpose of marketing their ideas and persons to potential voters. Here we meet the third type of Jobert's fora, 'political communication fora'. None of this has strict equivalents or counterparts at the EU level. EU law has quite different characteristics: despite the increasing role of the European Parliament, it is predominantly a 'judge-made' or 'praetorian' type of law (Scharpf 1999). Despite the flowering forms of Europeanisation in every domain (Favell and Guiraudon 2011), there exist no equivalents for national public spaces for debating and for a distinct, identifiable legitimising process within a polity and a political community via its own political language. The lack of a clear process takes many forms that the actors, both at the national and at the EU level, keep experiencing in their mundane dealings with EU law. 'How to assess the legitimacy of the various NGOs that are supposed to represent us in Brussels?' asks a French Director of a social association; 'these people focus on commas and dots, they are trapped in their own "circus" in Brussels.'[12]

In the last section of this chapter, we will come back to the difficult question of comparing EU and national law with respect to the empirical consequences of their basic characteristics upon the existence of a 'democratic deficit' at the EU level. As many have convincingly argued (Schmidt 2006), democracies experience similar limits at all 'levels'. In political science, it is common to distinguish between 'input legitimacy' and 'output legitimacy' (Scharpf 1999). However, in sociological terms, the objectification of legitimacy is definitely more empirically complex. In the next section we turn to the actors' experience when it is focused on social policy.

---

[12] Interview, March 2011.

1.4 THE OVERARCHING ASYMMETRY BETWEEN ECONOMICS AND 'THE SOCIAL'

Our research took place just after the French and Dutch referenda and the debate over the 2006 Service Directive in which actors and citizens for the first time voiced their discomfort with EU law and its impact on their social rights and social policies. This was an 'intermediary' period between the 'benign neglect' shown in the past by voters and the increased 'Euroscepticism' emerging from the crisis after 2008. The combined effect of negative integration on the one hand, and spill-over effects on the other, took time to really bite in the social domain (Ferrera 2005; Martinsen 2009; Barbier 2013), where positive integration has always been hardest to achieve. In the following we review the four dimensions which emerged as significant for social actors and at the same time were considered relevant by the legal scholars interviewed: the subordination of national law, the uncertain process of implementation, the opposition between economics and solidarity, and the limited hopes opened up by the Charter of Fundamental Rights and social citizenship at the EU level.

1.4.1 Subordination and the Practical Consequences of EU Law Supremacy

NGOs and unions, as well as non-profit organisations engaged in welfare provision, view social protection institutions as essential and key elements of the ordinary functioning of European societies, both politically and economically; social law is core for them because it is able to identify deserving individuals in order to organise redistribution on a legitimate basis. These organisations are disturbed by the immense contrast at the EU level where these realities are only seen as *legal exceptions* and funding for reasons of solidarity enjoys only marginal attention. 'The EU tends to see citizens as consumers on a market for indistinct services, but the associations have always made economic things their own way, which is different and not recognised legally', says a specialist of social services in a French NGO.[13] Furthermore, the contrast emerges not only between EU law and national legal orders, but also between the EU legal order and international labour and other social standards (Bercusson 2009; Supiot 2009; Akandji-Kombé and Leclerc 2001; Roman 2010). Contradictions remain among different legal orders

[13] Interview, May 2010.

and 'it is odd that the European Social Charter – Council of Europe – does not feature among the sources of EU law', a German law professor tells us.[14] The legal community is divided, a French law professor observes, especially with regard to the increasing role of economics in law: 'Economics is a fragile discipline, which is rejected by many legal scholars. Its intellectual value remains poor and ends up as contradicting the proportionality principle.'[15] For a specialist of human rights, and their internationalisation, the famous lawyer Mireille Delmas-Marty, the EU legal order lacked consistency because of fragmentation among the pillars introduced by the Maastricht Treaty (Delmas-Marty 2006, p. 264). She expressed her regret that respect for human rights cannot be invoked legally as part of a European public order against market rules and is not applicable to firms (Delmas-Marty 2004, pp. 151–2). For their part, national legal systems derive their consistency from the fact that under an autonomous constitutional order, they are covering all areas of law. Consequently, because of their long history and embeddedness in the social reality of member states' legislation, social rights and collective entitlements are fully recognised by the courts of the country and are a constitutive part of the legal system. These rights have legally binding effects and are fully 'justiciable' at the national level. This is not the case for social rights at the EU level; for instance for the right to collective action (Bercusson 2009). 'The right to strike is fundamentally jeopardised at the national level by the potential legal contestation of employers that draw arguments from EU law on freedoms of movement. This is especially visible in the United Kingdom.'[16] Similarly, the fear of collective authorities to be seen as trespassing EU law leads them to increase their recourse to cumbersome tenders putting associations in competition with all sorts of private actors, thus disadvantaging small associations.[17]

At the EU level, the role of social law (labour and social protection law) has remained marginal because it always was to remain, at least officially, the preserve of member states' jurisdiction. Despite the evolution of a social dimension, for example in the important domain of anti-discrimination legislation (de Schutter 2004), the initial, economic logic has prevailed in the European integration process and economic and social rights are still not treated similarly in EU law, even after the formal adoption of texts establishing social rights. Social rights are only relevant

---

14 Interview, April 2011.
15 Interview, February 2010.
16 Interview, unionist, Brussels, March 2011.
17 Interview, Brussels NGO, February 2012.

in relation to the functioning of the market (or, conversely, in case they affect negatively the market's functioning). Especially in the older member states, EU social law is often considered as marginal in comparison to national law. This is for instance the case, observes a unionist, for legislation on working time: 'the basics of legislation are national, and what we have in France is difficult application, but only in certain sectors'.[18] EU 'social legislation' often appears as if concentrated on general principles of little actual consequence, because of lack of 'justiciability' (Roman 2010). This is the case for the long list of rights that feature in the chapter 'Solidarity' of the European Charter of Fundamental Rights. 'There is a lack of innovation in the legal services of the Commission, but one needs to find new legal principles for protecting national social arrangements', a legal specialist in the Commission notes.[19] Seen through the EU legal angle, these rights remain de-contextualised, de-territorialised and, thus far at least, have never constituted a serious legal basis for upholding *justiciable collective rights* for a majority of European citizens, who are covered by their own national legislation.

1.4.2 The Vagaries of Implementation: What about Actual Rights?

Social actors are also dismayed at the extremely long and unpredictable process of implementation of EU law: only the strongest actors are able to summon sufficient financial resources and are well incorporated in EU fora and, even more, in arenas, where they are able to use this feature of EU law to their advantage. The main instrument is lobbying but litigation is another well-known strategy. The interminable revision of the Working Time Directive is a case in point here, which took five years and failed to pass (see Rogowski, chapter 6 in this volume). Unions are not able to wait for such long spans of time and they can only rely on their national regulations, but they fear difficult problems in the future, especially with regard to social protection schemes.[20] In social protection and in public as well as non-profit services, actors who contest the extension of EU competition law (because services are deemed to be of an 'economic' nature; see Koukiadaki, chapter 13 in this volume), have been waiting for the European Commission to introduce specific rules, but until December

---

18 Interview, French unionist, June 2011.

19 Interview, February 2011.

20 Interview, unionist, March 2011.

2011 with no result.[21] As a result, from the asymmetric point of view of EU law, social care or childcare services are still seen as comparable in principle with large service networks (the railways, electricity). It is one of the topics on which the legal community appears divided (Krajewski et al. 2009), but where private firms implement apparently successful strategies in order to delay the adoption of new provisions and increase their market share. Particularly in the Netherlands, the case of social housing is a controversial but typical case in point (Sol and Vos, chapter 12 in this volume).

More generally, as far as implementation of law is concerned, the process at the EU level is decidedly more arcane, obscure, uncertain and risky than the already obscure, specialised and uncertain process at the national level. This situation is, *inter alia*, the outcome of the length of the chain of actions that take place from the initial drafting to the eventual application (Falkner et al. 2005; Hartlapp 2007). A situation can easily prevail whereby, unless explicit litigation is started, EU law may remain a 'dead letter', as Falkner and Treib (2008) have observed for Central and Eastern European countries (see Sirovátka, chapter 14 in this volume). Actors in the social protection and non-profit organisations whose representatives we met in France and Germany reported that they had little, if any, 'grip' on the law-making process, all the more so as there is no homogenous 'public space' available in which to develop their usual strategies. 'The national adaptations of EU law are much more opaque than the counterpart processes for national law: associations were kept in the dark for instance, by the French government with respect to the transposition of the 2006 Service Directive.'[22] The fragmentation of the numerous fora and arenas where decisions are prepared and eventually taken may even lead to division within and among NGOs according to their fields of intervention,[23] which sometimes results in the fragmentation of issues debated in the European Parliament.[24] At times, this goes

[21] Several interviews with representatives of French and German non-profit organisations, October 2010. A large literature is devoted to the matter. See for instance Krajewski et al. (2009). See also Barbier (chapter 15 in this volume) for the failed attempts of cooperation between social actors in France and Germany in the late 1990s. On 20 December 2011, a new set of legislation was brought forward by the Commission (see also discussion later in this chapter).

[22] Interview, French NGO, social services expert, May 2011.

[23] Multiple interviews, French associations, September 2009, October 2010, March 2011.

[24] A case in point in this respect has been the creation of a special European Parliament group dealing with situations of extreme poverty (promoted by the

so far as to make EU law preparation and adoption appear as '*un procès sans sujet*' (a process without a subject): this is what a specialist in a French ministry, directly involved in the judicial discussions of case-law, tells us: 'EU law is in the life of every one of us, but no one really draws the consequences; this is the "steamroller" of EU law.'[25] It is striking to listen to high-level officials in the national administrations,[26] especially and directly concerned with the application of EU law, reporting that the whole process is beyond the control of its direct actors. A somewhat deterministic reading of recent jurisprudence in social matters (Supiot 2009; Scharpf 2010) also lends support to a view of EU law as a complex social process without identifiable authors. This impression is corroborated by the discovery that even with careful analysis of the production of legal texts it is difficult, if not impossible, to identify anything equivalent to the 'legislator's intention' that exists at the national level (Kjaer and Adamo 2011, p. 104, p. 109) and this situation is reinforced by the 'foreignness' of EU law for ordinary citizens.

1.4.3 Economics vs. Solidarity: Individual vs. Collective, Mobile vs. Immobile

When we meet social actors, they most often link this foreignness to a perception of EU law as being 'economic'. NGOs, for instance, are deemed to be 'undertakings' and to deliver 'social services of general economic interest', whereas in most countries they have historically been considered as contributing to public services (see Koukiadaki, chapter 13 in this volume). 'It is really a paradox that we, associations, are now part of economic law', says a specialist of social services in a French NGO.[27] This perception certainly does not contradict a significant part of the legal literature. In the economic point of view actively promoted by the CJEU (Neergaard 2009), market provision of social services is always a priori seen as the best outcome. In the words of one of the Commission's legal specialists, the best and most efficient way of providing social services consists in the universal recourse to 'vouchers' that allow

NGO ATD Quart Monde), as opposed to mainstream poverty action (interview, French association, March 2011; confirmed by another interview with the EU-level correspondent of the same NGO, April 2011).

25 Interview, legal expert, French ministry, February 2011.

26 Several interviews (September–December 2010) in the social ministries and in the Foreign Ministry in Paris.

27 Interview, May 2010.

consumers to buy their services from whatever providers they choose.[28] 'Economisation' of law is stressed by many lawyers. When it comes to 'public goods', for instance, among which social protection traditionally features, the CJEU uses a predominantly economic mode of reasoning (Prosser 2005; Supiot 2005, 2009; Deakin and Sarkar 2008; Neergaard 2009, pp. 44–7). As a consequence, individual rights are privileged for individuals, but also for firms, and collective entitlements are disregarded (Camaji 2008) when not directly combated, or considered as an exception to the rule, only legitimate in certain cases. The CJEU is active in promoting mainstream economic ideology which combines the promotion of the market for reasons of efficiency and transparency with the promotion of 'fundamental rights'. It is certainly not by chance that in its case-law this court has taken to declaring the free movement provisions 'fundamental freedoms', an expression that does not feature in the Treaty. In strategic terms the court thus strives to put 'fundamental rights' (as inherited from national legal systems and the international norms of the International Labour Organisation and the European Convention on Human Rights) (Roman 2010) and allegedly 'fundamental' economic freedoms on the same symbolic footing. This equivalence is directly challenged by a significant part of the legal literature, and the actors we meet are well aware of this contentious aspect of EU law. The majority of non-profit providers of social services or social benefits have had great difficulty, especially in certain countries (notably France, Belgium and Germany)[29] in finally accepting that the services they provide are 'economic'. Some still resist the qualification, as for instance the European Trade Union Congress (ETUC).[30]

What strikes social actors even more, in contrast to national law, is that, in spite of the rhetorical presence of 'solidarity' as a legal notion, there is little, if any, effective substantive solidarity at the EU level. To put it more strongly, solidarity is the essential legal category that allows for exceptions to economic law. The famous 1993 *Poucet-Pistre* rulings[31] constitute a key reference in this respect, because this case-law has

---

[28] Professor J.B. Cruz, conference on social services, Copenhagen, May 2011.

[29] Interview, French association, February 2010; German association, May 2011. See also Barbier (2013).

[30] Interview, February 2010, ETUC. In 2008, the ETUC made a proposal for a 'Social Progress Clause' Protocol aiming at counterbalancing the asymmetry between 'social' and 'economic' rights.

[31] Joined Cases C-159/91 and C-160/91 *Poucet and Pistre* [1993] ECR I-637 246, 250.

historically established (actually, created) the criteria of what can be seen as a typical social programme that is exempted from complying with competition rules. Ironically, far from being protected by the market, social protection is thus 'sheltered from the market' (see Koukiadaki, chapter 13 in this volume). This encapsulates the crucial de facto opposition in EU law between individual rights and collective entitlements. It should be stressed that the two crucial pillars of social security constituting essential tenets of the classic welfare state, namely state pensions and state healthcare, are not based on any provision of primary law, but on the fragile ground of a 1993 ruling that could be reversed (Driguez 2010). As a result of the gradual extension of the reach of EU law, non-profit providers of social services and their organisations report the dangers they see for the continuity and quality of the services they most often deliver to vulnerable people: 'With the inadequate levels of obligations for tenders, there is a growing fear of losing the contracts, thus a danger for the continuity and quality of services.'[32] They tell us that they feel powerless in this domain, because the only action possible is through lobbying and mobilising in fora where 'rules for representation are obscure'.[33] At worst, debate occurs only as a result of litigation, as in the *Laval* and *Viking* cases or in the 2010 'Commission versus Germany' case where national arrangements negotiated between social partners were threatened by the application of EU legislation on economic freedoms.[34] 'Negative' notoriety of EU law has thus recently provided the main opportunity for debating social policy across the Union. In contrast to the promotion of economic thought, the attention paid by EU institutions[35] to 'solidarity' is limited (Ferrera 2005; Barbier 2008). This process was exceptionally illustrated in 2014 during the preparation of the elections for the European Parliament.

1.4.4 The Ambiguities of European Citizenship and the Limits of the Charter

Despite general reluctance among social actors in seeing advantages of European citizenship when it comes to collective entitlements and social services, numerous NGOs among our interviewees are fighting for the

---

32 Interview, French NGO, September 2010.
33 Interview, French NGO, March 2011.
34 Interview, European Trade Union Institute (ETUI), March 2011.
35 Interview, DG Employment, December 2010.

promotion of individual rights and are keen on using litigation strategies.[36] National organisations are often taken aback, however, when, for instance, in the struggle against poverty and the support for social protection schemes, they experience contradictions between these two goals that are pursued together in a national context without difficulties.[37] They are also happy to obtain protection of their national systems purely on a national basis, with little consideration for the systems in other member states.[38] In actual fact, since its inclusion in the Maastricht Treaty, European citizenship has unfortunately remained, de facto, the preserve of only a limited number of citizens in Europe; for example, those who are able and willing to move. This is illustrated in the formulation of the Treaty: the only classic social rights presented in it are those of migrants (article 21.3 TFEU). In fact, one dimension that is perhaps difficult to understand for non-specialists, and the citizens themselves, is that EU law in the area of citizenship targets situations of movement between member states (Rodière 2008, p. 195, p. 265). One aspect of anti-discrimination is linked directly to movement – that is, the prohibition of discrimination on 'grounds of nationality'. However, other aspects are much more encompassing, because they concern all the most common grounds for discrimination ('sex, gender, racial or ethnic origin, religion or belief, disability, age or sexual orientation') (article 19 TFEU). Here again, the ambiguous 'Janus-faced' nature of EU citizenship appears: on the one hand, it pertains to fundamental rights. But on the other hand, all the major components of EU citizenship de facto concern citizens who are keen on moving and do actually move, except the right to vote for the European Parliament.[39] The main exception in terms of significant European influence on social and labour rights has been equality between men and women, because of the unexpected spill-over effects of the initial provisions in the Treaty of Rome (namely, ex-article 119; Davies et al. 2005). The great majority of the 26 legal experts we have interviewed since the 2009 implementation of the Lisbon Treaty share the view that the reference to the Charter of Fundamental Rights (its article 6 TEU) will not substantially modify this situation in

---

[36] As one French NGO member reports (January 2010), it has been easier so far to introduce litigation on the basis of the Convention on Human Rights, but his association expects new openings from the future extension of implementation of the Charter of Fundamental Rights (article 6 TEU).

[37] French NGO, interview, February 2009.

[38] German NGO, interview, May 2011.

[39] The number of people working in a country different from their own is estimated at between 1 and 2 per cent of the working age population.

the future. 'Despite face-saving exercises concerning some member states, the legal status of social rights is not modified by its reference in the new Treaty.'[40] The protection of the right to strike, however, is explicit in article 28 of the Charter, and unionists aim at influencing the application of law on this subject through systematic monitoring and intervention in legal cases before national jurisdictions.[41] As was already the case before the adoption and the reference to the Charter, in matters of human rights, the Court of Justice's case-law referred to legal sources originating in member states' legislation and constitutions, as well as to the European Convention on Human Rights.

Finally, the overall impression documented among our actors in the first and second groups of table 1A.1 is legal uncertainty as to the future sustainability of healthcare and pension systems, of labour law and collective agreements, and of social services of general interest, that is, public services. This impression is shared by a majority of the legal experts among the interviewees, but for lawyers, 'legal security' is a concept pertaining to their trade; what French law for instance calls *sécurité juridique*.[42] When sociologists, on the other hand, deal with legal uncertainty or insecurity, they are using a different notion that encapsulates the perceptions of actors.

1.5 CONCLUSION: THE BIFURCATED LEGITIMACY OF THE EU LEGAL ORDER

What conclusions can we draw from this exploration of the views and actions of social actors with regard to their relationship to EU law? The comparison of their points of view with in-depth discussion with legal experts (as well as the taking stock of focused case-law in social services and labour law) shows that the fears of social actors cannot be dismissed as imaginary. The sociological approach is able to document this. As the French president of an influential non-profit organisation told a conference organised by the social services of general interest (SSGI) lobby group in Paris, 'there exists real or alleged legal uncertainty'.[43] The range

---

[40] Interview, official, Council, March 2010.

[41] Interview, ETUC, February 2010.

[42] The French *Conseil d'État* speaks of '*qualité et prévisibilité de la loi*' in its *Rapport public* (2006); Craig and de Búrca, about 'legal certainty' (Craig and de Búrca 2008, p. 555).

[43] Collectif SSGI, A New Deal, the Almunia-Barnier 'package', Paris, 2 February 2012.

of actors that we have interviewed for the present exploratory study is obviously not representative of the full variety of social actors in the EU and national fora and arenas we have been targeting. The main bias of our survey is with regard to the Central and Eastern member states, despite the findings drawn from the Czech case studies (see Sirovátka, chapters 7 and 14 in this volume). A different bias has also been inherent to the angle chosen by the authors of the present chapter, since there is only a limited number of interviews with commercial actors which essentially are only used as a 'mirror' for the perceptions of traditional social actors, the non-profit and public ones. This second bias, however, is somewhat mitigated by the consideration of the UK, Dutch and Czech case studies, where private for-profit provision of services is considerably higher. All in all, the significant material collected draws a picture of endemic contestation by social actors, fears for their future work as non-profit service providers and fears for the future of their national labour law. Because of its exploratory nature, the material is nevertheless insufficient for a comprehensive discussion of the overall legitimacy of EU policies in the areas of social legislation. Yet it is interesting to consider in that it points to two essential conclusions.

1.5.1 Expected and Unexpected Alliances in the Fora and Arenas

First, EU law is far from being only legitimised by the legal discourse articulated by a small group of judges and lawyers. Support originating from commercial actors is documented at the national and the EU level by the literature on European integration (Scharpf 1999; Schmidt 2006) and confirmed by our survey. 'The growth of private provision in long-term care for the elderly is a result of legislation favouring more competition', a French for-profit firm tells us.[44] Two German lobbyists and a German law professor concur in praising the situation in this sector in their country: the 'flexibility of services for the elderly has been greatly increased since the reform of *Pflegeversicherung* which introduced competition', they observe.[45] Less expected, a priori, we also document support by NGOs at the EU level. Strongly supporting individual rights, the legal community, for its part, seems to be united, while, on the other hand, a minority of it points to the destabilising of collective arrangements (Bercusson 2009; Guinard 2009; Supiot 2009), or to the inconsistency of the EU legal order. Some of our interviewees in

---

[44] Interview, French long-term care provider, September 2009.

[45] Interviews, January 2012, March 2011, September 2010.

the 'legal services' of the Commission[46] report their preference for devising correcting mechanisms, in line with the normative aim of trying to 'nest' the systems of social protection (Ferrera 2009), put forward by political scientists or by lawyers (Bercusson 2009). Unions and social security actors are dismayed.[47] In times of crisis, they are joined by new political actors.[48]

But one of our main empirical findings is that NGOs and various advocacy coalitions enter in essential alliances with the legal community, because they share the substantive project of promoting the individual rights of a variety of groups, with the key support of the European Commission. The quest for this type of legitimacy was visible from the early stages in the life of the Court of Justice. This provided it with a key resource, 'moral high ground': the gradual extension of reference to 'human rights', or 'fundamental rights', on the other hand has disturbed the traditional references of traditional social actors, more accustomed to dealing with social rights, social protection and social services. An essential challenge for future sociological studies of the Europeanisation of law is to identify the changing social forces supporting/opposing the legitimacy of EU law in its ordinary functioning. A wealth of literature has insisted on the well-documented fact that economic interests and big firms are at the forefront of this support, and play a key role (Streeck 1998; Scharpf 1999). But what is less stressed in general is that, apart from the overall liberalising of the economy, consistent with the promotion of powerful cross-national economic interests, EU law has also decidedly promoted and safeguarded some rights of individuals from a liberal equality point of view, against classic *raison d'État*. A case in point is the prominent position of the 'anti-discrimination' principle in EU law, which features, along with the principle of equality between men and women, in the Treaty on the same level as European citizenship (article 2 TEU, articles 18 and following TFEU). Anti-discrimination is at

46 Interview, Commission, June 2010.

47 In order to counteract moves by member states, by employers or by the Commission, EU-level union representatives have started devising strategies of litigation in the hope of achieving a more balanced consideration of social rights as against economic freedoms (interview, ETUI, September 2010; see also Bercusson 2009).

48 An interesting case in point is Jérôme Vignon, the former Director of Social Cohesion in the DG Employment and Social Affairs, now retired. In the SSGI conference already mentioned above, addressing the Commission, he declared to the audience: 'Has the moment not arrived today, with the huge deficit of provision in social housing and childcare, for the EU to create new social safeties?' (2 February 2012).

the same time an excellent illustration of the Janus-faced nature of EU law. It is certainly not by chance, then, that its passionate defence is part of all the texts written by former judges of the ex-ECJ. Nor is it surprising to see how the European Commission has eagerly attached its political communication to this aspect of EU politics.[49] Nor is it by chance that the first Report on Fundamental Rights (2010) established by the Commission enumerated a list of individual situations that EU law was especially organised to protect: the rights of women to equality, the special situation of the Roma people, the rights of the disabled. Along the same lines, it is also quite logical that the Court and the Commission concur in defending the cause of marginal and excluded people: people asking for assistance, irrespective of their citizenship rights (Ferrera 2005), poor people, homeless people, and so on and so forth. The otherwise uncertain legitimacy of EU law, often criticised for its privileging powerful economic interests, has found a key basis for indispensable balance there. We just have to read Judge Mancini's plea to understand the logic of this support, when, with the hindsight of 30 years of case-law, he drew a list of individuals that had nominally benefited from the implementation of EU law – all chosen, note, in the realm of anti-discrimination:

> They will do well to look closely at the Court's case law and remember how many of Europe's citizens have benefited directly of the Court's rulings. They will for example remember the Belgian air hostess who claimed the right to the same rate of pay as her male colleagues [*Defrenne* – case 43/775 (1976)], the British nurse who objected to being compelled to retire several years earlier than a male [*Marshall* – case 152/84 (1996)], the German woman who was prevented from getting a job as a canteen assistant at Cagliari university by a practice of discriminating against non-Italians [*Scholz* – case 419/92 (1994)], the French student who wanted to study cartoon-drawing at an academy of fine arts in Belgium and was required to pay a fee not imposed on Belgian students [*Gravier* – case 293/83 (1985)], the Greek hydrotherapist who asked only that his name should not be distorted beyond recognition, when transliterated by an over-zealous German registrar of marriages [*Konstantinidis* – case 168/91 (1993)] and above all the millions of consumers who are the direct beneficiaries of a common market founded on the principles of free trade and undistorted competition. What citizen of Europe has not been assisted in some way by the rulings of the European Court in Luxembourg?
> (Mancini 2000, p. 193)

49 The promotion of the rights of the Roma people led to various conflicts between member states and the Commission.

This points to the existence of a rarely stressed alliance in favour of active support for EU law's legitimacy. Large economic interests motivated by the extension of the frontiers of the market are in fact allied with groups of citizens who have a particular stake and pursue the particular advocacy of a cause. For instance, an objective and paradoxical alliance exists between the EU Commission, presently promoting the interests of homeless people, the NGO which leads this advocacy coalition in Brussels (FEANTSA)[50] and the private for-profit providers of housing across the member states. This coalition stands directly against the interests of social housing corporations in the Netherlands – which, according to statistics and to the Commission's view – are 'abnormally' aimed at rich or middle class households (see Sol and Vos, chapter 12 in this volume). A similar political stance was presented in February 2012 by an official from DG Competition, when, in a conference, she told that when it came to 'upper class housing for the elderly',[51] the social character was doubtful. Another case concerns the NGOs promoting a better recognition of extremely rare diseases which were very active in the coalition of actors that eventually achieved the adoption of the 2010 Directive on cross-border healthcare.[52] A more systematic review of this phenomenon is called for.

1.5.2 Contestation and Uncertainty

Secondly, social actors – the unions, the non-profit providers of services, the key actors in the traditionally 'public' provision of social security benefits – have hardened their defiance and contestation of the EU master discourse. They are certainly not inactive and they are being increasingly heard, as the referendums have shown (Barbier 2008). More recently, a case in point has been the project of a renewed extension of the single market. The 2010 Monti Report to the president of the Commission is typical because it exemplifies a new consciousness among political arenas in Brussels: 'Member states, political groups and stakeholders', it writes, are 'conditional supporters' and it notes that 'a re-launch of the

---

[50] European Federation of National Organisations Working with Homeless People. A comparable social policy NGO is EAPN, the European Anti-Poverty Network, representatives of which we interviewed in France and at the EU level in March 2011. Normative and political conflicts abound among the EU-level NGOs.

[51] SSGI conference, 2 February 2012.

[52] Interview, March, 2011, French ministry.

single market is likely to meet serious opposition'.[53] The problematic situation is exacerbated by doubtful if not negative economic outcomes, the understanding of which goes far beyond the theme of the present chapter. The economic crisis provides a context in which uncertainty keeps increasing and EU and national elites appear divided. The moving and dynamic context in which we find our interviewees does not resemble an inexorable development just led by de-contextualised law, as Fritz Scharpf seems to conceive of it (Scharpf 2010). New proposals for legislation regarding the services of general economic interest put forward in December 2011 by the EU Commission provide an illustration of the fact that, however incremental, margins of manoeuvre are still available to actors in the social domain.[54] Nevertheless, with the hindsight of the previous 20 years (Barbier 2008, 2013) nothing is secured and initial 'social' hopes in the new Lisbon Treaty (Ferrera 2009) have failed so far to materialise decisively. In terms of the interaction between the various instruments of governance, law and macroeconomic coordination have undoubtedly dwarfed the role of the 'soft law' modes of governance. There is every reason to believe that this primacy will obtain for the medium-term future. As the fieldwork for this chapter had been completed in the years 2010–2012, many echoes of the concerns we identified were heard during the run-up to the European elections in May 2014.

BIBLIOGRAPHY

Akandji-Kombé, J.-F. and S. Leclerc (2001), *La charte sociale européenne*, Bruxelles: Bruylant.

Barbier, J.-C. (2008), *La longue marche vers l'Europe sociale*, Paris: PUF.

Barbier, J.-C. (2013), *The Long Road to Social Europe*, Abingdon: Routledge.

Bercusson, B. (2009), 'The impact of the case-law of the European Court of Justice upon the labour law of the Member States', *Labour Law and Social Europe: Selected Writings of Brian Bercusson*, Brussels: ETUI, pp. 459–90.

Camaji, L. (2008), *La personne dans la protection sociale, recherche sur la nature des droits des bénéficiaires des prestations sociales*, thesis, Paris: Dalloz.

Craig, P. and G. de Búrca (2008), *EU Law, Text, Cases and Materials*, Oxford: Oxford University Press.

---

53 'A New Strategy for the Single Market', that was to be followed by a Communication of the Commission in 2011 (COM 2011 206 final 13.4.2011).

54 Adaptations of the legislation by the Commission in December 2011 can certainly be seen as pertaining to these existing margins of manoeuvre.

Davies, P., A. Lyon-Caen, S. Sciarra and S. Simitis (2005), *European Community Law: Principles and Perspectives, Liber Amicorum Lord Wedderburn*, 2nd ed., Oxford: Clarendon Press.

De Schutter, O. (2004), 'The Implementation of the EU Charter of Fundamental Rights through the Open Method of Coordination', Jean Monnet Working Paper 07/04, New York School of Law.

Deakin, S. and P. Sarkar (2008), 'Assessing the long-run economic impact of labour law systems: a theoretical reappraisal and analysis of new time-series data', *Industrial Relations Journal*, **39** (6), 453–87.

Delmas-Marty, M. (2004), *Les forces imaginantes du droit (I): Le relatif et l'universel*, Paris: Seuil.

Delmas-Marty, M. (2006), *Les forces imaginantes du droit (II), Le pluralisme ordonné*, Paris: Seuil.

Dezalay, Y. (2007), 'De la défense de l'environnement au développement durable, l'émergence d'un champ d'expertise des politiques européennes', *Actes de la recherche en science sociale*, **166–7**, 66–79.

Driguez, L. (2010), 'Les institutions de protection sociale face au droit de la concurrence: confirmations ou inflexions?', *Revue de droit sanitaire et social*, **6**, 1048–59.

Falkner, G. and O. Treib (2008), 'Three worlds of compliance or four? The EU-15 compared to new member states', *Journal of Common Market Studies*, **46** (2), 293–313.

Falkner, G., O. Treib, M. Hartlapp and S. Leiber (2005), *Complying with Europe: EU Harmonization and Soft Law in the Member States*, Cambridge: Cambridge University Press.

Favell, A. and V. Guiraudon (eds) (2011), *Sociology of the European Union*, London: Palgrave Macmillan.

Ferrera, M. (2005), *The Boundaries of Welfare: European Integration and the New Spatial Politics of Social Protection*, Oxford: Oxford University Press.

Ferrera, M. (2009), 'The JCMS annual lecture: national welfare states and European integration: in search of a "virtuous nesting"', *Journal of Common Market Studies*, **47** (2), 219–33.

Guinard, D. (2009), *Réflexions sur la construction d'une notion juridique: l'exemple de la notion de Services d'intérêt général*, PhD thesis, Université Paris-Sud XI, Faculté Jean Monnet.

Hartlapp, M. (2007), 'On enforcement, management and persuasion: Different logics of implementation policy in the EU and the ILO', *Journal of Common Market Studies*, **45** (3), 653–74.

Hartlapp, M. (2012), 'Deconstructing EU old age policy: Assessing the potential of soft OMCs and hard EU law', in Jean-Claude Barbier (ed.), *EU Law, Governance and Social Policy*, European Integration Online Papers (EIoP), Special Mini-Issue 1, Vol. 16, Article 3, http://eiop.or.at/eiop/texte/2012-003a.htm. Accessed 22 May 2014.

Höpner, M. (2011), 'Der Europäische Gerichtshof als Motor der Integration: Eine akteursbezogene Erklärung', *Berliner Journal für Soziologie*, **21**, 203–29.

Jobert, B. (1998), 'La régulation politique: le point de vue d'un politiste', in J. Commaille and B. Jobert (eds), *Les métamorphoses de la régulation politique*, Paris: LGDJ, pp. 119–44.

Jobert, B. (2003), 'Europe and the recomposition of national fora: the French case', *Journal of European Public Policy*, **10** (3), 463–77.

Kjaer, A.L. and S. Adamo (eds) (2011), *Linguistic Diversity and European Democracy*, Farnham: Ashgate.

Koukiadaki, Aristea (2012), 'EU governance and social services of general interest: when even the UK is concerned', in Jean-Claude Barbier (ed.), *EU Law, Governance and Social Policy*, European Integration online Papers (EIoP), Special Mini-Issue 1, Vol. 16, Article 5 http://eiop.or.at/eiop/texte/2012-005a.htm. Accessed 22 May 2014.

Krajewski, M., U. Neergaard and J. van de Gronden (eds) (2009), *The Changing Legal Framework for Services of General Interest in Europe: Between Competition and Solidarity*, The Hague: TMC Asser Press.

Leibfried, S. and P. Pierson (eds) (1995), *European Social Policy between Fragmentation and Integration*, Washington: Brookings Institution.

Mancini, G.F. (2000), 'The making of a Constitution for Europe', in *Democracy and Constitution in the European Union, Collected Essays*, Oxford: Hart, pp. 1–16.

Martinsen, D.S. (2009), 'The Europeanization of healthcare governance: implementing the market imperatives of Europe', *Public Administration*, **86** (1), 169–84.

Neergaard, U. (2009), 'Services of general economic interest: the nature of the beast', in M. Krajewski, U. Neergaard and J. van de Gronden (eds), *The Changing Legal Framework for Services of General Interest in Europe: Between Competition and Solidarity*, The Hague: TMC Asser Press, pp. 17–50.

Piris, J.-C. (2006), 'Union européenne: comment rédiger une législation de qualité dans 20 langues et pour 25 États membres', *Revue du Droit public de la Science politique en France et à l'étranger*, **2**, mars, 475–91.

Prosser, T. (2005), *The Limits of Competition Law, Markets and Public Services*, Oxford: Oxford University Press.

Rodière, P. (2008), *Droit social de l'Union européenne*, Paris: LGDJ.

Roman, D. (2010), 'La justiciabilité des droits sociaux ou les enjeux de l'édification d'un État de droit social', in D. Roman (ed.), *Droits des pauvres, pauvres droits, recherches sur la justiciabilité des droits sociaux*, Paris: EHESP CREDOF, pp. 1–40.

Scharpf, F. (1999), *Governing in Europe: Effective and Democratic?*, Oxford: Oxford University Press.

Scharpf, F. (2010), 'The asymmetry of European integration, or why the EU cannot be a social market economy', *Socio-Economic Review*, **8** (2), 211–50.

Schmidt, V.A. (2006), *Democracy in Europe: EU and National Polities*, Oxford: Oxford University Press.

Streeck, W. (1998), 'De la construction du marché à la construction étatique? Réflexions sur l'économie politique de la politique sociale européenne', in S. Leibfried and P. Pierson (eds), *Politiques sociales européennes, entre intégration et fragmentation*, Paris: L'Harmattan, pp. 339–87.

Supiot, A. (2005), *Homo juridicus: essai sur la fonction anthropologique du Droit*, Paris: Seuil.

Supiot, A. (2009), *L'esprit de Philadelphie, la justice sociale face au marché total*, Paris: Seuil.

Vauchez, A. (2008), 'Integration-through-law: contribution to a socio-history of EU political commonsense', *EUI Working Papers* RCAS 2008/10, Florence: EUI.

Weiler, J.H.H. (1991), 'The transformation of Europe', *Yale Law Journal*, **100** (8), 2403–83.

APPENDIX

Table 1A.1 Relevant actors: Relationship to EU law and content of semi-structured interviews

Actors	Number of interviews	Relationship to EU law and participation in EU law making (soft and hard)	Topic (basis for semi-structured interviews)
'National' actors in national fora and arenas (1)	61		
Commercial actors/ businesses	6	Apply law/resist law/act for developing their share/litigate/negotiate with public/lobby authorities	Influence of EU law, role of competition and government
NGOs, associations and non-profit (social services)	20	Apply law/resist law/ negotiate with public/act for protecting their share/ lobby national authorities	Influence of EU law (public procurement, services directive, state aid), role of private competition and change, quality of services; OMCs*
Unions	5	Look for EU resources to use in national fora and arenas/lobby national authorities	Multi-level union action, evolution of labour law (national and EU); OMCs
Public authorities and ministries	20	Negotiate/transpose/ adapt/link to EU law decision/accommodate lobbies	Strategy with Commission, understanding and applying law, negotiation with actors, overall provision and change; OMCs
Legal experts: (social services) + labour law + EU law	9	Explain law; litigate on behalf of actors; apply law; interpret; create and discuss; work with authorities/lobby	Understanding of EU law; dynamic development; articulation of norms; role of legal categories; hard and soft law
Politicians	1	Use of EU law and EU policy resources	Role of the EU and local politics
'National' actors in the EU fora and arenas (2)	27		

Actors	Number of interviews	Relationship to EU law and participation in EU law making (soft and hard)	Topic (basis for semi-structured interviews)
Commercial actors	2	Lobby	Current situation of sector and EU law; actions
NGOs	5	Lobby	Current situation of sector and EU law; actions
Unions	3	Lobby	Current situation of social policy, labour law and social services, union action
Legal scholars	17	Interpret, create law; work with formal institutions; participate in fora and in EU arenas; lobby for EU law formulation	The EU legal order; specific topics being negotiated; understanding EU legal categories; hard and soft law; innovation
Formal institutions of the EU (3) Council and EU Parliament (politicians) Commission as executive and administration	12 2 10	Participate in EU politics and as EU 'legislators' Administer, negotiate, accommodate lobbies, politicise issues, communicate, write texts	Specific interviews Law-making process; present adaptation of governance of social policy (specific topics); soft and hard law
Formal institutions of the EU (4) CJEU and Commission as legal authorities	4	Take decisions and legal rulings, create case law	The making of EU law; EU and national law articulation; EU legal order; evolution of primary law
Persons involved in the translation of texts (EU institutions) (5)	6	Explain, interpret, translate, communicate	Role of EU languages; organisation of language policy for legislation

Notes:
Multiple interviews with the same person over the four year period (2009–2012) are counted as different interviews. The total number of interviews does not include 6 case studies (social services and labour law) conducted by colleagues in the Czech Republic, the Netherlands and the UK nor the 26 semi-structured interviews conducted with experts by M. Hartlapp (see chapter 4 in this volume).

* OMC, Open Methods of Coordination.

2. EU governance of sustainable development: Social and environmental policies[1]

Iain Begg

2.1 INTRODUCTION

The idea of sustainable development (SD) manifestly resonates widely with policy-makers and the public alike. Its roots are in the 1987 Brundtland report, which articulated the now well-known line that SD has to strike a balance between meeting the needs of the present without compromising the ability of future generations to meet their own needs.

There are three distinct facets of the Brundtland report definition that should be stressed. First, a balance has to be struck in depleting scarce resources so that today's generation can enjoy an adequate quality of life without depriving successor generations. 'Scarce resources' in this context comprises a mix of those that are lost irretrievably once consumed (such as oil stocks), those that can be re-cycled (many materials) and those that can be regenerated with competent management (fish stocks). While it might appear invidious to appear to be comparing workers to fish, an argument can also be made that social policies that promote life-long learning are about maintaining the stock of human capital.

Second, the present generation has to avoid leaving a legacy that is detrimental to the well-being of future generations. Environmental degradation is the obvious example here, with extreme forms associated with contamination of industrial sites that will take centuries to recover naturally. However, it is important also to recognise that there are social and economic dimensions to legacies. Extreme poverty or endemic disease are just as debilitating as a poisoned environment and will often be seen as more immediate political challenges. In many African

[1] I am grateful to Jérôme Gautié, Jean-Claude Barbier and other participants in GUSTO work package 5 for comments on a previous version of this chapter.

countries, the loss of such a high proportion of the prime age population to AIDS is having a devastating effect, not just on economic potential but also on social relations. At a political level, actual or perceived inequalities or social injustices can give rise to reactions that culminate in terrorism.

Third, there are the obligations to provide infrastructure and social capital for the future, just as previous generations have provided capital from which today's benefits. A specific element here is pensions and care for the elderly which, in ageing populations such as the EU, raise complex questions about the sustainability of inter-generational arrangements, and also have an international dimension. For many in the developed world, capitalised pension funds imply investment in emerging markets (indeed the rules in many countries impose a fiduciary duty on fund managers to seek the highest returns consistent with a level of risk). Such investment improves the availability of funding for developing economies that might struggle to finance investment, but also creates governance challenges to do with the sustainability of investment. It also implies future flows of income from poor to rich in the form of profits, dividends and interest.

EU policy towards sustainable development has had a chequered history. It has ranged from grand visions to rather empty combinations of objectives that lack much policy substance. SD is one of the fundamental aims of the European Union, prominently set out in article 3 of the Lisbon Treaty. There has been some re-wording compared with previous versions of the Treaty on European Union (TEU), with the new formulation stating that the Union 'shall work for the sustainable development of Europe based on balanced economic growth and price stability, a highly competitive social market economy, aiming at full employment and social progress, and a high level of protection and improvement of the quality of the environment'. Previously, the reference was to the achievement of 'balanced and sustainable development' (article 2, TEU) as one of a list of fundamental aims. What this suggests is that there has been a subtle switch of emphasis in which SD has become the over-arching aim within which other aims are nested. Yet it is also apparent that, while the concept is generally present, it often struggles to command immediate attention from policy-makers.

That there are shortcomings in the governance of sustainable development is undeniable, whether at global level, in the EU or in the approaches of individual states or other stakeholders, and it is evident that there is a pervasive reluctance to confront some of the more intractable challenges. The aims of this chapter are, first, to review the governance *of* sustainable development, focusing on the EU approach and whether it may have value for other parts of the world. Second, it tries to tease out ideas on policy developments that might enhance governance *for* sustainable development. Although climate change and the uncertainties surrounding the impacts of carbon emissions have rapidly become central to debate around sustainability, awkward conceptual and policy questions have to be posed about social sustainability. This chapter tries to link the analysis of shifts in underlying models with the manner in which policy has evolved, and in so doing asks whether the social dimensions of sustainability are given due weight.

2.2 DEFINING SUSTAINABLE DEVELOPMENT IN THE EU

Although the original conception was as much about economic development and social aims, SD is often more narrowly interpreted to be about environmental goals – especially climate change – and the quality of life in richer countries. An especially critical view is offered by Victor (2006, p. 93), who observes that:

> even as sustainable development has become conventional wisdom over the past two decades, something has gone horribly wrong. Because the concept stresses the interconnection of everything, it has been vulnerable to distortion by woolly thinking and has become a magnet for special interest groups. Human rights watchdogs, large chemical companies, small island nations, green architects, and nuclear power plant operators have attached themselves to the fashionable notion only to subvert it for their own ends. Instead of bringing together nature, the economy, and social justice, sustainable development has spawned overspecialized and largely meaningless checklists and targets.

Today, what Europeans want to sustain is a mix of the physical (notably the various environmental goals), the economic (an organisation of economic activity and a level of prosperity) and the socio-political (normative priorities such as a fair distribution of income or gender equality). It is a long-term ambition and not one that lends itself to easy quantification or a clear statement of when it has been attained. Rather, it is a direction for travel and a description of values, likely to be more readily captured in broader notions of well-being (as discussed, notably, by Stiglitz et al. 2009) or quality of life than conventional output measures such as GDP. Indeed, high levels of output, to the extent that they embody damage to the environment or detract from social cohesion, could be seen as antithetical to sustainability.

'Sustainable' as understood today has many strands to it that are – quite possibly by design – elided in much of the policy debate. The equation of sustainable with 'green' is perhaps the most readily understood and needs little elaboration. But there are also fiscal, macroeconomic and social dimensions to 'sustainable' that governance has to take into account. Much effort has gone into promoting the sustainability of public finances, not just as a response to recession and crisis, but also to deal with the medium- and longer-term threats to fiscal stability from changing public expenditure patterns. This has repercussions for social spending insofar as 'sound' public finances imply curbs on entitlements and categories of spending that have long been safeguarded.

The straightforward interpretation of macroeconomic sustainability is that it describes a trajectory for the economy that is not inflationary, but the identification of imbalances as a key determinant of the years of crisis since 2007 also points to competitiveness and the character of growth as equally important. An economy that is only able to grow by relying on excessive credit creation or demand from abroad is treading a perilous path. Dynamics are, therefore, pivotal. Certainly, the links between macroeconomic and environmental sustainability have to be better elaborated. A macroeconomic approach that depends on ever higher consumption, including a strong propensity to throw away last year's purchases (Jackson 2009), is going to be in conflict with calls to reduce resource use. But consumption is not always or necessarily resource intensive and one of the directions for development may be to promote services as the principal vector of future growth in more developed countries. A smart growth alternative is sometimes predicated on the opportunities for 'green' production and jobs to supplant the old activities. But this notion needs to be taken further.

'Social' sustainability is more complex. One way of looking at the social dimension could be to consider how the social environment might degrade. Pawlowski (2008, p. 83) maintains that such degradation could be shaped by shifts in 'a large number of factors, including customs and traditions, culture, spirituality, interpersonal relations and living conditions. Even human relationships with nature have their social dimension, since all the different kinds of activity oriented towards the environment are mediated via the socio-cultural models in place in a given society.' Social sustainability can also be linked to opportunity and mobility, as well as the issues that are usually at the forefront of European discourse, notably cohesion, equality, poverty reduction and job quality.

The social investment function of social protection has been identified by a number of authors as a novel though increasingly pervasive approach to welfare reform (Hemerijck 2012) in which the emphasis is on investing in the individual. Indeed, Taylor-Gooby (2008) maintains that in its idealised form, the social investment approach to welfare can bring together economic and social objectives in a self-reinforcing manner. However, he also notes that the practice falls short of the rhetoric, implying that rather than social investment, what has happened is 'negative activation'. He attributes this outcome partly to the weakness of unions and notes that there has been a disjunction between the emphasis on social investment in policy debates and the realities of what has been done within many countries. Nevertheless, the investment theme remains prominent, not least in the 'flexicurity' agenda. As such, it points to an important connection in SD policy that is only partly made explicit in the EU's policy approaches, although recent EU initiatives such as the 2013 social investment package suggest that the concept is making the jump from academia to policy-making.

A further consideration is that globalisation has links to sustainable development that warrant attention, many of which have been highlighted by the succession of crises after 2007. At a macroeconomic level, inter-connected economies are subject to disruption if imbalances reach unsustainable proportions. Any subsequent adjustments risk having pronounced effects across borders. Global markets for essential inputs like energy affect all countries, with major importers subject to price volatilities that can affect their competitiveness while also having social ramifications. Economic volatility, in turn, can affect migration flows and thus have social impacts. Many in the countries worst affected by the euro crisis which began in Greece late in 2009 would argue that social cohesion has been undermined by what became unsustainable macroeconomic policies. And so on ...

In assessing what is sustainable, another useful concept is what type of goods are under consideration, going beyond the classical dichotomy between pure public and pure private goods. Ostrom (2010), in her Nobel Prize lecture, revisits some of her earlier work and suggests that four main types should be distinguished: public goods, private goods, club (or, in her terminology, 'toll' goods) and common-pool goods. She proposes a two by two classification of these goods in which they can be portrayed as high or low on, respectively, the 'subtractability' of use (that is, the extent to which consumption by one user detracts from what others can access) and the difficulty of excluding potential beneficiaries.

Arguably the atmosphere is a common pool, even though it has only latterly been recognised as such, given that limits to its capacity to cope with increased greenhouse gases (GHG) are a comparative novelty – and remain contested in some quarters. But can the same be said of social cohesion, considering that it is much more amorphous as a 'good'? It has attributes that bring collective benefits (such as the greater security that stems from a crime-free environment), but can equally be predominantly about re-distribution. Social sustainability may, therefore, need to be broken down into different components to ascertain how it fits into the Ostrom classification. Trust is a facet that has to be considered in this regard, but (certainly in the EU setting) the underlying social model is also germane.

As a policy mandate, sustainable development is bedevilled by looseness of interpretation which, while it opens it to acceptance by a wide range of actors, also means that they can adopt very divergent policies under its banner (Burchell and Lightfoot 2004). The initial Lisbon agenda in the EU, arguably agreed at a time when globalisation was viewed as a positive force, sought to bring together competitiveness and social cohesion, with environmental goals subsequently added to give a three pillar definition of SD (Begg 2009). Faced with a more challenging international context, this conjunction has since been weakened, leading Magnusson (2010, p. 7) to fear that the perceived costs of dealing simultaneously with social and environmental dimensions will see the former side-lined: 'there is a clear danger that, for example, social cohesion and social equality will be accorded less priority and it is thus essential that the concept of sustainability should continue, in the future, to include both a social and an environmental dimension'. The upshot may well be that SD is supported so long as it does not intrude on immediate policy aims (Lenschow 2005) – a classic Catch-22. One key question is whether, given the limited constitutional mandate for social Europe, there is enough political support for a stronger European engagement. The unfolding of the economic crisis is testing the limits of solidarity, yet there is also ample evidence that what happens in one Member State has repercussions for others, be it through financial connections or prospective adjustment mechanisms with social effects such as migration, not to mention standard macroeconomic spillovers.

Sustainable development is bound to require an extensive range of policy metrics and initiatives rather than reliance on one or other approach. Instruments to promote a shift towards greater environmental sustainability are at once obvious and awkward. They include taxes, regulatory standards, various forms of price-fixing (such as lead-in prices), cap and trade systems, and so on. In all cases, the thrust and potential impact of the instrument can readily be anticipated, but there are inevitable side-effects that complicate policy choices. Taxes are sources of revenue for governments as well as means of altering economic behaviour through recalibration of incentives. Subsidies, similarly, have incentive properties, but also demand higher levels of public expenditure. All this raises issues of what to measure in appraising demands on, and outcomes of, policy, including how production and consumption are valued, as well as more general issues of measurement. Many of the subjects of policy to promote SD do not have well-defined prices. Air, water, well-being (as opposed to material production), health and so on are all hard to calibrate: some are commons, some are intangibles, some are measurable but not in terms easily amenable to a monetary unit of account.

Sustainability arguably adds urgency to the search for more nuanced and more diverse ways of measuring the performance of economies and the social consequences of economic trends. Output, income, well-being and (latterly) happiness are conceptually distinct approaches. The Stiglitz Commission is the most recent and comprehensive attempt to investigate these issues and it makes the emphatic point that 'it has long been clear that GDP is an inadequate metric to gauge well-being over time particularly in its economic, environmental, and social dimensions, some aspects of which are often referred to as *sustainability*' (Stiglitz et al. 2009, p. 8). Indeed, the report suggests that measurement shortcomings may be one explanation for the 2008–2009 economic crisis insofar as the data to which most attention was paid did not alert policy-makers to underlying problems. One of the key distinctions that the Stiglitz Commission stresses is between current well-being and whether that well-being can last over time; this echoes the Brundtland report formula.

Several factors come into play. Quality is a particularly contentious element of measurement in relation to sustainability. If quality improvements are not given sufficient weight, true output may be under-estimated and/or inflation may be exaggerated (and, obviously, vice versa). Some services are crudely measured by input rather than by what they yield in terms of facets of well-being, such as health or security.

The stock of capital is central to adequate measurement of well-being and its sustainability. A society that maintains its well-being by consuming its wealth can appear to be prosperous as measured by output or expenditure, but it does so at the expense of future generations. However, investment has to be interpreted subtly. Property bubbles of the sort seen in Ireland, Spain and the UK in recent years illustrate the problem: at its peak just before the crisis, fixed capital formation in Spain exceeded 30 per cent of GDP, the sort of figure normally associated with the fast-growing Asian tiger economies. But far too much of this investment was going into property, causing severe economic distortions, and an unsustainably high level of construction activity. Symmetrically, a society that builds up the 'right' kind of capital is providing for future well-being. In this regard, it is important to consider all forms of capital:

physical, human and social, as well as the environment. The interplay between the stock of wealth and the flows of new investment or consumption of capital is therefore at the heart of sustainability.

Balance sheets are often poorly presented for the public sector, especially in the EU where the criteria for assessing macroeconomic stability have been the ratio of public deficits or public debt to GDP, but no account is taken of how the money has been spent or on what, let alone whether it promotes or undermines sustainability. Public assets should enter into the calculations to give a better-rounded picture, raising challenges of appropriate valuation, including how to accommodate divergent views about true value. To some extent, the notion of the quality of public finances (Deroose and Kastrop 2008) addresses this facet of sustainability, emphasising that there are forms of public spending that enhance growth, while others may be a drag on it. One of the messages from this analysis is that it is important in assessing efficiency and effectiveness to look at out*comes* rather than out*puts*. But, the analysis is largely couched in terms of GDP, whereas (as the Stiglitz report stresses) more radical rethinking is needed to arrive at appropriate measures of well-being. A particular difficulty is that measurement of social and human capital is conceptually and practically much harder than measurement of the physical capital or natural resources, making it hard to arrive at a consensus on what to include in measures of well-being that embrace sustainability. The subjective nature of happiness – another metric that is attracting increasing interest – is harder still to quantify, although it has the potential to enrich understanding of sustainability.

Some environmental factors have an immediate impact on quality of life, such as pollution that has a negative impact on air or water quality, or the form of the built environment; some social indicators, such as exclusion, can be viewed in the same way. Other factors, such as the risks from high and growing carbon emissions, are latent, so that timescales have to be taken into account. A disjunction between the baskets of goods and services individuals secure and their well-being as measured by other metrics is pivotal. The Stiglitz report provides a careful survey of alternative ways of assessing sustainability and identifies four main approaches:

- What it calls the dashboard of indicators, which typically range from the very general to the highly specific.
- Composite indicators of well-being.
- Adjustments of basic indicators such as GDP to reflect unmeasured or inappropriately measured variables.

- Measures of over-consumption or under-investment that directly monitor sustainability.

None of these approaches offers comprehensive answers and all have their drawbacks. A key question remains, what is to be sustained? And are 'sustainability' and 'development' terms that can always be conjoined?

2.3 UNCERTAINTY AS AN ORGANISING THEME IN SUSTAINABLE DEVELOPMENT

Sustainable development exemplifies many of the governance issues that arise in trying to deal with uncertainty at the European level. As Crouch (2009, p. 4) notes in a conceptual paper that sets out general propositions around the GUSTO project, uncertainty has become a central principle for appraising flexibility and security in European policy debates over the past two decades. Crouch observes that 'reconciling these various policy goals and approaches is not easy, and there has been a need for considerable creativity among policy makers in order to do so'. Dyson (2014) makes a similar point in relation to how to interpret debt, arguing that 'good' and 'bad' debt, as well as whom to regard as 'saints' and 'sinners' in how debt is appraised are highly contentious governance issues. Crouch also stresses that the challenge is one of adapting systems of governance to the imperatives of sustainability and, especially, focusing on how to govern uncertainty. He concedes that the idea of 'the governance of uncertainty' may seem to be an oxymoron and should, instead, be presented as 'coping', but notes that many policy areas are characterised by approaches to the distribution of uncertainty or the burden-sharing associated with mitigating its effects or finding ways of sharing burdens. This implies using a political economy approach.

Among the uncertainties around SD is the lack of knowledge about when what is familiar and understood ceases to be tenable. In the environmental arena levels of pollution or concentrations of gases (GHG or, previously, the CFCs that were blamed for the hole in the ozone layer) can build up gradually with few visible effects, yet suddenly pass a tipping-point beyond which urgent remedial action is needed. Slow societal changes can suddenly mutate into pressing social problems or acquire high political salience, either of which demands a policy response.

New concepts and tools are needed to relate sustainability, uncertainty and the measurement of economic performance. Many of the risks associated with a lack of sustainability cannot readily be quantified. We know that carbon emissions are correlated with global warming, but can only speculate on the parameters of the relationship and on whether it is subject to significant discontinuities. There are no real historic data on which to base projections, nor are experiments other than simulations feasible, and the latter are inevitably vulnerable to the 'garbage in, garbage out' syndrome. Strange and Bayley (2008, p. 66) stress that models

> [cannot] tell us what as yet unforeseen solutions might appear on the horizon, but they can help us understand the possible consequences of decisions we make now. And these days they are sending a clear message: our current path of development is hurtling us towards major changes, changes that will affect almost every aspect of our lives.

2.3.1 Fairness

Uncertainty also arises in relation to notions of fairness and where the emphasis should lie in reconciling the tensions between different conceptions of it. This suggests that several overlapping 'justices' should be encompassed when discussing sustainable development (Begg 2009):

- *Social*, in a contemporary sense encompassing new balances of risks and an emphasis on incentives and empowerment, as well as distributive transfers (see, for example, Giddens et al. 2006).
- *Carbon*, taking account of the differences between richer and poorer nations in levels and historical responsibilities, notably in relation to demands from richer countries that others should reduce their emissions.
- *Inter-generational*, taking account of the Brundtland report aphorism about meeting the needs of the present without compromising the needs of future generations.
- *Developmental*, in balancing the evident priority that emerging economies give to reaching the higher income levels needed to make progress and to alleviate mass poverty, while cajoling them into accepting environmental commitments.
- *Knowledge*, in recognition of the imperative of more rapid innovation and its implications for the spread of intellectual property. In particular, is there a case for knowledge aid, as opposed to cash and technology transfers?

There are several parallels between the motivations for social policy and environmental policy which reflect uncertainties and ambiguities about what is fair and to whom. Meadowcroft (2008, p. 331) observes that 'both are political responses to long-term societal changes linked to industrialization, urbanization and democratization. Both have been called into being to wrestle with issues that cannot adequately be addressed by markets and voluntary action.' There is also a parallel between the trade-off between social protection's productive and protective roles and the equivalent in environmental policy between the opportunities from the green economy and the more traditional view of restricting damaging activities. However, Meadowcroft also notes that by comparison with the well-embedded welfare state, the putative environmental state is institutionally weak and he adds that it is difficult to conceive of an Esping-Andersen type of classification to describe emerging regimes. Like the present author, Crouch (2008) is sceptical of the reductionism to regimes that has become so common-place in analysing socio-economic development. It is nevertheless worth considering whether some social models are more amenable to sustainability than others.

2.3.2 Engaging Business Interests

The role of markets in securing or preventing sustainable development deserves scrutiny. In many respects, sustainability is on the agenda precisely because of market failures: exhaustible resources have not been priced to reflect their future scarcity, and emissions, especially of GHG, have been treated as costless. But market signals can also be vital in shifting patterns of consumption and production, and for an SD strategy to succeed it has to make sense to the corporate sector, and not just in the form of good citizenship implied by corporate social responsibility (CSR) commitments.

At a global level, sustainability can seem to be a preserve of the rich or a luxury to contemplate once more immediate priorities are dealt with. There is an obvious tension between economic development imperatives and climate change, and many developing countries have articulated resistance to curbing emissions, placing economic development as a higher priority. Energy is a lubricant of economic development and fossil fuels remain the fuel of choice in terms of cost and efficiency. But there are options and, in seeking to exploit some of them, business stakeholders are likely to be especially important in two respects: first for the actions they take themselves, and secondly in shifting the terms of political debate. It follows that political efforts to engage business are vital. One facet of uncertainty in relation to sustainable development concerns the incentives to invest. The lack of stability in policy intentions leaves investors in doubt about the wisdom of launching major long-term projects.

What would make sense, notably from a business perspective? Plainly, business craves and values certainty, and is, consequently, more likely to make the necessary long-term investments if a clear and enduring policy framework is in place. A governance imperative is, therefore, to work towards greater certainty. Second, policy has to deliver a tolerably level playing-field, or else there will be strong pressures to diminish policy-related costs that penalise production in locations that have imposed heavier taxes or restrictions, ultimately triggering a 'race to the bottom'. With the advent of fracking in the US and the dramatic energy cost advantage it has conferred on US exporters, EU policy-makers have come under pressures to ease energy policies and there are some who argue that the 2014 EU energy package is evidence of backsliding.

Choice of mechanisms is also central. Regulatory measures are often resisted because they distort the market, although that is often precisely why they are introduced. Taxes (or subsidies) are an alternative means of using price signals to shape behaviour. Here there are many issues to confront. Who pays, and is the incidence of taxes equitable, especially if there is a risk of 'fuel poverty'? What should be taxed or subsidised? By using the tax system to raise the costs of polluting activities or to subsidise social policies, the expectation would be that investment and consumption decisions would be altered. But taxes inevitably raise difficult political economy problems.

2.3.3 Burden-sharing in Governing Uncertainty

Burden-sharing is at the heart of strategies to promote sustainable development. Various models for allocating costs can be envisaged (discussed in depth by Llewellyn and Chaix 2007), deploying criteria such as:

- *Ability to pay*, implying that richer countries pay disproportionately.
- *Level of current emissions*, essentially the polluter pays principle, with a target for curbing the level, typically expressed per head of population.
- *Estimated volume of past emissions*, which entails working out retrospectively which countries bear the responsibility. Llewellyn and Chaix (2007) report that some 70 per cent of the stock of

carbon up to 2004 is attributable to the US, EU, Japan and Russia, with China and India accounting for just 10 per cent.

- *Distribution of benefits* in which the social, political or economic benefits of curbs are taken into account. A low-lying European country, for example, might have a higher welfare gain than, say, an upland Asian country.
- *Egalitarian principles* might be advanced to justify richer countries subsidising abatements in poorer countries, thereby going beyond the ability to pay principle.

Also relevant is how abatement policies are pursued. The choice between mitigation of carbon emissions and adaptation to climate change is part of the burden-sharing discourse, but with profound distributive consequences. Low-lying areas or regions subject to desertification have much to fear from global warming that raises sea levels and alters weather patterns. Access to fresh water threatens to become an increasingly acute source of insecurity and conflict. Emissions can be cut by direct action to cut the burning of fossil fuels (principally by investment in replacing energy-inefficient equipment and buildings), but also more indirectly by investing in technology developments. The US, for example, argues that it is in the forefront in the latter category, even if it lags behind in current abatement. The other side of the same coin is technology transfer and the related intellectual property right costs/benefits.

Similar analyses could be conducted about dealing with the costs of other facets of sustainability, such as world health, world poverty or what, to adapt a well-known EU term, might be called global economic and social cohesion. In the EU, cohesion is identified in article 2 of the Treaty on European Union as a fundamental objective. At a global level, there are various commitments, but these are generally more amorphous. There is, for example, a direct counterpart of the technology transfer issue referred to above in relation to drugs aimed at mitigating the effects of HIV. Drug companies, not surprisingly, want to charge prices that help to amortise the high costs of past and current research, implying prices much higher than the costs of marginal production, while impoverished nations are severely constrained in how much they can afford to pay. Although Bill Gates and Warren Buffett have led the way in showing that philanthropy can play a part in bridging this gap, it is an inadequate approach to the governance of such a major issue.

Finding an appropriate key for burden-sharing will be one of the most intractable governance problems. China has just overtaken the US as the world's biggest emitter, but its per capita emission rate is a quarter of the American one. Europe and the US are clearly responsible for the bulk of the build-up of stocks of GHG and other parts of the world have a justifiable case for asking them to shoulder most of the burden of mitigation, but their efforts risk being nullified if other parts of the world argue that development – entailing a growth in fossil fuel consumption – must come first.

Free-riding as an aspect of burden-sharing is bound to loom large, because it is easy to rely on others. Moreover, the polluters and the prospective victims of global warming are often the same people wearing different hats and there are so many separate channels through which small losses occur for the individual that they can become hard to measure against the much more obvious counterpart of, say, a higher price per litre of petrol or an airline's fuel surcharge.

2.4 THE CORE SUSTAINABLE DEVELOPMENT CHALLENGES

For the EU especially, much of the current debate concerns how to manage globalisation so as to make it consistent with a vision of sustainable development. The neo-liberal prescription of full-blown market opening as the best (or only) way forward for economic development has been harshly criticised by Stiglitz (2002), not least because the uneven playing-field leaves so many poorer nations unable to compete effectively. Anti-globalist campaigns by the likes of the anti-globalisation movement ATTAC have grown partly out of a reaction against the neo-liberal agenda and partly out of a wish to promote the interests of the excluded, but the danger in the prescriptions offered is that wealth creation is also inhibited in a way that ultimately militates against those interests.

This prompts the question of whether growth, itself, is the problem, rather than whether or not it is smart. The notion of a steady-state economy (Daly 2008) in which the emphasis is on capital that is renewable in a sustainable manner is one alternative. However, Jackson (2009) argues that there also has to be a new macroeconomics for sustainability. The latter may include a fresh look at sharing of the stock of jobs and will require attention to distributive issues. It also requires a re-assessment of many of the socio-political tenets of modern society, notably the deeply embedded assumption that more is always better. Jackson (2009, p. 11) offers a stark verdict: 'the narrow pursuit of growth represents a horrible distortion of the common good and of underlying human values. It also undermines the legitimate role of government itself.'

Somewhere in the middle is the mainstream European view captured in the Lisbon strategy (the original strategy launched in 2000), which calls for extensive supply-side reforms along with open markets, and the promotion of the knowledge economy, tempered by policies to assure social cohesion. It is a middle that lies between what Mandelson (2007) has called the standpoint of the hyper-globalists and that of the protectionists. He identifies – and rejects – 'hyper-globalism' which portrays globalisation as an irresistible economic force in which global capital imposes neo-liberal economic policies on all governments, with the implication that social policies have to be watered down. Yet the very success of some of the EU Member States with the most extensive social policies shows that a judicious mix of social, environmental and economic objectives is attainable.

There may also be new aspects of the notion of 'the common good' to be developed. Should new energy technologies, for example, be under the control of narrowly drawn 'communities of fate' or be more readily available for all? Should there be a parallel notion, perhaps equivalent to anti-matter, of 'communities of ill-fate' which act in ways inimical to sustainable development? Although sustainability conventionally concentrates on distribution between generations, a further message from the Brundtland report is that distribution within a generation is also germane. It follows that a focus on inequalities (especially, but not only, of income) and of different forms of equality (notably in the workplace) can reasonably be included as part of 'social' in sustainability.

In this context commons share some attributes with public goods, but with the difference that they are not necessarily the result of policy decisions or public investment. Rain forests, climate, carbon in the atmosphere and water are commons in the sense of natural endowments that are under challenge because of an approach to economic activity that has neglected sustainability. Commons can also, however, refer to the corpus of knowledge and culture, some of which is the result of public policy, some derived from corporate activity and some stemming from the citizen. Social values and norms are part of EU commons, encapsulated in the slippery expression 'European Social Model' – which can perhaps best be defined by reference to other models that it is not, rather than by an unambiguous statement of what it is. Commons have to be nurtured but are often exhaustible or suffer from a lack of maintenance, so that sustainability requires management of the 'common-pool'.

2.4.1 Mitigating Carbon Emissions

Climate change has manifestly imparted a new urgency to the narratives about reconfiguring socio-economic models and has already assumed centre-stage in policy-making. While the scientific evidence that human activity is now the principal cause of global warming is increasingly accepted, there are still sceptics who argue that the underlying science is far from clear-cut. Even if the latter view is discounted, the socio-economic implications are prone to be poorly analysed and interpreted. In part, the fear of disruption of existing growth models dominates policy responses. For example, the logic deployed by countries like China – which argue for development first, then sustainability later – is compelling. There are layers of collective action problems here.

The Stern Review (2007) has been very influential in translating the scientific debate into economic analysis. The Review, together with subsequent work by Stern (2008), also highlights the long timescales needed for action and thus the imperative of acting now, rather than waiting for the effects of climate change to show themselves. As Arrow (2007) makes clear, the economics of climate change are fairly straightforward, involving a mix of more rational pricing of carbon, suitable regulatory intervention and funding of public goods in response to market failures. What is needed is a well-judged mix of regulatory measures coupled with incentives in the form of subsidies and penalties. 'We know what needs to be done. We have the tools at hand. We only need the political resolve' (Stiglitz 2006, p. 4).

But political resolve also requires that thought be given to breaking free of the political and social traps that inhibit action at national, EU and international level. Although Europeans have made great play of their desire to confront climate change, they have hesitated to act because of fears about endangering competitiveness. Their initial, artful (or, perhaps, disingenuous) answer to the question of when to act was a form of conditionality: having struggled to an agreement on the 20–20–20 targets embodied in the Energy Policy for Europe agreed in 2007, the EU also signalled to the other main actors (above all, the US and China) that it would move towards 30 per cent emission reductions if others followed suit.

The limited outcome of the 2009 Copenhagen climate change conference suggests that this conditional approach failed, and in 2014 the EU agreed a new climate change package which appeared to scale back its ambitions to provide a global lead. A cynical perspective is that many of the calls for action to promote a low-carbon paradigm are motivated by distributive preferences. Certainly, it does not take much of a leap to see naked protectionism behind calls in Europe for border taxes on imports from countries that appear to be unwilling to act to curb emissions.

Decoupling – a reduction in the intensity of resource use per unit of GDP – is bound to be central to an EU policy response, but has to be looked at with care. As Jackson (2009) points out, it takes two conceptually different forms: relative decoupling refers to a decline in the ratio of resource use to GDP, but the aggregate impact will depend on whether the rate of growth exceeds the decline in resource intensity; whereas absolute decoupling entails a reduction in resource use. The former may slow the negative consequences of unsustainable resource use, but only postpone the day of reckoning, and although the trend for some raw materials has been encouraging, there are others for which the GDP intensity of resource use has been rising. Even with the economic stagnation seen since 2007, far faster rates of decoupling would be needed to stabilise emissions.

What constitutes a sustainable low-carbon energy system, yet one fit to meet the needs of consumers and producers alike, is a subject of controversy, but as Meeus et al. (2011) show, there are five main axes to consider:

- Improving energy efficiency, both by lowering demand (buildings being a prime target) and improving the transformation of primary sources into final energy use.
- De-carbonising electricity generation.
- Increasing the share of renewable energy, including the imperative of pushing new technologies to the market.
- Improving cross-border connections.
- Ensuring sufficient capacity-building in electricity generation, notably in providing back-up capacity that can facilitate the integration of intermittent supply from inherently unreliable renewable sources, such as wind or solar.

Meeus et al. also reveal the extent to which stakeholders differ in their basic assumptions about how the energy market will evolve, partly reflecting ideological standpoints (such as Greenpeace's rejection of nuclear energy), partly because of uncertainties about key variables (such as the long-term price of fuels), but partly also because policy interventions are uncertain (for example, the speed with which carbon capture and sequestration will be embraced and funded, so as to become a viable technology).

2.4.2 Social Investment or Social Protection?

The lack of a genuine social Europe can, to a considerable extent, be explained by the reluctance of governments to cede powers to regulate the market or to shape welfare provision. Indeed, it can be argued (Scharpf 2002) that once the choice was made in the 1950s to opt for 'negative' market integration rather than the politically more difficult path of 'positive' integration, the prospect of social integration was killed off. Barbier (2008), in his description of the long road to social Europe, attributes the lack of progress to the absence of a shared understanding of what 'social' encompasses and is sceptical about much that is discussed under the banner of social Europe. A more social EU can be justified, according to Ferrera and Sacchi (2009), because it would help to legitimate European integration, as well as for reasons of social justice and economic efficiency. But it is not enough just to find a rationale, as the case for a social Europe also depends on why and how it is advanced.

The incorporation of a social pillar in the approach to sustainable development could underpin a new approach to establishing a social Europe. A key consideration is that a delicate political and policy balance is needed, especially for social market economies, in adapting to the rapid and extensive shifts in the economic and social environment. Scharpf (2009) notes that these shifts are both internal and external and that they are unavoidably controversial in national politics, not least because of the long-run accommodations that have given rise to existing social regimes. The thrust of European law-making and its interpretation by the European Court of Justice (ECJ) has been to support openness and liberal values and can therefore be inimical to expensive welfare states. Scharpf argues that although judgments by the ECJ could prevail over national preferences, the court has never attempted to do so, and would struggle to justify any such intervention.

Perhaps the best lens through which to view the social dimension of SD is that of capital, both human and social. Human capital is increasingly seen as one of the most critical determinants of competitiveness, especially in what is loosely called the knowledge economy, and policy instruments oriented towards boosting it have mushroomed. Life-long learning and skills strategies have evolved to boost the potential for more productive work, while deficiencies in educational systems have been highlighted. However, for the individual, human capital is also the passport to social mobility and to self-improvement, so that it affects the probability of social exclusion. It follows that human capital developments will play a part in the achievement of social cohesion. Social capital is harder to pin down and risks being tautological if the definition of a cohesive society is one which possesses an above average level of social capital.

The social investment turn in welfare policies can be seen as a response to the threats to the financial sustainability of social protection systems that weigh too heavily on public finances, but also to the need to rebalance work and welfare in a way that is economically sustainable. In some respects, it is certainties rather than uncertainties that are driving welfare reform, especially demographic trends. Longevity combined with a reduced fertility rate reshapes the age profile of the population, rendering pay-as-you-go arithmetic less sustainable. But there are also uncertainties surrounding, on the one hand, the outlook for altering the employment rates of hitherto under-employed segments of society, and the receptiveness of Europeans to immigration as a means of boosting the working-age population.

A social investment approach can be subject to the charge that it is code for de-regulation and welfare cuts, although perceptive authors such as Taylor-Gooby (2008) argue that it is more about the interactions between social systems and employment opportunities in shaping how individuals sustain their human capital and labour market attributes. Central to the approach is how extended periods of unemployment or (increasingly in some models) inactivity can be avoided, and there is considerable interest in the means by which countries like Denmark and the Netherlands have achieved sustained increases in employment rates. In addition, the investment focus can be seen as consistent with the contention that employment is the best route out of poverty, with human capital as the key variable. Persistent poverty and its inter-generational transmission are also part of the narrative. An interesting study by Hudson and Kühner (2009) finds that, contrary to some expectations, some welfare states have been able to combine productive and protective aims. They also find that the presumption that welfare states have generally moved away from protective to productive is far from clear-cut, with countries like Portugal, Korea and Canada having moved in the other direction. It could be that this is attributable to a search for balance.

Analysis of transitions and of the probabilities of exiting from an adverse labour market status (Erhel, Gautié and Gazier, chapter 5 in this volume) adds a further strand to these arguments, since there is compelling evidence that attributes associated with human capital (notably educational attainment) are, in turn, associated with improved prospects for both employment and social standing. Meticulous sociological research is not needed to demonstrate that the workplace is much more than a location for carrying out work.

There is some suggestion that the impact of social protection and other welfare arrangements has led to a more fragmented distribution of benefits and costs and changes in both. One of the striking features of social protection in Europe is the stability of expenditure. Yet it is undeniable that the profile of benefits differs considerably across countries and has evolved over time. For today's working-age population, an increasing uncertainty is what will be on offer for them when they retire, because predicting who will be the winners and losers is hard. One possible outcome is that, rather than the national regimes that have dominated thinking on welfare states for at least the last 20 years, there may be a process of convergence in which some groups gain systematically (Palier 2010). For younger age cohorts, the uncertainty is compounded by the prospect of having not only to pay more for a larger mass of future retirees, but also to settle for lower income growth because of the constraints of global competition. This dual squeeze may then feed into choices about investments in housing and skills that bear on social sustainability.

2.4.3 Governance Dilemmas

Many of the key uncertainties with which sustainable development has to contend stem from trends and forces that no single Member State of the EU can confront unilaterally, providing a rationale for an EU-level response. Climate change is manifestly one while demographic changes (largely known or predictable, but no easier to accommodate despite this knowledge) constitute another, but so too are some of the underlying drivers subsumed under the shorthand of globalisation. Rapid technological change brings undoubted advantages, but can also have its victims; increased immigration can be part of an answer to the rise in the elderly dependent population, but creates social tensions; competition and free trade are portrayed as benefits, but have costs. In short, there are always going to be winners and losers, and it is no surprise that the latter always shout loudest.

The level at which the governance of SD takes place is a first dilemma. Solutions to many of the problems of sustainability cannot be found at the level of the individual country, but depend instead on international coordination. Today's EU of 28 Member States has the scope to make a substantial difference by adopting common policies, but for some of the global sustainability challenges, EU action will have to be nested within global coordination. This prompts the question of the intensity of coordination at different levels of governance and, more intractably, of the appropriate forms of burden-sharing at global level. In particular, the mitigation of carbon emissions has to reconcile historical and current responsibilities for the level and rate of increase of greenhouse gases.

Growth can be considered necessary for development but not sufficient to assure *sustainable* development. Moreover, context makes a difference. Relative income and inclusion matter much more in advanced economies such as the EU than absolute poverty, and what constitutes exclusion is a moving target: in 21st-Century Europe lack of access to broadband is a vector of exclusion, whereas access to running water might have been 200 years ago, or to a telephone 50 years ago. Tertiary rather than basic education has become the source of social mobility.

Environmental and distributive issues are often connected, as can be seen by considering food. Bailey (2011) presents a bleak report about the outlook for food prices, which are expected to rise inexorably in coming decades, with damaging consequences for equity. The price of many staple foods will increase by between two-thirds and 90 per cent in real terms under a baseline scenario, but by 120–180 per cent under an adverse climate change scenario. Food production faces further challenges. Bailey argues that the sustainability of food production has to be greatly increased, notably to emit less CO_2 and to make better use of dwindling water supplies. He also observes that the resilience of the food production system has diminished, through a combination of speculative bubbles in key commodities, weather-related events, and actions taken by governments to defend indigenous supplies or to divert production to other uses. A specific problem is the diversion of both investment and acreage to the production of bio-fuels. 'Since 2004, the amount of maize diverted to biofuel has soared: in 2010 nearly 40 per cent of US corn production went into engines rather than stomachs' (Bailey 2011, p. 39).

Labour standards, gender equality and social protection also come into the equation. An ILO Commission found compelling evidence that women are more likely to be adversely affected by globalisation. Migration has seen an upsurge in the last two decades and can, moreover, be seen as a facet of sustainability. The flood of would-be migrants from Africa, drawn by the EU, is a symptom of imbalance between labour supply and labour demand that, in turn, results from lack of economic development. In all these areas, there is a need to balance commercial, developmental and political interests, yet an absence of agreed mechanisms of governance for doing so. Nor do established international institutions appear to be equipped to be the answer.

Sustainable development does, however, pose more fundamental challenges than more targeted strategies (such as energy) because it has to bring together such disparate policy domains and reconcile so many interests. It also has to contend with far greater uncertainties than other strategies, encompassing not only scientific knowledge (climate change), but the attitudinal and behavioural changes that are likely to be induced. This calls for flexibility in governance, but also for mechanisms that can be nimble enough to recognise new problems and opportunities. As Strange and Bayley (2008, p. 132) put it, 'not only their goals, but the strategies and instruments used to achieve them must be sustainable, too. They must be rigorous enough to be effective, but flexible enough to adapt as circumstances and priorities evolve. In the face of uncertainty, governance itself has to be sustainable.'

2.5 EU POLICY APPROACHES

Despite the uncertainties around its definitions and political commitment to it, there can be little doubt that sustainable development is, and will remain, at the heart of policy-making in the EU. A key governance question for any major policy initiative is, however, how much attention it commands and, in this regard, the EU has been somewhat inconsistent. To a degree it has been a work in progress, with the initial launch of the Sustainable Development Strategy (SDS) at the Gothenburg European Council in 2001 and its re-launch in 2006. The latter updated the aims of the strategy that had been established five years earlier, and broke new ground by elaborating the governance mechanisms intended to advance its aims. It has now been integrated into the Europe 2020 strategy, which has, as its leitmotif, 'smart, sustainable and inclusive growth'. Individual Member States also have bodies with various roles in fostering or monitoring SD: in 2006, for example, the UK assigned a watchdog role to an independent commission, though it is perhaps telling that it fell victim in 2011 to the need for public spending cuts and was abolished.

These vacillations can, in part, be explained by the political currents of recent years and the fact that 'the crisis' has, since 2008, dominated policy thinking and attention (Begg 2013), but it is also pertinent to ask whether there are intrinsic obstacles. One issue is where responsibility for sustainable development sits in government structures. In some Member States there is a ministry directly responsible, but in most cases the lead ministry's main focus is the environment. In the European Commission, too, DG Environment has the lead in administering sustainable development, although the Secretariat-General is also engaged. It is less evident that there is strong leadership (as opposed to warm rhetoric) in pushing forward some of the sustainability agenda, and it is easy for grand ambitions to be let down by lukewarm implementation. More positively, the experience of other EU strategies (for example, on social inclusion) suggests that there is a gradual progression from lofty but impractical goals to much more concrete policy initiatives.

2.5.1 The Evolution of the EU Strategy

As noted above, sustainable development as an over-arching goal of the EU first appears in the Treaty on European Union. In the strategy agreed at the 2001 Gothenburg European Council, there appeared to be equal weighting given to the competitive, environmental and social dimensions of the strategy. Although the environmental dimension of sustainable development is well elaborated in EU policies, the connections to 'social' are much less so. Attempts to link climate change and social policy have been rare (for an exception, see Gough et al. 2008), although some of the likely effects can easily be anticipated. One possible inference to draw is that a much strengthened precautionary principle should shape the social responses to climate change, with provision for the adaptation costs of the most vulnerable. Another would be to reconfigure tax and spending programmes in anticipation of the possibility of fuel poverty: rises in fossil fuel prices may be deemed essential to curb emissions (Fischer-Kowalski et al., 2012) but are likely to have a regressive effect that would need to be offset by other tax or benefit changes if fiscal neutrality for the least well-off is to be assured. Similarly, investment in low-carbon physical capital (especially buildings but also more fuel-efficient appliances) will be least affordable by low-income households.

What is perhaps overlooked in these debates is that the social dimension of sustainable development is predominantly a national policy issue and that the battle-grounds are the national politics of distribution. Many environmental issues, by contrast, are intrinsically supranational. This is not to deny that there is a global social dimension to sustainable development, captured *inter alia* in the Millennium Development Goals and in the inclusion of social standards in trade policy negotiations. But the bulk of what is social is jealously guarded in the EU by Member States.

The 2006 re-launch of the SDS set out seven key challenges, four of which are facets of environmental sustainability and two of which are social, while a seventh refers to global poverty and sustainability. Despite retaining the three distinctive over-arching aims of the 2001 SDS, the 2006 strategy appears, in these seven challenges, to be dominated by environmental objectives, distinguishing it from, notably, the Millennium Development Goals. What is noticeably absent from this list are competitiveness, growth and employment – the primary objectives of the Lisbon strategy since 2005. For each of the seven challenges the Council presented a list of ongoing or new actions to be implemented and corresponding objectives and targets.

In 2005, the EU launched an innovative Emissions Trading System (ETS) through which emissions of CO_2 (and two other greenhouse gases) by industrial producers are regulated by obliging electricity generators and producers in other industries which are heavy users of fossil fuels to obtain permits for each tonne of carbon dioxide emitted. The ETS also set up a market in which permits could be bought and sold, a feature which established a carbon price. The ETS is now in a third phase launched in 2013 in which more permits are being auctioned rather than granted at no cost to existing producers. However, because too many permits were offered the carbon price has been low, with the result that incentives to adopt cleaner technologies have been limited.

2.5.2 Europe 2020

The adoption of the Europe 2020 strategy (Commission 2010a) marked a new departure for sustainable development policy, both in the core ambitions for growth to be 'smart, sustainable, inclusive' and in assigning sustainability goals to two of the strategy's seven 'flagship initiatives' (FIs) that constitute (along with five headline targets) the key components of the strategy. By placing sustainability at its heart, the strategy requires all actions under it to take account of the goal, although what is less evident is how any clashes between the three headline ambitions are to be resolved. The juxtaposition of the three pillars also implies an emphasis on the environmental dimension, with social more under 'inclusive'.

Yet scope for confusion and incoherence remains. The Commission Communication (Commission 2010b) on the review of the EU budget adopted a rather glib mapping of the aims of Europe 2020 to budget lines, equating 'sustainable' with the common agricultural policy, while alluding to mainstreaming of climate change policies. Inclusive growth appears to have taken over the mantle of social sustainability.

Two of the Europe 2020 FIs are intended to support the sustainability agenda. The first, dubbed 'Resource Efficient Europe' has an obvious remit to lower carbon emissions and to reduce the intensity of use of other raw materials. A key concept is decoupling in the sense of breaking the long-established pattern of energy and resource use rising in tandem with output growth. The second FI has a more oblique link to sustainability: 'An industrial Policy for the Globalisation Era'. It covers a wide gamut of policies around encouragement of small and medium-sized enterprises (SMEs) and development of new industries, and better regulation, but also mentions assisting EU businesses to become more sustainable and the EU leading the way globally in sustainable development.

What is immediately apparent from the Europe 2020 approach is that the interpretation of 'sustainable' largely excludes 'social'. In the industrial policy FI, there is a reference to corporate social responsibility, while support for restructuring of sectors in difficulty (including through the Globalisation Adjustment Fund) is among the points highlighted. Apart from these two instances, it is hard to identify other direct social aims. By contrast, the industrial policy FI frequently alludes to resource savings and fostering the green economy.

Instead, social aspects of the 2001 definition of SD have now been encompassed under the heading of inclusive growth, albeit with a strong connection to cohesion policy. There are two FIs to promote it, the first concerning new skills and jobs, and the second action against poverty. The new skills FI builds on the employability and flexicurity agenda that has been central to EU employment strategies in recent years, complemented by promotion of equality and work–life balance, plus new emphases on skills and qualifications. The anti-poverty FI is stated to be about economic, social and territorial cohesion, but much of its content can be found in the strategy for social protection and social inclusion it replaces. Intriguingly, while the European Social Fund is highlighted in relation to the anti-poverty FI, the European Regional Development Fund is not singled out in these social FIs.

It is instructive to look at how sustainability features in the other flagship initiatives. The FI on industrial policy is largely about a new approach to industry and is replete with statements about boosting the competitive position of EU companies, notably SMEs. There are frequent references throughout the document to making industry more sustainable, though the allusions are almost exclusively to sustainable use of raw materials and energy. Complementary statements about finding sustainable solutions are in the innovation union FI. There are occasional phrases in the industrial policy FI that suggest a broader interpretation, such as a statement in a section on CSR that contrasts short-term profit maximisation with 'sustainable value creation'. However, other than in the section on CSR – itself largely about environmental obligations as set out in the text – a social angle is barely visible in this FI.

The new skills FI does refer to sustainability in the context of 'an ambitious commitment to the sustainability of Europe's social model, welfare systems, economic growth and public finances'. It also refers to sustainable pensions, but in the rest of the communication, the principal references to sustainability are in ensuring that a lack of suitable skills and competences does not impede the attainment of sustainable growth.

In the poverty FI, there is a reference to 'ensuring sustainable job-intensive growth' as the 'safest' route out of poverty, and pension sustainability is again addressed, with active ageing championed. The section on pensions also notes the need for a balance to be 'struck between equity, efficiency and sustainability', implying that sustainability transcends the conventional dichotomy between equity and efficiency. However, one nuance in the poverty FI is to refer to the 'sustainable involvement' of nongovernmental organisations and citizens, notably the engagement of those experiencing poverty. The youth on the move FI barely mentions sustainability, except in relation to university finances and the wider public finances. Similarly, the digital agenda FI mentions sustainable healthcare, but with the stress on costs, rather than more overtly social aims, while the innovation union FI refers to the 'sustainability and efficiency of our social and health-care systems'. The digital agenda FI does, though, mention the role of public funding (including through the European Investment Bank), stating that 'funding instruments should be used for well targeted broadband investments in areas where the business case is currently weak and, therefore, only such focused intervention can render investments sustainable'.

Uncertainty again comes into play in relation to the direction for change of the social model. While Europe 2020 is sufficiently all-embracing to accommodate many social goals, it is much less clear how tensions will be mediated or where the political emphasis will be put. Although social aims are evident in the poverty and new skills FIs, as well as in the five headline targets, it is not obvious how other facets of the European Social Model will be integrated. Equality, for example, risks being lost in the traffic.

The manner in which sustainable development is encouraged and integrated with other policy initiatives is also salient. Among tools to have been deployed are impact assessment and so-called 'mainstreaming', the latter consisting of the obligation to take account of the theme in all policy areas both in the design of policy and in assessing its effects. A predictable flaw is that, by being notionally pervasive, it is also easily reduced to rhetoric rather than action.[2] Moreover, with many themes supposed to be mainstreamed, there is likely to be competition for attention and political space (Geyer and Lightfoot 2010), with the result

---

2 This was the experience of gender mainstreaming in the European Employment Strategy – see Begg et al. (2010).

that it is only those themes that resonate with policy leaders or are sufficiently resourced within the bureaucracy that make progress. They show that SD has often suffered in this regard, attracting sporadic interest, then fading from view when, for example, a new EU Presidency shifts tack or a core policy area (such as the Lisbon strategy (from 2005–2009)) takes precedence. However, on the evidence of the years since the euro crisis came to dominate the policy agenda, the Europe 2020 strategy has lost visibility, momentum and (perhaps most tellingly) political attention (Begg 2013; Diebold 2013).

2.5.3 Implementation of SD Policy

The conjunctions of change involved in moving towards a more sustainable Europe will involve a variety of transitions and resort to diverse forms of governance. The preferred form of implementation up to the crisis was soft coordination, with the bulk of the policy initiatives coming from the national level. Such coordination provides orientations to national policies without the heavy-handed application of legal restrictions, but is always vulnerable to the charge that it has only marginal effects. Equally, their impact may still be profound in shifting the thrust of social policy and the architectures of social systems. These impacts are cognitive as well as procedural. The 'flexicurity turn' in social protection policy (for an overview, see Mandl and Celikel-Esser, 2012), for example, can be seen as a template and a goal for Member State policies: while the logic of the open method leaves implementation firmly with Member States, it suggests an ideal-type towards which Member States should gravitate, with the implicit corollary that those which make the least progress need to do most to shift towards the model.

Yet a likely legacy of the crisis years will be a toughening of EU mechanisms of coordination. The 2012 Treaty on Stability, Coordination and Governance, ratified by 26 of the 28 EU Member States, is often equated with the Fiscal Compact, but also contains a section on coordination that presages closer oversight and more intrusive scrutiny of national supply-side policies. The so-called 'European semester', another of the governance reforms introduced, potentially gives the Commission a greater prescriptive role.

The timescales for the EU approach to SD are distinctive insofar as the objectives are long term and do not have specific milestones, but there are defined periods for action. In contrast to nation-states, the EU is much less bound by political cycles around elections. However, Goetz (2009, p. 209) argues that 'governing by timetable is a prominent feature of EU governance', and he observes that there can be intensive political bargaining around timetables for policies. Three year bargains became the norm under the first Barroso Commission for the revamped Lisbon strategy and were maintained for Europe 2020. Sustainable development lacked such precision in its original formulation in 2001, but the re-launch in 2006 adopted national action plans with three year horizons and annual updating. In Goetz's terms, this helps to establish a functional means of committing Member States to actions in a coordinated manner. Since 2010, however, an annual cycle has become the norm, and it is also striking that the European Council has emerged as the institution at the pinnacle of economic governance, with set points in the annual cycle for different initiatives, even though crisis management between 2010 and 2013 often derailed the timetable.

Even so, the political salience of SD is affected by other time-related variables, especially those emanating from Member States, leading Goetz to claim that EU time is sensitive, notably to factors such as the interplay between rotating presidencies and national political calendars. Manifestly, the momentum behind sustainable development has been affected by such considerations: Sweden in 2001 was able to make headway, but other presidencies have demurred or been unable to devote enough political time to it because of too many other, more immediate priorities. Timetables may also help to explain why sustainable development – with intermittent support and three year planning cycles – has struggled for explicit funding (despite the rhetorical flourish of labelling line 1 of the 2007–2013 and 2014–2020 budget packages as 'sustainable growth', largely comprising cohesion and research policies) from the EU budget.

Instruments associated with the open method of coordination (national plans, scrutiny by EU institutions, peer review, benchmarking, and so on) have their supporters and their detractors, but for the time being it is hard to see much alternative. Europe 2020 promised more effective governance than its Lisbon and SDS predecessors but, as always, the key will lie in delivery rather than structures, and the experience in the EU since the crisis erupted has not been encouraging. Some pointers may emerge from looking at labour market transitions, extensively analysed following on from the work reported in Schmid and Gazier (2002) – see also Rogowski (2008) – and it may be that SD policy can learn from these analyses. In production, the necessity of 'cleaner' technologies is understood, although it is less clear that the nature and sequence of transitions are. Consumers are increasingly receptive to calls to conserve energy or to favour sustainable goods and services, but the consistency of transition is often hard to discern.

2.6 CONCLUDING COMMENTS

Any sustainable development strategy has to navigate between competing demands, and the three pillar approaches of the EU's 2006 strategy as well as the three buzzwords of Europe 2020 exemplify the sorts of trade-off that have to be accommodated. With new or accentuated uncertainties, the parameters of any trade-off are subject to change. Barbier's (1999) distinction between strategic and political aims of actors can be helpful in understanding SD tensions. As he points out, discretionary political decisions are to be expected at the end of a process, and may impart a bias towards consensual decisions. While his focus was on evaluation, these arguments have a wider resonance.

Sustainability can be conceived of as achieving a balance between different goals and effects, but with the complication that in some cases there is the great unknown of the tipping-point at which concessions within a trade-off have asymmetric effects. For example, competitiveness aims may dictate some tolerance of environmental degradation, but if the degradation goes too far it can have non-linear effects – hence the need in some aspects of SD for timely interventions:

> When systems work, when they are in equilibrium, they tend to continually produce possibilities for renewal ... Wild species naturally replace themselves. But populations will crash, possibly to extinction, if they are overharvested. We can even extend this notion to humans and their interactions. Children who are well-nourished, educated and cared for tend to flourish, carrying with them a lifelong capacity to contribute to their community. Deprive them of those things and the outcome is likely to be quite different. The same is true at the societal and governmental level. Abuse, conflict or deprivation can cause entire communities to collapse. (Strange and Bayley 2008, p. 15)

Policy-making involves a combination of goal-setting, choice of instruments, implementation and various techniques for review of approaches (monitoring, evaluation, peer review) in what is typically a recursive process. But there are also periodic shifts in the underlying paradigm that transcend goals, and the conjunction of climate change and the wide-ranging re-assessments that have followed the succession of crises since 2007 may have instigated such a shift. Rather than dwelling on possible incompatibilities between competitive and social aims, perhaps a more useful breakdown would be between what might be called *wealth-creating* objectives (such as the single market, monetary union, and the promotion of scientific and technological advance) and *wealth-distributing and quality of life* ones (sustainable development, cohesion and quality of environment). This is the nub of approaching sustainability as a governance and social science issue, rather than one that is purely technological. Indeed, the call from the German Advisory Council on Climate Change (2011) – in a report on the way forward – for a new social contract concludes with the statement that 'science will play a decisive, although subservient, role'.

A specific aspect of this is the approach to be adopted towards growth. It is sometimes argued that an environmental imperative necessitates slower growth. Similarly, a long-standing narrative about social policy is that it can only be accommodated (or afforded) if growth creates a sufficiently large cake to allow a proportion of it to be allocated to distributive ends. But a sustainability perspective invites a more subtle analysis. Not all growth is good and the case for looking at a wider range of outcomes for well-being, as discussed in the Stiglitz report, is compelling. The Europe 2020 formula of smart, sustainable and inclusive has a certain Panglossian tone to it, and hard choices may have to be made about the overall growth rate and what it encompasses: more services and knowledge products; a focus on goods rather than 'bads'; and so on?

In the Europe 2020 strategy, sustainability has again become better integrated with economic aims, having lost ground under the post-2005 Lisbon strategy. In the terms of the GUSTO project, these shifts could constitute a shake-up in the governance of uncertainty. It is far from clear that it has adequate mechanisms or sufficient attention from policy-makers. Bearing in mind that economic reform requires consistency and perseverance, often with reforms having to be implemented in a sequence before they bear fruit, it would be regrettable if a lack of political attention at the highest level diminished commitments to reform. But perseverance with some of the difficult policy orientations that underpin long-run change can only be kept up if there is a demonstrable political pay-off. This may be the ultimate governance challenge for sustainable development.

2.6.1 Five Uncertainties

In conclusion, it is useful to return to the issue of uncertainty and how it connects to sustainability. Central to the governance of uncertainty, as explained by Crouch (2009), is how it could be diminished or redistributed to those better able to cope with it. Sustainable development is, however, subject to such diverse forms of uncertainty that its governability may be problematic. At least five aspects of uncertainty render SD hard to govern.

First, it is evident that, at the European level, the notion of sustainable development has lacked an agreed narrative and has waxed and waned in its importance in EU policy-making. Of itself, this engenders uncertainty about what policies to promote it are designed to achieve. As a result, it is all too easy for sustainable development to lose the attention of policy-makers, who find it easier to focus on policies or strategies with more immediate or more narrowly defined agendas. Indeed, since the eruption of the euro crisis in 2010, crisis management and the elaboration of a new euro governance framework have claimed the bulk of the attention of policy-makers, with longer-term sustainability largely neglected. The upshot of this policy uncertainty is that actors are not able easily to identify any sort of common vision of what sustainable means.

A second uncertainty surrounds how the tensions between the different axes of sustainable development are reconciled. With climate change still the most coherent driver of change, social goals are prone to be relegated to secondary importance. Indeed, in the EU lexicon, the adoption of the term 'inclusive' seems to have been a means of separating the social dimension from the ecological, with the latter in the ascendancy. But in the wake of crisis, the EU's 2014 Climate Change White Paper (Commission, 2014) saw some watering down of the commitments to energy savings in the transport sector. Concerns about the competitive threat from other parts of the world benefiting from much lower energy prices (for example, in the US where the shale revolution has been transformative) appear to have had some influence.

Third, there is uncertainty about how governance processes are supposed to operate. At EU level, sustainable development has been implemented principally by soft coordination, but may now need a different toolkit. National sensitivities must, though, be expected to constrain what is possible.

A fourth uncertainty is about winners and losers. Mitigation of climate change is likely to have notable distributive consequences, raising energy prices and demanding higher investment in energy efficiency. Adaptation to climate change will pose the greatest challenges for countries facing threats from rising sea levels, desertification or damagingly higher temperatures. But the incidence of many of these changes across social groups and nations is surprisingly hard to predict and means that many groups face not just insecurity, but a lack of predictability about how their circumstances are likely to evolve. Taxing carbon, for example, may raise the cost of oil and gas to the consumer, but reduce it for producers to the extent that it dampens demand. Government revenues would benefit, but how these windfall gains are used will depend on a complex web of other public policy decisions. The debate sparked by Piketty

(2014) about inequality has also been influential in raising questions about the fairness of contemporary models of capitalism.

Finally, there is an uncertainty about whether the growing realisation that 'business as usual' cannot work points to a new economic model with – however ill-defined at present – sustainability attributes. Crouch (2008) argued that a successor to the neo-liberal paradigm is yet to be found but will emerge, although he suggests that it will be dominated by large corporations that come under pressure to steer the economy more 'responsibly'. Sustainable development is hard-wired into the EU Treaty and has been circling around EU policy-making for over a decade, yet the vacillations in its definitions and priorities demonstrate that it is still some way from being a coherent model. It chimes with the well-being, as opposed to GDP, turn.

To end on a positive note, it should not be forgotten that uncertainty need not always be something negative, but can also be a source of creativity and opportunity. Is sustainable development becoming the basis for a new European capitalism? The *trentes glorieuses*, Keynesian model of the early post-war decades gave way from the 1970s to what Crouch (2008) depicts as the neo-liberal model, but the latter is arguably also now in retreat, albeit without a clear sense of what will supplant it. Being 'pro-green', Lenschow and Sprungk (2010) assert, has become part of the brand identity of the EU, so that even though the EU's performance in promoting ecological sustainability may fall short of its aspirations, it is still a potent legitimating narrative. Perhaps its time has come.

BIBLIOGRAPHY

Arrow, K.J. (2007), 'Global climate change, a challenge to policy', *Economists' Voice*, **4** (3), 1–5.

Bailey, R. (2011), *Growing a Better Future*, Oxford: Oxfam.

Barbier, J.-C. (1999), 'Inter-governmental evaluation: balancing stakeholders' expectations with enlightenment objectives?', *Evaluation*, **5**, 373–86.

Barbier, J.-C. (2008), *La longue marche vers l'Europe sociale*, Paris: PUF.

Begg, I. (2009), 'Paving the way for a strategy of sustainable development', in M.-J. Rodrigues (ed.), *Europe, Globalization and the Lisbon Agenda*, Cheltenham and Northampton, MA: Edward Elgar.

Begg, I. (2013), 'Socio-ecological transition in a period of crisis: how well is the EU coping?', NEUJOBS Policy Report No.1. www.neujobs.eu (accessed 8 December 2014).

Begg, I., C. Erhel and J. Mortensen (2010), *Medium-Term Employment Challenges of the Lisbon Strategy*, report for European Commission Directorate-General for Employment, Social Affairs and Equal Opportunities. http://www.ceps.eu/book/medium-term-employment-challenges (accessed 8 December 2014).

Burchell, S. and J. Lightfoot (2004), 'Leading the way: the European Union at the WSSD', *European Environment*, **14**, 331–41.
Commission (2010a) 'Europe 2020', COM (2010) 2020, Brussels, 2 March.
Commission (2010b) 'The EU budget review', COM (2010) 700, Brussels, 19 October.
Commission (2014), 'A policy framework for climate and energy in the period from 2020 to 2030', COM (2014) 015 final, Brussels, 22 January.
Crouch, C. (2008), 'What will follow the demise of privatised Keynesianism?', *Political Quarterly*, **79**, 476–87.
Crouch, C. (2009), 'The governance of uncertainty and sustainability: tensions and opportunities', GUSTO Paper 2.1. http://www.gusto-project.eu/index.php?option=com_content&view=article&id=68:gusto-paper-21&catid=35:academic-papers&Itemid=57 (accessed 7 December 2014).
Daly, H. (2008), 'A steady-state economy', *UK Sustainable Development Commission*. http://www.sd-commission.org.uk/data/files/publications/Herman_Daly_thinkpiece.pdf (accessed 8 December 2014).
Deroose, S. and C. Kastrop (eds) (2008), 'The quality of public finances: findings of the Economic Policy Committee–Working Group', European Economy Occasional Paper No. 37.
Diebold, C. (2013), 'Europe's sustainability strategy – a casualty of the euro crisis or an ambitious restart?', Bertelsmann Stiftung Policy Brief No. 2013/06.
Dyson, K. (2014), *States, Debt, and Power: 'Saints' and 'Sinners' in European History and Integration*, Oxford: Oxford University Press.
Ferrera, M. and S. Sacchi (2009), 'A more social EU: issues of where and how', in S. Micossi and G.-L. Tosato (eds), *The European Union in the 21st Century: Perspectives from the Lisbon Treaty*, Brussels: CEPS.
Fischer-Kowalski, M., W. Haas, D. Wiedenhofer, U. Weisz, I. Pallua, N. Posssaner, A. Behrens, G. Serrio, M. Alessi and E. Weis (2012), 'Socio-ecological transitions: definitions, dynamics and related global scenarios', NEUJOBS State of the Art Report No.6.
German Advisory Council on Climate Change (2011), *World in Transition: A Social Contract for Sustainability*, Berlin: WBGU.
Geyer, R. and S. Lightfoot (2010), 'The strengths and limits of new forms of EU governance: The case of mainstreaming and impact assessment in EU public health and sustainable development policy', *Journal of European Integration*, **32**, 339–56.
Giddens, A., P. Diamond and R. Liddle (eds) (2006), *Global Europe, Social Europe*, Cambridge: Polity Press.
Goetz, K.H. (2009), 'How does the EU tick? Five propositions on political time', *Journal of European Public Policy*, **16**, 202–20.
Gough, I., J. Meadowcroft, J. Dryzek, J. Gerhards, H. Lengfeld, A. Markandya and R. Ortiz (2008), 'JESP symposium: climate change and social policy', *Journal of European Social Policy*, **18**, 325–44.
Hemerijck, A. (2012), *Changing Welfare States*, Oxford: Oxford University Press.
Hudson, J. and S. Kühner (2009), 'Towards productive welfare? A comparison analysis of 23 countries', *Journal of European Social Policy*, **19** (1), 34–46.
Jackson, T. (2009), *Prosperity without Growth? The Transition to a Sustainable Economy*, London: Sustainable Development Commission.
Lenschow, A. (2005), 'New regulatory approaches in "greening" EU policies', in A. Jordan (ed.), *Environmental Policy in the European Union*, London: Earthscan, 295–316.

Lenschow, A. and C. Sprungk (2010), 'The myth of a green Europe', *Journal of Common Market Studies*, **48**, 133–54.
Llewellyn, J. and C. Chaix (2007), *The Business of Climate Change II*, London: Lehman Brothers.
Magnusson, L. (2010), 'After Lisbon – social Europe at the crossroads?', European Trade Union Institute Working Paper No. 1.
Mandelson, P. (2007), 'The European Union in the global age', *Policy Network*. http://trade.ec.europa.eu/doclib/docs/2007/march/tradoc_133798.pdf (accessed 2 December 2014).
Mandl, I. and F. Celikel-Esser (2012), *The Second Phase of Flexicurity: An Analysis of Practices and Policies in the Member States*, Dublin: Foundation for the Improvement of Living and Working Conditions.
McCool, S.F. and G.H. Stankey (2004), 'Indicators of sustainability: challenges and opportunities at the interface of science and policy', *Environmental Management*, **33**, 294–305.
Meadowcroft, J. (2008), 'From welfare state to environmental state', *Journal of European Social Policy*, **18** (4), 331–4.
Meeus, L., I. Azevedo, C. Marcantonini, J.-M. Glachant and M. Hafner (2011), 'EU 2050 low-carbon energy future: visions and strategies', EUI Working Papers RSCAS 2011/11.
OECD (2009), *Eco-innovation in Industry: Enabling Green Growth*, Paris: OECD.
Ostrom, E. (2010), 'Beyond markets and states: polycentric governance of complex economic systems', in Nobel Foundation (ed.), *Les Prix Nobels*, Stockholm: The Nobel Foundation.
Palier, B. (ed.) (2010), *A Long Goodbye to Bismarck: The Politics of Welfare Reform in Continental Europe*, Amsterdam: Amsterdam University Press.
Pawlowski, A. (2008), 'How many dimensions does sustainable development have?', *Sustainable Development*, **16**, 81–90.
Piketty, T. (2014), *Capital in the Twenty-First Century*, Cambridge, MA: Harvard University Press.
Rogowski, R. (ed.) (2008), *The European Social Model and Transitional Labour Markets*, Farnham: Ashgate.
Room, G. (2008), 'Social policy in Europe: paradigms of change', *Journal of European Social Policy*, **18**, 345–52.
Scharpf, F.W. (2002), 'The European Social Model: Coping with the challenges of diversity', *Journal of Common Market Studies*, **40** (4), 645–70.
Scharpf, F.W. (2009), 'The asymmetry of European integration, or why the EU cannot be a "social market economy"', *Socio-Economic Review*, **8** (2), 211–50.
Schmid, G. and B. Gazier (eds) (2002), *The Dynamics of Full Employment: Social Integration through Transitional Labour Markets*, Cheltenham and Northampton, MA: Edward Elgar.
Schmidt, V. (2002), *The Futures of European Capitalism*, Oxford: Oxford University Press.
Stern, N. (2007), *The Economics of Climate Change: Stern Review*, Cambridge: Cambridge University Press.
Stern, N. (2008), 'Key elements of a global deal on climate change', Working Paper, London, LSE.
Stiglitz, J. (2002), *Globalization and its Discontents*, London: Penguin.
Stiglitz, J. (2006), 'A new agenda for global warming', *Economists' Voice*, **3** (7), 1–4.

Stiglitz, J., A. Sen and J.-P. Fitoussi (2009), *Report by the Commission on the Measurement of Economic Performance and Social Progress*. http://www.stiglitz-sen-fitoussi.fr/documents/rapport_anglais.pdf (accessed 8 December 2014).

Strange, T. and A. Bayley (2008), *Sustainable Development: Linking Economy, Society, Environment*, Paris: OECD.

Taylor-Gooby, P. (2008), 'The new welfare state settlement in Europe', *European Societies*, **10**, 3–24.

van Zeijl-Rozema, A., R. Cörvers, R. Kemp and P. Martens (2008), 'Governance for sustainable development: a framework', *Sustainable Development*, **16**, 410–21.

Victor, D.G. (2006), 'Recovering sustainable development', *Foreign Affairs*, **85** (1), 91–103.

3. European social dialogue as multi-level governance: Towards more autonomy and new dependencies[1]

Paul Marginson and Maarten Keune

3.1 INTRODUCTION

Almost 20 years ago the Maastricht Treaty introduced procedures for European social dialogue (ESD), as part of a larger package of measures to strengthen the social dimension of European integration. ESD is considered to be one of the five main instruments that constitute the core substance of EU governance in the area of social protection and social rights, and hence a core feature of the European Social Model (Barbier, Rogowski and Colomb, in this volume). Through the Treaty provisions (Articles 154–155 TFEU), the European social partners received the competence to become, in principle, co-regulators of the European labour market. Two principal modes of governance were institutionalised. First, the European social partners have the right to negotiate framework agreements and then jointly request the Commission to start a process to convert these agreements into EU Directives such that they become formally incorporated into law. Secondly, they can conclude so-called 'autonomous framework agreements', the enforcement of which is not dependent on the European institutions but is their own responsibility. According to Article 155 TFEU, implementation of these autonomous agreements should be in accordance with the procedures and practices specific to management and labour and the member states. These two modes of governance apply both to the cross-sector ESD, which involves

[1] An earlier version of this chapter was published in European Integration online Papers 16 (1), 2012. A substantially modified version was published in the *British Journal of Industrial Relations* (Keune and Marginson 2013).

the peak-level European social partners, and the European sector social dialogue (ESSD), which today concerns some 40 sectors.

The conventional reading of the evolution of European social dialogue since its inception is that it has evolved from a relationship of dependency of the European social partners on the European institutions for the implementation of their framework agreements, towards a more autonomous position in which the social partners themselves take charge of implementation (Branch 2005; Léonard 2008; Smismans 2008). It is argued that in the second half of the 1990s several framework agreements were negotiated by the European social partners in the 'shadow of hierarchy' of the European Commission (Smismans 2008) and implemented through EU Directives. This pointed to a double dependency on the EU institutions: first on the 'threat of legislation' to reach an agreement and secondly on EU Directives to get it implemented. Since the early 2000s, the argument continues, the social partners have taken a more proactive and independent stance and opted to focus on autonomous framework agreements, concluded under TFEU Articles 154 and 155, and other 'new generation texts', including joint reports, recommendations, compendia of good practices, and so on, which are not directed at the European institutions in order to secure implementation. Autonomous agreements and other new generation texts are often considered to be 'soft' forms of governance since they do not rely on 'hard' European legislation. They are also taken as an indication of growing social partner autonomy since they rely on the social partners themselves for implementation (Weber 2010).

In this chapter we want to challenge and move beyond this rather linear and one-dimensional conceptualisation of the evolution of European social dialogue. Empirically, we will show that there has not been a straightforward move away from the 'implementation through Directive' mode in favour of autonomous agreements. Whereas this may seem the case if we take a view of the cross-sector dialogue only, the picture changes when we have a closer look and include developments in the ESSD in the analysis. Analytically, we will argue that framing the issue in terms of dependency *or* autonomy does not do justice to the complexity of relationships that are involved in ESD and ESSD, and in the implementation of framework agreements and other new generation texts. Also, it accords little attention to the role of power in the relationships involved. We draw on a multi-governance perspective to analyse the dynamics of European social dialogue, which allows us to capture the relevant multiple horizontal and vertical relationships, or interdependencies, between the European and national, and public and private, actors involved. Interdependency implies the presence of both autonomy *and* dependence in a relationship, and our central proposition is that these interdependencies simultaneously enhance and limit the capacity of the European social partners to make and implement agreements. We will show that the implementation of so-called 'autonomous agreements' entails multiple relations of dependency on national social partners and governments that limit the autonomy of the European social partners.

The structure of the chapter is as follows. In section 3.2 we discuss the added value a multi-level governance approach has for the analysis of European social dialogue, as well as the limitations of such an approach. In section 3.3 we present the horizontal and vertical relationships involved in ESD and ESSD. Section 3.4 summarises the types of agreement made to date under ESD and ESSD to establish if a shift from dependent to autonomous agreements has taken place. Section 3.5 examines the experience with the autonomous agreements under the ESD from a multi-level governance perspective whilst section 3.6 does the same with the new generation joint texts of the ESSD. Section 3.7 presents conclusions.

3.2 DEPENDENCY AND AUTONOMY IN EUROPEAN SOCIAL DIALOGUE: A MULTI-LEVEL GOVERNANCE PERSPECTIVE

In this section we will address the question of whether autonomous agreements provide the European social partners with increased autonomy compared with the dependency inherent in the implementation of agreements through Directives. 'Autonomy' here refers to self-government, to the possibility for a group – here the European social partners – to govern the actions of their own members through a collectively elaborated system of rules without intervention from an external authority over which they cannot exercise control. In the case of agreements implemented through Directives this external authority refers to the European institutions involved in adopting such Directives, most importantly the European Commission and the European Council. These external actors are indispensable to the transformation of a framework agreement into legal rules and hence its implementation, something which the European social partners cannot do by themselves. Hence, in this sense they become dependent on the European institutions, which seem to limit their autonomy. In the case of autonomous agreements the European social partners do not depend on the European institutions for implementation. This, then, seems to increase their autonomy. But is this really the case? To better understand these questions a multi-level governance perspective is required to get a grip on the relationships involved in European social dialogue and the implementation of its outcomes.

3.2.1 European Social Dialogue as Multi-level Governance

Because it captures essential features of the European Social Model (see Barbier, Rogowski and Colomb, in this volume) and of contemporary European industrial relations, a multi-level governance perspective has considerable analytical potential for understanding the development of the European social dialogue as well as European industrial relations more generally (Marginson and Sisson 2004; Leisink and Hyman 2005). Multi-level governance is both an 'outcome' of the effects of European integration on industrial relations, but it is also an intervening variable. As such it provides industrial relations actors who are grappling with the challenges and consequences of European integration with multiple options for regulatory intervention (and innovation), and choices between these. At the same time, applying a multi-level governance perspective to the European social dialogue holds the promise of contributing to the elaboration of the underlying concept. Analysis of the choices made by industrial relations actors in the face of multiple options invites consideration of power relations. Yet, 'the [multi-level] governance approach … has a strong bias towards effective and efficient problem-solving, and almost completely ignores questions of political power' (Jachtenfuchs (2001) cited by Leisink and Hyman (2005, p. 279)).

What, then, are the potential, and limitations, of the concept of multi-level governance for analysing European social dialogue? Originating in political science and European studies, two linked developments underpinned its elaboration as a conceptual framework: the emergence of new levels of governance at the supra-national, including the EU, and sub-national, including regions and territories, levels (Hooghe and Marks 2001); and the growing role of non-state actors in policy decision-making (Rhodes 2000). Accordingly, the multi-level governance concept contains both vertical and horizontal dimensions. Vertically it refers to increased interdependence between governance mechanisms at different levels, whilst horizontally it refers to growing interdependence between governmental (public) and non-governmental (private) actors (Marks and Hooghe 2004).

In terms of 'multi-level', the relevance to European social dialogue is readily apparent. European social dialogue as it developed after 1992 is in addition to, and does not displace, forms of social dialogue at national and sub-national levels. Moreover, multiple EU levels are involved – cross-sector, sector and (multinational) company – with multiple linkages to national and sub-national levels. In this chapter we focus on the cross-sector and sector dimensions of European social dialogue.

Concerning 'governance', the distinction typically made between government and governance (Jessop 2004; Sisson 2007) helps establish the relevance of the concept. Unlike government, governance is not nationally bound, and involves the supra-national and also the sub-national. Governance involves private institutions, which may be associations or individual organisations (e.g. corporations) as well as the public institutions of government. It therefore involves a range of social actors as well as the public authorities.[2] Regulation can be negotiated (via associations) or unilateral (via corporate hierarchies) as well as legally framed. Linkages between levels are not necessarily hierarchical, and links – or 'coupling' – between them tends to be loose rather than tight. In addition, the multi-level governance literature exhibits a focus on changing forms of governance, and associated scope for experimentation and innovation (Léonard et al. 2007). This includes changes in the nature and use of 'traditional' forms, including legal enactment and collective agreement, and the emergence of newer forms, such as 'soft' forms of joint regulation, including framework agreements and joint texts associated with European social dialogue, and the 'open method of coordination' associated with EU employment and social policy.

Specific features of the EU context, and of that framing European social dialogue, accentuate the relevance of the multi-level governance concept. As Leisink and Hyman (2005) observe, the EU has no executive apparatus of government, which raises uncertainty over who is the agent of governance and simultaneously creates scope for a range of private and public actors to exercise governance functions, including the social partners through European social dialogue. Secondly, the relationship between authority at the EU level and that at the national level is non-hierarchical, focusing attention on interaction between levels (Hooghe and Marks 2001). Reflecting this, the EU does not possess a vertically integrated industrial relations system which mirrors the national arrangements found in the majority of the former EU-15. The

[2] Cf. the work of authors like Hollingsworth, Crouch and Streeck (e.g. Hollingsworth et al. 1994; Hollingsworth and Boyer 1997; Crouch 2005). They argue in a broader way that economic action is coordinated through a series of coexisting modes of governance, ranging from the state and the market, to micro-hierarchies (firms, organisations), networks, associations and community.

corollary for European social dialogue is that there is no necessary relationship with forms of social dialogue at national and sub-national levels; the nature and extent of any interaction become crucial. Given this, attention needs to be paid to bottom-up dynamics, from national and sub-national levels to the European, as well as top-down ones. Third is the diversity in industrial relations institutions and governance arrangements across the member states, which has increased noticeably following the 2004 and 2007 eastern enlargements. An implication of such differences on the horizontal plane is that they shape the nature and extent of interactions between the European and national and sub-national levels. For example, the possible dynamics between the European level and the national level will differ if in a specific country the coverage rate of collective agreements is high or low, since this determines the capacity of the national-level social partners to implement agreements in their national context through such collective agreements.

In combination, these contextual features help account for the role of European social dialogue in experimenting with and developing some of the newer forms of governance on which the multi-level governance literature has focused. These include both the 'harder' binding agreements, which entail unparalleled rights for private actors in drawing up generally applicable measures, and 'softer' measures such as joint texts and autonomous agreements.

3.2.2 Limitations of the Multi-governance Approach

If the multi-level governance concept has evident potential for comprehending European social dialogue, under its current formulation it also has limitations. Chief amongst these is the absence of consideration of power relations. Accounting for the rise of multi-level governance as a prominent characteristic of contemporary European political systems, Marks and Hooghe's (2004) explanation is essentially based on the notion of scale efficiencies, augmented by democratic considerations. Their efficiency rationale is situated in the varying scope of the externalities arising from the provision of public goods. These can range from being global in scale, as in the case of climate change, to local in scale, as with municipal services. The scale of governance needs to reflect the varying scope of these externalities: accordingly, multi-level arrangements will be more efficient than a single level of governance. By implication, multi-level governance will also involve a separation of competences across levels. However, under a different line of transactions cost reasoning, competency on any given issue can be distributed across levels. A prime instance in European industrial relations is 'organised decentralisation' (Traxler 1995). This involves a centrally framed solution, or 'steer', which maps out the main principles but leaves the details to be determined at other levels, according to national and/or local circumstances. In this way the local parties do not each incur the transactions costs of drawing up the main principles of a solution, whilst also avoiding those arising from central specification of the details and mode of implementation. Put another way, similarity of interest on the issues of principle coexists with differences of interest on the details and modes of implementation. Concerning the European social dialogue, the option of implementation through national procedures and practices under Article 155 TFEU could be viewed as corresponding to this logic.

The democratic considerations identified by Marks and Hooghe (2004) relate to the enhanced capacity of multi-level arrangements to reflect heterogeneity of preferences amongst citizens, and to the benefits that may derive in terms of innovation and experimentation from having multiple governance units at any given level. Yet, as Regalia (2007) observes, democratic – or participation – advantages of multi-level governance do not necessarily equate with efficiency in economic terms, as they may increase overall transactions costs. For instance, the legitimacy of measures may be enhanced by the involvement in the governance process of (more) actors at more levels, although the more complex procedural arrangements which this requires necessarily increase transactions costs. In turn, this alludes to the role of power relations within multi-level governance arrangements.

Recalling that multi-level governance in European industrial relations is an intervening variable as well as an outcome, the evolving multi-level framework of governance presents actors with multiple options for regulatory interventions, both horizontally (different combinations of private and/or public actors) and vertically (various levels). Actors' choices – or manoeuvres – may well be informed by the efficiency and democratic considerations outlined above, but they will also be informed by power ones. Advantages can be secured in terms of power relations by pursuing one option rather than another. Moreover, the actors involved have differing power resources.

It follows that governance arrangements may well become a focus for contestation between the parties, as each strives to secure advantage. The optional European framework for transnational collective bargaining, proposed by the European Commission in the Social Agenda 2006–2010, provides an example of such contestation (see Keune and Warneck 2006). The European Commission proposed to develop such a framework to provide for the possibility to conclude transnational collective agreements at either enterprise level, that is, in multinationals with companies in more than one EU country, or sectoral level, that is, covering a certain sector in multiple EU countries. Its objective was to provide an innovative governance tool adapted to the increasingly transnational character of economic activity and labour relations and give legal status to transnational collective agreements. Within the context of the ESD the Commission started a consultation process with the European social partners on the issue. The European trade unions initially regarded the initiative with a certain degree of scepticism, but after internal debate the unions by and large support it, arguing that it will increase their capacity to act at this ever more important level. They did set out a number of basic conditions the framework should meet. From the outset, however, the European employers argued against the measure, since it aimed to facilitate collective bargaining above the national level. As such it was contrary to established employer preferences favouring further decentralisation of collective bargaining and, more generally, against further legal regulation of industrial relations. The employers' contestation of the initiative proved to be powerful enough to force the Commission to shelve its plans.

There may also be differences in preferences between the actors at European and national or local level, which will impinge both on the mandate to negotiate any European agreement and on its subsequent implementation, questions to which we return below. Alternatively, moves by actors in one sphere of governance may be connected to securing change in others. For example, the European Metalworkers' Federation (EMF) developed its initiatives in cross-border bargaining coordination in the first instance to strengthen the bargaining position of metalworkers' unions; however, an additional rationale for the EMF's initiative appears to have been to place indirect pressure on the Council of European Employers of the Metal, Engineering and Technology-Based Industries to change its stance on engaging in European social dialogue for the sector (Marginson and Sisson 2004). The scope for, and reality of, contestation underlines that there is no shared vision of the governance arrangements that should prevail within Europe's multi-level industrial relations framework. A further corollary is that the pattern of governance within this multi-level framework may not be consistent as, according to a calculus of power advantage, local solutions are opted for on some issues, national on others and supra-national on still others. Put differently, multi-level governance arrangements are themselves a source of governance uncertainty, but also offer multiple options or solutions that can be pursued by the different actors involved.

Introducing power relations into the multi-governance framework has implications for the evaluation of dependency and autonomy. Power relations are always two directional, involving autonomy *and* dependency for both sides, even where power is distributed unevenly (Giddens 1979). A consequence of this is that severing a relationship of dependency may implicate a loss of autonomy as well. In the case of European social dialogue, dependence on the European institutions to implement the outcome of negotiations via a Directive at the same time implies autonomy for the European social partners in relation to their national affiliates in order to realise implementation. The autonomy the European social partners attain through taking responsibility for implementing the agreements they conclude at the same time increases their dependence on their national affiliates. For instance, national affiliates which were reluctant to agree a mandate for a given negotiation are now also in a position to frustrate its implementation.

3.3 MULTI-LEVEL GOVERNANCE AND EUROPEAN SOCIAL DIALOGUE

Drawing on the above analysis leads us to consider European (sector) social dialogue as a constellation of horizontal and vertical relationships, as pictured in Figure 3.1. At the horizontal (EU) level, ESD and ESSD first of all concern horizontal relationships between European cross-sector and sector employers' organisations and trade unions. From the dynamics between these two sides, framework agreements (and other texts) may result. As mentioned earlier, two types of horizontal dependency relation with the European institutions are of importance. One is that the 'shadow of hierarchy' may play a crucial role in agreements coming about in the first place. Secondly, the European institutions are needed if the social partners want to achieve the transformation of their agreement into a Directive. In addition, a more basic dependency exists between the private actors which constitute the ESD and ESSD on the one hand and the EU's public institutions, in particular the European Commission, on the other. Both the ESD and the ESSD are dependent on the Commission for the resources that make their functioning possible in the first place. The Commission finances the meetings, studies and other activities without which ESD and ESSD committees would not be able to meet and operate. In the ESSD the dependence on the Commission has an additional dimension, concerning the mix of private and public actors involved (Léonard 2008). In formal terms, the ESSD is – like the ESD – a bi-partite process involving private actors. Yet public authority, in the form of the Commission, is deeply implicated in its functioning. The

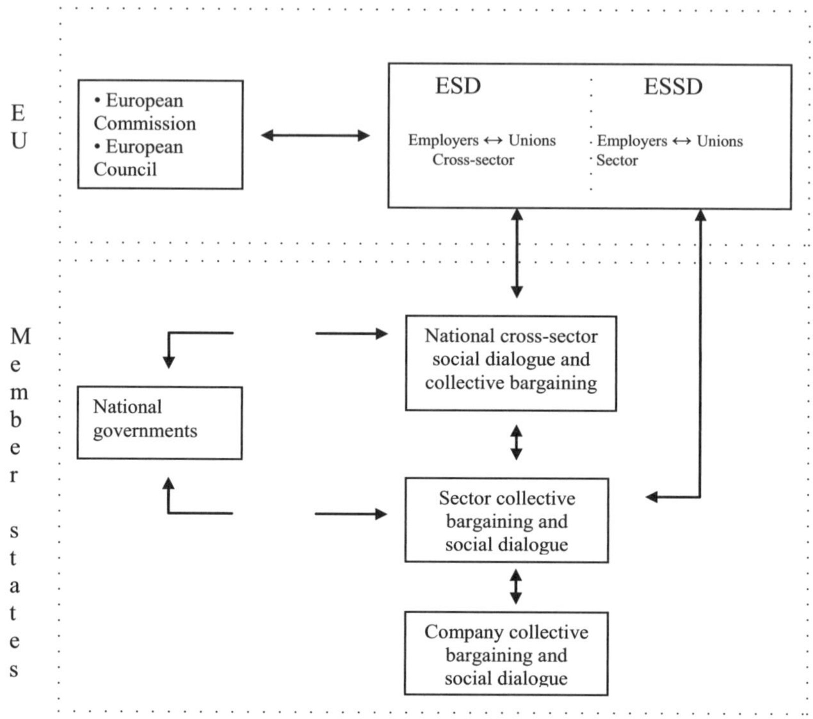

Figure 3.1 ESD–ESSD as multi-level governance

establishment of ESSD in any given sector is dependent on Commission authorisation, according to criteria established by the Commission.

The vertical relationships concern the relationships between the ESD–ESSD and the member state level. In formal (de jure) terms, the ESD relies on national (cross-sector) social partners for the mandate to engage in a European-level negotiation and, in the case of autonomous agreements, the subsequent implementation of the resulting outcome. In equivalent vein, the ESSD relies on the sector social partners at national level in respect of mandate to negotiate and subsequent implementation (if relevant). Yet, the relationship between the European and national social partners is non-hierarchical and, as established above, there is no top-down articulation mechanism. Indeed, social partners at the national level may have different preferences or priorities from their European counterparts. Hence, implementation is not guaranteed and ESD and ESSD are dependent on the cooperation, preferences and resources of national-level actors over which they cannot exercise control and that will differ substantially across the EU.

Moreover, de facto, the national social partners directly implicated by an autonomous agreement emanating from the ESD or ESSD, may be reliant on actions by other parties not directly implicated in the negotiation to secure implementation. Whether, and to what extent, this is the case depends on national institutional arrangements, which vary considerably. Under the ESD such a situation may arise where there is no institutional capacity or formal competence for negotiation at national, cross-sector level, and implementation rests on the actions of social partner organisations at sector level, or the parties at company level. Under the ESSD, the equivalent situation arises where there is no institutional capacity for negotiation at sector level nationally, and implementation rests on the actions of the parties at company level. In either instance, national social partners may turn to their national governments and request them to implement agreements through national legislation; a request to which governments may or may not respond favourably.[3]

From this analysis we can conclude that insofar as autonomous agreements increase the autonomy of the European social partners in respect of the European institutions, that they also entail relationships of dependency for their implementation, on social partners and governments in the member states. This seriously questions the prevailing reading of the evolution of the European social dialogue as moving from dependency to autonomy, something which is reinforced by the following section's review of the trajectory of agreements concluded under the ESD and ESSD. In the next section we will examine if there is indeed a shift from dependent to autonomous agreements. We then turn to demonstrate the potential of a multi-level governance perspective in informing analysis of the dynamics of the ESD and ESSD with a more empirical illustration of the issues discussed above. For the cross-sector level we will focus on the experiences with the autonomous agreements, whereas at the sector level we will examine the experiences with the new generation joint texts.

[3] In such a national adoption process it is of course possible that actors renegotiate the original agreement to some extent.

3.4 FROM DEPENDENT TO AUTONOMOUS AGREEMENTS?

A first issue to be resolved is if there is indeed a move from agreements implemented by Directives to autonomous agreements. Box 3.1 provides an overview of the agreements resulting from ESD and ESSD. Where the ESD is concerned, three Directives were adopted based on framework agreements in 1996, 1997 and 1999, whilst in 2009 an agreement was negotiated to revise the 1996 Directive on parental leave. Four autonomous agreements have been agreed, all in the 2000s. At first sight, this indeed suggests a move from a practice of implementation of ESD agreements through Directives to one of autonomous agreements. The 2009 agreement on the parental leave Directive to some extent contradicts such a trend, even though it concerns the revision of an earlier agreement. However, for the moment only four agreements of either type have been concluded and the conclusion of one further agreement to be implemented through a Directive would fatally undermine the linear portrayal.

BOX 3.1 FRAMEWORK AGREEMENTS RESULTING FROM ESD–ESSD

Cross-sector ESD

Agreements implemented by Council Directive
- Framework agreement on parental leave (revised) (2009)
- Framework agreement on fixed-term contracts (1999)
- Framework agreement on part-time work (1997)
- Framework agreement on parental leave (1996)

Autonomous agreements
- Framework agreement on inclusive labour markets (2010)
- Framework agreement on harassment and violence at work (2007)
- Framework agreement on work-related stress (2004)
- Framework agreement on telework (2002)

Sector ESD

Agreements implemented by Council Directive
- Framework agreement on decent working conditions in fishing (2012)*
- Framework agreement on health and safety in hairdressing (2012)*
- Framework agreement on the organisation of working time in inland waterways (2012)*
- Framework agreement on prevention from sharp injuries in the hospital and healthcare sector (2010)

- Framework agreement on the Maritime Labour Convention, 2006, and amending Directive 1999/63/EC (2009)
- Framework agreement on certain aspects of the working conditions of mobile workers engaged in interoperable cross-border services in the railway sector (2005)
- Framework agreement on the organisation of working time of mobile workers in civil aviation (2000)
- Framework agreement on the organisation of working time of seafarers (1999)

* Council decision pending following request from European social partners

Autonomous agreements
- Framework agreement on minimum contract rights for professional footballers (2012)
- Framework agreement on competence profiles in the chemicals industry (2011)
- Framework agreement on the implementation of European hairdressing certificates (2009)
- Framework agreement on the reduction of workers' exposure to the risk of work-related musculo-skeletal disorders in agriculture (2006)
- Framework agreement on workers' health protection through the good handling and use of crystalline silica and products containing it, 14 industrial sectors (2006)
- Framework agreement on the European licence for drivers carrying out a cross-border interoperability service (2004)
- European agreement on vocational training in agriculture (2002)

Moreover, the picture changes substantially when we consider also the ESSD. Here five agreements were implemented through Directives in the period 1999–2010 and five through the national procedures and practices mechanism. Yet two of the most recent framework agreements, concluded in 2009 and 2010 respectively, have both been implemented through a Directive. In short, there is no evidence of any shift from binding to autonomous agreements under the ESSD. Hence, taking the ESD and ESSD agreements together in terms of the number of agreements concluded, we cannot speak of a clear trend from agreements implemented through a Directive to autonomous agreements. In terms of scope, it might be argued that the Directives emerging from the ESSD are of less importance since they each cover only a small part of the economy and labour market. Nonetheless the ESSD experience clearly indicates that in the future we may expect new Directives to emerge from framework agreements.

3.5 EU CROSS-SECTOR SOCIAL DIALOGUE: AUTONOMOUS AGREEMENTS

Experience of the negotiation and implementation of the autonomous agreements on teleworking (2002) and work-related stress (2004) concluded under the European cross-sector social dialogue[4] underscores the challenges posed by non-hierarchical multi-level governance arrangements in framing and enacting measures which have the effects intended. Of particular interest from a multi-level governance perspective are the consequences and problems arising from the coupling of the European and national levels involved in Article 155's implementation mechanism via 'national procedures and practices specific to management and labour and the Member States'.

Interaction between the European and national levels occurs at different stages of the Article 154–155 negotiation and implementation procedures: the framing of the substantive negotiations; the procedural decision between the two possible implementation routes under Article 155 (giving an agreement binding force via a Directive or invoking 'national procedures and practices'); and the subsequent implementation of autonomous agreements within member states. The framing of the negotiations requires national member organisations to give their respective European social partners a mandate to negotiate on the issue in question. On telework, negotiations were prompted by proposals originally initiated by the Commission. The incentive for the social partners to contemplate negotiated European-level regulation on this, and the subsequent topics of work-related stress and workplace violence and harassment, probably lies in their status as newer industrial relations issues which are not (yet) subject to comprehensive regulation at national level. There are transaction costs advantages for national employer organisations and trade unions in framing a common approach at European level, and avoiding the additional resources involved in developing parallel initiatives in each member state (Marginson and Sisson 2004; Léonard et al. 2007). In the case of teleworking, the reasons why the social partners opted to negotiate with a view to implementation via the hitherto unused 'national procedures and practices' route reflected power, but also other considerations. According to Larsen and Andersen (2007),

[4] Reports on the implementation of the 2007 agreement on harassment and violence at work have yet to become available; whilst the 2010 agreement on inclusive labour markets has yet to become the focus of any evaluation of its implementation.

BusinessEurope (then the Union of Industrial and Employers' Confederations of Europe) and CEEP would not countenance a binding agreement, whilst the ETUC was initially divided between one group of affiliates which sought a binding agreement and another which preferred an autonomous agreement. The choice of implementation method, however, seems also to have 'reflected social partners' common wish to achieve increased autonomy from the European Commission and to show that they still had a role to play despite their failed attempt to reach an agreement on agency work [in 2001]' (Larsen and Andersen 2007, p. 184).

As a coupling mechanism, the 'national procedures and practices' implementation route is – by design – framed so as to accommodate diverse forms of implementation across countries, reflecting the diversity of national industrial relations arrangements. From a multi-level governance perspective the mechanism is consistent with the efficiency principle underpinning 'organised decentralisation' within national systems (Traxler 1995): the central actors agree on the principles and/or provide a steer, and leave decisions on the detail and implementation – which because of national diversity and therefore complexity risk jeopardising central-level agreement on the principles – to actors at lower levels. Consistent with this, both the 2006 joint evaluation of the implementation of the teleworking agreement undertaken by the social partners and the European Commission's own subsequent assessment find considerable variation in the mode of implementation amongst the 25 member states concerned (implementation in Bulgaria and Romania was still underway) (European Commission 2009, Table 5.2). The diversity apparent also points to differing mixes in terms of the respective roles of private actors – the social partners – and the public authorities. These different modes include national legislation, including incorporation in the Labour Code (e.g. Czech Republic, Hungary, Poland); inter-sector collective agreements, subject to legal extension (e.g. Belgium, France); sector collective agreements (e.g. Denmark); joint recommendations guidelines intended to prompt sector- and/or company-level negotiations (Finland, Spain); drawing up model company agreements (e.g. Germany – some sectors only); and adoption of joint guidelines and codes of good practice (e.g. Sweden, UK). Considerable variation in implementation mode is also evident from both the social partners' 2008 joint evaluation of the implementation of the work stress agreement, and the European Commission's (2011b) own subsequent evaluation report. Legislation was again the main implementing instrument in several member states (e.g. Czech Republic, Hungary, Poland); binding inter-sector agreements featured in others, subject to legal extension (e.g. Belgium, France, Romania); joint recommendations intended to prompt sector- and/or company-level negotiations featured in two (Finland, Spain); and adoption of joint guidelines and codes of good practice were adopted in several (e.g. Sweden, the UK). Whilst in almost all countries the preferred mode of implementation was the same for both agreements (European Commission 2011b, Box 6.6), the fact that social partners in four countries – Bulgaria, Estonia, Lithuania and Malta – have not reported on the implementation of either agreement underlines the dependence of the European social partners on the subsequent (in)action of their national affiliates.

This diversity of modes of implementation is, however, only partly attributable to the diversity in what might normally be considered 'national procedures and practices' (Larsen and Andersen 2007; Visser and Ramos Martín 2008; Prosser 2011). This draws attention to problems with operationalisation of 'national procedures and practices' as an implementation mechanism. Four kinds of problem have been identified (Larsen and Andersen 2007; Prosser 2007, 2011).

First are countries where the implementation mode adopted would seem to differ from conventional notions of the 'national procedures and practices' concerned. In this respect Larsen and Andersen cite Germany, where a mix of methods have been used, including sector collective agreements (e.g. local government and metalworking, corresponding to the conventional procedures and practices), drawing up model company agreements, joint declarations and the adoption of guidelines; and Sweden, where joint guidelines agreed at cross-sector level encouraged, but did not require, the conclusion of sector-level collective agreements (seen as the conventional procedure and practice). Indirectly this raises the second problem, which particularly arises in countries where sector-level agreements are a cornerstone of labour market regulation. 'National procedures and practices' may rely largely on (sector-level) actors not directly implicated in the negotiation and implementation of the autonomous agreement. Conversely, the cross-sector social partners who are directly implicated may not have domestic competence to conclude collective agreements. This applies to Denmark, as well as Germany and Sweden, where Prosser (2007) details how contestation arose between the national social partners over whether to conclude a cross-sector agreement recommending that their sector affiliates negotiate agreements. Ambiguities in the framing of the implementation mechanism thereby create scope for power relations to come into play. Thirdly, Prosser (2007) goes on to show how these ambiguities were exacerbated by previous interaction between European and national levels, since in

Denmark the practice of a cross-sector 'follow-up' agreement, as eventually concluded in the case of telework, was itself introduced into the Danish system as a means of implementing earlier binding agreements.

Fourth are countries where national procedures and practices are not well defined, leaving scope for contestation to emerge over implementation mode but also for choice and for innovation. Prosser (2011) cites the UK and many of the central eastern European member states as corresponding to this situation. These countries have neither strong national-level social dialogue structures and traditions, nor are sector-level collective agreements a central form of labour market regulation – either of which would constitute a well-defined national procedure and practice. Implementation of the teleworking and work-related stress agreements in the Czech Republic and Hungary was, at the request of the social partners, effected through the Labour Code. This choice was in fact consistent with established practice in both countries of social partner consultation over changes to the Labour Code. In contrast, in what amounts to an innovatory departure, the UK social partners concluded advisory guidelines on both occasions. On both occasions, the views of the peak employers' (CBI) and trade union (TUC) organisations differed: the TUC's proposal for an inter-sector agreement was opposed by the CBI on the grounds, amongst others, that there was no such tradition in the UK. The TUC was unable to mobilise the pressure required to secure its preferred course of action, and the alternative approach of agreeing non-binding guidelines – equally unfamiliar to UK tradition – was adopted (Prosser 2011). Crucially, the absence of well-defined national practices and procedures meant that the national social partners in these countries faced choices, which they exercised differently – with power relations shaping outcomes.

In addition to the dependency relationship between the European social partners and their national affiliates which is central to the national procedures and practices implementation mechanism, consideration of problems arising in its operationalisation bring to the fore the indirect dependencies depicted in Figure 3.1. These include sectoral employer and trade union organisations and also national governments.

Even if these various shortcomings in specifying the coupling between European and national levels were to be addressed (and it is not at all clear how the fourth, the absence of well-defined national procedures and practices, might be dealt with), the effect on policy and practice within companies and organisations would continue to rely wholly within the province of national-level actors, underlying the dependency of the European social partners on their national counterparts. On this issue, the 2005 multi-sector agreement on crystalline silica, concluded under

Article 155, but which does not rely on the 'national procedures and practices' transposition and implementation mechanism, goes considerably further (Léonard et al. 2007; European Commission 2009). Concluded between European employer and trade union federations representing 14 sectors, the agreement specifies a range of good practices to be implemented at sites across these sectors. To this end it directly implicates the company level in implementing and monitoring the agreement, through the establishment at each site of a joint monitoring committee comprising employer and employee representatives charged with promoting the good practices identified in the agreement, and periodically reporting to the European-level parties. In this way, the coupling between the European and national levels by-passes the national (sectoral) organisations, reaching down instead to the local level.

3.6 EUROPEAN SECTOR SOCIAL DIALOGUE: NEW GENERATION JOINT TEXTS

The experience of the ESSD points up the further challenges that are posed in giving effect within member states to regulatory initiatives which do not come under the negotiation and implementation provisions specified in the Treaty. Reviewing findings from two studies of the ESSD, Léonard (2008) draws attention to two problematic features. First, concerning the governance potential of the ESSD, Léonard reports that the social partners tend to hold rather different notions of the concept of 'social dialogue'. Employers' organisations tend to interpret dialogue as an exchange of views with a general presumption that it should not lead to regulation, whereas trade unions see dialogue as extending to negotiation and hold the aspiration that it may result in regulatory measures which have effects.[5] These differing perspectives are consistent with the idea of contestation over the role and outputs of these sector-level governance arrangements.

Second is the relationship with national industrial relations structures, and the social partners' national member organisations. Léonard highlights the nature of the coupling between national and European levels, which – as with the ESD – is non-hierarchical in nature, being two directional rather than top-down. ESSD committees are constrained in the scope of their agenda and their capacity to contemplate regulatory initiatives on the mandates that national member organisations are

[5] This equally applies to the ESD.

prepared to give them (as well as on the resources made available by these organisations, and by the Commission). In turn, transposition and effective implementation of any joint texts and agreements concluded by ESSDs 'largely depends on domestic dynamics over which the European social partners have little influence' (Léonard 2008, p. 408).

It is in this context that the period since 1998, when the ESSD was formally reconstituted by the Commission, has seen the emergence of 'new generation joint texts' characterised by increased emphasis on follow-up procedures involving monitoring and peer review, aimed at better ensuring transposition and effective implementation at national level (European Commission 2004). According to the Commission, the development embraces both framework agreements concluded under Articles 154 and 155 – either binding or autonomous – and 'process-oriented' texts such as frameworks of action, codes of conduct and guidelines. Whilst it remains the case that no more than ten framework agreements have been concluded under the ESSD (see Box 3.1), 55 process-oriented texts were concluded between 1999 and 2009 (Pochet et al. 2009; Weber 2010), with the incidence accelerating over the period, although the number of committees also increased from 24 to 40 in this period. Six types of follow-up procedure, sometimes used in combination, are identified by Pochet et al. (2009) amongst the texts concerned, which vary in the extent of the obligation they introduce on member organisations to report on implementation. At the 'harder' end of the spectrum are annual or periodic written reports, which through transparency and peer review entail the strongest obligation to demonstrate follow-up, whilst at the 'softest' end of the spectrum are presentations of good practice. Pochet et al. (2009) note that the extent of the follow-up obligation tends also to be related to the nature of the process-oriented text, being strongest for frameworks of action and least so for guidelines.

In multi-level governance terms, these procedures aim, to differing extent, to tighten the coupling between European and national levels. Indeed, Léonard (2008) confirms such intention on the part of the parties at European level: representatives of both employer and trade union federations interviewed saw transposition and effective implementation at national level as crucial for the long-term credibility of the ESSD. Yet practice would seem to fall some way short of intentions. In a study of ESSD in the electricity and commerce sectors, Weber (2010) concludes that inadequate 'level linkages' of two kinds are a major impediment to implementation of new generation texts in these sectors. Concerning the linkage between EU and national levels, she identifies the key role of the secretariats of sectoral European-level trade union and employer organisations in informing and communicating with national affiliates, and in steering their implementation activity. However, such activity tends not to be reciprocated in the other direction: the European-level organisations encounter considerable difficulty in eliciting information from national affiliates when monitoring implementation. This relates to the nature of a second, horizontal linkage at national level. Frequently awareness of ESSD is low or minimal, being confined to a single department or individual official in national affiliates. Put differently, ESSD would seem to remain detached from the mainstream activity of national social partner organisations.

Insofar as the follow-up procedures have the effects intended, these are likely to be more apparent in some countries than others, reflecting the diversity of industrial relations arrangements in any given sector across the EU. Attitudes to non-binding agreements and texts are, for example, more positive amongst affiliates in Denmark, where collective agreements are not legally binding but widely upheld, than they are amongst their counterparts in Germany, where collective agreements are legally binding and non-binding texts tend to be viewed as optional (Weber 2010). In those member states where sectoral structures for social dialogue and/or collective bargaining – and even member organisations – are weak or absent, including many of the central eastern European countries but also the UK, the capacity to ensure transposition and implementation is evidently limited. In contrast, in those countries where sector social dialogue and/or collective bargaining are well established such capacity exists and can be mobilised, as evidenced, for example, by the negotiations prompted in several countries by the 2002 agricultural sector agreement on vocational training (Léonard 2008).

3.7 CONCLUSIONS

The evolution of European social dialogue since its inception is often interpreted as a process that is moving from dependency on the European institutions towards more autonomy based on autonomous agreements. In this chapter we have shown that such a linear and one-dimensional view does not correspond to either empirical reality or the complexity of relationships that constitute the European social dialogue and the negotiation and implementation of its agreements.

Empirically, taking together the experience of the ESD and ESSD we cannot observe a trend away from agreements implemented by Directives and in favour of autonomous agreements. Even if the observation is confined to the ESD, the 2009 Directive giving effect to the revised parental leave agreement disrupts the trajectory which would constitute such a trend.

Whilst the negotiation and implementation of autonomous agreements may entail more autonomy from the European institutions, we have shown that their implementation also involves new dependencies on social partners and governments in the member states, reflected in a wide diversity of modes of implementation. The dependency *or* autonomy dichotomy presented in the conventional reading is a false one: negotiated regulation emanating from the European social dialogue rests on two-directional relations, between the European and national levels, involving autonomy *and* dependency at the same time. It also involves differing forms of horizontal interdependency between private actors – the social partners – and the public authorities according to the different institutional arrangements which prevail in member states. Further, implementation can also – in certain member states – rest on indirect dependencies in the shape of actors which are not directly implicated in the process, such as sectoral employer and trade union organisations. Power relations, which are conspicuously absent in the conventional reading, are integral to the playing out of these multiple interdependencies integral to European social dialogue as a mode of governance.

Grounding our analysis in a multi-level governance perspective has enabled us to capture key features of the two-directional vertical and horizontal relationships which European social dialogue involves. These include the central implication of the non-hierarchical vertical relationship between the European and national levels, which renders implementation of autonomous agreements dependent on the variable institutional geometry of national industrial relations; and the ambiguities in the specification of the coupling between the European and national levels which have arisen in operationalising the Treaty's 'national practices and procedures' implementation provision. The analysis also indicates ways in which the horizontal and vertical planes of interdependency which epitomise multi-level governance interact. As compared with binding agreements implemented through a Directive, autonomous agreements entail less horizontal interdependency at the European level (dependence of the European social partners on the European institutions) but greater vertical interdependency between the European and national levels, and possibly also increased horizontal interdependency at national level to the extent that national governments are called on to act. The outcome of these interactions is not predetermined but shaped by the preferences and power resources of the actors; contestation is an integral feature of multi-level governance arrangements, as our analysis has demonstrated. For this reason, multi-level governance arrangements are also a source of uncertainty in terms of the regulation that eventually results.

The central implication of our analysis of European social dialogue for existing conceptual work accounting for multi-level governance (e.g. Hooghe and Marks 2001) flows from the attention accorded to power relations, and hence the interplay between autonomy and dependency, in shaping governance arrangements and outcomes. Insofar as multi-level governance arrangements provide actors with choices and attendant scope for manoeuvre, our analysis concludes that outcomes will be contested with actors deploying their respective power resources to secure relative advantage. Considerations of power, as well as those of transactional efficiency and democracy, are integral to understanding the dynamics of multi-level governance arrangements.

REFERENCES

Branch, A. (2005), 'The evolution of the European social dialogue towards greater autonomy', *International Journal of Comparative Labour Law and Industrial Relations*, **21** (2), 321–47.

Crouch, C. (2005), *Capitalist Diversity and Change: Recombinant Governance and Institutional Entrepreneurs*, Oxford: Oxford University Press.

European Commission (2004), 'Partnership for change in an enlarged Europe', Communication from the Commission, COM (2004) 557. Brussels: European Commission.

European Commission (2009), *Industrial Relations in Europe 2008*, Brussels: European Commission.

European Commission (2011a), *Industrial Relations in Europe 2010*, Brussels: European Commission.

European Commission (2011b), 'Report on the implementation of the European social partners' framework agreement on work-related stress', Commission Staff Working Paper, SEC (2011) 241 final. Brussels: European Commission.

Giddens, A. (1979), *Central Problems in Social Theory: Action, Structure and Contradiction in Social Analysis*, London: Macmillan.

Hollingsworth, J.R. and R. Boyer (eds) (1997), *Contemporary Capitalism: The Embeddedness of Institutions*, Cambridge and New York: Cambridge University Press.

Hollingsworth, J.R., Philippe C. Schmitter and Wolfgang Streeck (eds) (1994), *Governing Capitalist Economies: Performance and Control of Economic Sectors*, Oxford: Oxford University Press.

Hooghe, L. and G. Marks (2001), *Multi-level Governance and European Integration*, Lanham, MD: Rowman and Littlefield.

Jachtenfuchs, M. (2001), 'The governance approach to European integration', *Journal of Common Market Studies*, **39** (2), 245–64.

Jessop, B. (2004), 'Multi-level governance and multi-level metagovernance', in I. Bache and M. Flinders (eds), *Multi-level Governance*, Oxford: Oxford University Press, pp. 49–74.

Keune, M. and P. Marginson (2013), 'Transnational industrial relations as multi-level governance: interdependencies in European Social Dialogue', *British Journal of Industrial Relations*, **51** (3), 473–97.

Keune, M. and W. Warneck (2006), 'An EU framework for transnational collective bargaining: an opportunity for European trade unions?', *Transfer: European Review of Labour and Research*, **12** (4), 637–41.

Larsen, T. and S. Andersen (2007), 'A new mode of European regulation?', *European Journal of Industrial Relations*, **13** (2), 181–98.

Leisink, P. and R. Hyman (2005), 'Introduction: the dual evolution of Europeanisation and varieties of governance', *European Journal of Industrial Relations*, **11** (3), 277–86.

Léonard, E. (2008), 'European sectoral social dialogue', *European Journal of Industrial Relations*, **14** (4), 401–19.

Léonard, E., R. Erne, P. Marginson and S. Smismans (2007), *New Structures, Forms and Processes of Governance in European Industrial Relations*, Dublin: European Foundation for the Improvement of Living and Working Conditions.

Marginson, P. and K. Sisson (2004), *European Integration and Industrial Relations*, Basingstoke: Palgrave Macmillan.

Marks, G. and L. Hooghe (2004), 'Contrasting visions of multi-level governance', in I. Bache and M. Flinders (eds), *Multi-level Governance*, Oxford: Oxford University Press, pp. 15–30.

Pochet, P., A. Peeters, E. Léonard and E. Perin (2009), *Dynamics of European Sectoral Social Dialogue*, Dublin: European Foundation for the Improvement of Living and Working Conditions.

Prosser, T. (2007), 'Europeanisation through procedures and practices?', FAOS Discussion Paper No. 77, Copenhagen: FAOS, University of Copenhagen.

Prosser, T. (2011), 'The implementation of the Telework and Work-Related Stress Agreements: European social dialogue through "soft" law?', *European Journal of Industrial Relations*, **17** (3), 245–60.

Regalia, I. (2007), 'Towards multi-level governance in industrial relations: mapping the field', Manchester: Plenary paper to IIRA European Congress, September.

Rhodes, R. (ed.) (2000), *Transforming British Government*, London: Macmillan.

Sisson, K. (2007), 'Revitalising industrial relations: Making the most of the institutional turn', *Warwick Papers in Industrial Relations* No. 85. Coventry: IRRU.

Smismans, S. (2008), 'The European social dialogue in the shadow of hierarchy', *Journal of Public Policy*, **28** (1), 161–80.

Traxler, F. (1995), 'Farewell to labour market associations? Organised versus disorganised decentralisation as a map for industrial relations', in C. Crouch and F. Traxler (eds), *Organised Industrial Relations in Europe*, Aldershot: Avebury, pp. 3–19.

Visser, J. and N. Ramos Martín (2008), 'A more "autonomous" European social dialogue: the implementation of the Framework Agreement On Telework', *International Journal of Comparative Labour Law and Industrial Relations*, **24** (4), 511–48.

Weber, S. (2010), 'Sectoral social dialogue at EU level – recent results and implementation challenges', *Transfer: European Review of Labour and Research*, **16** (4), 489–507.

4. EU governance on ageing: Older, wider and more influential than the OMCs[1]

Miriam Hartlapp

4.1 INTRODUCTION

There are good grounds to consider old age policy a least-likely issue to be dealt with at the EU level. Whereas pensions are the most important instrument to deal with ageing workers and old age security at the national level, governments are reluctant to transfer powers over pensions to the supranational level. Pensions are institutionally deeply entrenched (Schludi 2003), historically linked to nation building through welfare states (Korpi 1983) and highly salient, as can be seen in election disasters and high levels of mass mobilisation when reforms are on the agenda (Hartlapp and Kemmerling 2008). In addition, at the EU level a lack of financial resources renders distributive social policy a closed path. At the same time, decision making on social policy is an intricate matter given the growing diversity of Member States (Scharpf 2002), and the EU regulatory state continues to be characterised as limited (Majone 2005). Taking a closer look at this policy area, however, a number of instruments exist that influence national old age policies through soft coordination or hard legislation. Much of the existing political science research

[1] This is an extended and updated version of the online paper 'Deconstructing EU old age governance', European Integration online Papers, Special Mini-issue 1/16 (2012). I thank participants of the Berlin Colloquium on Social Policy, the lecture series 'Rescaling the welfare state', Centre Marc Bloch Berlin and collaborators in the GUSTO project, as well as Günther Schmid and Bernd Schulte for stimulating discussions and valuable comments and Jacob Düringer for research assistance. Financial support from the EU 7th Framework Programme as well as from a Schumpeter Fellowship provided by the Volkswagen Foundation is gratefully acknowledged.

in the area primarily debates the Open Method of Coordination (OMC) and in particular the OMC on pensions (De La Porte and Pochet 2002; Eckardt 2005; Lodge 2007; Natali 2009; Natali and De La Porte 2004; Pochet 2005). Starting from this observation, I critically ask how far the focus on soft governance via the OMC adequately reflects EU governance and its potential effect on old age policies.

Telling the story of how EU old age policy emerged, I will trace the form and substance of a range of EU instruments potentially impacting on national old age policies instead of focusing on the OMC as the most visible and most directly related instrument. This matters empirically as well as conceptually. First, analysing only the OMC on pensions is *too brief*. Going beyond an isolated assessment, this chapter argues that EU old age policy was initiated much earlier, unfolding over at least two decades. This is important for understanding whether EU governance has changed over time. Secondly, it is *too narrow*, because a number of (often less well known) instruments work in parallel, exerting direct influence (e.g. pension portability), belonging to the social policy context (e.g. age discrimination or participation of older workers in the labour market) or mattering for old age policy indirectly (financial services). Looking at their sum enables us to gain an adequate understanding of the different actors, arenas and interest constellations involved and thus of EU old age governance as a complex, at times contradictory and inherently political process. Thirdly, and following from the first two points, this has implications for the *depth and breadth of (potential) effects* on national social policy arrangements. While the governance capacity of the 'soft' OMC on pensions is typically overvalued, hierarchical influences of regulatory initiatives, for example via individual rights for non-discrimination or indirect influences of a fiscal logic on national social policy via the European Monetary Union (EMU), are often underestimated.

Section 4.2 outlines the analytical and methodological approach. What follows is a brief historical tracing of direct old age policy without formal competences since the 1980s (section 4.3). Turning to more recent policy developments, problem perceptions and actor constellations will be discussed. Here, legal instruments that exert their potential effect on old age through social legislation (anti-discrimination) or indirectly (financial services) (section 4.4) will be contrasted with soft governance instruments coordinating national policies in the area of employment and pensions (section 4.5). The final section (4.6) offers conclusions.

4.2 DECONSTRUCTING GOVERNANCE: SOFT OMCS AND HARD EU LAW, DIRECT AND INDIRECT INFLUENCE

In the late 1990s, the EU level witnessed the emergence of the OMC. Taking a starting point with the European Employment Strategy in 1994, it was constantly reformed and extended to other areas such as social protection and inclusion, education, youth and training but also taxation – all areas where Member State competence prevails. The OMC has attracted much interest from political science research fascinated with what was considered a new policy instrument. The dominant hope was that learning among Member States would be possible through coordination, negotiation and soft steering. Concrete measures centre on jointly identifying and defining policy goals to be reached, measuring performance with new instruments, and exchanging best practices (for examples, see De La Porte and Pochet 2002: 13; Regent 2003: 191). Many believed this could lead to a form of discursive democracy for the benefit of the integration process and European societies more generally (drawing on 'democratic experimentalism' established by Cohen and Sabel 1997; Dorf and Sabel 1998; see e.g. Jacobbson and Schmid 2003; Zeitlin and Trubek 2003). Empirical work has in the meantime drawn a much more nuanced picture, critically reflecting the effect of the OMC (Barbier 2008; Kröger 2009). Surely, national actors often alter their frames of reference with respect to policy goals established at the EU level, and this might in turn influence what is conceived or discussed as feasible reform at the national level. It is much more difficult, though, to show concrete and direct effects on complex national reforms or outcomes of policy change that result from the OMC (cf. different chapters in Kröger 2009).

With OMCs taking a prominent place in the EU governance literature generally, this can also be claimed more specifically for the OMC on pensions. When it comes to EU old age policy in the last decade, much of the political science literature has engaged primarily with the OMC on pensions, later reformed into the OMC on social protection, reframed as the OMC on social inclusion, pensions and health care, and integrated in the European Semester (De La Porte and Pochet 2002; Eckardt 2005; for an exception, see Haverland 2007, 2011; Lodge 2007; Natali 2009; Natali and De La Porte 2004; Pochet 2005). In contrast, this chapter deconstructs EU old age policy understood as different instruments in different policy areas exerting potential effect on national pension policies including transitions from the labour market. I employ the notion potential effect or potential influence to underline that, although in some cases influence can be documented easily, systematic judgement on de facto effect and influence requires a different research perspective. First, a specific national situation would need to be assessed before tracing and judging the respective changes flowing from EU policy.

One way to approach governance is through a perspective focused on instruments (cf. Bähr et al. 2007). In this view, the OMC is characterised as a coordinative governance instrument understood to matter by triggering learning in deliberative processes (e.g. Zeitlin 2005). This contrasts with legislative policymaking under the community method. Here, common EU standards exist and are implemented through legislative instruments (typically directives, regulations or decisions) as part of a regulatory framework. Consequently, looking at the different instruments, I differentiate between coordinative interventions (mainly OMCs) and hard steering though legislation.

Turning to the policy areas where we can observe EU governance on old age, table 4.1 places pensions as the core area of respective policies at the nation-state level. Existing EU policy instruments matter directly where they target national pension policies explicitly. However, we need to look at other policy areas too, and not just the ongoing reform efforts to bring private elements into old age security. Where EU instruments do not address pensions but nevertheless impact on their form or their substance, they can be classified as having indirect influence. Among EU instruments exerting indirect influence, market regulation is quite important (Haverland 2007), as are macroeconomic policies in the context of the EMU and more specifically the revamped Stability and Growth Pact.[2] Finally, between them we can observe instruments from the social domain (equal treatment and employment). When it comes to actors involved in governance, this perspective implies focusing not only on the EU pension policy arena, where typically the Commission Directorate General (DG) for Employment and Social Affairs interacts with representatives from pension institutions, employer organisations and trade unions, but also on other areas and actors. In the Council, matters are negotiated and decided among Social Ministers and the respective

[2] The research was conducted as part of a large project (http://ec.europa.eu/research/social-sciences/projects/398_en.html) which consciously decided to abstain from systematically including the EMU in EU old age policy analysed. However, it has been shown that the EMU constrains Member States' abilities in anti-cyclical macroeconomic policies by limiting budgets and spending policies on social protection (e.g. Featherstone 2005). What is more, it influences retrenchment and reform of pension systems, especially of single pillar systems (Hering 2006).

Employment and Social Affairs Committee in the European Parliament. Other portfolios and organised interests both at the national and supranational level add to the picture of actors and arenas, for example the DG for Internal Market or DG for Economic and Financial Affairs and their respective stakeholders, such as industry organisations.

Table 4.1 EU old age policy: Instruments and areas (not exhaustive)

Instruments/ areas	Legislation	Coordination
Direct	*Supplementary Pensions* Portability when moving in the EU (98/49/ EC, revised proposal pending)	*OMC Pensions* (today: social inclusion, pensions and health care)
Social	*Anti-discrimination* Employment Framework Directive (2000/ 78/EC) and proposal for Equal Treatment in Services (pending) Association Belge des Consommateurs Test-Achats ASBL (C-236/09) Römer (C-147/08)	*European Employment Strategy* Stockholm and Barcelona target
Indirect	*Supplementary Pensions* Institutions for Occupational Retirement Provisions (2003/41/EC) Denkavit International (C-170/05) Robins (C-278/05)	*Stability and Growth Pact*

Source: Author's own compilation.

In the following sections, I describe EU old age policy since the 1980s. What comes of the understanding of EU old age governance as a complex and contested area with a number of instruments is that this mapping exercise can hardly be complete. However, the examples have been chosen to allow an understanding of the breadth and depth of the policy instruments, actors and interests constituting EU old age governance. They will be classified along the conceptual lines of instruments and areas.

Policy analysis is interested in 'What Governments [here the EU, MH] do, why they do it, and what difference it makes' (Dye 1976). To this aim the chapter traces policy developments for each single instrument and analyses them along the lines of 'actor-centered institutionalism' (Scharpf 1997). This implies that actors are considered rational and acting autonomously in correspondence with their beliefs and preferences. The institutional setting in which they operate provides opportunities and constraints. For example, is the European Commission as an actor interested in making policies but is dependent on the Council where legal initiatives will be approved or rejected on the basis of defined rules, such as unanimity or qualified majority.

The material for the analysis is drawn from primary and secondary sources. Twenty-six semi-structured expert interviews were conducted with EU policymakers (2006–2009).[3] To avoid bias due to sectoral or organizational foci these individuals were selected from different DGs (Employment and Social Affairs, Economic and Finance, Education and Culture, Internal Market) and hierarchical levels in the European Commission. In addition the information provided was controlled through interviews with interest group representatives. Although this selection entails a potential bias in favour of supranational policymaking it is justified in light of the interest in EU-level policymaking and its (potential) effect as compared with national policy developments. All interviews were fully transcribed and coded with the software Atlas.Ti. On this basis separate case studies for each instrument were prepared, which then served as the basis for the more encompassing chapter at hand.

4.3 POLICYMAKING WITHOUT COMPETENCES: EARLY DEVELOPMENTS FROM THE FOUNDING DAYS TO THE 1990S

Approaching policy instruments in a historical sequence, we start with equal treatment rulings of the Court of Justice of the European Union (CJEU)[4] that substantially changed national pension arrangements. In the 1980s, *Defrenne* (C-149/77), *Marshall* (C-152/84) and *Barber* (C-262/88) put in place the equal treatment of men and women with respect to retirement age. The *Marshall* case disqualified the widespread practice that women could not claim compensation for unfair dismissal after age 60 due to their lower retirement age. The *Barber* ruling in turn established that employers and occupational pension schemes are generally required not to discriminate on the grounds of gender when offering pension benefits.

---

[3] In order to preserve anonymity, I refer to these interviews as 'COM1', 'NGO2', and so on.

[4] For reasons of clarity I refer to the CJEU throughout the text although in some instances ECJ would be the correct historical term.

Even today, it can be argued that this ruling unfolds great effect at the national level and changes continue even 30 years later since the complexity of pension arrangements and the costs and liabilities any reform entails hamper clear-cut implementation of the equal treatment principle. An example is the 2010 request of the former Labour government in the UK to equalise pension schemes which retain liability for Guaranteed Minimum Pensions – hitherto believed to be unaffected by EU legislation. In any case, national policies on ageing have been moving in the same direction with a view to the equal treatment of the sexes – moderate convergence can be asserted. We note, however, that this instrument was not intended or specifically looked at as EU old age policy, but can be situated in the social area.[5] This is in juxtaposition to the following developments that directly address old age but are of very limited effect.

In the early 1990s, a combination of interests and initiatives in the European Commission and the European Parliament prepared the ground for the *First Action Programme for the Elderly* (1991–1993). Earlier instruments had only touched upon older persons indirectly. The *Action Programme* put forward by DG Employment and Social Affairs focused on preventative strategies to face economic and social consequences of an ageing society and called for a new old age policy instrument by implementing the (non-binding) *Charter on Fundamental Rights of Workers*. Here, older persons were addressed as a separate group of people with specific rights, such as the right to resources to afford a decent standard of living, minimum income, and medical and social assistance (Article 24 and Article 25). An *Action Programme* focused on preventative strategies to face economic and social consequences of an ageing society and proposed measures to develop the potential of older people. It culminated in the *European Year of Older People and Solidarity between the Generations* (1993). Though they were barely visible politically, in substance these initiatives mark issues that even today – about 15 years later – still appear innovative at the national level (e.g. flexible retirement age). Influence on national policies took place through altering discourses and by offering some very limited financial incentives.

---

[5] Another early EU old age policy instrument in the social area is the coordination of national social security systems (1612/68/EEC). Although the instrument explicitly covers pensions, its potential influence is limited since comparability between national systems is sought without interfering in national policies.

In preparing these initiatives and ensuing regulatory policy, the European Commission consciously altered the constellation of actors involved in old age governance. Lobbying activities for policy on older people at the EU level started in 1982 with the founding of Eurolink Age, whose agenda includes organising the exchange of information, expert consultation and direct contact with EU institutions via the 'Liaison Group on the Elderly' and 'Intergroup Ageing'. However, as an EU-wide network of national non-profit organisations, Eurolink Age was not directly involved in EU legislative policymaking. FERPA, by contrast, an organisation for retired trade unionists, which had a large membership, was clearly rooted in a corporatist policy understanding. When it came to the formulation of EU old age policy, FERPA was a difficult partner for the European Commission to engage in innovative policymaking. According to interviewees, FERPA was by and large not very enthusiastic about EU-level initiatives for ageing workers, an issue whose place was clearly seen at the national level (interview COM18 2008). In this situation, the proactive involvement of civil society groups and the broadening of stakeholders by DG Employment and Social Affairs can be understood as a strategic move, 'trying to generate the pan-European interest group network on an NGO basis, which could sustain us and which would give some coalition partners which we could use against the Council' (interview COM22 2008). What matters for EU governance in this area is that the move decisively altered the number and orientation of actors involved in future policymaking. To this day, trade unions are reluctant to shape EU old age instruments, while NGOs are very active in the field. The most recent example is responses to the public consultation on the *European Year for Active Ageing* (2012), where NGOs participated in higher numbers than public institutions, and only two trade unions raised their voice (European Commission 2011).

Drawing on these developments, a second *Action Programme* was proposed under Commissioner for Social Affairs Flynn in 1995. Intended to triple the financial volume of the first *Action Programme*, it was rejected by Member States.[6] As a result, the European level was left with a vacuum in terms of how to approach the issue through regulatory activities directly aimed at old age. According to an interviewee, this situation raised the question: 'Should one imagine that Europe would have a typical dossier of older people like Member States had, with

[6] The German and UK governments were reluctant to agree out of a matter of principle to block spending policies and create any precedence of *Action Programmes* respectively.

everything that applied to older people, with certain policies for certain age groups, or should we have something else, and what were the other instruments?' (interview COM22 2008). The question was not decided consciously, but answered incrementally under changing interest constellations within the given set of institutional constraints. In the following, I discuss where and how 'bypasses to social Europe' (Obinger et al. 2005) were taken to address questions of ageing societies and old age security even when direct and formal competences were lacking. They constitute the purposive intervention of EU-level actors exerting potential effect on national pension policies including transitions from the labour market and can be situated alongside legal and coordinative instruments in different policy areas.

4.4 LEGISLATIVE INSTRUMENTS

4.4.1 The 'Social' Sphere: Prohibiting Age Discrimination

Anti-discrimination has been a particularly active field for EU policy-making since the founding days. Yet for a long time, equal treatment was thought of in the context of discrimination for reasons of nationality and sex. The Amsterdam Treaty first called 'to combat discrimination based on sex, racial or ethnic origin, religion or belief, disability, *age* or sexual orientation' (Article 13, now 19, on the negotiation process; see Flynn 1999). A short time later, the Commission presented a proposal for a general framework for equal treatment in employment and occupation (2000/78/EC, short: Employment Framework Directive; Hartlapp et al. 2014, pp. 64–71). Anti-discrimination standards that had been established for the sexes were extended to other areas. The directive was adopted when a window of opportunity emerged through the critical stance many governments took towards the election of populist right leader Haider in Austria (e.g. Tyson 2001). However, the form and substance of the directive had been prepared prior to this when DG Employment and Social Affairs strategically developed the policy area (and with it the EU legal order), in an interplay with the CJEU and strengthening actors that would support the directive. This instrument prohibits direct and indirect age discrimination in the workplace. Its effects are visible in the disappearance of age limits in job postings – although the *Wolf* case (C-229/08) has recently underlined that genuine occupational requirements exist and that in these cases age restrictions may be justified. The

German practice of restricting application to the fire service to persons under the age of 30 due to 'especially high physical capacities' can thus continue.

However, Member States successfully pushed for more relaxed rules that allow discrimination when it is objectively and reasonably justified or seeks a legitimate goal (Article 6). A short time after the transposition deadline was reached, the CJEU clarified in a first indicative case that, regardless of the exemptions, equal treatment was given priority over enhancing labour market opportunities for older workers. In what is known as the *Mangold* (C-144/04) case, a 56-year-old employee questioned the German *Teilzeitbefristungsgesetz*, which relaxes temporary contract limits for workers over the age of 52 to improve their incorporation into the labour market. The CJEU held that older workers should in principle be treated equally to other workers, even though this might worsen the situation for older unemployed persons. A number of rulings have followed since and compulsory retirement is at the heart of many of them. With cases such as *Palacios de la Villa* (C-411/05), *Petersen* (C-341/08), *Rosenbladt* (C-45/09) or *Prigge, Fromm, Lambach* (C-447/09) and most explicitly *Age Concern* (C-388/07), the CJEU has developed a view where discrimination in the form of fixed retirement age is justified where the legitimate aims are social policy objectives such as employment, labour market or vocational training – but not purely individual reasons such as increasing competitiveness that are particular to an employer's situation.[7] Judicial policymaking may have clarified that in specific cases fixed retirement ages are still allowed under EU law. This is the case for Mrs Rosenbladt (C-45/09), a cleaner who was dismissed at the end of the month when she turned 65, just as the collective agreement for the German cleaning sector established. Nevertheless, overall the directive is clearly challenging fixed retirement age. This is clearly visible where defining legitimate exemptions to compulsory retirement was abolished in the UK as of 1 October 2011 and was replaced by a need to justify retirement even in old age. Anti-discrimination policy is increasingly considered fundamental rights at the EU level (Geddes 2004), implying that rather than an employee in a labour relationship any individual in European societies is the

---

[7] Note though that the CJEU on issues other than fixed retirement insisted that differential treatment on the basis of age is unjust (e.g. *Andersen* [C-499/08], where an employer had to pay his long-term employee a statutory compensation after dismissal even though he was old enough to draw an old age pension).

addressee.[8] A case in point is the most recent Commission proposal for a directive that seeks to extend protection against discrimination beyond employment to the social sphere (COM[2008]426 final; cf. Hartlapp et al. 2014, pp. 77–80). In the case of adoption, age discrimination is prohibited in social security (including social protection and health services), education and access to and supply of services. Examples cover barrier-free access to public transport and credit – insurance companies and banks are no longer allowed to use age-based actuarial factors as practised before. The directive faces vehement opposition from Germany as well as a number of other Member States (including Czech Republic, Italy, Lithuania and Malta; cf. EUobserver 2010). Concerns centre on how to ensure that characteristics potentially linked to the reasons for discrimination can be used in assessing the risk portfolio of customers without turning them into a blank justification for different assessments. Arguments about the likely outcome of this second directive therefore seem premature. However, in the case of adoption, the insurance industry would have to change its practices considerably. Risks of individuals with very different characteristics would have to be pooled in much broader baskets. This line has been supported by CJEU rulings made during the course of legislative negotiations, most importantly in *Association Belge des Consommateurs Test-Achats ASBL* (C-236/09, cf. also *Römer* [C-147/08]).

4.4.2 Indirect Influence: Supplementary Pensions as Financial Market Instruments

With reform trends increasing the importance of schemes involving a second and third pillar (Ebbinghaus 2011), we can observe the emergence of EU policy for supplementary pensions. Traditionally, pensions are an issue for social actors. However, where pensions are seen as financial service instruments, they fall under the Single Market, and EU regulations seek to prevent distortion of competition between national and external providers. Earlier instruments of DG Internal Market on supplementary pensions had been blocked in the Council where there was a clash between proponents of a pension fund culture (Ireland, Great Britain, to some extent the Netherlands) favouring investment freedoms

[8] In *Mangold* (C-144/04) and *Kücükdeveci* (C555/07) the ECJ rulings even suggest equal treatment to be a general principle of Community law, implying that rather than an employee in a labour relationship any individual in European societies is the addressee and may invoke the rights through horizontal direct effect.

and Member States with an insurance culture (France, Germany) highlighting the need to protect the insured (Haverland 2007). Faced with a continuous stalemate, even an amended version (COM[93] 237final, 26 May 1993) had to be withdrawn in December 1994. When a couple of years later, financial interests and markets took centre stage with the *Financial Action Service Plan* (1999–2004), the context was favourable for a new proposal on *Institutions for Occupational Retirement Provisions* (IORP, 2003/41/EC). The directive sets prudential rules on operation and investment strategies of IORPs. It harmonises requirements on supervision authorities, their intervention rights and coverage rules. Influence in Member States is likely to be substantial. Ferrera (2005, p. 30) says that 'the institutions affected by the Directive cover about 25 per cent of the EU labour force and manage assets worth €2,500 billion, or about 29 per cent of the EU GDP'. The directive is best understood not as a social policy but as a financial market instrument, since questions touching upon typically controversial (re)distributive implications as we know them from social policymaking are excluded from the debates and directive (Mabbett 2009: 776). However, regarding unsolved questions, we may expect the CJEU to drive further policy developments. Cases in point are the rulings *Denkavit International* (C-170/05) on unequal taxation of dividends from transferred pension funds, and *Robins* (C-278/05) on accrued pension rights in case of insolvency. In this case entitlements of British employees were considerably reduced, as the assets of the supplementary company or intercompany pension schemes were not sufficient, raising the issue of conditional state liability. Given these developments, EU old age policy could gain more influence in the years to come through legal decisions on supplementary pensions.

4.4.3 The Same but Different: Direct Influence through Supplementary Pensions

Supplementary pensions as regulatory substance are also critical to legislation concerned with the free movement of persons. What happens to supplementary pensions when a worker decides to move to another Member State? Are pensions taxed twice – once when acquired and once upon consumption? Are acquired rights maintained? Here, a lack of coordination between supplementary pension schemes might substantially curb worker mobility. Problems arise in situations where a worker has spent her working life in a country where occupational pensions are taxed when paid into a fund, but she decides to spend retirement in a country where taxes are due upon consumption of benefits.

Policy developments in this area have been characterised by input from a network of Member State experts on supplementary pensions (since 1992), the 'Veil' High Level Group (set up in 1997) and the Pension Forum (composed of Member State representatives, social partners, NGOs and insurance stakeholders). They reported to DG Employment and Social Affairs as well as to DG Economic and Financial Affairs on multiple occasions that the prospect of a loss of supplementary pension rights is a clear disincentive to mobility and represents a serious obstacle to the exercise of the right of free movement as foreseen by the EC Treaty. Taking up these arguments, DG Employment and Social Affairs proposed a directive 'safeguarding the supplementary pension rights of employed and self-employed persons moving within the Community' (98/49/EC). The directive regulates that acquired rights must be maintained in cases of cross-border movement. All EU nationals have to be treated equally and benefits should be portable to the territory of other Member States. As for the IORP Directive, differences between Member States impeded the adoption of more far-reaching standards proposed by the Commission, for example on equal tax treatment for contributions by workers paying in the home Member State from the host Member State. This left room for functional arguments finally to curb the continuing problems and arguments stressing that more social policy instruments were needed to assist the free movement of persons.

A second directive on the *Portability of Supplementary Pension Rights* was proposed in 2005 and after lengthy negotiations has recently been adopted (2014[50]EU). It establishes that pensions can be accumulated even on the basis of short employment periods and at the beginning of a working career, and that they can be carried over to another scheme when taking up a new job. Moreover, the directive safeguards dormant rights through inflation and salary adjustments. The Council pressed for substantial changes, especially on compulsory age and vesting periods. Germany and the Netherlands have been among the strongest opponents (European Industrial Relations Review 2005). Consequently, a revised proposal put forward by the Commission in 2007 appeared substantially watered down. Replacing harmonisation requirements with minimum standards, introducing compromises on minimum age (now 23 years) and the necessary length of employment relationships (two years), the proposal was described by a Commission official as 'now lacking any portability' (interview COM18 2008, translation MH). Finally adopted in April 2014, the directive substantially challenges national occupational pension schemes, with considerable implications for any worker taking up a new job – not just in cross-border cases. It could alter the traditional purpose of supplementary pensions in Member States such as Germany, which is to bind employees to their employer (cf. Mabbett 2009).

4.5 COORDINATIVE INSTRUMENTS

4.5.1 Indirect Impact: Older Workers in the European Employment Strategy

Taking a look at coordinative EU old age policy, the *European Employment Strategy* comes first in the sequence of instruments. First established in the early 1990s, it has been the 'role model' for other OMCs. The instrument can be situated in the social area, and for the focus of this chapter it is interesting to see how employment of older workers moved from the sidelines to become a core goal of the OMC.

In the beginning, older people – in stark contrast to young people – did not receive specific attention. Older people are targeted in the employment guidelines for the first time in 1999. The respective recommendations issued at Member States put a lot of emphasis on the pull factors and incentives from the tax and benefit systems. If these were removed – the message went – the market could easily solve the (un)employment problem of older workers. Two years later, a specific guideline, 'Developing a policy for active ageing' was adopted at the Stockholm Council. Member State governments agreed to quantify the employment target for older workers to reach 50 per cent by 2010. Looking at the workers that could cause the greatest obstacle to that goal (women, young and old workers), and addressing them with specific measures, were seen as functional to reach the overall employment goal of 70 per cent, as set in the Lisbon Agenda (interview COM14 2006). A second quantitative target of '65 as the average exit age by 2010' was adopted a year later (Barcelona target). The ambitious goal to increase the average exit age by five years had been pushed for by the Spanish president with support from Great Britain (interview COM22 2008).

The means for reaching these targets have developed over time. We find a catalogue of measures such as continuous training, adoption of working conditions, phase retirement, internal flexibility measures, tutoring where experienced workers can pass on know-how and awareness-raising, as well as the call on the Commission to organise an exchange of information, experience and good practice concerning employment of older workers. Their effects have to be seen in the context of the Lisbon Process at the time, which set the goal for the EU to become 'the most dynamic and competitive knowledge-based economy in the world'. For the elderly, the most coherent notion developed was that of 'active ageing' policy, understood as an individual and societal strategy of working longer, retiring later and being active after retirement.[9] Two aspects seem distinct to the EU's 'active ageing' as a policy approach. First, (early) retirement is not seen as a beneficial achievement and due right of workers. Secondly, older workers are perceived as a resource to be mobilised to participate in the labour market. This perspective contrasted with policies and practices in most of the Member States adhering to the continental welfare state model. Here, in the late 1990s, the typical answer to ageing societies was still to shed older workers and provide for living through insurance and allowances at a relatively early age (Hartlapp and Kemmerling 2008). In contrast to these practices, the broad idea of the European Employment Strategy and 'active ageing' clearly carries with it that participation in the labour market is the (perceived) best way to prevent social exclusion and to maintain social cohesion (Schäfer 2005). It needs to be stressed that the goals set and policies proposed are mediated through national institutions and integrated into national programmes. Concrete effects remain unclear; all that can be said is that where influence is traceable, it most likely carries with it the notion of re-commodification.

4.5.2 OMC on Social Protection and Inclusion: Between Direct Implications and EMU

Finally, we turn to the OMC on pensions – the starting point for the argument presented. From the mid-1990s onwards, debates on social protection issues, especially pensions as well as health and long-term care for the elderly, started to gain momentum at the national and international level. At the EU level discussions were dominated by financial players from 1999/2000 on (interview COM18 2008). They stressed increasing pressures on public spending and highlighted the need for sustainable public finances in the context of the EMU. These concerns are reflected in progressive policy and structural developments. With respect to structure, in 1999 an Ageing Population subgroup was set up in the influential Economic Policy Committee, which is made up of experts from national administrations, DG Economics and Financial Affairs, the European Central Bank and the OECD, and which publishes forecasts on Member State public pension expenditures (interview

---

[9] Official documents lack a clear definition of 'active ageing' but note that the expression gave the name to the European Year 2012 ('European Year for Active Ageing').

COM13 2006). With respect to policy content, the long-term sustainability of public finances was to be assessed as part of the *Stability and Growth Pact*. From this point on, the *Broad Economic Policy Guidelines* (BEPG) were to contain recommendations for public pension systems (Agence Europe N°7986, 18 June 2001). The dominant discourse at the EU level was: 'we must control public spending on benefits' (interview COM19 2008) and that EU policies therefore have to address pensions. With the financial crisis these arguments have been reinforced and figure prominently in reform requirements to stabilise deficit countries.

Shortly after the BEPG had become the entry point for EU policy developments on pensions, the Council reacted decisively. Member State governments showed an interest in addressing questions of pension systems by highlighting concerns other than long-term financial sustainability, notably 'employment and social concerns' (Vandenbroucke 2002, p. 8). Supported by the Social Council formation, DG Employment and Social Affairs developed EU pension policy goals focusing on health insurance, social security and an ageing population. Under the Belgian Presidency in 2001, budget orientation and the focus on adequate pensions were integrated. The Social Protection Committee and the Economic Policy Committee cooperated (for the first time) to agree on the process and goals of the OMC on pensions. The emergence of the OMC on pensions has been described in more detail elsewhere (e.g. Lodge 2007; Pochet 2005). What is important for the focus of this chapter is that conflict lines ran between economic and financial players and social players rather than between the supranational and the national level. Put differently, the emergence of EU-level pension policy – hitherto the exclusive domain of the national level – is best understood via the intrusion of EU fiscal and economic concerns into social policies. This is most convincingly argued by the director of the responsible department at DG Employment and Social Affairs: 'If the Open Method of Coordination was not used in the area of social security, pension systems would be almost exclusively analysed in negative terms on the European level; as a risk to public finances and an obstacle to raising employment rates' (Vignon 2003, p. 14).

Summarising developments of the OMC on pensions describes how decision-making difficulties among Member States that are especially sensitive where EU policy impinges upon national welfare state institutions are more likely to be overcome under specific constellations. This is the case where advancing economic integration exerts pressure on national welfare states, thereby changing the fall-back option of Member States. Turning to the effects at the national level it first needs to be stressed that concrete changes in national pension systems are difficult to attribute to the OMC. Reforms have proven highly complex processes where EU influence interacts with a number of other factors. Taking Greece as one of the countries where OMC benchmarks called for substantial changes year after year, its effects are nevertheless limited to altering 'Greece's interest in reform (credibility, reputation), while serving to impact on domestic ideas (policy learning, mimicry, benchmarking). … Yet, the reform achievement has been modest and slow' (Featherstone 2005, p. 746).[10] Referring to the findings of empirical works that compare OMC effects across countries, we can state that 'there is some evidence of convergence (together with persistent differences) between … the social insurance systems, and … multi-pillar systems' (Natali and De La Porte 2004, p. 256). Further developments will most likely impact on the relative balance between actors involved in ageing policy. The influence of the ministry of finance as well as related arenas should increase relative to social and labour policy.

4.6 CONCLUSION

In deconstructing EU old age policy, this chapter has mapped different instruments. These can be classified as legislative or coordinative instruments that exert direct influence, that matter through social policy or that impact on Member States indirectly through other policy areas. While the political science literature has paid much attention to the OMC on pensions, the analysis carried out in this chapter shows that a number of different instruments exist in the legislative area. This is a very dynamic area of EU governance, as a number of highly relevant CJEU rulings illustrate. The analysis also emphasised that EU policy on old age is carried out through other coordinative instruments beyond the OMC on pensions. Summarising the most relevant empirical and conceptual implications, we observe the following.

EU old age policy started about two decades earlier than what is typically assumed as the starting point for the OMC on pensions, 2001. Over time, the substance of policymaking changed from attempts to develop a genuine EU old age policy to one that includes a diverse bundle of instruments ranging from financial service regulation to freedom of movement, labour law and equal treatment. Each instrument

[10] Reform finally took place as a result of the rescue plans for Greece making financial support conditional upon the introduction of a two-tier system with a basic (flat rate) pension granted on a 12-month basis and a contributory pension based on the lifetime earnings principle.

emerged in a different arena among different actors and follows different goals. It remains an open question whether EU old age policy would have looked different had Member States agreed to more far-reaching genuine social instruments at some earlier stage – for example, a second *Action Programme* for the Elderly leading to a number of alternative (hierarchical) instruments.

Closely related to this observation is the fact that influences exerted on national pension policies including transitions from the labour market are unclear and partially contradictory (e.g. case law on equal treatment and employment). In a recent *Green Book on Pensions* attempts have been made to integrate other measures to increase coherence among existing EU instruments, for example economic and social concerns on pensions, in a separate OMC.

Based on the analysis, I argue that coordinated EU policy seeking to trigger reforms in the area of pensions or the employment of older workers is typically overvalued. In contrast, we tend to underestimate how much the EU shapes national room to manoeuvre through legislative instruments establishing individual rights and requiring equal treatment regarding age or free movement of capital and persons. Finally, this chapter has only touched upon the limits the EMU sets for national policies on old age. It is highly likely that fiscal concerns are the most substantial EU influence on national ageing policies, and this has become even more tangible during the crisis.

Although at the national level we are inclined to think of old age policies as belonging to the social arena, at the EU level, market and economic policy instruments substantially affect the substance and content of EU old age policy. Interests, actor constellations and available Treaty bases better enable the adoption of instruments that strengthen economic concerns over social concerns and (neo)pluralist interest involvement over corporatist arrangements. With respect to actors, EU old age policy differs crucially from what we know about the making of national welfare states linked to nation building and class alignment. This is likely to alter the balance of power between actors and interests at the national level.

Finally, there are good reasons to believe that this assessment should not be limited to old age policy. It is likely to apply to other areas of social policy, such as health care. Here too, we see a substantial amount of legislative developments linked directly (e.g. patient mobility or cross-border health care) and indirectly (anti-discrimination instruments and service provision) to EU governance. As for EU old age policy, these developments bring to the fore a number of different actors and arenas, interest constellations and conflict lines. More generally, we may thus conclude that a broader perspective would be beneficial, wherein we understand EU governance as a complex, at times contradictory and inherently political process.

REFERENCES

Bähr, H., O. Treib and G. Falkner (2007), 'Von Hierarchie zu Kooperation? Zur Entwicklung von Governance-Formen in zwei regulativen Politikfeldern der EU', *Politische Vierteljahresschrift*, **40**, PVS-Sonderheft 2007/2, 92–115.

Barbier, J.-C. (2008), *La longue marche vers l'Europe sociale*, Paris: Presses Universitaires de France.

Cohen, J. and C. Sabel (1997), 'Directly-deliberative polyarchy', *European Law Journal*, **3** (4), 313–42.

De La Porte, C. and P. Pochet (2002), 'Introduction', in C. De La Porte and P. Pochet (eds), *Building Social Europe through the Open Method of Co-ordination*, Brussels: P.I.E. Peter Lang, 11–26.

Dorf, M. C. and C. Sabel (1998), 'A constitution of democratic experimentalism', *Columbia Law Review*, **98** (2), 267–473.

Dye, T. R. (1976), *Policy Analysis: What Governments Do, Why they Do It, and What Difference It Makes*, Tuscaloosa, AL: University of Alabama Press.

Ebbinghaus, B. (ed.) (2011), *Varieties of Pension Governance: Pension Privatization in Europe*, Oxford: Oxford University Press.

Eckardt, M. (2005), 'The open method of coordination on pensions: an economic analysis of its effects on pension reforms', *Journal of European Social Policy*, **15** (3), 247–67.

European Commission (2011), *Public Consultation in view of a Possible Designation of 2012 as European Year of Active Ageing and Intergenerational Solidarity*, Brussels: Employment, Social Affairs and Equal Opportunities DG European Commission.

European Industrial Relations Review (2005), 'Directive on supplementary pension rights', *European Industrial Relations Review*, **382**, 2.

EUobserver (2010), 'Belgium keeping alive EU anti-discrimination bill', *EUobserver*, 6 October, available at http://euobserver.com/890/30977 (last accessed 23 May 2014).

Featherstone, K. (2005), '"Soft" co-ordination meets "hard" politics: the European Union and pension reform in Greece', *Journal of European Public Policy*, **12** (4), 733–50.

Ferrera, M. (2005), *The Boundaries of Welfare: European Integration and the New Spatial Politics of Social Protection*, Oxford: Oxford University Press.

Flynn, L. (1999), 'The implications of Article 13 EC – after Amsterdam, will some forms of discrimination be more equal than others?', *Common Market Law Review*, **36**, 1127–52.

Geddes, A. (2004), 'Britain, France, and EU anti-discrimination policy: the emergence of an EU policy paradigm', *West European Politics*, **27** (2), 334–53.

Hartlapp, M. (2007), 'Intra-Kommissionsdynamik im Policy-Making: EU-Politiken angesichts des demographischen Wandels', *Politische Vierteljahresschrift*, **40**, PVS-Sonderheft 2007/2, 139–60.

Hartlapp, M. and A. Kemmerling (2008), 'When a solution becomes the problem: the causes for policy reversal on early exit from the labour force', *Journal of European Social Policy*, **18** (4), 381–94.

Hartlapp, M., J. Metz and C. Rauh (2014), *Which Policy for Europe? Power and Conflict inside the European Commission*, Oxford: Oxford University Press.

Haverland, M. (2007), 'When the welfare state meets the regulatory state: EU occupational pension policy', *Journal of European Public Policy*, **14** (6), 886–904.

Haverland, M. (2011), 'Policies of the EU towards occupational pensions: limits to regulation', in L. Leisering (ed.), *The New Regulatory State: Regulating Pensions in Germany and the UK*, Basingstoke: Palgrave Macmillan, 175–90.

Hering, M. (2006), 'The politics of structural pension reform in Western Europe: does the EU matter?', Chicago, IL: 15th International Conference of the Council for European Studies, 29 March–2 April 2001.

Jacobbson, K. and H. Schmid (2003), 'The European Employment Strategy at the crossroads: contributions to the evaluation', in D. Foden and L. Magnusson (eds), *Five Years' Experience of the Luxembourg Employment Strategy*, Brussels: Peter Lang, 111–40.

Korpi, W. (1983), *The Democratic Class Struggle*, London: Routledge.

Kröger, S. (2009), 'What we have learnt: advances, pitfalls and remaining questions of OMC research', *European Integration online Papers*, **13**, special issue 1, available at http://eiop.or.at/eiop/texte/2009-005a.htm (last accessed 23 May 2014).

Lodge, M. (2007), 'Comparing non-hierarchical governance in action: the open method of co-ordination in pensions and information society', *Journal of Common Market Studies*, **45** (2), 343–65.

Mabbett, D. (2009), 'Supplementary pensions between social policy and social regulation', *West European Politics*, **32** (4), 774–91.

Majone, G. (2005), *Dilemmas of European Integration: The Ambiguities and Pitfalls of Integration by Stealth*, Oxford: Oxford University Press.

Natali, D. (2009), 'The open method of coordination on pensions: does it de-politicise pensions policy?', *West European Politics*, **32** (4), 810–28.

Natali, D. and C. De La Porte (2004), 'OMC pensions: what role for Europe in co-ordinating the reform of different pensions systems?', in H. Jørgensen and M. Baerentsen (eds), *European Trade Union Yearbook 2003/2004*, Brussels: ETUI, 255–82.

Obinger, H., S. Leibfried and F. G. Castles (2005), 'Bypasses to a social Europe? Lessons from federal experience', *Journal of European Public Policy*, **12** (3), 1–27.

Pochet, P. (2005), 'The open method of co-ordination and the construction of social Europe: a historical perspective', in J. Zeitlin and P. Pochet (eds), *The Open Method of Co-ordination in Action: The European Employment and Social Inclusion Strategies*, Brussels: Peter Lang, 37–82.

Regent, S. (2003), 'The open-method of coordination: a new supranational form of governance?' *European Law Journal*, **9** (2), 190–214.

Schäfer, A. (2005), *Die neue Unverbindlichkeit: Wirtschaftspolitische Koordinierung in Europa*, Frankfurt/M.: Campus.

Scharpf, F. W. (1997), *Games Real Actors Play: Actor-Centered Institutionalism in Policy Research*, Oxford: Westview Press.

Scharpf, F. W. (2002), 'The European Social Model: coping with the challenges of diversity', *Journal of Common Market Studies*, **40** (4), 645–70.

Schludi, M. (2003), 'Politics of pension reform: the French case in a comparative perspective', *French Politics*, **1** (2), 199–224.

Tyson, A. (2001), 'The negotiation of the European Community Directive on Racial Discrimination', *European Journal of Migration and Law*, **3** (2), 199–229.

Vandenbroucke, F. (2002), 'The EU and Social Protection: What Should the European Convention Propose', MPIfG Working Paper 02/6, edited by Max-Planck-Institute for the Study of Societies, Köln.

Vignon, J. (2003), 'The "Open Method of Coordination" in the field of pensions: a strengthened cooperation at the European level', in VDR (ed.), *Open Method of Coordination in the Field of Pensions – Quo Vadis?*, Berlin: Verband Deutscher Rentenversicherungsträger, 12–14.

Zeitlin, J. (2005), 'The open method of coordination in action: theoretical promise, empirical realities, reform strategy', in J. Zeitlin, P. Pochet and L. Magnusson (eds), *The Open Method of Co-ordination in Action: The European Employment and Social Inclusion Strategies*, Brussels: Peter Lang, 447–503.

Zeitlin, J. and D. Trubek (eds) (2003), *Governing Work and Welfare in a New Economy: European and American Experiments*, Oxford: Oxford University Press.

5. In search of a European Employment Strategy: The construction of the 'job quality' agenda as an illustrative case

Christine Erhel, Jérôme Gautié and Bernard Gazier

The European Employment Strategy (EES) is a key pillar of risk management at the European level. It was first introduced to cope with the risk of unemployment, and extended later to the risk of non-employment, with an increasing focus on activation and the need for maximising the employment rate of the working age population. But since the beginning of the 1990s, the qualitative dimension of employment growth has also become a cause for concern at the European level. Getting a job of bad quality is indeed a social risk which must be taken into account. It may have consequences on a worker's income level, job satisfaction, career prospects, and affect well-being as well as physical or psychological health.

The 'job quality' agenda was first introduced in 2001 and has had fluctuating fortunes, from having a central role to official neglect. The topic is highly political as well as technical. It deals with key aspects of everybody's working lives, such as wages, working conditions, employment security, gender equality, the importance of part-time work, access to training and career progression, and so on, and it interferes with other European priorities such as 'activation'. It also involves the choice, implementation and use of a common set of statistical indicators, and is a typical area of dialogue among experts and debate involving different stakeholders at European level: Member States and the European Commission, but also social partners. Overall, the 'job quality' agenda is a good illustration of the construction of an important component of the EES, in terms of its conception and implementation.

The purpose of this chapter is to explore the evolution of this agenda.[1] The corresponding field of research is heterogeneous and burgeoning, and includes official reports at the EU level, as well as a related 'grey' literature (memoranda, notes, etc.), policymakers' initiatives and debates at various levels, along with other actors' reactions (such as union leaders) and proposals.

Three methodological choices have been made, in order to keep this diffuse set of information and data manageable. The first is to focus on the EU-level elaboration process, and to add some selected complementary observations made at national and/or regional levels. The second is to exploit the considerable variations which occurred during the decade 2001–2011, in order to explore the changing content and meaning of the 'job quality' agenda. The persisting difficulties of EU construction in the 2000s, as well as the current economic crisis which exploded in 2008, may be seen as revealing processes, through which the objective has been re-examined and re-evaluated almost permanently. The third is to link official documents to the comments of concerned actors or informed observers. These views are collected either from the existing literature or by interview.

The chapter is organised in three sections. Section 5.1 develops a framework to analyse the EES 'soft' governance process under review, and to analyse the interactions between political targets and indicators that make up the political agenda. The second section focuses on the difficulty of constructing such an agenda for the 'job quality' objective at the European level, in terms of a conceptual (or cognitive) framework, operational indicators and political priorities. Section 5.3 introduces other governance levels (Member States, regions, social partners), and briefly considers how the corresponding actors interact with the European 'job quality' agenda.

5.1 THE EES: FROM EMPLOYMENT GOVERNANCE AT THE EU LEVEL TO ESTABLISHING INDICATORS

We first present a brief overview of some of the issues raised by the multilevel 'soft' nature of the EES governance (5.1.1) and then focus more specifically on the interactions between targets and indicators (5.1.2).

---

[1] We will not try here to evaluate its impact in terms of effective job quality in the member countries.

5.1.1 A Brief Overview of Employment Governance at the European Level

Despite important changes and the existence of different political phases, the period opened by the 1997 Luxembourg Summit has been characterised by the emergence of a European governance of employment policy.[2] Although the subsidiarity principle still applies to this matter, the opportunity opened by the Maastricht Treaty to develop some European competences about this question 'of common interest' has led to several policy innovations. This implies a variety of policies and levels of intervention, from regional policies and the use of structural funds to support local employment, to the Commission's direct initiatives (reports, specific financing, for instance through the PROGRESS programme, which is controlled by DG Employment). From a procedural point of view, the main innovation is the European Employment Strategy. It appears primarily as an exercise in policy coordination, based on soft law and a policy learning process (according to the principles of the 'Open Method of Coordination' or OMC). The EES involves the definition of common goals (employment guidelines), the writing of a report presenting national policies (National Action Plans until 2005, National Reform Plans thereafter), to be discussed with the European Commission, and the participation in mutual learning processes. Indicators play an important role in this framework, to monitor the guidelines and follow up national trends. Although the EES is a non-constraining policy, the choice of indicators is a strategic one for governments, and the debates around them have been important within the Employment Committee (EMCO).[3]

In the academic literature, the EES is often conceptualised as a governance mode (Heidenreich and Zeitlin 2009), or a governance architecture (Borras and Radaelli 2011).[4] According to Borras and Radaelli (2011), governance architectures are made up of ideational and organisational components. Indeed, the EES builds an ideal-type as a model for policy reforms and implementation, and follows a range of procedural goals, encompassing enhanced coherence across administrations in charge of labour market policy, as well as better participation of

---

[2] Along the lines that were drawn by the White Paper in 1993 and the Essen Summit in 1994, which highlighted five main goals for the development of labour market policies in Europe: vocational training, flexibility, wage moderation, reduction in labour costs and labour market policy activation.

[3] The EMCO was created in 2000. For an overview of the first stages of the EES, see for instance Barbier and Sylla (2004).

[4] In their article, this concept is applied to the Lisbon Strategy as a whole.

social partners and civil society. Assessing the impact of this governance mode on national policies raises many methodological problems and leads to diverging results in the empirical literature (Kröger 2009). First, some EES goals are based on concepts that can be implemented in very diverse ways, depending on the characteristics of national labour market policy and/or social protection. Such diversity has been shown for 'activation' strategies, and more recently for 'flexicurity' (Barbier et al. 2009). Secondly, there are various sources of policy change and innovation, including common competitive trends in the world economy (putting pressure on labour costs) and the influence of international organisations on ideas about labour market reforms (especially the OECD). Finally, soft law mechanisms may lead to bi-directional influences, from EU to national policy (the 'top-down' perspective), but also from these policies to the European level. Therefore, whatever the relationships and correspondences revealed by empirical analysis, there is no easy way of establishing causality and a global impact of the EES on labour market policy reforms and outcomes. Empirical analysis needs to be aware of these limitations and challenges, and should in practice focus on processes that are related to EU coordination: guidelines, indicators, national policy reports (National Action Plans and National Reform Plans), and actors' behaviour and perceptions.

From this perspective, several effects have been confirmed by national case studies and comparative research (Pochet and Zeitlin 2005; de la Porte 2008; Mailand 2008; Begg et al. 2010; Zeitlin and Heidenreich 2009). Despite important differences across countries, there is evidence of some diffusion of the EU priorities in national policy agendas (activation, lifelong learning, gender mainstreaming, social inclusion, etc.). Indicators and benchmarking processes also play a role in the diffusion of policy goals (see the reference to employment rates in countries that were far behind the Lisbon targets). Secondly, learning manifestly does happen, as Member States are aware that they may provide lessons for others, and also find new solutions in what others have done. It is, however, open to question how far this goes and whether such learning as occurs stems directly from the Lisbon process or would have happened anyway. Thirdly, the OMC has affected the implementation of national labour market policies, at various levels. With regard to this, Zeitlin (2009) stresses the use of the process as a means of enhancing the steering capacity of national administrations, including through the better use of statistics. Depending partly on the constitutional framework, there can be more systematic approaches to engagement between levels of government, including how important agencies such as public employment services are run. Some cases of social partners' increased participation have also been reported. Institutional and coordination effects therefore seem important, but mainly concern administrations and some groups of experts. Contrary to the hypothesis of a 'deliberative' strategy, the diffusion to social actors and public opinion remains very limited. Finally, comparative analyses reveal that the interactions of the EES with national systems differ significantly across countries, depending on the characteristics of their social participation and political systems.

5.1.2 Some Remarks on the Possible Interactions between Policy Targets and Indicators

In the context of the multilevel 'soft law' mechanism presented above, the EES as a whole (in its different successive versions) may be conceived of as a more or less coherent coexistence or succession of several 'agendas' centred on labour market policies and labour market reforms. Other agendas have been proposed at the same time or slightly earlier: the 'Decent Work agenda' set out by the International Labour Organisation (ILO) (1999); the OECD (1994) 'Job Strategy' agenda, which focuses mainly on flexibility. As a piece of policy discourse, an agenda consists in elaborating and combining rationales, principles and indicators.[5]

Setting an agenda goes beyond a simple collection of proposed measures with a timetable (a 'plan'), and is tantamount to proposing an organised set of reasons and measurements underlying several policy measures. An agenda is not directly deduced from one precise and unique theoretical perspective, nor simply emanates from practice and experience. Policy agendas may be considered as an intermediate body of more or less strictly interrelated arguments indicating and illustrating one (or several interrelated) broad policy direction(s), and classifying priorities accordingly, in a more or less strict hierarchical order. A set of policy perspectives can become a policy agenda if three conditions are met:

1. It possesses and develops three kinds of ingredient: ends, means and indicators.

---

[5] For a comparison of four labour market reform agendas before the 2008 crisis, the International Monetary Fund (IMF) and OECD's 'flexibilisation' agenda, the EU's 'flexicurity', the ILO's 'Decent Work' and 'Transitional Labour Markets', see Auer and Gazier (2008). For a general reflection on the role of political and policy discourses, with an application to the EU Lisbon and Europe 2020 strategies, see Barbier and Sylla (2004) and Barbier (2011).

2. It integrates them in a relatively autonomous way.
3. Arguments and indicators impose a form of evidence in favour of a given broad policy option.

To understand the development of policy agendas, it may be useful to refer to the concept in political science of 'institutionalised cognitive frames' (in French: *référentiel*) (Jobert and Muller 1987; Jobert 2003; Muller 2005). In initial formulations, the concept has two different meanings. First, the 'global system of references' is a global and dominating vision of the world. Secondly, 'normative' or 'sectoral' systems of references are sets of representations and principles of action, providing the overall orientation of a given economic or social sector. Public policies are then understood as the result of an adjustment process of the normative/sectoral systems of references to the global one. In more recent elaborations (Jobert 2003; Muller 2005), 'institutionalised cognitive frames' (*référentiels*) comprise values, norms and causal relationships that actors adopt when they confront their interests. They are cognitive and normative frameworks which, once adopted, seem evident to the actors concerned. From a wider perspective, this conception belongs to the cognitive analysis of public policies (Hall 1989):[6] ideas and changes in underlying paradigms are essential to understand the dynamics and changes of policies. Policy agendas may be seen as deliberate interventions aimed at transforming existing systems of references in a given field, in favour of some new direction. They have much in common with 'normative/sectoral systems of references', and they seek to provide a form of evidence for policy through concepts, values and evaluations. But some differences exist: as we have seen these are more or less deliberate, emanating from experts and policymakers, and refined through debates. They appear in a pluralistic and less determinate context, which implies that they are diverse and also competing with each other.

This short discussion may shed some light on the relationships between agendas and indicators. The development of indicators is most often understood as driven by the development of an agenda. But indicators may be connected to several agendas. And they undergo their own specific transformation process: the construction, combination and use of a set of indicators depend on their practical feasibility as well as on the possible consent or dissent about their meaning and interpretation

[6] Even if the normative dimension of the notion of 'referential' put forward by Jobert and Muller introduces a difference with the common concept of 'paradigm' used by Hall, which is more focused on the cognitive dimension.

among experts, the actors concerned and in public opinion. This may contribute to an active feedback influencing existing agendas, connecting them, leading them to other transformations, and to different positions over time.

One of the central tasks of this study is to identify the possible interactions between the justification, implementation and evolution of the EES and the elaboration and use of operational indicators, and to illustrate the fluctuations and the difficulties of the construction of a coherent agenda.

5.2 THE CONSTRUCTION OF THE 'JOB QUALITY' AGENDA: AN ONGOING, COMPLEX PROCESS

The concern about job quality is not new in European countries (Gallie 2007), even if it has been less important due to the focus on the unemployment issue since the 1980s. At the end of the 1960s, social mobilisations emerged against bad working conditions along with criticisms of the Taylorist work organisations. In the 1970s and 1980s, the rise of non-regular employment (fixed-term contracts, temporary agency work) called for attention and became an important social issue in some continental European countries. But it is only from the beginning of the 2000s that job quality was constituted as an issue at European level, and even more, as an 'agenda'.

In the European arena, the 'job quality' agenda was first developed by the European Commission, especially in 2001, following the Lisbon Summit and the Nice Council. But this framework experienced uneven success until the recent Europe 2020 agenda. However, some other actors, which we are going to study in the next section, have also contributed to the definition of the concept and of some relevant indicators.

5.2.1 A Blurred Conceptual Framework, Contested Indicators and Fluctuating Political Priorities at the European Commission

The introduction of employment quality into the European debate about labour market performance and labour market policy dates back to the Lisbon Summit in March 2000, which put forward the objective of 'more and better jobs for all'. The importance of 'quality' was also stressed at the Nice Council in December 2000, which included employment quality in the European Social agenda, and made it an objective of the European Employment Strategy.[7]

This launching of the job quality issue in the European coordination of employment policies was driven by several factors, the respective weights of which are difficult to assess. The existence of an ILO Decent Work agenda as of 1999 provided an incentive to deal with these matters.[8] The economic upturn and the importance of job creation over the period 1997–2001 displaced interest from quantitative employment growth to other dimensions of the labour market. The European political context, characterised at the turn of the century by a majority of social democratic governments and a concern for employment and social issues in order to balance the focus on European Monetary Union, also appears to be crucial in understanding these dynamics. Finally, some countries which had a tradition of paying attention to job quality issues in social dialogue (especially the Nordic countries, for instance Sweden, but also Austria and the Netherlands) played an important role in putting the concept on the policy agenda.

The Laeken Summit in December 2001 played a key role in the building of the new agenda, as it defined indicators of 'job quality' (European Commission 2001a) by stressing the multidimensional nature of the concept. It was based on ten dimensions, including, among others, skills, working conditions, equality, and reconciliation between private and work life. This Laeken definition also includes labour market performance indicators (like employment rates, transition rates) as well as qualitative indicators (training rates, job satisfaction, in work accidents, etc.) – therefore mixing a macro perspective, concerning the performance of employment systems, and a micro perspective, focusing on job quality as narrowly defined.

The Laeken approach relied on a very wide approach to job quality. The concept itself was quite blurred, as the terminology used in debates and publications was varied: 'quality *in* work', 'quality *at* work', 'quality *of* work' 'employment quality', 'quality of employment' are all used.[9]

---

[7] According to this principle, the new formulation of the EES in 2003 includes job quality among its priority goals, namely 'full employment', 'employment quality and productivity', 'social inclusion and social cohesion'.

[8] Defined as promoting the 'opportunities for women and men to obtain decent and productive work in conditions of freedom, equity, security and human dignity' (ILO 1999).

[9] As Barbier and Sylla (2004) pointed out, the translation of the concept in other idioms may also be varied.

It is also important to stress that the relative consensus over including employment quality goals was accompanied by sharp debates about its definition: at the Laeken Council no agreement was met on the 'social dialogue' dimension or on the key indicator for intrinsic job quality. Moreover, the UK as well as the Nordic countries were opposed to the introduction of any reference to wage levels, and alternative solutions had to be found, like considering job satisfaction or wage mobility indicators (Davoine 2007).[10] But other key dimensions of job quality were also missing, in particular concerning work content and working conditions (lack of indicators on occupational disease, stress at work, work intensity, extent of autonomy granted to workers, etc.).

Overall, the Laeken approach was far from building a coherent conceptual and operational framework. Nevertheless, employment quality was set as a political agenda, and the various Laeken indicators, as well as their relationships with economic growth and performance, were investigated in four successive yearly reports by the DG Employment, from 2001 to 2004.[11] As well as the Commission, other European actors took part in this process, in particular the Dublin Foundation that proposed in 2002 a framework including four dimensions of quality of work and employment: career and employment security; skills development; reconciliation of working and non-working life; and health and well-being.

But this growing interest in quality issues in the field of employment began to show signs of fading in the second half of the 2000s.

For instance, the 2005 *Employment in Europe* report by the European Commission did not include any specific chapter devoted to employment quality, contrary to the four previous years. The report by Wim Kok in 2003 (entitled *Jobs, Jobs, Jobs*), which dealt with employment and labour market policies, focused mainly on the quantitative aspects of employment (and especially the employment rate and incentives to work). Since 2006, the focus on 'flexicurity' also tended to eclipse other goals, even if its definition as a combination of labour market flexibility and security

---

[10] The UK government was afraid of being singled out because of high levels of low-wage work. As for the Nordic countries, the refusal derived from the autonomy of social partners concerning wage bargaining and wage fixing: it is usual practice for policymakers not to interfere in wage bargaining.

[11] European Commission, *Employment in Europe*: (2001), Chapter 4, 'Quality in work and social inclusion'; (2002), Chapter 3, 'Synergies between quality and quantity in European labour markets'; (2003), Chapter 4, 'Flexibility, security and quality in work'; (2004), Chapter 4, 'Labour market transitions and advancement: temporary employment and low-pay in Europe'.

through lifelong learning and active labour market policy seemed to synthesise some of the previous EES priorities (European Expert Group on Flexicurity, 2007). The driving forces behind this change in priorities have been well described in the literature about the 'relaunch' of the Lisbon Strategy in 2005, and include factors such as changes in political majorities, with a liberal orientation, but also in the composition of the European institutions during the enlargement process. Besides, from 2003–2004 and until recently, direct initiatives by the Commission in the field of employment policies were developed and tended to avoid previous OMC processes: the role of external experts (intervening at the Commission's demand) like Wim Kok or the Flexicurity Experts Group was prominent, and some priority initiatives were disconnected from the EES or the OMC, like the creation of the Employment Globalisation Adjustment Fund in 2007 and the New Skills for New Jobs Initiative in 2008 (see also below).[12] It seems that these changes in the governance of employment policies at the EU level also took place to the detriment of the job quality agenda.

Nevertheless, if the issue of the quality of work was in a way crowded out by the focus on 'flexicurity' from the mid-2000s onwards, it never totally disappeared from the European agenda.

According to a key member of the EMCO during the period 2005–2010,[13] the interest in the quality of work issue, and more specifically, the job quality issue, never disappeared at Member State level. But there seems to have been a shift on the dimensions of quality on which their attention has focused. At the beginning of the 2000s, the focus was wide, with a particular interest in working conditions. At the end of the 2000s, the focus was more narrow, restricted mainly to 'employment conditions' (employment status, working time and pay levels), in connection also with the phenomenon of the working poor. The contributions of the European Foundation may be an indicator of this shift: whereas at the beginning of the 2000s it was mainly based on the exploitation of the European Working Conditions Survey, at the end of the 2000s, in the 'more and better jobs' contribution, the dimensions of job quality were restricted mainly to relative pay (i.e. pay levels in the quintiles of pay distribution) and employment status (with a specific focus on part-time work, fixed-term contracts and self-employment) – see European Foundation for the Improvement of Working Conditions (2008) and Hurley et al. (2011).

---

12 See European Commission (2008b).

13 Interview, May 2011.

Overall, as pointed out above, at the European level (in both the Commission and the EMCO), the interest in the quality of work was less obvious in the second half of the 2000s and up to 2010 (no specific follow-up of the indicators, contributions on the issue in the *Employment in Europe* annual publication based on occasional external contributions, etc.). Among the EMCO group, there was no specific interest in the issue. Belgium, which was a leader in the first period, seemed much less proactive at the end of the decade.

5.2.2 Continued Interest in other Arenas, besides the European Commission

The interest in job quality never totally disappeared from European debate, but seemed to be driven by the ILO's Decent Work agenda rather than the EU Laeken agenda of the early 2000s.

As mentioned above, the ILO, through its Decent Work agenda, had indeed been very active in calling attention to the qualitative dimensions of employment. From the beginning of the 2000s, several seminars on this issue have been held in Geneva, involving also the United Nations Economic Commission for Europe (UNECE) and Eurostat. In April 2007, the fourth joint UNECE/ILO/Eurostat seminar recommended the creation of a 'task force' in order to continue the conceptual work by building a 'systemic set of indicators on quality of employment statistics' (UNECE 2010, p. 1). This task force was mandated by the Conference of European Statisticians, and was further institutionalised in 2011, becoming an 'expert group'.

This work referred as a starting point to three previous frameworks (i.e. sets of indicators) on the issue: the ILO 'Decent Work' and two EU frameworks – a distinction being made between the European Commission's set of indicators for monitoring the labour market policies on the one hand, and the European Foundation framework based on the European Survey on Working Conditions on the other. But the document stated that 'while several related frameworks exist, each suits a particular purpose or policy agenda. None attempts to produce a broad, overall framework for the measurement of quality of employment as such' (UNECE 2010, p. 15).

The approach promoted here focused on 'quality of employment as such', measured from the perspective of the worker. Strictly speaking, it was closer to the common 'job quality' concept, rather than the broad concept defined by the Laeken initiative, which adopted a macro (or 'societal') rather than a 'micro' perspective. The proposed set of indicators did not include general context indicators (such as total employment and unemployment rates, gender segregation by sectors, etc.).

The approach referred to no 'particular purpose or policy agenda'. In fact, it even called for what could be labelled, in a way, as a form of 'measurement without theory' – that is, the building of statistical indicators without any explicit underlying institutionalised cognitive frame. The introduction of the report which presented the indicators, and the pilot country reports implementing them, stressed the fact that the goal was not to set any kind of recommendation, nor even to allow any kind of international comparison.[14] But, in spite of these caveats, the phrasing of the report was not considered cautious enough. Chapter 1 of the report, the so-called 'concept paper', was revised following discussion at the meeting of the Bureau of the Conference of European Statisticians (CES) in February 2010, and the term 'framework' was removed from the document, and 'any possible implication for defining quality of employment in it was avoided' (UNECE 2010, p. iii). Instead, the summary memorandum presented four months later at the 58th plenary session of the CES, which relies heavily on the initial concept paper, introduces some preliminary considerations: 'Quality of employment is a subjective concept which cannot become concrete without injecting some value judgement into the discussion [...] It is not possible for statisticians to define subjective issues like good, bad, quality, etc.' (UNECE–CES 2010, p. 4). In practice, the framework was designed to be purely descriptive, which excludes any weighting of sub-indices or construction of composite, summary indicators.[15] Besides, it was intended for national use, since comparisons were considered to be difficult and would have required better harmonisation.[16]

Overall, the potential political dimension of the UNECE/ILO initiative has been completely 'neutralised', and the definition of the relevant

[14] 'It is important to note that what is presented below should not be interpreted as a formal international recommendation that requires countries to produce statistics. The primary goal of this effort is to develop tools to measure and understand the quality of employment within a country, rather than facilitate international comparisons' (UNECE 2010 p. 3). 'Again, the goal is not to establish an international reporting requirement for National Statistical Organizations' (UNECE 2010, p. 8).

[15] Presentation, Brussels, 15 December 2011.

[16] A final report will be produced in 2015, and in the meantime it should be implemented at the country level by National Statistical Offices (examples exist in Germany and Switzerland).

dimensions and indicators of the quality of employment was presented as a purely statistical issue. In other words, there was no real 'political agenda' here as defined in Section 5.1.2 above, but rather a potential source of inspiration for the European community.

The European Trade Union Congress (ETUC) was another arena where the employment quality issue remained an important concern during the second half of the 2000s. In December 2006, the ETUC organised a conference about Decent Work. It referred to the ILO agenda, and criticised the orientations of European policies after 2005, disregarding the political (inside Europe and on the international scene) and social importance of job quality and increasing competition among European workers through deregulation.[17] The European Trade Union Institute (ETUI), which is the research agency of the ETUC, elaborated a job quality index based on Laeken indicators and some complements to monitor the dynamics of job quality in Europe (Leschke and Watt 2008).

5.2.3 Job Quality in the 2020 European Agenda: A New Start?

Within the new agenda 'Europe 2020', the promotion of 'inclusive growth' has been defined as a key priority. For this purpose, two 'flagship initiatives' have been adopted – one on skills and employment, the other on poverty. The first – the 'agenda for new skills and new jobs' – includes a chapter on 'improving the quality of work and working conditions'. The final document states that 'efforts are also needed to review the EU definition and common indicators of quality of work, and make them more operational for the evaluation and benchmarking of Member State policies in this area' (European Commission 2010, p. 15).

But signs of a new interest in the issue of job quality had appeared before the launch of the EU 2020 initiative. In the 2008 edition of *Employment in Europe*, a chapter reviewed the EU concept elaborated in Laeken, and indicated major weakness and omissions of the Laeken indicators (mainly those pointed out in Section 5.2.1 above, concerning especially the level and distribution of pay, social dialogue, and indicators concerning some key dimensions of work content and working conditions).

During the spring of 2009, the Indicators Group of the EMCO started to discuss a review of the state of the art concerning quality of work in the EU, but with no concrete outcomes, according to one of its key

---

[17] See John Monks, introductory speech, available at http://www.etuc.org/speeches/decent-work-conference#.VJRMHsCA (accessed 19 December 2014)

members.[18] The issue was relaunched one year later by the European Commission, during the thematic review of June 2010. The Commission proposed to open the debate to reach a 'more focused' quality of work approach. According to this initial proposal, the concept should be simplified around four dimensions. A 'quality job' could be defined as one that: 'provides adequate earning; offers opportunities for skills upgrading, life-long learning and career progression; ensures safe and healthy working conditions; [and] combines a high level of both security and flexibility, including flexible arrangements allowing for the reconciliation of work and private life' (EMCO 2011b, p. 4).

It may be asked whether a more focused 'job quality' approach was going to replace the wider but more vague approach of 'work quality' (or 'employment quality'), that had been promoted by the European Commission since 2001. The short report that was issued by the Ad Hoc Group of the EMCO after the thematic review did not bring any clarifications. Retracing the genesis and the evolution of the quality of work approach, it recalled the distinction between 'two broad dimensions' (Ad Hoc Group 2010, p. 2), the first referring to 'job characteristics' and the second to 'the work and wider labour market context'. There was apparently a distinction here between 'job quality' and the wider 'employment quality'. But the 'work and wider labour market context' dimension included not only contextual dimensions (non-discrimination, gender equality, etc.), but also dimensions that one would associate more spontaneously with job quality in the usual sense of the term (such as health and safety).

Still, the EMCO adopted a new road map for 2011. Its objective was to end the year (November 2011) with a revised concept of the quality of work (proposed by the Ad Hoc Group) and a revised set of indicators (built by the Indicators Group). In its first meetings (see EMCO 2011a), the Indicators Group decided to take stock of existing materials and recent research, starting with the Laeken indicators, and referring to recent UNECE work, as well as ILO work on the measurement of Decent Work[19] and the proposals of the ETUI concerning the job quality index (Leschke and Watt 2008 – see Section 5.2.2 above).

---

[18] Interview, May 2011.

[19] It must be noted that the cooperation between the European Commission and the ILO had been reinforced since 2006. Indeed, after initial support at the turn of the century, official EU support for the Decent Work agenda was emphasised and reasserted in several communications; see: the 2001 Communication on core labour standards, the 2004 Communication on the social dimension of globalisation; the 2006 ECOSOC ministerial declaration on 'Creating an

The proposals of the Indicators Group to make 'the EU definition and common indicators of quality of work more operational for the evaluation and benchmarking of the member state policies in that area' were issued at the end of October (EC, INDIC/18/271011/EN). They rely heavily on the proposals for modifications of the Laeken indicators put forward in the dedicated chapter in *Employment in Europe 2008*. Four dimensions were identified (see Appendix table 5A.1): socio-economic security (including adequate earnings, and job and career security); education and training (including skills development and employability); working conditions (health and safety at work, work intensity, workers' autonomy and working practices, collective interest representation); and work–life balance and gender balance. For each item, a precise indicator and source are given.

Overall, many dimensions missing from the Laeken indicators have been introduced. The approach was also more focused on 'job quality', strictly speaking, at the micro level. But it still included a more macro perspective, as features of the employment and social protection systems, as well as public policy, were taken into account.[20]

The report of the Dublin Foundation released at the end of 2011 also focused on job quality, using the 2010 European Working Conditions

---

environment at the national and international levels conducive to generating full and productive employment and decent work for all, and its impact on sustainable development'; the 2006 Communication on 'Promoting decent work for all'; and the Council Conclusions on 'Decent work for all', 30 November and 1 December 2006.

The Commission proposal for the Community Lisbon Programme 2008–2010, dated 11 December 2007, asserted, in particular: 'The Community is committed to shape globalisation with a view to maximising its benefits and sharing it with its partners. The Community needs to further engage with key trading partners, including neighbour countries and the emerging economies, and should further promote regional economic integration with its neighbourhood … . These negotiations, together with enhanced policy dialogues, can also contribute to further promoting sustainable development in partner countries, to promoting common values and internationally agreed social and environmental standards, including decent work.'

[20] For instance: one indicator of the 'job and career security' item was social protection expenditure by function (in per cent of GDP); the 'employability' item encapsulates indicators concerning the outcomes of the initial educational system (such as the share of early leavers from education and training, and the percentage of the working age population having completed at least upper secondary education).

Survey, returning to the multidimensional framework of the early 2000s.[21] It included four dimensions: earnings (fairness and level); employment quality; intrinsic job quality (work quality/social environment/physical environment/work intensity); and work–life balance.

At the time this chapter was being written (first quarter of 2012), discussions were thus on the table. The social partners had been welcomed to participate. The intention of the Commission (DG Employment) was to use these indicators for annual monitoring of labour markets and for the Joint Assessment Framework. There seemed to be a clear restoration of the 'job quality' agenda. But the effectiveness of this new start remained to be confirmed, as, at the beginning of 2012, the European Council seemed to be much more focused on the reinforced Stability Growth Pact and the debates around the new set of rules concerning economic and financial surveillance (the so-called 'six-pack'); and as the 2012 work programme of the Employment Committee referred only marginally to the issue of job quality.[22]

5.3 MULTILEVEL INITIATIVES AND GOVERNANCE

In this complex process, some actors have been quite active in other arenas and decision-making areas, in separate ways: national or local states and governing bodies (Section 5.3.1), and at the various levels of the social dialogue in the EU (Section 5.3.2). We shall focus on several developments which seem to be typical of what could become a (partial and uneven) 'bottom-up' process.

5.3.1 Isolated but Ongoing, Structured Developments in National States and Local Communities

5.3.1.1 Some separate national initiatives

Following UNECE recommendations, *Germany* has implemented a monitoring system of job quality. The Federal Statistical Office of Germany has started publishing information and statistics about job quality (aimed

---

[21] A first draft was presented at a meeting in Brussels on 14 December 2011. See Green and Mostafa (2012) for the final report.

[22] In the 22 page document (1 February 2012), the issue is mentioned only once, on page 18, where it is mentioned that the Indicator Committee 'will also continue its work on the monitoring and integration into the JAF [Joint Assessment Framework] of multidimensional policy concepts (e.g. Flexicurity or Quality in Work)'.

at a large audience) that should be released every year. The publication is entitled *Quality of Employment – Earning Money and What Else Counts*.[23]

This encompasses seven dimensions that are similar to the UNECE framework: safety and ethics of employment; income and benefits from employment; working hours and balancing work and non-working life; security of employment and social protection; social dialogue; skills development and training; and workplace relationships and work motivation. The work also includes extensive analysis of these different dimensions, including for instance the number of days on vacation per year in the income and benefits dimension, but also several indicators concerning working time (annual working time, overtime hours, night and weekend work, commuting time, involuntary part-time work, parents' employment rates and part-time work), and different ways of analysing the workplace relationships (relationships with colleagues, satisfaction at work). Like the UNECE initiative, the German monitoring of job quality is largely 'a-theoretical' and does not correspond to any policy agenda at the national level. The success of this initiative and its diffusion to a larger audience is impossible to measure at this stage, and the probability that this kind of process would be extended to other national statistics offices in the EU remains low.

In the *Netherlands* and *Flanders*, job quality is identified through another model, called the '4As Model'. It includes four main dimensions: work content (nature and autonomy of tasks/autonomy, on the job training, etc.), working conditions, employment relations (interactions between employees and employers), and employment conditions (wages, contracts, training, etc.). These dimensions are evaluated on the basis of a specific questionnaire, called the 'Experience and Evaluation of Work' (Dutch abbreviation: VBBA) (Van Veldhoven and Meijman 1994). This questionnaire is designed to be implemented through occupational health services in the Netherlands. Apart from general questions about working and employment conditions, it aims at identifying health problems and stress at work. This questionnaire was first implemented in 1996–2000.

Therefore the issue of job quality has been a concern in the Netherlands (and also in Flanders, with a similar methodology) for more than a decade. But the concept is more health oriented than the European and ILO frameworks.

---

[23] See Federal Statistical Office of Germany (2011).

Job quality appears as an important topic in *Austria*, from a political as well as from an academic point of view, involving numerous publications.[24] Quality of work and working conditions have been monitored since 1997, through the Austrian Working Climate Survey (*Arbeitsklimaindex*).[25]

The main focus of the Working Climate Survey is on job and workplace satisfaction, as well as satisfaction with working life in general. The survey covers questions on the type of employment contract, in particular in relation to temporary agency work, along with questions on job satisfaction, feelings of security or insecurity with regard to the future, working time, job tenure, work–life balance and work strains. In total, 26 different thematic indicators are collected, which are then combined into four sub-indexes (society, company, work and expectations) and subsequently an overall indicator. As the survey started in 1997, the index points of the first survey equal 100 and the following surveys are calculated on the basis of the first index points. The standardised survey is based on a representative sample of about 900 to 1,000 respondents and is collected four times a year.

The *Austrian* Working Climate Survey is commissioned by the Upper Austrian Chamber of Labour (*Arbeiterkammer Oberösterreich, AK*) and carried out by the Institute for Empirical Social Research (*Institut für Empirische Sozialforschung*) and the Institute for Social Research and Analysis. It is published regularly for a large audience on the Chamber of Labour website.[26]

5.3.1.2 Job quality between evaluation and reciprocal commitments: Regional initiatives in France, as an illustration

Two regional initiatives in France are considered here: the *Charte bretonne de partenariat pour la qualité de l'emploi* of the Région Bretagne (2008) and the *Charte d'engagement des entreprises* of the Région Rhône-Alpes (2007–2011).

The starting point is the same in both cases: using the allocation of subsidies and other modalities of help to firms as a lever to reach sustainable employment targets. Given the domains of intervention attributed to the French regions (which include economic development,

---

24 See WISO 3/2011 (September 2011) Schwerpunkt: 'Arbeitsbedingungen und Qualität von Erwerbsarbeit', available at http://www.isw-linz.at/publikationen/wiso/publikationsuebersicht/115#wiso_03_2011(accessed 19 December 2014).

25 Ibid.

26 Available at http://www.arbeiterkammer.com/gesundheit/arbeitsklima.htm (accessed 19 December 2014).

professional training, but exclude most labour market policies), the funds are either directly given to firms, or, most often, given to collective inter-firm projects, for example for export development, social innovation and expertise with company restructuring. Some of them are matched with European grants (European Social Fund, European Regional Development Fund) and co-managed by central government (the French State).

The basic idea is to tie the allocation of funds to commitments signed by firms in the domain of employment, social dialogue and environment. Both *Chartes* group together several targets of employment quality and environmental preservation (a choice which brings them close to the issue and style of Corporate Social Responsibility, integrating some core elements of job quality into a wider context).

The main stake for the Région Rhône-Alpes was and still is the accountability of such a policy, and especially the measurement of the employment outcomes of the various types of support given to firms. Two committees were set up, the first (2004) composed of experts, policymakers (members of the Regional Assembly) and of members of the regional administration, devoted to a 'generalised process of evaluation'; and the second (2005) adding members of the social partners (Commission SUEVAL, 'de suivi et d'évaluation des fonds régionaux accordés aux entreprises').

Officially adopted in 2007, the *Charte* has not been implemented because the financial and economic crisis has led to other emergency measures. During spring 2011, it underwent a revision and reformulation process by the Commission SUEVAL, in order to become operational in the autumn 2011.

Accompanying this process, the regional authorities of Rhône-Alpes have started a long-term process of selection and testing of regional indicators of job quality, since 2009. It mirrors the EU indicators, seeking local equivalents. As part of a seminal study proposing such a list (2010), a multi-actor process has been initiated, with representatives of different directorates of the region and of the regional offices of central government Departments, members of the regional agency of the INSEE (French National Institute of Statistics) and of other bodies and networks in the fields of training and employment. The first results were published in March 2012 (Dupré and Labosse 2012) and provide a regional overview of job quality, using a series of indicators that are close to European reports (especially the *Employment in Europe* 2008 report). In a second stage (2012–2014), a feasibility study has been undertaken by a private evaluation institution, focused on firms' behaviour regarding job quality targets and indicators. The aim was twofold: to ensure that the targets are meaningful for firm managers, while also checking the consistency and coverage of the items considered (see Besret 2013).

5.3.2 Job Quality as a Fluctuating Priority for Social Partners at National Level

Decent work has been endorsed by the ETUC as one of its priority goals, and remains on the top of its agenda.[27] Its research Institute (ETUI) is developing and monitoring a job quality index (Leschke and Watt 2008). But in recent years, the ETUC's priorities have been challenged by the crisis and the massive rise in unemployment, leading to a renewed focus on job creation and the quantitative performance of the labour market.

The situation of national trade unions with regard to job quality appears very diverse. Some interesting initiatives to measure job quality trends through specific surveys have been developed in Belgium (Flanders, 'workable work'), in Germany and in Austria. But in other countries, like France, it remains a secondary concern for trade unions.[28]

French trade unions seem to be more concerned with Corporate Social Responsibility than with the Decent Work agenda. One reason for the weak relationships with European concepts might be the more general institutional context and the low participation of French social partners in the EES and more generally European processes. This trend seems to have worsened since 2010, as a result of internal processes and of the substitution of National Reform Plans (NRPs) by the National Action Plans (NAPs) of the Lisbon process.

Indeed, the participation of French social partners in European coordination processes in the field of labour market policy has been weakening since 2010. This trend is related to both European and national factors. At the European level, the relaunch of the Lisbon Strategy in 2005, and the integration of the employment guidelines with macroeconomic policy guidelines in the NRPs, have contributed to limit the role played by employment actors, including social partners. This trend was reinforced by national reforms: employment issues were

---

[27] See the speech given by Bernadette Ségol, ETUC General Secretary Designate, at the 'March for an Alternative' in London on 26 March 2011: 'You want, need and deserve jobs, good jobs', as well as the Athens resolution (ETUC Congress, May 2011).

[28] Interview, Confédération Française Démocratique du Travail, 7 January 2011; interview, Force Ouvrière, 16 December 2011.

transferred to the Ministry of Economy and Finance in 2007, thus putting this Ministry in a leading position concerning the Lisbon Strategy and the EES.

In practice, since 2006 social partners have no longer been systematically invited to the presentation and discussion of the French NRP with the Commission, despite the fact that these meetings were unanimously considered a success (according to both social partners and officials). It remains unclear if this limitation is due to a change in the EU's attitude, following the enlargement that has increased the administrative burden related to the NRP process, or to the French government's attitude. Anyway, it seems clear that the social partners are willing to discuss the NRPs with the Commission: 'The presence of social partners at bilateral discussions between the French government and the Commission has enhanced their awareness of European matters. But since the enlargement these meetings have been suppressed, even though they were extremely useful.'[29]

Besides, social partners' participation in the most recent NRPs has been reduced, since their comments are no longer attached in the appendices, nor included in the text. Indeed, the practice has varied since 1997: social partners' comments were first included in the text, under the corresponding item of the NAPs, and then they were put in an appendix. But over the last two years, their contributions have not been presented. Therefore, it is possible that the apparent low level of interest of French social partners in job quality issues at the European level is explained by their low level of participation in the European Employment Strategy.

Overall, the French case is a good illustration of the difficulty in implementing an agenda defined at the European level, when social partners do not feel concerned about it.

The observations and analyses made in this section remain sketchy. However, they suggest, as plausible hypotheses connected to the question of EU risk management governance, four ideas. First, the observed contributions to a job quality agenda and measurement process start from various departure points and inspiration sources: more often the ILO and the UNECE than the EES as international sources. Secondly, the intensity and durability of the agenda-making processes are quite uneven, from strong and lasting commitments to sporadic attempts. Thirdly, the union coordination process at the EU level remains weak regarding this issue, and did not stimulate (up to now) a generalised concern in national unions. Fourthly and finally: it has been shown that some regional

[29] Interview, December 2008.

experiences (at least in France) do make explicit references to EU policies and orientations.

5.4 CONCLUSION

Thus the job quality debate and its fluctuations over time appear to have been permanent in the European arena, since 2000, although the leading actors and the intensity of publications and events have changed. This topic clearly reveals the transformations of employment policy governance at the EU level and changes in political priorities. As a result, the political treatment of risks in work and in the labour market has been unstable.

Ten years after the Laeken Summit and the definition of indicators, job quality remains a complex issue in the European labour market policy debate, major uncertainty on the denomination and definition of the concept ('job' versus 'employment' versus 'work' quality), as well as concerning the dimensions to be examined. Our analyses (although still incomplete) show that the process around job quality is characterised by major uncertainty at the European level, but also by a semi-autonomous process, which can be described as a bottom-up, deepening of the issue. The ideas of multilevel governance and political agenda seem particularly adequate to understand this process. Uncertainty at the European level can be understood as the result of competing agendas. The EES can be considered an intermediate process between two extremes: the 'flexibilisation' agenda promoted by the OECD and the IMF, and the Decent Work agenda promoted by the ILO. Initially, the dominant agenda was 'flexibilisation', expressing the pressures of globalisation.

The crisis changed this situation and induced what can be termed a 'swing of the pendulum' among agendas. In 2009, the 'flexibilisation agenda' was largely discredited, and the ILO agenda (closer to job quality) has been temporarily perceived as prominent. Based on economic and financial arguments that were promoted by economic actors at the national and European level, evolution after 2010 seems to have brought back austerity and budgetary discipline (including cuts in labour market policy budgets), as this may re-introduce more 'quantitative' and market discipline concerns. Other possible intermediate agendas may be developed, such as 'Transitional Labour Markets', in which 'social risk management' is explicit and prominent (Schmid 2006), but up to now they have remained confidential.

But many actors at different levels seem to have committed themselves to a deepening process, which may influence the ongoing debate at the

European Commission level: a semi-bottom-up process, illustrating the way a more or less shared set of indicators may influence policy priorities in a 'soft' multilevel governance process.

BIBLIOGRAPHY

Ad Hoc Group (2010), *Ad Hoc Group Report on the 2010 Thematic Review, Part 2, 'Quality in Work'*, Employment Committee reports, issue 6, November.

Auer, P. and B. Gazier (2008), 'Flexicurity as a policy agenda', CESIfo Dice Report, *Journal for Institutional Comparisons*, **6** (4), Winter, 3–8.

Barbier, J.-C. (2008), *La longue marche vers l'Europe sociale*, Paris: PUF.

Barbier, J.-C. (2011), 'Change in political discourse from the Lisbon Strategy to Europe 2020: tracing the fate of "social policy"?' *ETUI Working Paper* 2011.01.

Barbier, J.-C. and N.S. Sylla (2004), 'La Stratégie Européenne pour l'Emploi, genèse, coordination communautaire et diversité nationale', *CEE Rapports de Recherche*, October, no. 16.

Barbier, J.-C., F. Colomb and P. Madsen (2009), 'Flexicurity – an open method of coordination, at the national level?', *Documents de travail du CES*, 2009.46.

Begg, I., C. Erhel and J. Mortensen (2010), *Medium Term Employment Challenges of the Lisbon Strategy*, DG EMPL VT/2008/010, CEPS, Bruxelles. Available at: http://ec.europa.eu/social/main.jsp?catId=101&langId=en (accessed 21 May 2014).

Besret, V. (ed.) (2013), 'Mesure et suivi de l'effet emploi des politiques de développement économique', Euréval.

Borras, S. and C. Radaelli (2011), 'The politics of governance architectures: creation, change, and effects of the EU Lisbon Strategy', *Journal of European Public Policy*, **18** (4), 463–84.

Davoine, L. (2007), *La qualité de l'emploi: une perspective européenne*, thesis, Université Paris 1.

De la Porte, C. (2008), *The European Level Development and National Level Influence of the Open Method of Coordination: The Cases of Employment and Social Inclusion*, Thesis, European University Institute, Department of Political and Social Sciences.

Dupré, A. and L. Labosse (2012), 'Rhône-Alpes: des conditions d'emploi de bonne qualité malgré certains facteurs de fragilité'. Available at: http://insee.fr/fr/themes/document.asp?reg_id=8&ref_id=18411 (accessed 11 May 2012).

EMCO (2011a), 'Indicators on quality in work: taking stock of existing material and indicators', INDIC/08/110311/EN.

EMCO (2011b), 'Quality of work: exchange on views with the social partners. Steering note', ADHOC/12/030511/EN.

Eurofound (2002), 'La qualité du travail et de l'emploi en Europe. Enjeux et défis'. *Cahiers de la Fondation*, no. 1, février, Luxembourg: Office des publications officielles des Communautés européennes.

European Commission (2001a), *Employment and Social Policies: A Framework for Investing in Quality*, Communication from the Commission to the Council, Brussels, COM (2001) 313 final, 20 June.

European Commission (2001b), *Promouvoir un cadre européen pour la Responsabilité Sociale de l'Entreprise*, Livre Vert, DG Emploi et Affaires Sociales, unité Empl/D1.

European Commission (2005), *Employment in Europe*, Luxembourg: Office for Official Publications of the European Communities.

European Commission (2006), *Implementing the Partnership for Growth and Jobs: Making Europe a Pole of Excellence on Corporate Social Responsibility*, COM (2006) 136 final, Brussels, 22 March.

European Commission (2008a), *Employment in Europe*, Luxembourg: Office for Official Publications of the European Communities.

European Commission (2008b), *New Skills for New Jobs: Anticipating and Matching Labour Market and Skills Needs*, Communication from the Commission to the European Parliament, the Council, the European Economic and Social Committee and the Committee of the Regions, COM (2008) 868 final, Brussels.

European Commission (2010), *An Agenda for New Skills and Jobs: A European Contribution towards Full Employment*, COM (2010) 682 final, Strasbourg, November.

European Expert Group on Flexicurity (2007), *Flexicurity Pathways: Turning Hurdles into Stepping Stones*, June.

European Foundation for the Improvement of Working Conditions (2008), *More and Better Jobs: Patterns of Employment Expansion in Europe*, Luxembourg: Office for Official Publications of the European Communities.

Federal Statistical Office of Germany (2011), 'Quality of employment – earning money and what else counts'. Available at: https://www.destatis.de/EN/Publications/Specialized/LabourMarket/QualityEmployment.pdf?__blob=publicationFile (accessed 21 May 2014).

Gallie, D. (ed.) (2007), *Employment Regimes and the Quality of Work*, Oxford: Oxford University Press.

Green, F. and T. Mostafa (2012), *Trends in Job Quality in Europe*, Dublin: Eurofound.

Guergoat-Larivière, M. and O. Marchand (2012), 'Définition et mesure de la qualité de l'emploi: une illustration au prisme des comparaisons européennes', *Economie et Statistique*, 454, 23–42.

Hall, P. (ed.) (1989), *The Political Power of Economic Ideas*, Princeton: Princeton University Press.

Heidenreich, M. and J. Zeitlin (eds) (2009), *Changing European Employment and Welfare Regimes*, London: Routledge.

Hurley, J., D. Storrie and J.-M. Jungblut (2011), *Shifts in the Job Structure in Europe during the Great Recession*, Report, Eurofound, Luxembourg: Office for Official Publications of the European Communities.

ILO (1999), *Decent Work*, Report of Mr. Juan Somavia, ILO Director-General, 87th session of the International Labour Conference, 1999.

ILO (2012), *Decent Work Indicators – Concepts and Definitions*, ILO Manual, Geneva, first version, May.

Jobert, B. (2003), 'Europe and the recomposition of national forums: the French case', *Journal of European Public Policy*, **10** (3), 463–77.

Jobert, B. and P. Muller (1987), *L'Etat en action. Politiques publiques et corporatismes*, Paris: Presses Universitaires de France.

Kok, W. (2003), *Jobs, Jobs, Jobs: Creating More Employment in Europe*, Brussels: European Commission.

Kok, W. (2004), *Facing the Challenge: The Lisbon Strategy for Growth and Employment*, Brussels: European Commission.

Kröger, S. (2009), 'The Open Method of Coordination: underconceptualisation, overdetermination, depoliticisation and beyond', in Sandra Kröger (ed.), *What we have Learnt: Advances, Pitfalls and Remaining Questions in OMC Research. European Integration online Papers (EIoP)*, Special Issue 1, Vol. 13, Art. 5. Available at http://eiop.or.at/cgi-bin/erpa-search.pl?cmd=search&datefrom=2009&dateto=2009&format=EIoP&site=EIoP (accessed 17 October 2014).

Leschke, J. and A. Watt (with M. Finn) (2008), 'Putting a number on job quality? Constructing a European Job Quality Index', *ETUI-REHS Working Paper*, March.

Mailand, M. (2008), 'The uneven impact of the European Employment Strategy on member states' employment policies: a comparative analysis', *Journal of European Social Policy*, **18**, 353–65.

Muller, P. (2005), 'Esquisse d'une théorie du changement dans l'action publique. Structures, acteurs et cadre cognitif', *Revue Française de Science Politique*, **55** (1), 255–75.

OECD (1994), *The OECD Jobs Study: Facts, Analysis, Strategies*, Paris: OECD.

Pochet, P. and J. Zeitlin (eds) (2005), *The Open Method of Coordination in Action: The European Employment and Social Inclusion Strategies*, Brussels: PIE-Peter Lang.

Schmid, G. (2006), 'Social risk management through Transitional Labour Markets', *Socio-Economic Review*, **4** (1), 1–33.

UNECE (2010), *Measuring Quality of Employment. Country Pilot Reports*, ECE/CES/2010/9.

UNECE-CES (2010), 'Potential indicators for measurement of quality of employment. Note by the secretariat', Fifty-eighth plenary session, Paris, 8–10 June.

Van Veldhoven, M. and T.F. Meijman (1994), *Het meten van psychosociale arbeidsbelasting met een vragenlijst: de vragenlijst beleving en beoordeling van de arbeid (VBBA)* (*The Measurement of Psychosocial Work Load with a Questionnaire: The Questionnaire Experience and Evaluation of Work (QEEW)*). Amsterdam: Dutch Institute for Working Conditions.

WISO – Wirtschafts- und SozialpolitischeZeitschrift, *Job Quality Special Issue*, 3/2011. Available at: http://www.isw-linz.at/component/content/article/34-wiso-dokument/115-wiso-2011 (accessed 21 May 2014).

Zeitlin, J. (2009), 'The open method of coordination and reform of national social and employment policies: influences, mechanisms, effects', in J. Zeitlin and M. Heidenreich (eds), *Changing European Employment and Welfare Regimes*, Abingdon: Routledge, pp. 1–25.

Zeitlin, J. and M. Heidenreich (eds) (2009), *Changing European Employment and Welfare Regimes*, London: Routledge.

APPENDIX

Table 5A.1 An overview of job quality indicators by dimensions according to international approaches

Dimensions	ILO (1999, 2012)	European Commission (2001a)	EC–EMCO (2011a)	Eurofound (2002)	UNECE (2010)
Health and security at work, working conditions	5. Work forms to be abolished 7. Equality 8. Security at work	3. Gender equality 4. Health and security at work 9. Diversity and non-discrimination	3.1. Health and security at work 3.2. Work intensity 4.2. Gender equality	Health and well-being	Security and work and ethics
Earnings	2. Adequate earnings	1. Intrinsic quality of jobs	1.1. Appropriate wages	Income	2. Earnings and advantages related to employment
Working time and work family reconciliation	2. Decent hours 3. Work, family and private life reconciliation	7. Work organisation and work–life balance	4.1. Work–life balance	Work and private life reconciliation	3.1. Working time and work/private life reconciliation
Job security and social protection	6. Job stability and security 9. Social protection	5. Flexibility and security	1.2. Employment security and career prospects	Employment status and social protection	4. Employment security and social protection
Social dialogue	10. Social dialogue and workers'/ employers' representation	6. Social dialogue and workers' participation	3.4. Collective representation	Workers' rights	5. Social dialogue
Lifelong learning		2. Lifelong learning and career progression	2. Competences development and employability	Competences development	Lifelong learning and competences development

Dimensions	ILO (1999, 2012)	European Commission (2001a)	EC–EMCO (2011a)	Eurofound (2002)	UNECE (2010)
Other dimensions	1. Employment opportunities 10. Economic and social context for decent work	1. Labour market integration 10. General work performances (productivity)	6. Work autonomy		7. Workplace climate and work motivation

Source: Translated and adapted from Guergoat-Larivière and Marchand (2012).

PART II

The regulation of working time in Europe

6. Sustainability and uncertainty in governing European employment law – the community method as instrument of governance: The case of the EU Working Time Directive[1]

Ralf Rogowski

The case of the EU Working Time Directive (hereafter WTD) will serve in the following as an example of assessing potential and limits of the so-called ‘community method’ as a method of governance in European social and employment law. The overall question asked in the chapter will be how the community method contributes to overcoming and/or creating uncertainty in order to sustain European employment law. For this purpose the chapter will evaluate the four case studies on the implementation of the WTD that were carried out within the context of the workpackage on European Governance of the FP7 project GUSTO (Governance of Uncertainty: Meeting the Challenges of Economic Uncertainty and Sustainability through Employment, Industrial Relations, Social and Environmental Policies in European Countries). The results of the workpackage are outlined in chapters 7, 8, 9 and 10 in this volume. The countries under comparison are the Czech Republic, France, the Netherlands and the United Kingdom.

The chapter contains five sections. The first section gives an overview of the main features and structural deficits of the community method, including some remarks on the community method as a specific form of

---

[1] I would like to thank Mark Hall and Ania Zbyszewska for comments and Christian Mecklenburg-Guzman and Falk Mäde-Heck for research assistance. A previous version of this chapter was published as Chapter 9, ‘Reflexive Implementation of EU Employment Law – a Case Study of the Working Time Directive’, in R. Rogowski (2013), *Reflexive Labour Law in the World Society*. Cheltenham and Northampton, MA: Edward Elgar, pp. 207–26.

governance in European labour law. The second section outlines the WTD and efforts to reform it. Section 6.3 presents results of the four case studies mentioned above. The final sections draw conclusions from the case studies for a discussion of sustainability and uncertainty in relation to the community method as a method of governance.

6.1 THE COMMUNITY METHOD[2]

What characterises the community method? From a political science perspective it is a unique form of governance based on the principle of 'balanced representation of national and supranational interests'.[3] This assessment concentrates on aspects of legitimation and democracy and in particular on problems of cooperation of European institutions and member states in creating legislation. What this view largely neglects is the implementation perspective.

From a legal perspective the community method is a means to generate so-called 'hard law'. The three binding legal instruments that constitute the core of the community method – Regulations, Directives and Decisions – are considered hard because the Commission can take legal action in case of non-compliance. Thus from a legal perspective implementation is a central issue. Once a legal Act comes into force, member states can be forced to obey it. Herein lies the main difference with soft law.

The Commission is formally responsible for overseeing the 'application'[4] and the enforcement of EU law. Once it has received information on non-compliance, it has powers to start the enforcement procedure outlined in Article 258 of the Treaty on the Functioning of the EU (TFEU). The first step of the procedure is informal. The Commission approaches the member state with an informal letter that warns about a possible violation of its obligations under EU law. Usually the member state will be given a time limit of two months to respond to the initial letter.

---

[2] The notion of Community Law was replaced by Union Law within the official European Law discourse when the Lisbon Treaty came into force on 1 December 2009. Accordingly the dominant official governance method should probably now be named 'union method'. However, community method is still the common term used in the literature and will be maintained in the following.

[3] Majone (2005), pp. 42–63 (here p. 59) and further references in Ch. 3 of Majone's book entitled 'The Community Method'.

[4] See Article 17(1) Treaty on the European Union (TEU).

If the member state does not respond satisfactorily, the Commission can start the formal procedure by sending a Letter of Formal Notice (*lettre de mise en demeure*, *Mahnschreiben*). This letter contains a brief legal summary of the alleged infringement that should provide enough information for the member state to prepare its legal defence.[5] Under normal circumstances the member state is given a further two months to respond to the Letter of Formal Notice.

If the Commission considers the member state's response to its Letter of Formal Notice insufficient, it sends a Reasoned Opinion to the member state. This Opinion is the binding legal statement in which the Commission lists in detail the allegations of infringement of EU law. It constitutes the formal indictment (the Commission now acts as the prosecutor) and has to indicate all legal arguments the Commission intends to use in front of the Court of Justice of the European Union (hereafter CJEU). The Reasoned Opinion is in fact the document that the Commission must use if it decides to go to the CJEU and spells out clearly the measures the Commission expects the member state to take to end the infringement. Usually the member state will be given a further two months to respond or react. After this period elapses the Commission has to decide if it will proceed to the CJEU.

The relatively clear and straightforward procedure aims to create certainty for member states in terms of what to expect from the Commission and how to respond. However, it has to be emphasised that the main characteristic of the enforcement procedure is total discretion on the part of the Commission, which can decide to abandon the procedure at any stage. The Article 258 procedure aims at cooperation and recognises the fact that there is an on-going relationship between the Commission and the member state which is based on dialogue. Here we can detect an element of legal uncertainty in the very nature of the enforcement procedure. The member state cannot simply rely on the Commission to use its discretion to stop the procedure. The member state has to show at least willingness to continue the dialogue with the Commission in order for the threat of being dragged in front of the CJEU to disappear. What actually convinces the Commission to stop the procedure in case it is difficult for the member state to obey remains uncertain (Tallberg 2003).

From a sociological perspective the enforcement procedure is characterised by a capacity deficit that leads to decisional outsourcing and functional differentiation. According to Poul Kjaer (2010), the capacity

---

5 Case C-274/83 *Commission v Italy*, [1985] ECR 1077.

deficit results from the EU's severe limitations of competences, a relatively low level of cognitive resources and a lack of real control mechanisms. In Kjaer's conclusion reflexive structures, in particular new forms of governance, are 'nurtured by the EU in order to off-set its structural deficits' (Kjaer 2010, 48).

However, these deficits can also be seen as strengths insofar as they force the Commission to become creative in influencing implementation processes. We can detect features of reflexive implementation strategies that promise greater success than formal legal enforcement. Reflexive implementation forms part of strategies of reflexive harmonisation (Barnard and Deakin 2001). From a reflexive law perspective it is crucial that the Commission has to realise its dependence on the member states' ability and capacity to regulate themselves. Reflexive implementation is in this view regulation of self-regulation (Rogowski 2013, Ch. 2).

The question whether the community method creates uncertainty in member states is rarely asked in European labour law. Since hard law, including directives, is designed to send out clear expectations, its objective is to create certainty. Indeed problems of uncertainty are usually not encountered at the level of formal legal transposition of directives, which are the main legal instruments used in EU labour law. However, if we use the model of three phases in implementing EU law (transposition, enforcement and application) that was introduced by Falkner and her team in studying compliance in the EU (Falkner et al. 2005), uncertainty is more likely to occur at the levels of national enforcement and application of EU measures (see also Hartlapp 2005; Treib 2004).

In the domain of labour law, the fact that European law might pose problems for national legislation, administrative practices, company policies and employee rights was for a long time neglected, with the exception of the outsider voice of the UK of course. National labour law, including industrial relations and collective bargaining, co-evolved more or less happily with community (now union) law. These areas of regulation were seen as operating in different realms. However, this coexistence has been challenged by recent case law of the CJEU. The awareness of impacts of European labour law on industrial relations and national approaches in protecting employee interests has been sharpened in particular by the *Viking* and *Laval* cases. These cases and their judicial aftermath brought into sharp focus that national social and employment protection systems are not exempt from scrutiny and can be declared illegal if not compatible with EU law (see Deakin and Rogowski 2011).

As result of these developments central actors in the field, in particular the trade unions and also the employer associations, increase their engagement with EU law. They begin to realise that European law and policies may create specific risks and general uncertainty regarding their status and their rights, as well as the nature and quality of employment protection they defend by their policies. Ideological and political battles that target privatisation and negative consequences of rampant competition policies are likely to increase.

For academic observers the area of European social and employment policy has never been without tensions. The original neglect of labour law in the 1950s was intentional, as was the reversal of this attitude in the 1970s when a Social Action programme was enacted that led to important legislation at the supranational level (Barnard 2006, 8–11; Bercusson 2009, 107–120). In particular the adoption of the Charter of Fundamental Social Rights of Workers in 1989 raised the hope among trade unions and employees in general that European law would establish a floor of rights that is capable of improving the situation for workers in the EU as a whole by forcing member states to adopt adequate measures of protection and by harmonising national legislation (Bercusson 2006). Even the transformation of the policy focus from employment protection to employment promotion in the 1990s[6] and the introduction of new forms of governance of employment did not fundamentally alter the positive attitude of the trade union movement towards European labour law.

Nevertheless, the situation was always slightly different in relation to implementation of European law in national contexts. In the following, the use of the community method in governing and implementing European labour law will be discussed in relation to the example of the WTD. The Directive regulates weekly hours of employment and is situated at the crossroads of health and safety regulations, employment protection and labour market policy. It also crosses over to the field of industrial relations insofar as regulation of working time falls in some member states, for example Germany, into the constitutionally protected domain of 'autonomy of collective bargaining (*Tarifautonomie*)' (Article 9(3) of the German Basic Law).

In the next section the chapter provides brief information about the Directive and its context. This is followed by an overview of the findings of the four case studies on implementation of the WTD that were carried

---

6 On the regulation of new forms of employment in Europe see Schömann et al. (1998) and on new forms of governance, including the concepts of the Open Method of Coordination (OMC) and flexicurity, see Rogowski (2007).

out as part of the research undertaken by the GUSTO workpackage on European governance.

6.2 THE WORKING TIME DIRECTIVE

The WTD was first introduced as Council Directive 93/104/EC on 23 November 1993. It was amended by the so-called 'Horizontal Amending Directive' 2000/34/EC of 22 June 2000 and adopted in its current form on 4 November 2003 as Directive 2003/88/EC concerning certain aspects of the organisation of working time. The WTD is officially a measure to protect the health and safety of workers and regulates specifically hours of work.

6.2.1 Scope and Content of the WTD

Key features of the WTD are the limitation of the maximum length of a working week to 48 hours in 7 days, a minimum rest period of 11 hours in each 24 hours, at least 4 weeks' paid holiday a year and protection in the case of night work.

The 1993 Directive was stated to apply to all areas of economic activity as defined by the Framework Directive on Health and Safety,[7] but then went on to exclude certain sectors: 'air, rail, road, sea and inland waterway and lake transport, sea fishing, other work at sea and the activities of doctors in training' (Article 1(3)). These excluded sectors were removed by the Horizontal Amending Directive of 2000, and additional directives were put in place for specific sectors. This resulted in special rules for mobile workers in sea, road and air transport. With effect from 1 August 2003, non-mobile workers in these sectors, in addition to all workers in rail transport and all workers in other forms of work at sea (such as offshore oil and gas workers), gained the full protection of the 1993 Directive, and mobile workers in road transport received the benefit of the provisions governing paid annual leave and health assessment for night work. Furthermore, Directive 2003/88/EC extended the coverage to doctors in training but granted member states transition periods for introducing national legislation in this area. In effect Directive 2003/88/EC only enlarged the scope of Directive 93/104/EC; otherwise the provisions are materially identical to those of the 1993 Directive.

---

[7] Council Directive 89/391/EEC of 12 June 1989 on the introduction of measures to encourage improvements in the safety and health of workers at work.

A special and controversial feature of the WTD is the possibility of an individual opt-out. According to Article 22(1)(b)(i) (former Article 18(1)(b)(i)) WTD member states can grant workers the right to opt out of the 48-hour rule on a voluntary basis. The fact that this opt-out is often presented as an individual right of the employee disguises the fact that it is companies and employers who have an interest in the opt-out and who are the real beneficiaries.

The 2010 Report of the European Commission on the implementation of the WTD provides the following assessment of the use of the individual opt-out by member states:

> In 2000, the UK was the only member state to make use of the opt-out. However, by 2003, other member states (France, Germany, the Netherlands and Spain), had introduced, or were introducing, opt-outs. These were limited to workers who performed extensive on-call work, and were thus intended to alleviate in the short term the problems posed for health systems seeking to absorb the implications of the CJEU's rulings regarding on-call time in *SIMAP* and subsequent cases.
>
> Following recent enlargements, the use of the opt-out within the EU has expanded further, and a total of sixteen member states now explicitly provide for use of the opt-out (including one which is currently legislating to allow its use).
>
> Bulgaria, Cyprus, Estonia, Malta, and the United Kingdom allow use of the opt-out, irrespective of sector. The Czech Republic, France, Germany, Hungary, Latvia, the Netherlands, Poland, Slovakia, Slovenia, and Spain allow for use of the opt-out in certain jobs which use extensive on-call time. Belgium is currently legislating to allow use of the opt-out by doctors and some other health professionals. (European Commission 2010a, 87–88)

6.2.2 CJEU Case Law on the WTD

The above quote from the 2010 Commission report on implementation of the WTD refers to case law of CJEU interpreting the Directive. It indicates that CJEU case law was the driving force behind the expansion in the use of individual opt-out clauses. In general this case law has to be distinguished into two types of case: those that challenge the legal basis of WTD and those seeking interpretation of specific WTD concepts.

As reported in chapter 10 in this volume, the UK government of the day sued the Council in the mid-1990s, arguing that the WTD had a defective legal basis.[8] The UK government claimed that the Directive

[8] Case C-84/94 *United Kingdom v Council of the European Union* [1996] ECR I-5755 and Industrial Relations Law Reports (IRLR), Vol. 26, No. 1, January [1997] 32.

should have been adopted on the basis of former Articles 100 or 235 EC Treaty, which required unanimity within the Council, rather than Article 118a EC Treaty which allowed a health and safety measure to be adopted by majority vote. According to the UK, the connection of the areas regulated by the WTD with the health and safety of workers was too tenuous and not supported by scientific evidence. In the UK's view, the WTD contributes to the improvement in living and working conditions of employees and thus is part of the Community's social policy; it went further and called the WTD disguised labour market policy. The CJEU rejected the UK view and held that the principal objective of WTD was the protection of the health and safety of workers within the meaning of Article 118a EC Treaty. 'It does not follow from the fact that the directive falls within the scope of Community social policy that it cannot properly be based on Article 118a, so long as it contributes to encouraging improvements as regards the health and safety of workers.'[9]

Specific provisions of the WTD were clarified and interpreted in a number of rulings of the CJEU, for example the calculation of the duration of working time. However, the most notable cases have been the *SiMAP*[10] and *Jaeger*[11] judgments of 2000 and 2003 concerning on-call duties of doctors in hospitals. In the *SiMAP* judgment the CJEU defined, for the purposes of work and rest calculations, all time when a worker is required to be present on site as actual working hours. Times when the worker is on call, but not on site, do not count as working time. The *Jaeger* judgment confirmed that all time doctors spend at their place of work counts as working time, even if workers are allowed to sleep during their services, although periods when the doctor is not working should be treated as rest periods. These judgments have had practical effects, particularly for junior doctors and care home workers who traditionally work on nightshifts and are required to be resident on site when on call. The Court's interpretations were confirmed in later judgments, for example the *Dellas* case.[12]

In addition to on-call work, the CJEU clarified on a number of occasions WTD requirements that need to be met for an individual opt-out to be

---

[9] Ibid., IRLR at 36.

[10] Case C-303/98 *Sindicato de Medicos de Asistencia Publica (SiMAP) v Conselleria de Sanidad y Consumo de la Generalidad Valenciana* [2000] ECR 1-7963.

[11] Case C-151/02 *Landeshauptstadt Kiel v Norbert Jaeger* [2003] ECR I-8389.

[12] Case C-14/04 *Abdelkader Dellas and others v Premier Ministre* [2005] ECR I-10253.

legal. It decided in *Fuß*,[13] a case in which national laws at regional (*Land*) level required firefighters to work a standard 54-hour working week, that the WTD did not apply because the *Land* had not transposed it adequately by creating measures for the use of the individual opt-out. In *Pfeiffer and others*,[14] emergency workers working for the German Red Cross challenged work rosters regulated by a collective agreement. The collective agreement permitted a working week of up to 49 hours if time spent on call at the workplace amounted to at least 3 hours per day. The Court argued that 'the worker's consent must be given not only individually but expressly and freely'.[15] Consent granted collectively in a collective agreement is not sufficient (see also Barnard 2006, 589–90).

Summarising the case law on individual opt-out, the following conditions must be met for the opt-out to be legal: the member state must have clearly introduced the 'necessary measures' for the use of the opt-out mentioned in Article 22(1) WTD. The individual workers concerned must have expressly and freely granted their consent to the opt-out; a blanket endorsement by collective agreement is not sufficient, unless the collective agreement expressly regulates the measures mentioned in Article 2(1) WTD. The employer must keep records for all opted-out workers, available for inspection on request of health and safety inspectors.

6.2.3 Reform of the WTD

Since 2004 the European Commission has been trying to reform the WTD. It has been put under considerable pressure by member states and other interest groups and is particularly concerned about reactions in member states to CJEU rulings on on-call work which led to the adoption of opt-out provisions in the majority of member states. The Commission tries to find a way to reconcile general opposition to the WTD, for example regularly voiced by the UK, which insists on maintaining a strong opt-out clause, and efforts, for example by the European Parliament, to strengthen the WTD by abolishing any opt-out clause.

The Commission put forward a proposal to amend WTD in 2004 (European Commission 2004). It was the result of a broad consultation in two phases. During both phases, there was a major stalemate in the negotiations between the social partners. It was only after the responses to the second phase of consultation arrived and were so divergent that it

---

[13] Case C-243/09 *Fuß v Stadt Halle* [2010] ECR I-9849.

[14] Joined Cases C-397/01 to C-403/01 *Pfeiffer and others* [2004] ECR I-8835.

[15] Ibid., para. 84.

was clear that there would be no agreement between the social partners. The Commission then proposed the draft directive that went to the co-legislators, the Parliament and Council.

In the 2004 proposal the Commission suggested, among other things, that inactive on-call time should not be considered working time. This proposal was blocked by the European Parliament with a counter-proposal which suggests removing the possibility of opt-out from the WTD altogether and that the entire period of any time spent on call, including the 'inactive part', should be considered as working time.[16] In its response to the consultation, the Parliament urged the Commission to encourage further negotiations between the social partners as the preferred route to revision. The Commission reacted with an amended proposal (European Commission 2005), which considered some of the amendments suggested by the European Parliament but did not accept the Parliament's proposed amendments regarding the two contested issues: the individual opt-out clause and on-call time.

It took the Council until 2008 to reach a political agreement on amending the WTD.[17] During 2005 and 2008 the Commission tried a number of strategies to reach a compromise. For example, it proposed a time limit for the opt-out to run out. When this idea encountered massive opposition, in particular coming from the UK, it was abandoned and replaced with a proposal to strengthen the reporting and evaluation requirements for member states that use the opt-out. An agreement was finally reached by qualified majority at the Employment, Social Policy, Health and Consumer Affairs Council in June 2008.

However, this agreement was again rejected by the European Parliament, which continued to insist on removing the opt-out clause from the WTD. A second reading of the amending proposal under the co-decision procedure became necessary. A Common Position was formally adopted by the Council in September 2008 and transmitted to the European Parliament. The Parliament adopted a Resolution in response in December 2008, proposing a number of amendments to the Common Position, some of which were in turn accepted by the Commission in its Opinion issued in February 2009.[18] The Council, however, decided to reject the

[16] Opinion of the European Parliament A6/2005/105. The European Parliament was not opposed to the possibility of exempting inactive on-call time from coverage by the WTD if this was accepted in collective agreements.

[17] For details on the negotiations see the analysis in Nowack (2008).

[18] Opinion of the Commission pursuant to Article 251(2), third subparagraph, point (c) of the EC Treaty on the European Parliament's amendments to the Council's Common Position regarding the proposal for a Directive of the

changes proposed by Parliament. In the following conciliation procedure an agreement could not be reached between the co-legislators – the Council and the Parliament – within the required six weeks. The result was that the legislative proposal lapsed.

In September 2009, the Commission announced its intention to carry out a new review of WTD, based on a detailed impact assessment[19] and on a consultation of the European social partners in accordance with Article 154 TFEU. The Commission in fact stated exploring the possibility of using the Social Dialogue for the reform of the WTD. It launched the first phase of the consultation of the European social partners in March 2010, asking whether they saw a need for action at EU level, what in their view could be its scope, whether they considered that the Commission should launch an initiative to amend the Directive, and whether they wished to consider entering a dialogue of the European social partners under Article 155 TFEU on any of the issues raised. The second stage of consultation started in December 2010, leading to a formal agreement of the social partners in November 2011 to negotiate on EU working time rules. These negotiations are conducted by the main cross-sectoral social partners at EU level, which are BUSINESSEUROPE, CEEP (French acronym for Centre européen des entreprises à participation publique et des entreprises d'intérêt économique général or European Centre of Enterprises with Public Participation and of Enterprises of General Economic Interest) and UEAPME (French acronym for Union Européenne de l'Artisanat et des Petits et Moyennes Entreprises or European Union of Handicraft and Small and Medium Enterprises), representing employers, and the European Trade Union Confederation (ETUC), representing employees.

6.3 IMPLEMENTATION OF THE WORKING TIME DIRECTIVE

This section analyses results of the case studies presented in chapters 7 to 10 of this volume. The case studies evaluate the implementation of WTD in four countries: the Czech Republic, France, the Netherlands and the

---

European Parliament and of the Council amending Directive 2003/88/EC concerning certain aspects of the organisation of working time amending the proposal of the Commission pursuant to Article 250(2) of the EC Treaty COM/2009/0057 final.

[19] Results of the impact assessment were presented in a Commission Staff Working Paper, European Commission (2010a).

United Kingdom. The reports used a grid that was agreed upon in discussions of the workpackage on European Governance. The grid consists of the following dimensions:

- General characteristics of the national labour law system
- General information on the national approach in implementing EU law
- Description of the concrete legal measure of implementation
- Behaviour and attitude of national courts towards WTD
- Problems in specific industries, for example doctors
- General political awareness or discussion of WTD.

This grid also constitutes the basis for the information provided in summary fashion in Table 6.1.

6.3.1 Czech Republic

The implementation of the WTD in the Czech Republic followed a pattern well known in this region of the European Union, which consists of former Socialist countries (Falkner et al. 2008). As Tomáš Sirovátka reports in chapter 7 of this volume, the community method has created a 'world of dead letters' in the Czech Republic. In this world the transposition record of EU directives is good, but problems exist in their actual implementation.

6.3.1.1 General characteristics of the Czech labour law system

Czech labour law has a long history that dates back to the beginning of the 20th century. It never lost its identity and has granted significant employment protection before, during and after the Communist period. Czech labour law is to some extent shaped by international labour law due to the Czech Republic's longstanding membership of the International Labour Organisation; its conventions were duly implemented. There are no labour courts.

6.3.1.2 National approach in implementing EU law and national measure of implementation

The Czech Republic transposed EU labour law into national legislation rather mechanically after it signed the association agreement with the EU. The Labour Code was amended in one big sweep in 2000. This included the 1993 WTD. The social-liberal governments between 1998 and 2002 endorsed the view that EU directives were supreme over national legislation and insisted on directives being adopted by Parliament as they were. It meant that harmonisation of domestic law became a somewhat technical ('copy and paste') affair.

Important implementing laws were Act No. 118/2000 Coll. on protection of employees in the case of the employer's insolvency, and the amendment of the Labour Code (Act No. 155/2000 Coll.) which adopted 28 EU directives ('harmonisation amendment'). This harmonisation amendment also implemented the WTD fully without exercising the right to opt out from any of its articles. The amended WTD of 2003 was transposed in 2006 (Labour Code Act No. 262/2006 Coll.). Due to the mechanical implementation process, the impact of EU labour legislation is hard to assess. There seems to be a huge gap between formal transposition of EU law and enforcement and application.

6.3.1.3 Czech courts and their reaction

A particular problem in the case of the WTD arose from the fact that under Czech law every individual employment contract must be interpreted separately, making it possible to work longer than 48 hours per week on a second employment contract. Since the EU Directive is silent on this issue, the Czech legislators did not see a need to change the legislation. However, there is no evidence that this has led to an increase in labour law cases in Czech courts.

6.3.1.4 Problems in specific industries

The limits imposed on overtime work have brought specific problems for several industries such as transport, restaurants and hotels, and hospitals and emergency services. For hospitals, a specific problem emerged in 2006 when the amended WTD regulating on-call duty following the *SiMAP* and *Jaeger* cases was transposed. Hospitals sometimes reacted by either adding an overtime work clause to the labour contract of doctors or through additional 'free contracts/agreements outside the labour contract', both routes enabling the total working time to transcend the legal limits on the length of working time. Furthermore, some hospitals established a separate legal entity within the hospital for staff working on call so that they cannot be considered being 'at the workplace'.

6.3.1.5 General political awareness or discussion of the Directive

Discussion of the WTD started after the 2006 election when the Czech centre-right government proposed a new Labour Code and embraced the idea of a revised WTD in the context of flexibilisation of labour legislation. Since then the general political direction concerning labour law in the Czech Republic has been represented by a strong tendency towards flexibilisation. In 2011 the re-elected Conservative-led government proposed revisions of the Labour Code in Parliament that allow overtime to be included in negotiations of wages and salaries and expand the work day from 9 to 12 hours.

6.3.2 France

The French debate on the WTD is embedded in a wider discussion of working time as a means of regulating work and the labour market. France is the EU member with the shortest average collectively agreed working week. As demonstrated in chapter 8, the implementation of the WTD had both a sectoral and a national impact on French labour law.

6.3.2.1 General characteristics of the French labour law system

France is a country in which the trade union movement has not managed to adopt a unified structure. However, despite union competition collective agreements are a major source of regulation of employment protection including working time, although the length of the working time per week is regulated by statute. The main basis of statutory labour law is the *Code du travail*. It distinguishes between provisions on employment contracts (book 1) and working conditions (book 2). Statutory rights are enforced by the labour courts (*conseils des prud'hommes*), which are lay courts and rarely engage in policy-making. Statutory interpretation and leading case law on working time regulations is produced by higher-ranking ordinary courts.

6.3.2.2 National approach in implementing EU law and national measure of implementation

The WTD was implemented by amending the *Code du travail* and the *Code de l'action sociale et des familles*. French legislation limits the maximum working time per week to 35 hours, though overtime is possible and there are exceptions. The working day may not exceed 10 hours, but can be extended up to 12 hours by collective agreement.

6.3.2.3 French courts and their reaction

French judges have interpreted the Directive and its transposition into French law since the early 2000s. In particular in reaction to the CJEU's *SiMAP* (2000) and *Jaeger* (2003) rulings, problems of calculating working time for on-call work became an issue. Under French law, on-call duty which was spent on site was not regarded as working time, so that effectively a working time up to 60 hours per week was possible. The *Conseils d'Etat* referred a case to the CJEU on calculating on-call working time and the CJEU decided in the *Dellas* case[20] that all time spent at the workplace must be regarded as working time and therefore falls within the 48-hour limit of the WTD.

6.3.2.4 Problems in specific industries

As is made clear in chapter 8 of this volume, there were a number of unexpected consequences of the application of the EU WTD in France. The *Dellas* ruling of the CJEU led to problems for example in hospitals and care homes. The health and transportation sectors reacted with changed collective agreements.

6.3.2.5 General political awareness or discussion of the Directive

The 35-hour week is a controversial political topic in France. It is upheld as an achievement of welfare legislation by left-wing parties and trade unions, but opposed by conservative parties and employer associations. However, the WTD has not been the centre of political campaigns like, for example, in Great Britain.

6.3.3 The Netherlands

As reported in chapter 9 of this volume, the Netherlands was a pioneer in regulating working time. Largely due to initiatives of the Dutch trade union movement, an active policy on working time, both on the grounds of job creation in situations of high unemployment and on the grounds of health and safety, had been introduced long before the WTD was implemented.

6.3.3.1 General characteristics of the Dutch labour law system

Dutch labour law and labour market policy pay particular attention to atypical forms of employment. In relation to working time the Netherlands has been on the whole successful in regulating and actually significantly increasing the number of part-time employees.

6.3.3.2 National approach in implementing EU law and national measure of implementation

The WTD was implemented through separate legislation on working time, the Working Time Act (*Arbeidstijdenwet*), 1996 which regulated maximum hours of work, breaks and minimum rest periods in accordance with the original WTD. It was accompanied by the Working Time Decree

---

[20] Case C-14/04 *Abdelkader Dellas and others v Premier Ministre*, European Court of Justice [2005] ECR I-10253.

(*Arbeidstijdenbesluit*) that contained exceptions and additions to the Working Time Act. There are general exceptions that apply to certain employees and certain situations and exceptions that apply to certain sectors, such as health care or mining. The reform of the Working Time Act in 2007 reflected the changes introduced in the WTD of 2003. It adopted the method of calculation over a period of 16 weeks in order to calculate an average 48-hour working week.

The Netherlands adopted the possibility of an individual opt-out. However, it only applies to the maximum standard duration of the working week for jobs which make extensive use of on-call time, such as in health services and emergency services. The Working Time Act regulates 'on-call duty' as well as 'standby duty' in the health care sector. In the event of on-call duty and standby duty, the hours during which an employee can be called are not considered working hours. In conformity with EU case law, all hours during an on-site standby shift, which requires mandatory presence at the workplace, count as working time.

6.3.3.3 Dutch courts and their reaction

There are no labour courts in the Netherlands. Civil and administrative courts have produced some case law, for example regarding the definition of on-call time. The Working Hours Act 1996 formerly defined inactive on-call time at the workplace as rest time. However, the national courts applied *SiMAP* and *Jaeger* about the treatment of on-call time as working time. In particular on-call working time of firefighters and ambulance workers was brought in line in this way.

6.3.3.4 Problems in specific industries

In the Netherlands, there are several specific sector regulations based on the Working Time Decree, which in principle can only be applied by collective arrangement. Derogations and exceptions to the general rules on the organisation of working time by collective agreements are found in a number of sectors, for example health care and mining.

6.3.3.5 General political awareness or discussion of the Directive

The implementation of the WTD in the Netherlands has not been controversial. Trade unions were dissatisfied with the consultation process during the national transposition of the Directive. They deem that the Directive has been transposed into national law in a way which reduced the level of protection previously available. Trade unions consider that the 2007 changes to working time legislation worsen the previous law as regards overtime, night work and co-determination. Employers on the contrary praise legislative changes introduced in the Working Time Act of 2007 for simplifying working time obligations, but consider the protection for night workers as still set too high.

While the evaluation of the implementation of the Directive by the Dutch government was in general positive, it indicated that the Directive has had a negative impact on the use of on-call working time in some sectors. The government also stated that revision of the Directive regarding the treatment of on-call time, the timing of compensatory rest and the extension of reference periods to 12 months by legislation remain a major and urgent priority.

6.3.4 United Kingdom

Implementation of the WTD in the UK reveals a certain exceptionalism that is partly ideological but also reflects the lack of statutory legislation in the area of working time regulation prior to the transposition of European law.

6.3.4.1 General characteristics of the UK labour law system

The common law-based labour law of the UK had few statutory regulations on working time at the time of implementation of the WTD in 1998. In contrast to most member states, statutory limits on weekly working hours of 48 hours or less and statutory minimum holiday entitlement of 4 weeks or more were lacking in the UK. The Directive drove significant new statutory intervention in an area hitherto largely characterised by voluntarism in the UK.

6.3.4.2 The UK approach in implementing EU law

There is a split between political and legal attitudes towards implementation of EU law in the UK. In general the approach is characterised by political reluctance but legal obedience. The WTD was implemented via secondary legislation. However, this was not unusual since most EU directives are implemented in the UK by delegated (or secondary) legislation in accordance with the Statutory Instruments Act 1946. Secondary legislation in the form of Statutory Instruments has equal effect in law.

6.3.4.3 UK measure of implementation

The UK measure of implementation of the WTD was the Working Time Regulations (WTR), which came into force on 1 October 1998. These regulations have been amended on several occasions since.

Article 5(4) of the WTR includes the possibility of granting workers the right to opt out of the 48-hour rule. The UK was in 1998 the only member state since the enactment of the WTD in 1993 that made use of the Directive's blanket opt-out for workers to voluntarily decide on their working hours.

6.3.4.4 National courts and their reaction

As reported in chapter 10 in this volume, the WTD increased working time claims in British Employment Tribunals significantly. They have been consistently among the highest group of applications since 2005 and outnumbered all other areas of jurisdiction during the 2010–2011 statistical period. There was no outright opposition of UK courts towards the WTD or WTR.

6.3.4.5 Problems in specific industries

The judgments of the CJEU in *SiMAP* and *Jaeger*, requiring that the time doctors spend 'on call' should count as working time, had practical effects upon doctors, who have traditionally been required to be resident on site when on call, particularly junior doctors and care home workers. There was wide-scale resentment and vociferous opposition to change of practices in the hospital sector.

6.3.4.6 General political awareness or discussion of the Directive

Although the WTR follow in legal terms relatively closely the text of the WTD, the fact that the WTR expressly include the possibility of individual opt-out somewhat contradicts and undermines the aim of the WTD. This fact also expresses the general hostile attitude towards regulation of working time in British politics. The Conservative Party openly opposes this regulation, and this view is, although less vociferously, shared by the dominant market-friendly core of the Labour Party ('New Labour'). The Conservative-Liberal UK government has announced on several occasions since 2011 that it will propose further exemption from EU social and employment law as part of their overhaul of British employment laws and of renegotiations of Britain's position in the EU, with a particular focus on the WTD.

Table 6.1 summarises the findings of the country studies on the implementation of the WTD.

Table 6.1 Implementation of the WTD in the Czech Republic, France, the Netherlands and the UK

	National approach to implementation	National measure of implementation	National courts' reaction and practical enforcement	Problems in specific industries	General political awareness and discussions
Czech Republic	Rather technical (copy and paste) transposition; problems with enforcement and application	'Harmonisation amendment' of the Labour Code (No. 155/2000 Coll.); Act No. 118/2000 Coll.; Act No. 46/2004 Coll.; Act No. 435/2004 Coll.; The new Act on Labour Inspections (No. 251/2005 Coll.); Act No. 262/2006 Coll.	No labour courts; delays in civil courts; rarely request ruling from CJEU; Labour Inspectors lack expertise and capacities for effective enforcement	Hospitals operating with on-call personnel; transport sector with working time records	Opposition from the centre-right governments since 2006; proposals for labour law flexibilisation
France	No problems with transposing WTD standards	Amendments to the *Code du travail* and the *Code de l'action sociale et des familles*	Interpretation of WTD and reference to the CJEU in the *Dellas* case	Health and transport sectors	On-going controversy over 35-hour week
Netherlands	WTD had only minor impact due to existing high level of regulation	Working Time Act (*Arbeidstijdenwet*); Working Time Decree (*Arbeidstijdenbesluit*); considerable possibility to opt out via collective agreements	No labour courts; some case law of civil and administrative courts applying CJEU rulings	Special regulations of work time by collective agreement in compliance with WTD in several sectors like hospitals and mining	WTD has not been very controversial; criticism from trade unions; employers praise the changes
United Kingdom	Delayed transposition by secondary legislation, Statutory Instruments Act	The Working Time Regulations (1998); making use of individual opt-out, Article 18(1)(b) WTD	Large number of claims based on WTD in Employment Tribunals	Health sector (NHS); significant influence on working time of junior doctors	Hostile attitude to regulation of working time, including CJEU rulings; major opposition to WTD displayed by the Conservative-Liberal government

6.4 THE GOVERNANCE OF WORKING TIME IN THE EU: SUSTAINABILITY AND UNCERTAINTY IN REGULATING WORKING TIME

The WTD has to be understood in the wider context of governing working time in the European Union. Working time policies play a central role in European labour market policies. They reach far beyond regulations on the limitation of the maximum length of the working week, the focus of WTD. We can distinguish in this respect the supranational governance context and the labour market policy context, including the regulation of new forms of employment.

6.4.1 Regulating Working Time through alternative Methods of Governance

The community method constitutes only one of four methods of governance of employment law at the supranational level.[21] In addition to (a) the community method, which is traditionally seen as the ordinary route of legislation and was used to create the WTD, there are: (b) the Social Dialogue, (c) governing employment through fundamental rights, and (d) governing employment through new forms of governance, in particular the use of soft law like the OMC in the context of the European Employment Strategy.

The Social Dialogue is a governance method to create legislation through agreements between social partners. The Social Dialogue is the responsibility of the European social partners (BUSINESSEUROPE, CEEP and UEAPME, representing employers and ETUC, representing employees). Once the social partners have established a so-called 'framework agreement', the Commission will use it to create a proposal for a Directive that is usually endorsed by the Council without discussion (and no input from the European Parliament!). As we saw above, this second route of legislation was and is currently explored by the Commission for the revision of the WTD. A number of important directives regulating working time arrangements, like those on parental leave, fixed-term contracts and part-time work, originate from the 'collective route' (Barnard 2006, 88–104) of legislation.

Governing employment through fundamental rights has been significant since the adoption of the Charter of Fundamental Social Rights of

[21] On the four 'strategies' to govern European labour law see Bercusson (2009), Part II, pp. 99–255.

Workers in 1989 and became a great hope for reform with the adoption of the Charter of Fundamental Rights in 2000. With the introduction of social citizenship, constitutionalising employment rights was seen to enlarge Social Europe to 'the excluded peoples of Europe … the poor, the unemployed, the old, the ethnic minorities and others whom the common market has excluded' (Bercusson 2006, 19–20). Article 31(2) of the Charter of Fundamental Rights states one of the rights to fair and just working conditions: 'Every worker has the right to limitation of maximum hours, to daily and weekly rest periods and to an annual period of paid leave.' It has been suggested that upgrading the WTD regulations to fundamental rights puts the possibility of excluding certain sectors of employment and derogations in the Directive and in national implementing laws into question (Blanke 2006, 374–75).

Probably the most promising way to influence working time policies at member state level is through soft law. The European Employment Strategy establishes through the use of the OMC an on-going dialogue between member states and the Commission about objectives of labour market policies. Guideline 21 of the Employment Guidelines 2008, for example, states as an objective of European employment policy the promotion of flexibility combined with employment security. In this context flexibilising working time arrangements has been identified as an important policy goal. However, whether this transition from protection to promotion in European employment policies (Rogowski 2008; Rogowski 2013, Ch. 8) will be successful remains to be seen. To some extent the economic crisis of 2008 has revealed its limits (Rogowski et al. 2011).

6.4.2 WTD and other Working Time Arrangements

For an assessment of the WTD at the European level as well as the national level of implementation of WTD, it is vital to relate this regulation to other regulations and policies concerning working time. Working time is an important policy within the European Employment Strategy that aims at coordinating labour market policies and their reform in the member states. The 'hard' law of the WTD interacts with 'soft' law measures that regulate labour market policies. Furthermore, at the national level implementation of the WTD has to be seen in the wider context of regulating working time arrangements that provide employees with real autonomy over their working times. New demands for more flexible working time arrangements result from an increased participation of female employees in the labour market. Demands for changes also result from the introduction of new technologies at the place of work. A number of types of working time arrangements can be distinguished.

6.4.2.1 Flexitime arrangements

Flexitime arrangements are promoted within the European Employment Strategy as forms of flexibilisation of employment. They are working time arrangements with no fixed start and end of a working day. They include working time banking, that is, a system of accumulation of hours around the standard number of weekly or monthly hours. It can mean that an employee can work more hours in exchange for taking the equivalent time off at some time in the future. Two options can be distinguished: working time banking with the possibility only to take hours off and working time banking with the possibility to take full days off. Flexible working time arrangements include the option of a flexible start and end of the working day and the possibility to fully determine one's own working schedule. In addition, there is a category 'other', which often includes the case of a fixed start of the day until the work is finished (see European Foundation for the Improvement of Living and Working Conditions 2010).

6.4.2.2 Part-time work

Part-time employment has been increasing in Europe for the past two decades. This is especially true for countries where different working time arrangements have been discussed among policymakers and social partners as a way to increase flexibility.[22] Part-time work is promoted as a strategy for balancing work and family life in certain life phases, although no reliable data exist on the amount of involuntary or forced part-time work. Our case study on the Netherlands reports that part-time work has been the focus of working time policies for some time and has been successful in increasing the number of part-time employees in the Netherlands. Part-time work is regulated in the Part-Time Work Directive 97/81/EC that aims at prevention of discriminatory treatment in part-time work. WTD also applies to part-time work.

6.4.2.3 Annualised Hour and Working-Time Accounts

Working time accounts are growing in popularity among EU member states (Wotschack 2011). Annualised hours' schemes are a popular means of achieving working time flexibility. They allow working time (and pay) to be calculated and scheduled over a period, for example a year. Article

---

[22] For an overview see O'Reilly and Fagan (1998).

18 WTD, which creates scope for derogations by means of collective agreements, including the length of the reference period which may be extended by up to 12 months, opens up the opportunity to implement annualised hour schemes in order to adapt to changes in demand.

6.4.2.4 Fixed-term employment

Fixed-term employment is increasing in the European Union and has been central in European employment policies that aim at flexibilising employment and increasing labour market efficiencies through deregulation policies (Schömann et al. 1998; Rogowski 2013, ch. 6). In a legal perspective fixed-term employment is defined as a contractual arrangement whereby the contract ends automatically when a specific event occurs, a specific task is finished or simply the contractually arranged date is reached. Fixed-term employment is regulated at the European level by the Fixed-Term Directive 99/70.

6.4.2.5 Overtime

Overtime, that is, hours worked above a certain threshold of working time for an extra payment, is an important flexibility tool, favoured in particular by employers. It is often an important source of extra income for employees. WTD establishes a threshold for the maximum of allowable overtime by establishing a weekly limit for working hours that cannot be exceeded.

6.5 WTD, LEGAL UNCERTAINTY AND LONG-TERM SUSTAINABILITY

WTD is a good example of the paradox that characterises law in modern society according to social systems theory: when law creates certainty by reducing complexity, it unavoidably increases complexity at the same time and creates new uncertainty (Luhmann 2004, 317).

There are a number of ways in which law produces uncertainty; three can be highlighted here. First, vague legal programmes may render law merely symbolic without becoming effective in society. Secondly, statutory law can become uncertain if it is not or only partially enforced or implemented. Thirdly, statutory provisions can become ambivalent due to legal or judicial interpretations or failure to learn from implementation problems.

The example of the WTD can provide evidence of legal uncertainty on all three levels. The WTD has increased uncertainties in national law (see also Sypris 2007, 141–42). Some of our case studies report that the failure to reach agreement on reforming the WTD at the European level has created anxiety and uncertainty at the national level.

Furthermore, legal uncertainty can be the result of CJEU rulings. Insofar as labour law in general is concerned, the *Viking* and *Laval* cases are the most prominent examples of creating uncertainty. And legal uncertainty has certainly been the result for employers and national governments regarding the organisation of on-call work after the intervention of the CJEU in *SiMAP*, *Jaeger* and other cases on behalf of junior doctors and care workers.

However, despite these uncertainties it has to be emphasised that law is a key, and probably the most important, means to guarantee sustainability in European social and employment law and policies. In particular the community method has this function. Its success depends on it being able to become reflexive. As the case of the WTD shows, in order for hard law to be effective it has to be reflexive, both in the sense of realising its limits as a regulatory instrument and the context in which it operates. Political opposition as well as labour market developments shape its application and limit its effectiveness. Regulation of working hours is part of a wide range of regulations of working time arrangements at member state level. The Dutch example shows that focussing regulation on part-time employment is an alternative way of reducing long working hours.

The context at the European level consists not only of other directives regulating working time (for example, fixed-term and part-time employment, temporary work and parental leave), but also of other modes of governance used for reducing uncertainty in employment. The Social Dialogue has been used on several occasions for reforming WTD, although it has to be said that the failure in coming to an agreement in the pre-2004 consultation aptly demonstrates the limits of this form of governance when the parties are polarised, as they were in relation to the opt-out and other items on the reform agenda. The current use of the Social Dialogue could be another example of its limits in resolving an essentially political deadlock over the WTD at the European and even more so at the national level.

The regulation of the length of working time, including holiday pay and rest periods, thus has to be interpreted in the context of a wide range of issues related to working time. Working time has become an important matter for labour market policy. This policy area has witnessed significant transformations related to changes in work organisation and labour market composition. The traditional model of a male breadwinner working an 8-hour day is no longer the dominant model. Increasing female labour market participation has led to more flexible forms of work organisation and changing working time preferences. To tackle the regulatory problems that derive from these trends, the focus of the WTD has to be transcended. In fact a mix of methods of governance is necessary to address problems arising from demands for new working time arrangements. And for this, reflexive laws and policies are needed.

BIBLIOGRAPHY

Barnard, C. (2006), *EC Employment Law*. Third edition. Oxford: Oxford University Press.

Barnard, C. and S. Deakin (2001), 'Market Access and Regulatory Competition', Jean Monnet Working Paper No. 9/01. New York: NYU Law School.

Bercusson, B. (2009), *European Labour Law*. Second Edition. Cambridge: Cambridge University Press.

Bercusson, B. (ed.) (2006), *European Labour Law and the EU Charter of Fundamental Rights*. Baden-Baden: Nomos.

Bercusson, B. (2002), 'The European Social Model Comes to Britain', *Industrial Law Journal*, **31** (3): 209–44.

Bercusson, B. (1996), A Study of Working Time: Extent of Coverage of Sectors and Activities excluded from the Working Time Directive in National Regulations of the member states of the European Union, Brussels. Available at http://ec.europa.eu/social/BlobServlet?docId=2418&langId=en (last accessed 15 December 2014).

Blanke, T. (2006), 'Fair and Just Working Conditions', in B. Bercusson (ed.), *European Labour Law and the EU Charter of Fundamental Rights*. Baden-Baden: Nomos, pp. 357–58.

Bosch, G. (2001), 'Working Time: From Redistribution to Modernization', in P. Auer (ed.), *Changing Labour Markets in Europe*. Geneva: ILO, pp. 55–107.

Deakin, S. and R. Rogowski (2011), 'Reflexive Labour Law, Capabilities and the Future of Social Europe', in R. Rogowski, R. Salais and N. Whiteside (eds), *Transforming European Employment Policy – Labour Market Transitions and the Promotion of Capability*. Cheltenham and Northampton, MA: Edward Elgar, pp. 229–54.

European Commission (2010a), 'Detailed report on the implementation by member states of Directive 2003/88/EC concerning certain aspects of the organisation of working time ("The Working Time Directive")', Commission Staff Working Paper, SEC(2010) 1611 final.

European Commission (2010b), 'Reviewing the Working Time Directive', Communication, COM(2010) 801 final.

European Commission (2005), 'Amended proposal for a Directive amending Directive 2003/88/EC concerning certain aspects of the organisation of working time', COM(2005) 246 final.

European Commission (2004), 'Proposal for a Directive amending Directive 2003/88/EC concerning certain aspects of the organisation of working time', COM(2004) 607 final.

European Commission (1998), 'On the organisation of working time in the sectors and activities excluded from Directive 93/104/EC of 23 November 1993', Communication, COM(1998) 662 final.

European Foundation for the Improvement of Living and Working Conditions (2010), *Comparative Analysis of Working Time in the European Union.*

Falkner, G., E. Holzleithner and O. Treib (2008), *Compliance in the Enlarged European Union: Living Rights or Dead Letters?* Aldershot: Ashgate.

Falkner, G., O. Treib, M. Hartlapp and S. Leiber (2005), *Complying with Europe: EU Harmonisation and Soft Law in the Member States.* Cambridge: Cambridge University Press.

Grant, C. with K. Barysch and H. Brady (2009), *Cameron's Europe: Can the Conservatives Achieve their EU Objectives?* London: Centre for European Reform.

Hartlapp, M. (2005), *Die Kontrolle der nationalen Rechtsdurchsetzung durch die Europäische Kommission.* Frankfurt and New York: Campus.

Kjaer, P. F. (2010), *Between Governing and Governance: On the Emergence, Function and Form of Europe's Post-National Condition.* Oxford: Hart.

Luhmann, N. (2004), *Law as a Social System.* Oxford: Oxford University Press.

Majone, G. (2005), *Dilemmas of European Integration.* Oxford: Oxford University Press.

Moffat, G. (1997), 'Competition, Competitiveness and Re-regulating the Labour Market: The Working Time Directive', *Nottingham Law Journal,* **6** (1): 46–68.

Nowack, T. (2008), 'The Working Time Directive and the European Court of Justice', *Maastricht Journal of European and Comparative Law,* **15** (4): 447–71.

O'Reilly, J. and C. Fagan (eds) (1998), *Part-Time Prospects: An International Comparison of Part-Time Work in Europe, North America and the Pacific Rim.* London: Routledge.

Rogowski, R. (2013), *Reflexive Labour Law in the World Society.* Cheltenham and Northampton, MA: Edward Elgar.

Rogowski, R. (ed.) (2008), *The European Social Model and Transitional Labour Markets: Law and Policy.* Aldershot: Ashgate.

Rogowski, R. (2007), 'Flexicurity and Reflexive Coordination of European Social and Employment Policies', in H. Jørgensen and P. K. Madsen (eds), *Flexicurity and Beyond: Finding a New Agenda for the European Social Model.* Copenhagen: DJØF Publishing, pp. 131–53.

Rogowski, R., R. Salais and N. Whiteside (eds) (2011), *Transforming European Employment Policy – Labour Market Transitions and the Promotion of Capability.* Cheltenham and Northampton, MA: Edward Elgar.

Schömann, K., R. Rogowski and T. Kruppe (1998), *Labour Market Efficiency in the European Union: Employment Protection and Fixed-Term Contracts.* London: Routledge (Studies in the European Economy 6).

Sypris, P. (2007), *EU Intervention in Domestic Labour Law.* Oxford: Oxford University Press.

Tallberg, J. (2003), *European Governance and Supranational Institutions – Making States Comply.* London: Routledge.

Treib, O. (2004), *Die Bedeutung der nationalen Parteipolitik bei der Umsetzung europäischer Sozialrichtlinen.* Frankfurt and New York: Campus.

Wotschack, P. (2011), 'Working-Time Options over the Life Course: Challenges and Company Practices', in R. Rogowski, R. Salais and N. Whiteside (eds), *Transforming European Employment Policy – Labour Market Transitions and the Promotion of Capability.* Cheltenham and Northampton, MA: Edward Elgar, pp. 96–114.

7. The EU Working Time Directive in the Czech Republic[1]

Tomáš Sirovátka

This chapter analyses the impact of EU labour law on the Czech system of labour law with particular reference to the case of the EU Working Time Directive (WTD). It assesses whether the transposition and implementation of the EU directive into the national labour law has provided workers with more certainty or not. There are several reasons why the EU legislation might rather have increased uncertainties in national law systems (see Rogowski, in this volume, and Barbier, in this volume).

The chapter is divided into four sections. In section 7.1 the Czech approach to the transposition and implementation of EU law is explained. Section 7.2 analyses how the WTD was transposed and implemented. In section 7.3 the political debate over the directive in the Czech Republic is examined. In the last, concluding section (7.4) the findings are discussed in a broader societal and political context.

7.1 THE CZECH APPROACH TO IMPLEMENTING EU LAW

There is a strong continuity in Czech labour law from the beginning of the 20th century until today. Since labour law was first codified during the time of the Austrian empire it maintained its general 'protective function' during the interwar Czechoslovak Republic and surprisingly even during the communist regime between 1948 and 1989 (except for some specific 'formulas' like 'violation of the socialist moral' as a reason of notice) as well as after the Velvet revolution in 1989.

[1] The writing of this chapter was supported by the Czech Grant Agency (Project No. P404/11/0086) Modernisation of the Czech Social Policy.

Protection of the labour force was even stronger in some areas before 1989 under the communist regime, which praised itself as a 'working class regime'. For example, in addition to the standard three month notice period common in the EU, a 'protective' period of six months was obligatory both for the employer and the employee, which could be shortened if specific reasons applied like ill health or care for children or other family members. Furthermore, Czech labour law was shaped by international standards. As a member of the International Labour Organisation the Czech Republic officially transposed ILO conventions during the communist regime.

This continuity of the labour law is the main source of its legitimacy today. The EU law did not bring substantial improvements in 'social standards' or more protection – its role in this respect may be assessed as 'neutral'.[2] Nevertheless, new tools were incorporated into the Labour Code by EU directives that enable easier enforcement of law, for example in the field of discrimination. However, in practice, such expectations remained largely unfulfilled (compare Falkner et al. 2008). On the other hand, hardly any conflicts emerged in implementing EU directives either.

The Czech Republic became obliged to transpose EU labour law into national legislation when it signed its Association Agreement with the EU. Important implementing laws were Act No. 118/2000 Coll. on protection of employees in the case of the employer's insolvency, and the amendment of the Labour Code (Act No. 155/2000 Coll.), which adopted 28 EU directives ('harmonisation amendment'), including the directives on rights to information and consultation, protection against collective redundancies, maximum length of working time, parental leave, part-time work, posting workers, and health and safety at work. The second EU amendment of the national Labour Code (Act No. 46/2004 Coll. of March 2004) included directives on equal treatment and anti-discrimination (direct and indirect). Furthermore, Employment Act No. 435/2004 Coll. transposed principles of EU labour and employment legislation and, in addition, the new Labour Code that was adopted in 2006 (Act No. 262/2006 Coll.) introduced remaining aspects of EU labour law (see below).

However, it can be questioned whether EU legislation was transposed appropriately within the national context. It seems that, in general, EU law was often transcribed only mechanically and too quickly into

---

2 This opinion was voiced during an interview conducted by the author of this chapter with an academic lawyer and specialist on labour and social protection law.

national legislation, without considering the boundaries which EU law aims to define and alternative ways of transposing EU law appropriately within the national context.[3]

This failure does not of course create grounds for effective implementation of EU law. Basically, although the EU labour legislation was transposed promptly, its impact is hardly visible in practice. The process of transposition, implementation and practical impact of the EU on Czech labour law has to be understood with regard to the specific features of the national context: the generally positive perception of the legitimacy of the national labour law among lawyers; and the generally low level of legal awareness, low respect for legislation and neglect of the labour law in practice, with little (or insufficient) intervention from the responsible bodies. Compliance with EU legislation in general was rather formal and problems with implementation of the law in practice followed.

Falkner et al. (2005) and Falkner et al. (2008), who studied the transposition of three EU directives in the EU member states (one of them being the WTD as enacted in 1993), elaborated a typology of 'compliance cultures' (characterised by shared interpretative schemes, sets of cognitive rules and recipes, and implementation patterns). The Czech Republic, clustered by them together with countries like Hungary, Slovenia and Slovakia, belongs to the 'world of dead letters' where the transposition record in legislation is relatively good, better than in many of the old EU states, with, however, problems in implementation.

Although formal transposition of EU law was excellent due to a 'joining-the-club effect', implementation into practice after accession represented the real test of compliance with EU law: a huge gap arose between the formal transposition of EU law, on the one hand, and enforcement and application, on the other. A lack of institutional capacities is recognised as an obstacle, including a missing labour court system, long proceedings of the civil courts, deficient personnel capacities of the responsible institutions such as courts and Labour Inspectorates, and a lack of resources provided to them. Secondly, cultural factors are at play, such as a weak civil society, low prestige and weak influence of the trade unions, lack of legal awareness and low trust in institutions, combined with people's fear of unemployment and dismissals and a lack of case-law tradition. Lastly, in the case of the Czech

---

[3] This information was obtained during an interview conducted by the author of this report with an academic lawyer and specialist on labour and social protection law.

Republic, the well-documented Euro-scepticism of some influential political actors also implies anti-European institutional practices when it comes to enforcement and application of the directives.

Apart from the above problems, the often discussed inconsistency between the more binding EU economic criteria and less binding EU social policy agendas implies in practice that the requirements placed on the new member states by the Stabilisation and Growth Pact largely restrict their possibilities to implement soft 'social agendas'. In the case of the WTD, the economic pressures on competitiveness and balanced public budgets seem to directly push political actors to support the employers' position of keeping labour costs low and being reluctant in consistently enforcing and applying the directive. These circumstances implied from the beginning the failure in the new member states to respect the EU case law concerning the *Jaeger* case (recognition of time spent at the workplace on call as working time).

The introduction of the market economy has brought enormous liberalisation in employment practices in the Czech Republic in terms of labour flexibilisation. The motivation behind the transformation to a market economy has sometimes been described as an 'escape from lawyers'[4] or a strategy of 'switched off lights' in order for a new economy based on private ownership to be established quickly. It entailed that a substantial amount of property was transferred to new owners in a problematic way and that corruption became a widespread phenomenon.[5] National legislation formulated during the 1990s was extremely liberal. For instance, the new national legislation on collective dismissals admitted that those acts by employers which were not in concord with the law were still valid and could only be cancelled by civil courts (Nekolová 2008). Furthermore, it is a fact that many labour laws are often not respected in practice or are being circumvented. Večerník (2009) reports common practices of avoiding legislation that were on the line between the formal and informal economy. In the case of collective dismissals, for example, employers often circumvent their duty to inform the Employment Office and Trade Unions by dismissing one employee less than specified in the law (Nekolová 2008).

---

4 We remind the reader of the famous quote by Prime Minister Václav Klaus from the early 1990s: 'There is no dirty money'.

5 In 2010, for example, the corruption perception index of Transparency International was 4.6, with only Slovakia, Italy, Latvia, Bulgaria and Romania ranking worse in the EU (the Czech Republic ranked 53rd out of 178 countries); see http://www.transparency.org/policy_research/surveys_indices/cpi/2010/results (accessed 15 December 2013).

7.2 NATIONAL MEASURES FOR IMPLEMENTATION OF THE WORKING TIME DIRECTIVE

The transposition of EU labour law did not start before 1998 because the political scene was dominated by Václav Klaus's Euro-sceptic ODS Party (Civic Democrats) during the 1990s. In 1998, pro-European parties won the support of the electorate and the majority of seats in Parliament; they formed successive governments and were in power in the period before and during accession. During 1998–2002 there was a minority Social Democratic government, and between 2002 and 2006 a coalition of Social Democrats, Christian Democrats and Liberty Union (US–DEU, a centre-right party which emerged in 2001 after unification of the Liberty Union party and Democratic Union party). This prompted acceleration of the process of accession and transposition of the EU legislation, which included the WTD. Between 1998 and 2002, Vladimír Špidla, later a European Commissioner, was the Minister of Labour and Social Affairs. He advocated that the EU directives were supreme over national legislation and insisted that these directives be adopted by Parliament as they were. Thus harmonisation of domestic law was regarded as a somewhat technical procedure ('copy and paste') (see also Falkner et al. 2008).

Representatives of business and employers and also the centre-right ODS opposition party tried to change large parts of the Harmonisation Amendment, and especially the new provisions of the WTD, calling for 'more flexibility' in the workplace. These proposals were not taken into consideration and did not influence the process of prompt transposition. The WTD of 1993 was implemented, together with several other directives in the area of labour law, by the already mentioned 'Harmonisation Amendment' (Act No. 155/2000 Coll.) to the Labour Code of 1965.

Before implementation in 2006, statutory working time according to the Czech Labour Code had been 42 hours and 30 minutes, including five rest periods of 30 minutes each. This was simply changed to 40 hours of effective working time, with no provision concerning the rest period included. In some respects, Czech law had been more generous than the European WTD: there was a daily rest period of 12 hours per 24 successive hours in the law, while the WTD only demands 11, and a break after five hours of work, while the WTD only demands a break after six hours. On the other hand, the minimum length of holidays increased from three to four weeks per year and the minimum weekly rest period increased from 32 to 35 hours. Most significantly, the extent of overtime work was reduced to eight hours per week (150 hours per year), while previously no limit on overtime had been stipulated in legislation. The employer is allowed to negotiate an agreement with the employee on overtime beyond the limit of 150 hours but only if the maximum overtime of eight hours per week and 416 hours per year is respected. The regulations governing night work were also fully transposed (a maximum of eight hours of work between 10 pm and 6 am within 24 hours is possible). However, the amendment imposed a new obligation on employers to keep records of employees' working time. The Czech Republic did not exercise the right to opt out from any of the articles of the WTD and transposed it fully.

Nevertheless, some problems remained unresolved until 2006 and some continued to exist even after 2006. The government did not consider the European Court of Justice's (ECJ's) case law – that is, the *SiMAP* and *Jaeger* cases, which imply that time spent on call at the workplace must be regarded as working time, although the trade unions were calling for respecting these rulings. As Falkner et al. (2008) explain, the main reason for this neglect was fear that it would be 'expensive' for the state since, for example, hospitals would have to count on-call time as working time and reward doctors during on-call night shifts appropriately. When the EU explicitly regulated in Directive No. 34/2003 that on-call time at the workplace constitutes working time, the Czech Republic transposed this article into the new Labour Code (Act No. 262/2006 Coll.).

An obstacle arose from the fact that under Czech law every individual employment contract must be interpreted separately. This means that it is possible that employees who have a second employment contract may effectively work longer than 48 hours per week. The only limitation in the Czech Labour Code is that the second labour contract has to be on shorter working time than the main labour contract (but it is not defined how much less working time this should be). Since the EU directive is silent on this issue, the Czech legislators did not see a need to change the legislation although in fact the emerging practice is going against the objectives of the EU directive. Furthermore, there have been serious problems with application and enforcement which have remained unaddressed by responsible bodies. The Czech courts rarely request a preliminary ruling from the ECJ, and prefer instead to refer to the Higher Court of the Czech Republic.[6]

---

[6] As Falkner et al. (2008, p. 45) explain, one of the first preliminary rulings was related to doctors' work/on-call duty at hospitals. This was only submitted in February 2006 although the WTD had been implemented in 2000 in the Czech Republic (and the amended EU WTD of 2003 had already been in force).

The widespread low respect for labour legislation encourages practices of contravening or circumventing the WTD. Probably the most frequent is violation of the employer's obligations related to overtime work.[7] Employers tend not to adequately compensate employees for overtime work (the overtime rate should be higher when working on Saturdays or Sundays), nor do they properly compensate for overtime by time off in lieu. This is typical in the food industry, in hospitals and also in other industries, including the construction sector. Employers often force employees to agree to specific equivocal clauses, such as that the general salary, agreed upon in the labour contract, includes overtime.

In some cases employers do not compensate for overtime work at all. Since it is quite common practice to pay low wages to employees officially and give them pocket money on the side, it is difficult to identify how appropriately overtime work is rewarded (Večerník 2009). Although there is a general obligation for employers to keep records of individual employees' working time, overtime work, stand-by and night work, many of them keep incomplete records or none at all. This makes it difficult to check the enforcement of the WTD articles related to overtime work.

The right to a rest period during working time is often violated in the case of salespersons in small stores (one-person enterprises) or night nurses where employees cannot take breaks due to organisation of work at their workplace. However, although the abovementioned practices are in conflict with the transposed WTD, they in fact represent a general violation of Czech labour law, rather than specifically a violation of the EU legislation. Only in the cases of overtime work and on-call time at the workplace have violations of the law become more frequent and more important since the WTD imposed new and stricter standards.

Enforcing rights is expensive and risky since the Czech judicial system does not provide employees with effective ways to enforce their rights (compare Falkner et al. 2008). No labour courts exist and the proceedings at civil courts are long, sometimes lasting longer than three years; even five years is not an exception (due to the understaffed and underfinanced public administration and its ineffective performance). A 'vivid legal culture' hardly exists in the Czech Republic. Even in cases where employees know their rights and entitlements well, they are not willing to go to court. Similarly, complaints to the Ombudsman in the area of labour law are rare (Veřejný ochránce práv 2009, 2010, 2011). With respect to EU law this means that old Czech legislation is often

[7] This is also referred to in Falkner et al. (2008).

applied instead of new legislation based on the transposed EU law. Cases are being referred to higher courts of the Czech Republic rather than to the ECJ (Falkner et al. 2008, p. 45). This situation is to a large degree due to political decisions to support businesses by constraining public administrations from taking effective action. For example, the Labour Inspectorate's strategy is to refrain from immediately imposing fines. Similarly, the guidelines of the Ministry of Labour and Social Affairs suggest that efforts to reach consensus with employers should have priority (Falkner et al. 2008, p. 54). The labour law cases submitted to civil courts, rare in number considering the volume of violations of law (see below), tend to deal with invalid notices and accidents at work. Furthermore, there is no developed case-law tradition in the Czech Republic and judges prefer references to continental European law, which is closer to legal positivism than to modern EU law (Kuhn, in Falkner et al. 2008, p. 51).

In addition, the control mechanisms of the state are as ineffective as courts when it comes to violation of labour law. Until July 2005 (the first year after accession), Public Employment Services had been responsible for monitoring labour law enforcement. The new Act on Labour Inspections (No. 251/2005 Coll.) shifted the competences for monitoring labour law to new Regional Labour Inspectorates. However, Labour Inspectorates have a weak position against employers, who take advantage of 'political support'. On top of that, the quality of staff is disputable because Employment Offices tended to release rather less competent staff for the new institutions.[8]

These circumstances are reflected in the performance of Labour Inspectorates. Nekolová (2008, p. 49) mentions their low professional expertise and insufficient material capacity. These problems were discussed at a conference of social partners in 2006, where the government promised to take measures, but it has failed to adopt any (in 2006, a new centre-right government was elected which replaced the government led by Social Democrats).

In such a weak 'legal environment' the influence of hostile ECJ judgments does not seem very significant. There is a certain circle of lawyers who are aware of the decisions of the ECJ although these are not important for domestic legal practice.[9] These decisions could potentially

[8] Source: interviews by the author at employment offices.
[9] Source: interview with a lawyer, an academic specialist on EU law.

destabilise the social standards introduced by the EU labour law directives. However, this is not the case due to ineffective implementation of labour law in the Czech Republic, including the EU directives.

The limits imposed on overtime work have brought specific problems for several industries such as transport, restaurants and hotels, and hospitals and emergency services. In some industries, in particular small shops, it proved difficult to guarantee appropriate break schedules. For hospitals, a specific problem emerged with the new Labour Code of 2006 which transposed the EU regulation of overtime work and on-call duty. For this reason, in September 2008 an amendment to the Labour Code was put into effect, aiming to soften this regulation. The amendment allows agreement between employer and employee on overtime work in the health sector: up to an additional eight hours per week and 12 hours per week for emergency service/ambulances (Article 93a of the Labour Code), in line with the exemption from the regulation of overtime work provided by the European Parliament, in effect up to the end of 2013.

In any case, since implementation of the new legislation is not accurate, the practical impact on employers is not so significant. This trend has been corroborated by the uncertainty over the long-term viability of the Directives of 1993 and of 2003 (negotiations of new legislative proposals followed between 2004 and 2009) and by attempts of the Czech centre-right government to revise the Labour Code under an umbrella notion of 'flexibility' that started in 2007.

Labour Inspectorates suffer from understaffing (there are less than 350 labour inspectors in a country with a labour force of about five million) and often low competences. For this reason, the work plan of monitoring violations of labour law, including working time cases, does not systematically cover all industries/sectors. In 2009, for example, only a few specific themes/areas were inspected; these included accommodation and catering services as well as health and emergency services and acute care units in hospitals. The inspectors completed more than 11,000 inspections concerning labour law and labour conditions under the scheme of 'planned inspections' (this is 33 inspections per inspector, which might be considered a low performance standard). It is interesting that the number of labour law violations was higher than the number of subjects/employers examined: about 7,000 violations concerning the signing of, changes to and terminations of the labour contract; more than 5,000 violations concerning rewarding employees (especially with respect to overtime work), and 2,250 violations (this is about 20 per cent of the cases examined) concerning working time and rest periods, and so on (about 19,000 violations in total). It is also interesting that less than 1,000 penalties were imposed on employers, which means that only 5 per cent of violations were sanctioned. Not only the number but also the amount of penalties was low; only about 25 million CZK (one million EUR) was exacted in total (for data, see Státní úřad inspekce práce 2010).

In addition to their own investigations of violations of labour law, Labour Inspectorates dealt with appeals submitted to them concerning violations of the labour law: they examined 669 appeals regarding violations of regulations of working time and rest periods. In these cases, 2,251 violations of labour law regulations were recorded (this means that in many cases several violations were found at once). The most common was neglecting the duty to record working time, overtime and on-call duty (nearly 1,000 violations). Next, more than 500 violations of the rest period regulations were identified, and about 360 violations of regulations on working time (and overtime). These problems applied to more than half of the cases examined. Problems with keeping records of working time and violations of working time rules were most widespread in the transport sector.

Since 2009, Labour Inspectorates have also examined emergency health services and acute care units in hospitals, with a close eye on the institution of 'additional negotiated overtime work' in the health sector: when they inspected 47 employers in 2009 they found 48 violations by 22 employers (nearly half of the examined cases) regarding working time, rest periods, overtime and on-call duty. Similar inspections of 49 employers in 2010 found 73 violations by 31 employers; in fact, an increasing trend in violations (compare Státní úřad inspekce práce 2010, 2011). It seems that employees mostly agree to additional overtime work beyond the limit of 150 hours since they are interested in additional rewards. The inspections revealed the practice of circumventing legislation. Hospitals sometimes reacted to the 2003 WTD (transposed in 2006) by either adding an overtime work clause to the labour contract of doctors that allows them to work an additional 416 hours per year (this means 832 hours altogether), or through additional 'free contracts/agreements outside the labour contract', both routes enabling the total working time to transcend the legal limits on the length of working time. Since the employees are financially interested in such arrangements, it is difficult to penalise these practices, even if some of them circumvent legislation. It is also a common practice to violate law deliberately. This practice became apparent to the public when in December 2010 and January 2011 doctors protested against low pay in healthcare by submitting notices in high numbers (an action initiated by their Trade Unions). Softer forms of protest included the refusal to sign new amendments to labour contracts about overtime. The doctors revealed that in reality they work between 800 and 1,200 hours of overtime per year (see Moravský deník 2011) but this practice did not change much until the end of 2013 (Havlíčskobrodský deník 2014). Furthermore, some hospitals have established a separate legal entity within the hospital in order that staff working on call are not by law considered to be 'at the workplace'.[10]

Due to these practices, the scope/amount of time worked or overtime work did not significantly drop in the Czech Republic during 2004–2008, despite implementation of the WTD. During this period the average number of working hours per full-time employee remained stable, at 41.3 hours per week, and the average proportion of employees working overtime dropped by only a fraction, from 5.6 per cent to 4.6 per cent. If we put these two figures together, they may even indicate more hours per employee working overtime (European Commission 2010).

7.3 GENERAL POLITICAL AWARENESS AND DISCUSSION OF THE DIRECTIVE

When the WTD was first transposed to Czech labour law there was little discussion of the issue. The governments led by Social Democrats between 1998 and 2006 did not pay much attention to the complaints of the centre-right opposition, who were critical of the WTD and demanded more 'flexibility' in the labour market. It is interesting that although Trade Unions agreed with most of the articles of the WTD they did not accept the rule of including time worked in a second/other job(s) into the total amount of working time. The main reason was that they perceived the necessity of two labour contracts as a widespread strategy to secure an 'appropriate living standard of employees' households'. The centre-right coalition government that emerged from the elections of 2006 was committed to changing almost every previous public policy of the former government, including revising the Labour Code by adopting more flexible arrangements. This intention corresponded well with the ongoing discussion on the revision of the WTD during 2005–2008 at the level of the EU (see Rogowski, Chapter 6, in this volume).

The Czech centre-right government proposed a new Labour Code and embraced the idea of a revised WTD in the context of flexibilisation of labour legislation. The Czech government was supportive of organisations representing the interests of businesses at the level of the EU,

[10] Source: interview with a lawyer, university lecturer, experienced with 'faculty hospitals'.

such as Eurochambers, BusinessEurope, the Central European Energy Partners (CEEP) and the European Association of Craft, Small and Medium-Sized Enterprises (UEAPME), all of which lobbied for the Council's common proposal of June 2008 to make working time more flexible with respect to on-call time and overtime.[11]

At the national level the government proposed several crucial changes in a new Labour Code, in accordance with its Government Programme Declaration of January 2007 (Government 2007) that aims to increase labour market flexibility. One important proposal touched the field of working time indirectly. The government suggested that all employees should be allowed to negotiate their wage/salary with respect to potential overtime work (limited to a maximum of 150 hours per year), while until then this had only been possible for managers and a limited group of employees.

The trade unions (and the political opposition – Social Democrats and Communists) criticised the proposal for a new Labour Code, arguing that it was incompatible with the EU concept of 'flexicurity'. According to them, the suggestions only increase the number of 'precarious labour contracts' and reduce employees' substantive securities. Similarly, they refused the proposal to include overtime work in negotiations of wage/salary as harmful to the right of workers to be rewarded appropriately for overtime work. The centre-right government had to resign in April 2009 because it lost the unstable coalition majority but a Conservative-led government was re-elected in May 2010. The new government succeeded in 2011 in ratifying a revision of the Labour Code aiming to flexibilise the labour market. Among other things, from 2012 it became possible for employer and employee to make an agreement that a wage includes a reward for overtime work of up to 150 hours per year; in the case of workers in managerial positions, overtime work could be beyond this limit; and the work day limit was expanded from nine to 12 hours (Article 114 (3) of the Labour Code).

7.4 CONCLUSIONS

Czech labour law paid close attention to international standards even before 1989, and in some areas provided stronger protection than EU law. Thus EU law has brought only minor improvements in labour law. Although EU labour legislation was transposed promptly, its impact was

---

[11] In January 2009, the European Parliament again refused the Council's proposal of June 2008.

hardly visible in practice due to the generally low level of legal awareness, generally low respect for legislation and neglect of labour law in practice. There was little (or insufficient) intervention from the bodies responsible for enforcement, due to inappropriate institutional means and lack of political commitment.

During the 1990s national legislation focused on liberalisation and this facilitated the rapid development of practices to circumvent legislation. Because these practices are widespread, the actors involved do not need to seek support of the ECJ in order to oppose labour law legislation. Furthermore, hostile ECJ case law has so far not interfered with Czech labour law.

There are two circumstances that contribute to a legislative uncertainty associated with the regulations of the EU WTD. The first is the problem of the inconsistent position of EU bodies such as the European Parliament, European Council, European Commission and ECJ concerning the directive. This may not be surprising, since all regulations adopted by the EU bodies are subject to the political process both at the national and the EU level.

Secondly, in the case of the Czech Republic, a major problem of the EU WTD is that there are serious failures in its implementation and enforcement. These problems are particularly pertinent with respect to overtime work, on-call time regulations, and combined working time of a first and a second labour contract. In addition, the WTD is openly refuted in certain sectors, such as in hospitals. The general political direction concerning labour law in the Czech Republic is represented by a strong tendency towards flexibilisation, as expressed in the political programmes of the centre-right governments since 2006 that are implicitly supporting liberalisation as well as the practice of circumventing labour law.

BIBLIOGRAPHY

European Commission (2006), *Green Paper on modernising labour law to meet the challenges of the 21st century*. Brussels: European Commission – MEMO/06/439 22 November 2006. Available at: http://europa.eu/rapid/press-release_MEMO-06-439_en.htm (accessed 18 October 2012).

European Commission (2010), *Indicators for monitoring the Employment Guidelines including indicators for additional employment analysis. 2010 compendium, Update 20 July 2010*. Brussels: EC, DG Employment, Social Affairs and Equal Opportunities. Available at: http://www.bing.com/search?q=European+Commisssion+(2010)%2c+Indicators+for+monitoring+the+Employment+Guidelines+including+indicators+for+additional+employment+analysis.+2010+compendium%2c+July.&PC=MALC&QS=n&first=11&FORM=PERE (accessed 15 December 2013).

Falkner, G., O. Treib, M. Hartlapp and S. Leiber (2005), *Complying with Europe: EU Harmonization and Soft Law in the Member States*, New York: Cambridge University Press.

Falkner, G., O. Treib and E. Holzleithner (2008), *Compliance in the Enlarged European Union: Living Rights or Dead Letters?*, Aldershot and Burlington: Ashgate.

Havlíčkobrodský deník [online newspaper] (2014), *Nemocnici chybějí lékaři, zákon silně omezuje práci přesčas* [The hospital lacks doctors, the legislation restricts strongly the overtime work]. 28 January 2014. Available at: http://havlickobrodsky.denik.cz/zpravy_region/nemocnici-chybeji-lekari-zakon-silne-omezuje-praci-prescas-20140128.html (accessed 8 February 2014).

Moravský deník [newspaper] (2011), *Lékařská revolta: konec s přesčasy* [The revolt of doctors: ending the overtime work]. 19 January, p. 1.

Nekolová, M. (2008), *Flexicurity – hledání rovnováhy mezi flexibilitou a ochranou trhu práce v České republice*, Praha: VÚPSV.

Programové prohlášení vlády [Programme declaration of government] (2007). Available at: http://www.vlada.cz/cz/clenove-vlady/historie-minulych-vlad/prehled-vlad-cr/1993-2007-cr/mirek-topolanek-2/prehled-ministru-24440/ (accessed 20 September 2013).

Státní úřad inspekce práce (2010), *Zpráva o činnosti Státního úřadu bezpečnosti práce za rok 2009,* Opava: SÚIP. Available at: http://www.suip.cz/rocni-zpravy/ (accessed 12 June 2012).

Státní úřad inspekce práce (2011), *Zpráva o činnosti Státního úřadu bezpečnosti práce za rok 2010*, Opava: SÚIP. Available at: http://www.suip.cz/rocni-zpravy/ (accessed 12 June 2012).

Večerník, J. (2009), *Czech Society in the 2000s: A Report on Socio-economic Policies and Structures*, Prague: Academia.

Veřejný ochránce práv (2009), *Souhrnná zpráva o činnosti veřejného ochránce práv za rok 2008*, Brno: Veřejný ochránce práv/Ombudsman. Available at: http://www.ochrance.cz/zpravy-o-cinnosti/zpravy-pro-poslaneckou-snemovnu (accessed 8 February 2012).

Veřejný ochránce práv (2010), *Souhrnná zpráva o činnosti veřejného ochránce práv za rok 2009*, Brno: Veřejný ochránce práv/Ombudsman. Available at: http://www.ochrance.cz/zpravy-o-cinnosti/zpravy-pro-poslaneckou-snemovnu (accessed 8 February 2012).

Veřejný ochránce práv (2011), *Souhrnná zpráva o činnosti veřejného ochránce práv za rok 2010*, Brno: Veřejný ochránce práv/Ombudsman. Available at: http://www.ochrance.cz/zpravy-o-cinnosti/zpravy-pro-poslaneckou-snemovnu (accessed 8 February 2012).

8. The unexpected consequences of the application of the EU Working Time Directive in France

Fabrice Colomb

In some respects, studying European policy resembles a discourse analysis whose impact on the daily lives of ordinary actors is hardly apparent, if not non-existent. In contrast, European action relating to working time is a clear example of regulatory output in social policy, which does have a major impact on the lives of European workers.

It must be asked what exactly is to be expected from the transposition of the European Directive into French law. From some points of view, the effects could be minimal, given that French regulations already complied with standards set out by the Directive. The current research draws on a sociological survey to show up the strategies of national actors *vis-à-vis* European institutions. It also shows that certain standards of France's law on working time have indeed been significantly modified.[1] In fact, it is impossible to examine the dynamics of the legal transposition by only looking at the level of correspondence between European and national standards. But this 'mechanical' relationship has a blind spot. It denies the political legitimacy of national actors within their respective countries. Governance of social policies, be it at the European or national level, is not 'apolitical'. It must therefore account to society (the citizens) and to actors (high-level civil servants, union representatives, politicians, etc.) involved in the political regulation and public policy.[2] This is all the

[1] This work is based on written manuscripts (reports by the European Commission, legal texts, etc.) and on interviews conducted with French actors in the Ministry of Labour and experts working with the Commission, as well as French and EU union leaders.

[2] See the contribution of Jean-Claude Barbier and Fabrice Colomb, Chapter 1 in this volume.

more so as national actors have responsibility for arguing their case and translating European legal obligations to establish their domestic political legitimacy. The transposition of European texts into national laws is thus a complex process. Indeed, it is necessary to take into account domestic political and social constraints in order to understand the thrust of working time policy at the national and EU level. From this perspective, a non-mechanical approach integrates the influence of Member States on European standards. I will draw on these prerequisites to grasp the specificities of the transposition of the Directive in France.

The analysis here must therefore relate to the issues raised by European governance of social policies and their consequences on Member States. In particular, the approach taken here is based on the assumption that the Court of Justice of the European Union (CJEU) plays a decisive role in setting and defining European – and potentially national – standards concerning working time. This function is in fact shared with the political branches of the EU's government (the Commission and the Council), as will be seen, as well as the judicial branch of Europe's institutional framework (the CJEU). The construction of European policy on working time follows the succession of sequences whereby the judges of the CJEU 'reply' to the authors of directives.

Indeed, the CJEU plays a decisive role in generating European guidelines relating to working time. Through constant decisions since the early 2000s, the judges have considerably participated in challenging the Directive, as well as its transformation into French law. The *SiMAP* (2000) and *Jaeger* (2003) rulings thus led to two lots of negotiations in 2004 and 2010 (Box 8.1). In fact, the ruling highlighted problems of interpreting the Directive in national law. The Court's decisions have created tensions for both the Commission and national laws.

To understand how French law and actors have translated and interpreted European requirements, this chapter begins by showing to what extent France complies with European recommendations (Section 8.1). This will make it possible to present situations in which European categories are in contradiction with French standards (Sections 8.2 and 8.3). Thereafter, the chapter will show how France seeks to influence negotiations in progress to introduce its own categories, to deal with guidelines that contradict its own working time regime (Sections 8.4 and 8.5).

BOX 8.1 THE *SIMAP* AND *JAEGER* RULINGS

- *The* SiMAP *ruling.*[3] The 1993 Directive distinguishes two types of 'time': working time and rest time. At the end of the 1990s, a Spanish medical union objected to the Ministry of Public Health's policy on the issue of on-call time. The Spanish courts raised a series of questions concerning the distinction between active and inactive on-call time. The main issue was whether both types of on-call time could be considered as working time, as defined by the Directive. The CJEU replied positively for active on-call time and negatively for inactive on-call time.
- *The* Jaeger *ruling.*[4] This case was practically identical to *SiMAP*. Again, the issue revolved around whether doctors on call at their place of work were working as defined by the Directive. The Court concluded in a similar way to *SiMAP*: active on-call time had to be counted as part of working time.

8.1 FRENCH LAW IS GENERALLY 'ON TRACK'[5]

A summary comparison on Union and French standards indicates a large degree of correspondence. Article 15 of the Directive stipulates that Member States can 'apply or introduce laws, regulations or administrative provisions more favourable to the protection of the safety and health of workers'. In fact, in most situations, France respects the European Directive. Its transposition of European positions concerns maximum weekly working time in particular. Elsewhere, French standards are more favourable to workers than the minimal prescriptions of European law. Yet, there is a clear discrepancy between the number of categories defined in France and in the EU. 'Weekly working time', 'inactive on-call time' and 'equivalent hours' are not defined within the Directive (Table 8.1).

---

[3] CJEU ruling of 3 October 2000, in case C-303/98, Sindicato de Médicos de Asistencia Pública (SiMAP) against Conselleria de Sanidad y Consumo de la Generalidad Valenciana.

[4] CJEU ruling of 9 October 2003 in case C-151/02, set to the Court by the Landesarbeitsgericht Schleswig-Holstein in the law suit pending in this jurisdiction between the Landeshauptstadt Kiel and Norbert Jaeger.

[5] The French expression was 'dans les clous', and means that a person is crossing a road on a pedestrian crossing. It was used during an interview by a representative of France's employers' federation.

Table 8.1 French and EU categories of working time

	French law[1]	European law[2]
Working time	'Effective working time': effective working time is the length of time that a person is available to his/her employer and carries out the employer's orders without being able to attend freely to his/her personal affairs	'Working time': 'any period during which the worker is working, at the employer's disposal and carrying out his activity or duties, in accordance with national laws and/or practice'[3]
Weekly working time	35 hours	–
Maximum weekly working time	48 hours 44 hours over a 12-week reference period	48 hours 48 hours over a 16-week reference period
Rest time	–	Any period of time which is not working time
Daily rest	Every employee is entitled to a daily rest time of 11 hours	Member States take the necessary measures to ensure that every employee benefits from at least 11 consecutive hours of rest during a period of 24 hours
Night work	Any work between 9 pm and 6 am is considered as night work. Another period of nine consecutive hours, between 9 pm and 7 am, including in any case the time between 12 midnight and 5 am, may be substituted for the period mentioned in the first paragraph by a convention or collective agreement extended to a company or establishment agreement	'Night-time': any period of at least seven hours, as defined by national legislation, including in any case the time between 12 midnight and 5 am
Inactive on-call time	An inactive on-call period occurs when the employee, though not being at the permanent and immediate disposal of the employer, has to remain at home or close by in order to carry out work for the company if necessary. The duration of this period is considered as effective working time	–

	French law[1]	European law[2]
Equivalent hours	A period of time equivalent to legal working time may be implemented in professions and for specific jobs, including periods of inactivity. It may be set by decree, in the wake of a collective bargaining agreement, or through a branch agreement, or by a decree by France's Council of State (*Conseil d'Etat*), which also acts as the public sector's highest court. These periods are paid according to usage or to collective agreements	–

Notes:

1. See L. 312.1 of France's Labour Code.
2. Article 2 Directive 2003/88.
3. Article 2(1) WTD.

The discrepancies between EU and national categories make it difficult to have a 'mechanical' understanding of the transposition of European laws. Some interpretative work always needs to be carried out by national actors to arrive at a domestic reading. This national translation leads to legal insecurities in as far as French actors have to modify domestic regulations as well as adapt certain sectoral measures. Two cases illustrate these mechanisms.

8.2 THE '*DELLAS* RULING': A PRECEDENT THAT MAY BE EXTENDED – THE CASE OF SOCIAL AND HEALTH PROFESSIONS

The first influence of the 2001 Directive concerns night work by women (Box 8.2). The '*Dellas* ruling' put pressure on French regulations, in as far as the latter were in contradiction to European guidelines.

BOX 8.2 THE FIRST INFLUENCE OF THE DIRECTIVE ON FRENCH REGULATION: NIGHT WORK BY WOMEN

- Since 2 November 1892, women have not been allowed to work in industry at night to spare them harsh working conditions.[6] For a century, a series of adaptations were adopted progressively to allow women to work at night. For example, in 1987 night work was made possible as part of collective agreements, under several conditions:[7] the reasons must be exceptional, the work must be organised in successive teams, and negotiations need to take place at the branch and company level.
- These French practices became contradictory both with the two European Directives relating to working time and with CJEU decisions. In fact, the 1976 Directive and the 1993 Directive recalled the principle of non-discrimination between men and women.[8] Thus, the first indicates that access to work, training and promotion must be applied equally to women's and men's work. The second recalls that protective measures must cover all employees. The CJEU interpreted EU law in this way in the *Stoeckel* ruling of 1991; the 1976 Directive also created an obligation for Member States to implement non-discriminatory measures concerning work.
- In view of these Directives and Court decisions, the European Commission launched infringement proceedings against France in 1996, on the grounds that French legislation did not respect EU rules.[9] The CJEU backed the Commission, leading to two possible domestic solutions: either France outlawed night work for men or it allowed it for all employees. The second solution was adopted by the government in 2001, and led to the passing of a law governing the night work of women and men more precisely.[10] The latter fits in with the lines of the Working Time Directive by stipulating in particular that night work covers any activity between 9 pm and 6 am.

The question raised by the *Dellas* affair is similar to the *Jaeger* and *SiMAP* rulings (see above). In 2002, a specialised educator challenged the way his working time was calculated by his teaching, established before the Council of State. In fact, since the Decree of 2001 relative to non-profit health institutions, working time is calculated using a weighting system according to whether or not the employee is active or inactive.

---

6 Article L.213-1 of the French Labour Code.
7 Law no. 87-423 of 19 June 1987.
8 No.76/207/CEE.
9 Ruling C-197/96 of 13 March 1997.
10 Law no. 2001-397.

This allowed, *de facto*, the working week to run to 60 hours. The Council of State opted for a stay of judgment, and sent the case to the CJEU for a preliminary ruling on the conformity of domestic law with EU law.

In 2005, the Court ruled against France, noting that according to the continuity of jurisprudence, any time spent in a place of work should be counted as part of working time, as defined by the Directive. This meant that activities carried out at work could not last more than 48 hours per week.[11] Anticipating the decision of the CJEU and the Council of State, the French government repealed the Decree.

While this procedure clearly is effective in this case, it raises fears in the French administration of being widely applied. In fact, systems using equivalent hours are a measure used to compensate inactive periods in the workplace, at lower rates. Health, transport, social work, security and entertainment organisations are directly affected. For members of France's Labour Department resolving this issue is a matter of urgency, as the French system faces legal uncertainty with non-negligible financial consequences.

Pending a potential decision to this effect, the *Dellas* ruling has indirect consequences for certain sectors. In the health sector, and especially in transport, companies have revised their collective agreements to make up for the extra costs of conforming to European regulations.[12] Furthermore, the government has overhauled its Decree so that it meets European requirements. In 2007, it published a new decree allowing for equivalent hours, though not exceeding 48 hours per week. Accordingly, it modified the Code of Social Action and Families, providing that: 'Use of the equivalence regime […] may not lead to infringement: to an average working week of more than 48 hours for employees, counted hour by hour over a period of four consecutive months.'[13] In this way, the Directive has direct and significant impacts on French regulation. It is a clear case of the national transposition of European law. The Directive led France's Labour Department to adapt French regulations in a most constraining manner, limiting the working week.

Infringement proceedings or questions concerning preliminary rulings are all legal means that have shown their effectiveness in transposing European law. However, these means have in fact been relatively little used. It may be thought that infringement proceedings constitute a strong

---

[11] Ruling C-14/04 of 1 December 2005.

[12] http://www.fnts.org/images/pdf/3-magazine12.pdf.

[13] Article 1 of Decree no. 2007-106 of 29 January 2007.

political decision on behalf of the Commission. Yet the latter avoids such proceedings where they may have major consequences on the organisation of companies in Member States which use on-call systems. The Commission actually opted for new negotiations rather than considering that the 1993 Directive was set in stone. Questions prior to rulings have also been little used, as far as the author is aware. However, the relevant French government administrations fear a proliferation of court cases based on the *Dellas* ruling. Decisions challenging French regulations have been accompanied by a series of repeated positions taken by the European Committee on Social Rights. To put it simply, these decisions raise the question of competing European legal norms, and whether the Social Charter or the Directive has primacy.

8.3 THE CONTRADICTORY STANDARDS OF THE CHARTER OF SOCIAL RIGHTS AND THE DIRECTIVE RELATING TO MANAGERS

The adaptation of domestic law to European law may even have unexpected effects, especially for executives paid *per diem*. In fact, a new version of Article L. 3121-48 of France's Labour Code states that employees paid a 'daily rate' are not subject to working week regulations or limits on working time. Instead, they are covered by weekly and daily rest time obligations, which means that they are authorised to work up to 78 hours per week.[14] The Working Time Directive does not apply to 'managing executives or other persons with autonomous decision-taking powers'.[15] However, French unions have challenged this position, on several occasions, before the European Committee of Social Rights (ECSR) of the Council of Europe, which is responsible for assessing conformity with the European Social Charter (revised), or ESC (revised).[16]

On 23 June 2010, the ECSR stated that such working time was 'actually too long to be qualified as reasonable'. This institution has only limited powers as it has only a consultative role. It is thus for the Minister's Committee to set out a recommendation for France in conformity with the Charter. The French government has asked for more time to produce new elements.

---

[14] Article L3121-48 of 22 August 2008.

[15] Article 17.

[16] Miné Michel, 2011, 'Le droit du temps de travail à la lumière de la Charte sociale européenne', *Semaine sociale Lamy*, no. 1475.

This raises the question of the hierarchy of European standards. If, on the one hand, the Working Time Directive authorises exemptions for managers, but on the other hand the Charter challenges unreasonable working hours, then the question becomes, with which standards should Member States comply? One possibility would be for the Directive to integrate the recommendations of the Charter and to consider that self-employed workers and managers are also subject to 'reasonable' standards, or at least to the same standards relating to weekly working time. The coming months will provide indications about the way in which domestic laws will negotiate these contradictions.

In the last resort, it is possible to see how European unions have drawn on the contradictions of European standards to challenge the working time regime for managers. Again, the Working Time Directive is part of the regime, but the transposition failed to take into account union activity. The position of the union may thus lead to feedback effects whose consequences are relatively unknown.

8.4 FRANCE'S INFLUENCE ON EUROPEAN WORKING TIME POLICY

It is impossible to understand French attempts to influence the European Directive without at the same time referring to the changing justifications of the Commission relating to proposals for overhauling the Directive. Indeed, between 1993 and the 2000s, defending employees' security gave way to promoting flexibility.

The ambition of the November 1993 text was to promote minimal standards relating to maximum working time, the conditions of night work, paid leave and rest time.[17] The Working Time Directive was clearly designed as an instrument to help prevent the negative repercussions of flexibility on employees' health. From this point of view, it is a tool for protecting workers in the face of the construction of the Single Market. The aim was to create a common reference 'base',[18] defining minimal common standards which guaranteed work in conditions that were not dangerous for the health and safety of employees. The Directive was thus a 'safety net'.

---

17 COM(90) 317 final, pp. 2–3.
18 Ibid.

The modification of the Directive was however broached from a completely different perspective in 2004.[19] The 'social interlude' was clearly over. Between 2003 and 2010, the Commission published a series of propositions to modify the 1993 Directive.[20] These reforms envisaged major transformations in the original orientations of the Directive (see Table 8.2).

Table 8.2 One of the scenarios put forward by the Commission

Reference period	The aim was to facilitate exemption from the four-month reference period in the 1993 Directive
Multiple-contract workers	The limits to working time for workers holding several contracts simultaneously should be 'by worker' and not 'by contract'
The Directive's field of application	The point is to distinguish mobile workers (truck drivers) from immobile workers, especially in terms of night work and rest
'Opt-out'	The proposal aims to make 'referral to this measure less necessary', by lengthening the reference period and introducing the notion of on-call time into the Directive

Source: COM (2010) 106 final.

These proposals challenge the whole thrust of European policy on working time. Thus, henceforth ensuring workers a 'high level of health and safety protection in respect of working time' is juxtaposed with 'giv[ing] firms and Member States more flexibility in the way they manage working time'. For the Baroso Commission, the Directive thus becomes one of the instruments necessary for greater flexibility in the organisation of work, as it meets both the needs of employees and employers. If the 1993 Directive was designed as a safeguard against flexibility and if flexibility was viewed largely as being imposed by employers, then the intentions of the Commission in the early 2000s were indeed very different. Accordingly, a new argument was put forward partially justifying the desire of employees for greater flexibility, namely by 'improving compatibility between working and family life'. Indeed, 'greater flexibility in the organisation of working time would meet the

[19] COM(2004) 607 final.

[20] See, in particular, 2003/88/CE and COM(2010) 106 final.

growing needs of workers, particularly those with dependent children or elderly relatives, as well as the interests of companies'.[21]

The whole argument turns around the question of improving labour flexibility. The Commission's document only raises the possibilities of improving workers' security in the Directive as a side line. Its priority is to justify the maintenance of the 'opt-out'. The trend was the same in 2010: the Directive is promoted both to ensure worker security but also to promote labour flexibility.[22]

In sum, the Commission's discourse on the Working Time Directive has shifted from an approach protecting workers towards favouring labour flexibility. This has gone so far that all the significant new aspects of the Directive mentioned above (lengthening the reference period, maintaining the 'opt-out' and on-call time) have been shaped to improve labour market flexibility. This is part of the trend towards neo-liberal economics which dates back to the early 2000s. In the wake of the Single Act, various European initiatives sought to counteract economic considerations: the two successive proposals by the Commission concerning working time have taken the opposite position.

Faced with this changing discourse, French actors have not remained passive and have sought to influence European policy on working time. From this point of view, the construction of a European policy is not the work of civil servants locked up in the Commission buildings in Brussels. On the contrary, the principle of formulating European public policies is one of co-production between Member States and EU institutions. Each country seeks systematically to introduce national measures into EU policy, in order to orient such policy towards domestic practices, especially when the thrust of EU policy contradicts national trends.

The French agenda in negotiations on the new version of the Directive has been to promote the introduction of 'grey time'. This has been a constant strategy since 2003. At the time, both France's Department of Labour and the General Secretariat of European Affairs sought to incorporate a definition of 'on-call time' into the Directive. The aim was to make France's system of equivalent hours applicable to several professions, and which had been made incompatible with the Directive following the *Jaeger*, *SiMAP* and *Dellas* rulings.

French institutions appear to be driven by a twofold motivation. First, they are responding to the 'reality principle': if EU jurisprudence is applied in all areas in which on-call time is counted as equivalent time,

---

21 COM(2010) 801 final.

22 Ibid., pp. 9, 11, 17.

then the economic situation of these professions is badly threatened. Thus, from their point of view, it is legitimate to consider that effective working time is not the same as inactive working time. The Labour Department disagrees with France's unions on this point. The CGT and the CFDT claim that an employee is always in a subordinate relationship at his/her place of work, whether he/she is active or inactive. For the Labour Department, it is important to be pragmatic and political, and argue that France has effective solutions which can be transposed to the European level. Also, this strategy seeks to stop the spread of 'opt-outs'. France is consistently among the countries which contest the principle of regimes that authorise exemptions to agreements between workers and employers which are not included in collective agreements. This position seeks to favour the use of equivalent hours in order to make the use of 'opt-outs' obsolete. Ultimately, France is defending a certain conception of working time policy in which exemptions for employees must be included in collective agreements. France is thus partly opposed to recent leanings by the Commission. Indeed, as we have seen, the Commission has been putting forward proposals that do not just favour workers' protection but also promote flexibility. France's strategy on this is to defend the principle of equivalent hours, both by modifying its decrees so that they correspond to European rules, while also seeking to introduce its domestic working time categories into the Directive.

8.5 CONCLUSION

Two key factors stand out following from this analysis of the effects of the Working Time Directive on French regulations. They contradict views of a 'mechanical' transposition of European standards. First, national standards are not adapted in an unexpected manner, especially in the medical–social field, in which the time equivalence regime had to be dropped. Similarly, managers' working time may be called into question due to contradictions between the European Social Charter (revised) and the Directive. These feedback effects were unexpected as ultimately European standards end up by redefining actors' strategies which do not necessarily imply the direct application of EU orders. At the same time, as has been shown here, French actors – led by the Labour Department – have been seeking to modify the Directive to bring it in line with the French regime. The introduction of 'grey time' is part of this. These various actions lead to legal uncertainties in as far as each Directive is constantly being submitted to renegotiation, while guidelines are unstable.

Ultimately, it may be considered that France takes its own road in applying the Directive, when compared with the Netherlands, the Czech Republic and the United Kingdom.[23] In these countries, minor adjustments have been followed, and there have been no modifications or radical challenges. France, however, is more affected by the Directive, as European regulation is both of sectoral and national importance to French labour law.

BIBLIOGRAPHY

Barbier, J.-C. (2008), *La longue marche vers l'Europe sociale*, Paris: PUF.

Conseil économique, social et environnemental (2010), *Le travail de nuit des femmes: impact sur les conditions de travail et de vie des salariés*, Report, 30 June. Available at: http://www.decisionsante.com/fileadmin/uploads/Actualite/Enquete_travail_de_nuit_CES.pdf (last accessed 12 May 2014).

Deloitte Consulting (2010), *Study to support an Impact Assessment on further action at European level regarding Directive 2003/88/EC and the evolution of working time organisation*, Final Report, 21 December.

European Commission (1990), 'Proposal for a Directive concerning certain aspects of the organisation of working time', COM(90) 317 final, September.

European Commission (1993), 'Proposal for a Directive concerning certain aspects of the organisation of working time', COM(93) 578 final, 16 November.

European Commission (2004), 'Proposal of a Directive of the European Parliament and of the Council', COM(2004) 607 final, 22 September.

European Commission (2010a), 'Proposal of reviewing of the working time directive, first phase', COM(2010) 106 final, 24 March.

European Commission (2010b), 'Proposal of reviewing of the working time directive, second phase', COM(2010) 801 final, 21 December.

Falkner, G., O. Treib, M. Hartlapp and S. Leiber (2005), *Complying with Europe: EU Harmonization and Soft Law in the Member States*, New York: Cambridge University Press.

Ferrera, M. (2005), *The Boundaries of Welfare, European Integration and the New Spatial Politics of Social Protection*, Oxford: Oxford University Press.

Leibfried, S. and P. Pierson (eds) (1995), *European Social Policy between Fragmentation and Integration*, Washington: Brookings Institution.

Rodière, P. (2008), *Droit social de l'Union européenne*, Paris: LGDJ.

Scharpf, F. (1999), *Governing in Europe, Effective and Democratic?*, Oxford: Oxford University Press.

[23] See the contributions of Els Sol and Nuria Ramos Martín, Tomáš Sirovátka and Ralf Rogowski in this volume.

9. Governance of EU labour law: Implementation of the EU Working Time Directive in the Netherlands[1]

Els Sol and Nuria Ramos Martín

9.1 INTRODUCTION

Debates over challenges that European law poses for national legislation and practices may be relatively new, but the general aspects of working time are a long-time and hotly contested field in the governance and implementation of EU law. This field of regulation of weekly hours of employment is situated at the crossroads of health and safety regulations and employment protection. It is also of concern for industrial relations insofar as it falls into the domain of autonomy of collective bargaining. The length of working time is a fundamental element of the employment contract and the limitation of daily working time is a longstanding union demand. The European Union has acknowledged this need to regulate and limit working time in several legal instruments such as the Community Charter of the Fundamental Social Rights of Workers of 1989 and the Charter of Fundamental Rights of the EU. In secondary EU legislation, the Directive 2003/88/EC aims to protect workers predominantly against the health and safety risks of long and irregular hours by setting up a framework on the organisation of working time.

In the European perspective the Netherlands has pioneered working time regulations. In the 20th century the Dutch trade union movement successfully claimed an active policy on working time, both on the grounds of job creation in situations of high unemployment and on the grounds of health and safety. Since this has resulted in protective Dutch regulations, the implementation of the Working Time Directive (WTD) has had less impact in the Netherlands than in some other countries.

[1] The authors would like to thank Klara Boonstra and Suhendra Leon for comments made and Kea Tijdens for providing data from the WageIndicator.

Much has already been regulated at national level in statutes and collective agreements. The major arrangement is the Dutch Working Time Act of 1996, which underwent major changes that came into force on 1 April 2007.[2] The Working Time Act determines the rules of the maximum working hours and minimum rest periods and sets a series of other standards. Also the Act gives effect to the WTD (2003/88/EC).[3]

In addition to the Working Time Act, other legal provisions regulate the adjustment of working hours in the Netherlands. The Adjustment of Working Time Act 2000 (Wet Aanpassing Arbeidsduur)[4] gives employees the right to request a decrease or an increase in the number of hours they work (Kuip and Verhulp 2000). This legislation is weighted in favour of the employee (Jacobs and Schmidt 2001).[5] As a rule, employers are obliged to grant a working time adjustment request unless there is a substantive business reason to refuse, and they should arrange the pattern of working time in line with the employee's wishes unless the employer proposes an alternative pattern that would better suit operational needs. In this case, employees should be 'reasonable and fair' in trying to accommodate the employer's request. Moreover, employers are not generally allowed to demand to know the reasons behind the request. Currently, the government is discussing a legal proposal on 'Modernising leave arrangements and working time', proposing amendments to the Adjustment of Working Time Act and the Work and Care Act.[6] In the context of the new tripartite social agreement adopted in 2013, the Minister of Social Affairs is planning to organise a summit with the social partners to discuss ideas on how better to reconcile work and care which might lead to amendments of that proposed legislation.[7]

---

[2] Law of 23 November 1995, last amended in July 2013, State Bulletin of the Netherlands, 236.

[3] In addition to ILO Conventions 14 and 106, the European Social Charter and the Youth Council Directive (94/33/EC). Since the Treaty of Lisbon the right to limitation of working hours, daily and weekly rest, and paid leave is bound by the Charter of Fundamental Rights of the European Union.

[4] State Bulletin of the Netherlands, 114, 2000.

[5] See case law: Rechtbank Zwolle, Sector Kanton, 12/10/200, KG 200, p. 235; Rechtbank Haarlem, sector Kanton, 12/05/2001, JAR 2001, p. 117; Kantonrechter (Ktr.) Groningen 23/03/2001, JAR 2001, p. 87; Ktr. Haarlem 17/05/2001, JAR 2001, p. 117; Ktr. Breda 30/03/2001, JAR 2001, p. 85; Ktr. Maastricht 02/02/2001, JAR 2001, p. 49; and Rechtbank Groningen, sector Kanton, 23/03/2001, JAR 2002, p. 140.

[6] State Bulletin of the Netherlands, 2013, 236.

[7] Labour Foundation of the Netherlands, 'Perspectives for a Social and Entrepreneurial Country: Leaving the Crisis, with Quality Work, on the way to

This chapter presents working time issues related to debates concerning the EU Working Time Directive. After an introduction of the Dutch part-time work model and working hours arrangements (section 9.2), section 9.3 first explains the Dutch legal approach towards implementing EU law. Section 9.4 focuses on relevant aspects of the WTD in terms of regulation, implementation and practice. In this chapter we use empirical data from the Labour Force Survey (LFS) and the WageIndicator database. Sections 9.5 and 9.6 deal with derogations and exceptions respectively in general (section 9.5) and in specific industries (section 9.6). Section 9.7 focuses on case law. Furthermore, section 9.8 gives an overview of the appreciation of WTD by the relevant actors. Finally in section 9.9 the chapter ends with some concluding remarks.

9.2 WORKING HOURS ARRANGEMENTS AND GENERAL HISTORIC CONTEXT OF PART-TIME WORK

During the 1980s, the growth of part-time employment accelerated simultaneously with the rise in female labour market participation, concentrated heavily in the service sector. The initial rise in part-time employment was mostly the unintended result of the late entry of Dutch women into the labour market following rising education trends and changes in cultural values regarding mothers and paid work outside the home (Visser and Yerkes 2008). The growth in part-time work was stimulated by the economic situation at the time, with fewer employment opportunities, with wage moderation taking place and policy pressures towards a redistribution of employment. From the employers' point of view, part-time work was a means of increasing flexibility, and offered an individual, rather than a collective solution to working time reduction. One of the main advantages of part-time work for employees was that it supposedly offered the flexibility needed to combine paid work with caring responsibilities (Visser 2002; Visser and Hemerijck 1997; Visser and Yerkes 2008).

Table 9.1 presents an overview of the part-time working hours arrangements for employees for the Netherlands and for four benchmark countries, each representing different arrangements in Europe: France,

---

2020'. <http://www.rijksoverheid.nl/documenten-en-publicaties/kamerstukken/2013/04/11/bijlage-perspectief-voor-een-sociaal-en-ondernemend-land-uit-de-crisis-met-goed-werk-op-weg-naar-2020-stichting-van-de-arbeid.html> Accessed 1 May 2014.

the United Kingdom, Denmark and the Czech Republic, using LFS data. A majority of men stipulate they work on a fulltime hours per week basis. As the table shows, the Netherlands' figures for fulltime work are the lowest. Compared with earlier LFS data of 1999 all countries have reduced fulltime working hours.

The part-time-work history of the Netherlands as the country noted for its part-time economy is clearly reflected in the figures (Table 9.1). In 2010 the Netherlands' share of part-time hours (24.2 for men and 76.82 per cent for women) for both men and women stand out as remarkably high against 2.2 and 9.1 per cent in the Czech Republic (lowest) and 14.1 per cent in Denmark for men and 42.5 per cent in the United Kingdom for women (second highest score). And the percentages still rise. All percentages of employees with part-time hours contracts rose from 1999 to 2009.

Table 9.1 Part-time working hours' arrangements of employees as a share of total employment in the Netherlands and four benchmark countries (%), 1999–2009

Part-time hours per week	Males		Females	
	1999	2009	1999	2009
Czech Republic	2.4	2.1	9.9	9.1
Denmark	10.4	14.1	34.7	38.6
France	5.5	6.4	31.4	29.8
Netherlands	18.0	24.2	68.9	76.2
United Kingdom	8.8	11.0	44.0	42.4

Source: Labour Force Survey data.

We can typify the Netherlands against its benchmark countries' working time participation model using a typology developed by Anxo and Boulin as a maternal part-time work model (Anxo and Boulin 2006):

- 'Maternal part-time work' model. Characteristic is that women, after they have children, continue to participate in the labour market in a part-time appointment. Part-time is seen as the norm for mothers, even if the children are older. The Netherlands is an example of the 'maternal part-time work' model, along with, to a smaller extent, the United Kingdom. Both the Netherlands and the United Kingdom have a large percentage of women working part-time: 75 per cent in the Netherlands and 41 per cent in the UK (OECD 2009).

- 'Universal breadwinner model'. Characteristic for this model is that women's employment throughout the life cycle is high and women generally work in large (20 hours or more) part-time jobs or work full time. In most families both partners work. Denmark, the Czech Republic and France practise this model.

9.3 NATIONAL LEGAL APPROACH TO IMPLEMENTING EU LAW

In general terms, the Netherlands can be defined as a parliamentary representative democracy and a constitutional monarchy. The legislative process in the Netherlands is based on a bicameral system with a Second Chamber (House of Representatives) that discusses and adopts the bills and a First Chamber (Senate) that assesses bills by reference to its own criteria after they have passed through the Second Chamber. When describing the legislative process in the Netherlands, it is important to mention the existence of some bi- and tripartite advisory boards. In fact, trade unions and employers are represented in the Social-Economic Council (Sociaal Economische Raad, SER), the Stichting van de Arbeid (Labour Foundation), and the Council for Work and Income.

When dealing with EU-related matters, the Second Chamber does not usually adopt resolutions on EU proposals, nor does it give mandates to the government to take a certain position in the Council of the European Union. Instead, there is a consultation and reporting procedure, according to which ministers incorporate Parliament's views by discussing their position with MPs before every Council meeting. The government outlines its position on important EU proposals in explanatory memorandums (so-called BNC fiches) that are sent to the Standing Committee on European Affairs of the Parliament. These include an assessment of the proposal's financial and other implications for Dutch interests and regulations. In principle, the role of the Committee on European Affairs is limited mainly to 'horizontal' EU issues, like the adoption of new treaties or the Lisbon process, and each specific committee (in the case of the organisation of working time, the Committee on Social Affairs and Employment) deals with the EU proposals in its own area.

9.4 RELEVANT ASPECTS OF THE WORKING TIME DIRECTIVE: IMPLEMENTATION AND PRACTICE

This section discusses the major topics of discussion concerning issues related to the WTD and its implementation, notably annualised hours, flexible hours, the opt-out from the WTD, on-call work and shift work. It gives figures related to these topics for the Netherlands benchmarked against four other countries.

Working time in the Netherlands is mainly regulated in the Working Time Act (Arbeidstijdenwet) and in the Working Time Decree (Arbeidstijdenbesluit).[8] The Working Hours Act stipulates how many hours per day and week an employee may work and also regulates breaks and minimum rest periods. These legal texts apply for the employed over the age of 18 but there are special regulations applicable to children under 16 and young workers aged 16 and 17. In addition, special rules concerning working time apply to women who are pregnant or who have recently given birth. In principle the Working Hours Act applies to everyone who works for an employer, so for all employees, including interns and temporary employees. However, workers who earn three times or more the minimum salary are excluded from the scope of the legislation (unless they are engaged in dangerous work, night work or shift work, or when they work in non-managerial positions in the mining sector). This exclusion has been criticised by some researchers (Knegt et al. 2011). In a number of cases the Working Hours Act also applies to the self-employed (i.e. in the transport sectors). Finally, there are also specific regulations on working time for several sectors, that is, healthcare and mining.

9.4.1 Definition of Working Time and Rest Time

In the Netherlands, until a legislative change introduced by Law of 22 November 2012, there was no clear definition of working time or resting time.[9] This legislative lacunae was criticised in 2009 by a decision of the Administrative Law Division of the Council of State.[10] This Administrative institution decided on appeal that whereas the definitions of working

---

[8] Decree of 4 December 1995, last amended in August 2012, State Bulletin of the Netherlands 2012, 397.

[9] State Bulletin of the Netherlands 2012, 604.

[10] JB 2009/99 Council of State, 04-03-2009.

time and rest period included in Article 2 of the WTD are not implemented in the domestic law and, as long as the proper description and explanation of these definitions are decisive in a given case for answering the question whether there has been a violation of law, it is against the principle of legal certainty to apply the doctrine of interpretation in conformity with EU law. This led to the conclusion that the Ministry of Social Affairs had no power in that case to impose a fine on a company for non-compliance with the working time and resting time imposed by that Directive. After this decision, new definitions of working time and rest period were included in Article 1.7 K and L.[11] Working time is now defined in the national law as 'the time that the employee performs work under the authority of the employer' and rest period means 'any period which is not working time'. This new definition of working time does not seem to fully correspond with the wording of the WTD, which is more elaborate and defines working time as 'any period during which the worker is working, at the employer's disposal and carrying out his activity or duties, in accordance with national laws and/or practice'. Therefore, this lack of full compliance could lead to further litigation in the case of on-call workers – see below – or, eventually, to a submission of a preliminary question to the Court of Justice of the EU (CJEU) in order to clarify if the term 'the authority of the employer' is equivalent to the EU law terminology, 'the employer's disposal'.

9.4.2 The Length of the Working Week

The length of the working week is at the heart of the working time controversy between governments, employer associations and the trade union movement in the EU (Van Klaveren et al. 2008). The debate has been intense during the discussion of the European Commission's proposals for revising the WTD (European Commission 2005). These proposals aimed at counteracting the effect of the CJEU's decisions in the cases *SiMAP*[12] and *Jaeger*,[13] which held that on-call duty performed by doctors when they are required to be physically present at their working place must be regarded as working time.

---

[11] An amendment of Article 1.7 of the Working Time Act was introduced by State Bulletin of the Netherlands 2013, 236.

[12] Case C-303/98 *SiMAP v Conselleria de Sanidad y Consumo de la Generalidad Valenciana. [2000] ECR 1-7963.*

[13] Case C-151/02 *Landeshauptstadt Kiel v Norbert Jaeger*. Judgment of 9 October 2003.

Table 9.2 presents an overview of average usual working hours per week for the Netherlands, broken down by industry, for 2010.

Table 9.2 Distribution of overtime payment arrangements

	Netherlands
Agriculture	39.5
Manufacturing	41.1
Utilities	41.3
Construction	42.1
Wholesale/retail	37.4
Hotels, restaurants, catering	36.3
Transportation	40.6
Finance	39.2
Other community services	39.2
Public admin.	39.1
Education	38.0
Healthcare	34.2
Other	36.2
Total	38.7
N	27759

Source: WageIndicator data 2010.

Compared with previous years (September 2004–March 2007), the average number of hours for the Netherlands rose from 36.4 to 38.7 per cent. The construction industry has the longest working week, with 42.1 hours.

Regarding rest periods, the legislation in the Netherlands establishes that after a working day, an employee must have 11 consecutive hours of resting time. This rest period may be shortened to 8 hours once in a 7-day period if the nature of the work or the business circumstances so require. In a regular week of 5-day work, an employee is entitled to enjoy 36 consecutive hours of resting time after the end of the working week. A longer working week is also possible, provided the employee has at least 72 consecutive hours of resting time within a period of 14 days. This period may be split into two periods of at least 32 hours each. Moreover, the legislation in the Netherlands stipulates that an employee who works more than 5½ hours per day is entitled to at least a 30-minute break each day. This may be split into two 15-minute breaks. Furthermore, if an employee works for more than 10 hours, he must have at least a 45-minute break. This may be split into several breaks, each of which must be at least 15 minutes. These breaks can be modified by collective agreement, also to the detriment of the employee.

9.4.3 Individual Opt-out

The WTD allows, providing that the conditions set up in Article 22 are fulfilled, for a worker to sign an agreement with the employer to work more than 48 hours per week. In this case the WTD explicitly forbids any kind of victimisation of the worker who is not willing to give his agreement to perform such work. In addition, the Directive contains recording and information obligations of the employer concerning all workers who carry out such work. The Netherlands applies the individual opt-out to the maximum standard duration of the working week for jobs which make extensive use of on-call time, such as in health services and emergency services. However, the introduction of the opt-out has been controversial; trade unions complain that it amounts to a regression from the levels of protection and co-determination which applied previously, while employers disagree. Municipal authorities and public service unions reached an agreement in May 2010 on allowing the use of the opt-out during the period 2009–2011 for emergency services, subject to approval by union members. The agreement would allow working time of up to 50 hours per week, and maximum daily working time would not exceed 11 hours (see also court cases below).

9.4.4 Annualised Hours

The issue of annualisation of working hours relates to the reference periods for the calculation of maximum weekly and daily working time and for minimum rest periods. Nevertheless, derogations to the maximum length of night work and of the reference periods set up in the WTD are admitted in many cases.

Table 9.3 presents personal characteristics of employees with annualised hours, their Collective Labour Agreement (CLA) coverage and the percentage of employees with annualised hours. The table reveals that the Netherlands has a major CLA coverage.

Table 9.3 Personal characteristics of employees with annualised hours, breakdown by CLA and percentage of employees with annualised hours, 2010

	Percentage female employees	Average age	Percentage covered by coll. agreement	Firm size workplace	Percentage with annualised hours
Netherlands	70.2	41.2	95.8	4.81	0.8

Source: WageIndicator data 2010, employees with an employment contract.

9.4.5 Overtime Payment

As Table 9.4 reveals, the Netherlands scores poorly on the payment of overtime as regular hours plus overtime compensation and well on additional overtime hours paid as normal hours.

Table 9.4 Distribution of overtime payment arrangements and average contractual working hours by arrangement, 2010

Distribution of arrangements	Netherlands
1 Overtime paid as normal hours plus overtime premium	8.6%
2 Overtime paid as normal hours	16.9%
3 Time off in lieu of overtime hours	31.4%
4 Partly paid, partly compensated with time off in lieu	14.3%
5 Not compensated	28.7%
Total	*100%*
Average contractual working hours	
1 Overtime paid as normal hours plus overtime premium	36.8
2 Overtime paid as normal hours	30.2
3 Time off in lieu of overtime hours	34.6
4 Partly paid, partly compensated with time off in lieu	34.5
5 Not compensated	37.8

Source: WageIndicator data 2010, employees with an employment contract.

In the Netherlands time off in lieu of overtime hours is most common, reflecting the high value attached to leisure time.

9.4.6 On-call Work

The case law of the European Court of Justice has established that on-call working time, when the employee must be available at the workplace, should be regarded as working time. Due to the dissatisfaction of some Member States, including the Netherlands, with the need to implement the *Jaeger* doctrine, the European Commission amended proposal for revising the WTD suggested the introduction of a new category of on-call time, the 'inactive' part of on-call time (COM 2005 246 final).

In the Netherlands, even if an employee is not at the workplace, he may be called on to go to work if unforeseen circumstances arise. This is referred to as 'on-call duty' in the Working Time Act. 'Standby duty' is also regulated in that Act, and the difference between the two is that being called to work is a normal part of the job for someone with standby duty, for example in the healthcare sector (Ministry of Social Affairs and Employment 2010). In the legislation in the Netherlands in the event of on-call duty and standby duty, the hours during which an employee can be called are not considered working hours. However, if an employee is called and must go to work, this time does count as working hours. A call counts for at least a half hour of working time, even if the employee only actually works for 15 minutes. If an employee is called once again within a half hour after he has finished his work following a call, the interim time also counts as working time.[14]

In addition to on-call duty and standby duty, the Working Time Decree regulates another form of on-call work, the so-called 'on-site standby duty'. This form refers to cases when the employee must be present at

[14] The Dutch Working Time Act establishes that an employee who works on on-call duty may not work more than 13 hours per 24 hours, including the hours arising from calls. An employee may be on on-call duty for a maximum of 14 days during a 4-week period and must have at least two consecutive days in every 4-week period in which he is not working and also not on on-call duty. Furthermore, an employee may not be on on-call duty immediately before or immediately after a night shift nor in the 11 hours preceding a night shift or during the 14 hours after a night shift. If an employee is on on-call duty between midnight and 6 am 16 times or more within a 16-week period, he may not work more than 40 hours per week on average during that 16-week period. However, the legislation foresees an extension to 45 hours per week under the following conditions: the employee has 8 consecutive hours of rest immediately after the last night call during which he is not working or on on-call duty or, if that is not possible, 8 consecutive hours of rest on that same day (before midnight in any case).

the workplace (similarly to the situation in the *Jaeger* and *SiMAP* EU cases). In the Netherlands, special rules apply to on-site standby duty. During on-site standby duty, an employee must remain at the workplace, so that he can start working as quickly as possible after being called. This is only permitted if the type of work requires such presence and the work cannot reasonably be organised in a different way (i.e. in healthcare or in the fire brigade). Moreover, working on-site standby shifts must be agreed in a collective arrangement. The specific regulation of this type of labour performance only applies if the employee does not regularly work an on-site standby shift. Otherwise the standard working time regulations apply.[15]

An on-site standby shift may not last more than 24 hours, including hours of waiting or sleeping, and an employee may work an on-site standby shift a maximum of 52 times in 26 weeks. In conformity with EU case law, all hours during an on-site standby shift, which requires mandatory presence at the workplace, count as working time. In principle, an employee working on-site standby shifts may work at most on average 48 hours per week in a 26-week period. However, since 2005, the employee and employer may also make use of the individual opt-out to the maximum duration of the working week and agree on an arrangement to work up to 60 hours per week. This exception follows the opt-out option provided by Article 22 of the WTD and it was included in the national legislation to limit the impact of the *Jaeger* ruling. If an employee agrees to the opt-out, he must state his agreement in writing and his consent is valid only for a period of 26 weeks and is subsequently tacitly renewed for the same period, unless he explicitly states that he does not want to continue the agreement.

---

[15] The ruling is as follows. There must be a period of at least 11 hours of rest before and after every on-site standby shift. This rest time may be shortened to 10 hours once per week and to 8 hours once per week if necessary due to the nature of the work or the business circumstances and providing that it is collectively agreed. The shorter rest times may not be planned to follow each other. A shortened rest time between two shifts must be compensated for in the following rest period. Moreover, after a shortened rest period, the very next rest period must in that case be extended by the number of hours by which the previous one was shortened. In addition, in every consecutive period of 7 times 24 hours, the rest time must amount to a minimum of 90 hours and it must contain at least one uninterrupted rest period of at least 24 hours, as well as four uninterrupted rest periods of at least 11 hours, one uninterrupted rest period of at least 10 hours, and one uninterrupted rest period of at least 8 hours, whereby uninterrupted rest periods may follow one another.

9.4.7 Shift Work

According to national Dutch law, an employee works a night shift if he must work for more than 1 hour between the hours of midnight and 6 am. This regulation improves the protection provided by the WTD, which considers as a night worker any worker who, during the night time, works at least 3 hours of his daily working time. The legislation in the Netherlands stipulates that a night shift may not involve more than 10 hours of work, whereas the WTD sets up that limit at 8 hours but exceptions are allowed. If a night shift ends after 2 am, this must be followed by a minimum of 14 hours of non-work time. This may be shortened to 8 hours a maximum of once per week if the type of work or the business circumstances justifies this. If a night shift ends before 2 am, it must be followed by 11 consecutive hours of resting time. An employee may work a 12-hour night shift a maximum of five times per 2 weeks and 22 times per year. After a 12-hour night shift, he must have at least 12 hours of resting time. After a series of three or more night shifts, an employee must have at least 46 hours of resting time.

The legislation in the Netherlands regulates also the maximum number of night shifts that an employee may work during a reference period of 16 weeks.[16] Collective agreements might increase the number of night shifts from 117 to 140 night shifts per year if there is justification based on the type of work or due to special business circumstances. Furthermore, if the employee only works on the 'edge of the night', for example if the working day starts at 4 am, then the collective agreement may establish that the employee may work a maximum of 38 hours every 2 weeks between the hours of midnight and 6 am. Since the new Working Time Act came into effect on 1 April 2007, the transitional scheme for permanent night work applies in the Netherlands indefinitely.[17]

---

[16] In principle, an employee may work a maximum of 36 night shifts in a 16-week period. Moreover, an employee may not work more than seven consecutive shifts if one of these shifts is a night shift. This maximum may be extended by collective agreement to eight shifts if the type of work or business circumstances justifies it. If the employee only works a night shift occasionally (less than 16 times in 16 weeks), the regular rules for day shifts apply, namely: on average 48 hours of work per week during a reference period of 16 weeks. Finally, if an employee regularly works night shifts (16 times or more during a 16-week period), he may not work more than an average of 40 hours per week within those 16 weeks.

[17] According to that scheme, if an employee already worked mainly at night before 1 January 1996, he/she may continue this work pattern after 1 April 2007

Concerning the obligation established in Article 11 WTD of taking all necessary measures to ensure that an employer who regularly uses night workers brings the information to the attention of the competent authorities, the legislation in the Netherlands seems to comply with that requirement. However, concerning the obligation of Article 12 WTD on ensuring health and safety protection, prevention services and facilities which are appropriate to the specific nature of night work or shift work, the European Commission has pointed out that the reference of the Dutch government to the general legislation on health and safety of workers might not suffice to fulfil that duty (European Commission 2010). A large proportion (51 per cent) of Dutch employees regularly work in the evenings, and this figure is rising. According to the WageIndicator, the percentage of employees who regularly work at night increased from 43 per cent between 2004 and 2007 to 51 per cent in 2010. Compared with the previous period (September 2004–March 2007), the percentage of employees that regularly works on Saturdays or Sundays rose sharply from 30 per cent to 43.6 per cent and 18 per cent to 28.9 per cent respectively.

9.5 THE USE OF DEROGATIONS AND EXCEPTIONS

The most frequently used derogation of the WTD is Article 17.3 WTD, which allows Member States to derogate from the Directive's requirements regarding daily and weekly rests, rest breaks, length of night work and length of reference periods in a detailed range of specific situations or activities (European Commission 2010).

In principle, the legislation in the Netherlands regarding daily breaks and rest periods complies with the minimum rest periods set up by Articles 3 to 5 of the WTD. Also the derogations allowed by the national regulation comply with the EU legal framework as far as they are included in the derogations provided by Articles 17 to 18 WTD. These derogations are applicable when, on account of the specific characteristics of the activity concerned, the duration of the working time is not measured and/or predetermined or can be determined by the workers themselves, and in particular in the case of managing executives, family workers and workers of religious communities. Provided that alternative equivalent periods of compensatory rest or appropriate protection are afforded to workers by means of regulation or collective agreement,

providing that in every period of 4 consecutive weeks he/she is not working more than 20 night shifts (Ministry of Social Affairs and Employment, 2010).

derogations to the general resting periods set up by the WTD are also admitted for activities which imply distant/offshore work, security and surveillance activities, for activities needing continuity of service or production (i.e. healthcare, residential institutions and prisons, docks and airports, press, radio, television, postal services, fire and civil protection services, gas, water and electricity production, transmission and distribution, research, agriculture, transport of passengers, etc.); when there is a foreseeable surge of activity (i.e. agriculture, tourism and postal services); and in several activities in railway transport and in cases of accidents or risk of accident. Finally, derogations to the minimum daily and weekly rest periods are admitted in the case of shift work activities when the worker is changing shifts and in the case of activities involving periods of work split up over the day, particularly those of cleaning staff.

In the case of the Netherlands, the Working Hours Decree contains exceptions and additions to the Working Time Act. There are general exceptions that apply for certain employees and certain situations, and exceptions that apply for certain sectors, such as healthcare or mining. These sectors therefore are subject to the general regulations of the Working Hours Act and the Working Hours Decree and the separate sector regulations. Moreover, several provisions of the Dutch Working Time Act and the special and sectoral regulations on working time can be modified or adapted by collective agreements (CLAs or company level between the employer and the works council).[18] This possibility is foreseen by Article 18 WTD, which allows derogations from the breaks, minimum daily and weekly resting time, and references periods set up by the Directive as long as those derogations are made by means of collective agreements concluded between the two sides of industry at national or regional level or, in conformity with the rules laid down by them, by means of collective agreement or agreements concluded between the two sides of industry at a lower level. These derogations are allowed on the condition that equivalent compensating rest periods are granted to the workers concerned or, in exceptional cases where it is not possible for objective reasons to grant such periods, the workers concerned are granted appropriate protection.

---

[18] Unless otherwise stated in the law, the application of exceptions in on-site standby duty, on-call during breaks, break waived, longer night shift during the week and reference period extended to 52 weeks, is only possible by collective agreement (Ministry of Social Affairs and Employment 2010).

9.6 SPECIFIC INDUSTRIES

According to Directive 2000/34/EC from 1 August 2004, the Working Time Directive applies to all sectors of activity, unless other Community instruments contain more specific requirements on the organisation of working time for certain occupations or occupational activities. The previously excluded workers who are now covered by the Directive include doctors in training, offshore workers, workers on seagoing fishing vessels, non-mobile workers in civil aviation, workers in inland waterway or lake transport, most rail workers and some workers in local road transport. Special provisions of the Working Time Directive apply to some of these groups.

As has already been mentioned, the WTD also foresees derogations and exceptions to the applicability of the general rules on the organisation of working time. The derogations may be adopted by means of collective agreements or agreements between the two sides of industry in the case of certain activities, such as security and surveillance activities intended to protect property and persons; activities involving the need for continuity of service (hospital care, agriculture and media); and where there is a foreseeable surge of activity (agriculture, tourism, postal services and railway transport).

In the Netherlands, there are several specific sector regulations based on the Working Time Decree. In principle, unless otherwise stated, application of the specific regulations is only possible by collective arrangement. The sectors where special regulations on working time are found are the following (Ministry of Social Affairs and Employment 2010): audio-visual productions, dredging activities, cinemas, performing arts, boarding schools for children of bargees and occupational travellers; winter maintenance work; exhibition construction and ship repair; mining industry; bakeries and patisseries; defence; and young employees, hospitality industry, volunteer police and non-nautical inland navigation personnel.

Other sectors with special regulations regarding working time are:

1. *Fire brigade*. The derogation applies to the municipal fire brigade and company fire brigades, and both volunteer and professional fire brigades. In this case, the specific regulations concern exclusively the regulations for on-call duty and on-site standby duty. Normal activities, such as extinguishing fires, are subject to the regulations of the Working Time Act. For the volunteer fire brigade the maximum working time for on-call duty is 14 hours in every period

of 24 consecutive hours and 48 hours of work (main occupation plus fire brigade work) on average per week, measured over 16 weeks (also in the case of on-call duty partly at night). The normal restrictions on on-call duty apply to the volunteer fire brigade, except if the individual is head or deputy head of the fire brigade. Among other more specific arrangements on on-site standby duty, a worker must not have more than one on-site standby shift per 7 consecutive days. For professional firemen a system of a maximum 62 presence shifts in any period of 26 consecutive weeks applies. In this case the regular rules over resting periods for on-call work are applicable, unless the number of workers needed to ensure the unimpeded progress of the service is below the required minimum. In that case, the minimum rest period of 11 hours between shifts is not compulsory. There has been some case law ruling that the current practice at the town halls of using rosters of 54 hours per week for the fire brigades is against the regime established by the Working Hours Decree – in line with the WTD – of a maximum 48 hours per week working time. In this case, the court has allowed the employer to offer the firemen to sign an individual 'opt-out' agreement, on the basis of which the maximum working time can be up to 60 hours per week on average – including, of course, payment of overtime compensation. This agreement was seen as a transitional solution until a uniform national agreement for the working time of the fire brigade is reached.[19]

2. *Health sector*. A number of specific regulations apply to work in the healthcare sector, for nurses and workers in care (i.e. physical therapists, laboratory assistants, and workers in home care and maternity care), doctors, midwives and for ambulance employees. These regulations replace the corresponding regulations in the Working Time Act. In this sector the use of standby duty and on-site standby duty occurs regularly. If an employee first works a normal, scheduled shift and a period of exclusively standby time follows that, both periods together constitute a standby shift. The regular regulations for on-site standby duty apply for on-site standby duty for nursing and care.

   'Doctors in training' is a special group within the healthcare sector that deserves attention. Doctors in training were expressly excluded from the scope of Working Time Directive 93/104/EC (Article 1.3). However, this was changed by the amending Directive

---

[19] Judgment of the Court Haarlem, 13-04-2007, 133140/KG ZA 07-115.

2000/34/EC. Therefore, doctors in training are now covered by the Working Time Directive in the same way as other workers, except in the Netherlands (and Hungary and the UK), which have chosen to use extended transitional arrangements, in accordance with Article 17.5 WTD. Accordingly, in the Netherlands, the working time of doctors in training may amount to up to 52 hours per week, averaged over not more than 6 months, until 1 August 2011. This extension was subject to the national social partners reaching agreement on a joint plan for achieving a 48-hour average weekly working time in hospitals by 1 August 2011.

There are also specific rules on working time for midwives (including midwives working in extramural healthcare and midwives in training).

9.7 CASE LAW

In 2012 the Working Time Act was reformed to include a new definition of the concepts of 'working time' and 'rest period'. This legal amendment was the result of a number of cases where there was a discussion on the lack of proper definition of working time in Dutch law and when an interpretation in conformity of the national law and the WTD was denied because it could jeopardise the principle of legal security.[20] For example, it was unclear whether travel time during working hours was counted as working time. Also, in some professions, such as fire-fighters or in the care sector, the employees often spend the night at work, under on-call duty. According to EU law, this falls under working time, even if the workers sleep during this duty. By amending the Working Hours Act the definition of 'working time' was clarified. The law states now that working time is when the employee performs work 'under the authority of the employer'. However, the different terminology used by the Dutch law might still lead to some confusion. Whether travel time is considered working time depends on whether the employee travels 'under the authority of the employer' – in other words, whether the employee is during that trip 'at the disposal of the employer'. Other important elements to determine if travel time is working time are also whether the agreement reached between employer and employee includes this issue, or whether under the collective agreement applicable those hours or

[20] JB 2009/99 Council of State, 04-03-2009; Judgment of the Court Utrecht, of 19-01-2010, SBR 08/966; and judgment of the Court Breda, of 28-04-2008, AWB- 07_3585, inter alia.

wages should be paid.[21] This issue is often dealt with in collective agreements or company arrangements.

In general the subject of working time has not very often led to litigation. Relevant cases that are available tend to relate to conflicts between CLA actors, as the individual worker does not go to court for problems over working time in fear of conflict with the employer which might make things worse. Only in case of dismissal might one consider to do this.

The most relevant national case law dealing with the implementation in the Netherlands of the WTD relates to the definition of on-call time. The Working Hours Act 1996 formerly defined inactive on-call time at the workplace as rest time. However, the Court of Justice's decisions about on-call working time were applied by national courts in a number of cases brought by fire-fighters and ambulance workers about the treatment of on-call time as working time. Consequently, the Working Time Decree 605/2005 amended national law to define inactive on-call time at the workplace as working time, with effect from 1 June 2006. According to national law, collective agreements which pre-date the Decree are now void, to the extent that they define inactive on-call time other than as working time. This case law has considerable implications for sectors using extensive on-call time, such as health, residential care, nursing homes, support services for people with disabilities, midwifery, ambulance and fire services, and defence forces. As a temporary measure, the Netherlands has introduced a temporary and limited opt-out, under which workers in services using extensive on-call time may agree to work up to 60 hours per week including on-call time, averaged over 6 months (see section 9.4 on on-call work).

What is more, in the case of on-call time, the Working Time Decree 2005 provided for a minimum of 11 hours' daily rest before and after each period of on-call duty at the workplace. However, a shorter rest could be applied for 'objective reasons', or a collective agreement could provide for the worker to take extra remuneration instead of the 11-hour immediate rest. The Arnhem Court of Appeal held in January 2007[22] that these rules failed to respect the minimum daily rest required under the WTD following the *Jaeger* case. Consequently, the Working Time Decree was amended, and now sets an obligatory rest period of at least 11 consecutive hours immediately after an on-call duty at the workplace. In

---

[21] Advice by the Council of State, N0.W12.11.0120/III, The Hague, 9.06.2011.

[22] LJN: AZ6434, Arnhem Court of Appeal, 2006/1110.

exceptional cases where this is objectively impossible, this may once a week be reduced to 10 hours and once a week to 8 hours, on condition that the next rest is extended by a corresponding number of hours. Such a reduction must be agreed under a collective agreement, or between the employer and the works council. In any event, each week must contain a minimum of 90 hours' rest consisting of six daily rest periods of at least 11 hours, and one weekly rest period of at least 24 hours.

Also following the *Jaeger* judgment, both the court in Rotterdam in 2006[23] and The Hague[24] on 27 February 2007 put in the right a fire-fighter who wanted full pay for 48 hours instead of 54 hours. Both courts found that the workweek of fire-fighters may take up to 48 hours and no more. The Fire Department, as a good employer, should be offering the fire-fighter a schedule of 48 hours for a full salary.

Finally, there is also relevant domestic case law about how employers should comply with the obligation to register working hours applicable in some sectors and on enforceable entitlements for leave during illness (Art. 7 WTD). The ruling on *Schultz-Hoff/Deutsche Rentenversicherung Bund*, and *Stringer and others versus Her Majesty's Revenue and Customs*,[25] has resulted in administrative-law and civil-law jurisdiction at national level. Regarding civil law, Article 7:635 subsection 4 of the Dutch Civil Code provides that sick employees can only accrue holiday rights over the last 6 months of their sick leave and that partially disabled employees can only accrue holiday entitlement over hours worked. This is contrary to Article 7 of the Directive. Since citizens cannot make a direct appeal to this Directive,[26] the legislator must amend the aforementioned Act. On 24 May 2011, the Upper House agreed to a legislative bill to abolish[27] the distinction in the way sick and healthy employees accrue paid leave.[28] The new Act took effect on 1 January 2012. Regarding administrative law, on 18 July 2011 the Central Appeals

---

[23] Sector kanton Rechtbank Rotterdam, 743949 LJN: AZ2887.

[24] Court case Hague Administrative Sector, 27 February 2007, LJN: AZ9327.

[25] *Gerhard Schultz-Hoff v Deutsche Rentenversicherung Bund* (C-350/06) and *Stringer and Others v Her Majesty's Revenue and Customs* (C-520/06), Court of Justice of the European Union, 20 January 2011, Dutch Law Reports 2009.252.

[26] Court of Amsterdam, 10 November 2009, National Case-Law Number BK4648.

[27] Proceedings of the *Upper House* 2010-2011, no. 28, item 7.

[28] It can be agreed in writing to depart from this provision for the accrual of paid leave above the minimum set out in Article 7 of the Directive.

Tribunal ruled[29] in proceedings involving civil servants[30] that legal status regulations[31] restricting the accrual of paid leave entitlement during sick leave, without a guaranteed minimum of 4 weeks, are contrary to EU law.

A last case worth mentioning is one in response to questions of German and British judges about the interpretation of the Working Time Directive of the European Court of Justice on 20 January 2009 ruling on the interpretation of Article 7 of the Directive. It ensures an employee's annual leave with pay for 4 weeks, which cannot be replaced by an allowance, except in case of termination of employment. The ruling of the Court of Justice EC is that it is contrary to Article 7 of the Directive as a sick employee is not able to make use of his right to annual leave with pay and therefore will not receive financial compensation. In a dispute in Utrecht between an employer and employee on the amount of accrued leave during disability,[32] the magistrate acknowledged that the judgments of the European Court of Justice have no direct effect in the relationship between an employer and an employee. However, the magistrate did see room for a Directive-conforming interpretation. The Cantonal Court does not interpret a Directive to a compliant implementation of Article 7:635 paragraph 4, Civil Code (in short: 'accrual of holidays during the last six months of disability') as against the law (*contra legem*), since Article 7:638 paragraph 1 Civil Code stipulates that the employer is required to allow the employee each year the holiday to be taken under Article 7:634 Civil Code which he is entitled to as a minimum (i.e. the 4 weeks' holiday required under the Working Time Directive are guaranteed). In a ruling of 10 November 2009, the Amsterdam Court held that conformity with interpretation leads to an application of the law '*contra legem*' and therefore is not possible.[33]

9.8 GENERAL POLITICAL AWARENESS AND APPRECIATION OF THE DIRECTIVE

Recently, the European Commission has presented an evaluation report on the implementation by the Member States of Directive 2003/88/EC.

---

[29] Highest Civil Service Tribunal.

[30] Central Appeals Tribunal 18/07/11, National Case-Law Number BR0268.

[31] In this case, the General Legal Status (Police) Decree.

[32] District Court Utrecht, 14 October 2009, www.rechtspraak.nl, LJN: BK0017 (accessed 14 January 2013).

[33] District Court Amsterdam, 10 November 2009, www.rechtspraak.nl, LJN: BK464 (accessed 14 January 2013).

On the occasion of the elaboration of that report the social partners were consulted on their opinion of the implementation at national level of the EU rules on working time. In the Netherlands trade unions were dissatisfied with the consultation process during the national transposition of the Directive. They deem that the Directive has been transposed into national law in a way which reduced the level of protection previously available. Trade unions consider the recent changes to working time legislation make it less favourable than the previous law as regards overtime, night work and co-determination.

Employers, on the contrary, praise legislative changes introduced in the Working Time Act in 2007[34] for simplifying working time obligations, but considered the protection for night workers as still set too high.

The evaluation of the implementation of the Directive by the Dutch government was in general positive. However, the government indicated that the Directive has had a negative impact on the use of on-call working time in some sectors. The problems arose from major difficulties with transposition of the European Court of Justice's interpretation in the *SiMAP* and *Jaeger* cases regarding on-call time and immediate compensatory rest, particularly in specified sectors (healthcare, defence forces, services for persons with disabilities, emergency services and firefighters). Transport was also mentioned as a sector where working time rules were considered to present particular difficulties of application in the Netherlands, especially on the inland waterway transport sector (though this might be solved in the short term as the social partners are currently discussing a possible agreement for this sector). The government also stated that revision of the Directive regarding the treatment of on-call time, the timing of compensatory rest and the extension of reference periods to 12 months by legislation remains a major and urgent priority. Moreover, the government pointed out the convenience of streamlining the content of the WTD with more specific directives in the transport sector (European Commission 2010).

The implementation in the Netherlands of the WTD has been considered by some scholars as 'non/in-flexible' in comparison with other EU Member States, especially because in the Netherlands collective agreements play an important role in implementing the Working Time Directive (Boonstra and Schaapman 2004).

---

34 State Bulletin of the Netherlands, 2006, 632.

9.9 CONCLUSIONS

Despite some problems, the implementation of the WTD in the Netherlands has not had a major impact nor has it been controversial. However, some discrepancies between the EU law and domestic definitions of the crucial concept of working time do persist which could lead to further litigation in this area in the case of on-call work. In general terms, the implementation of the WTD has left the main problem relating to working time in the Netherlands, its 'successful' part-time model, untouched. Until the 1990s the Netherlands considered this to be the 'ideal' model both for a combination of work and care and for employment growth ('The Dutch Miracle'; see Visser and Hemerijck 1997). However, part-time work in the Netherlands is gendered; the unequal division in household and caring tasks remains and the constraint of motherhood is not lessened. The long-term effects of part-time work are far from ideal (O'Reilly and Fagan 1998; Wattis et al. 2006; Yerkes 2009), resulting in diminished career prospects, lower income and, in many cases, reduced rights to social security benefits such as pensions (Lewis 2002). From an employer's point of view, part-time availability means less labour available in a labour market situation of labour shortages to come.

The combination of paid work and other responsibilities increasingly provides time bottlenecks. More and more Dutch workers experience significant time constraints and lack of time. This is related to the fact that more people have multiple responsibilities and thus divide their time on paid work, housework, care, volunteering and other activities. In addition, there is a continual acceleration rate in both economy and society due to developments in ICT and international markets. Companies need flexible deployment of personnel to survive in an international market and to respond to new customer needs. The combination of these factors leads to a need for flexibility, but a significant change in a way that addresses this new reality is missing. Within the organisations the growth of part-time work made it possible that a distinction could be made between operating time and working time, so relatively few innovative arrangements such as a flexible start and end times or opportunities to plan the work over the week have been introduced in the Netherlands (SER 2011). As a result, a majority of workers between 20 and 65 years of age do feel having time constraints/pressure a couple of times a week or month (Cloïn et al. 2010). Up till now this problem of dealing with time constraints has been solved through more part-time work. However, this leads to a part-time work paradox: part-time constraints as a coping strategy keep the traditional time format – one of the main causes of time constraints – intact. As such, part-time work is a lazy catch-all to avoid modernising work organisation. The cost for society is considerable: time pressure, anxiety among civilians, under-utilisation of human resources, traffic jams and under-utilisation of buildings and equipment outside rush hours (SEOR 2010). Unfortunately the WTD as it stands does not provide solutions to this problem.

BIBLIOGRAPHY

Anxo, D. and J.-Y. Boulin (eds) (2006) *Working Time Option over the Life Course: New Work Patterns and Company Strategies*. Dublin: European Foundation for the Improvement of Working Life and Working Conditions.

Barnard, C., S. Deakin and R. Hobbs (2003a) 'Opting out of the 48-hour week: employer necessity or individual choice? An empirical study of the operation of Article 18(1) (b) of the Working Time Directive in the UK', *Industrial Law Journal*, 32 (4): 223–52.

Barnard, C., S. Deakin and R. Hobbs (2003b) '"Fog in the Channel, continent isolated": Britain as a model for EU social and economic policy', *Industrial Relations Journal*, 34 (4): 461–76.

Boonstra, C. and M. Schaapman (2004) 'Arbeidstijdenwet in Europees perspectief', *ARBO Magazine*, September: 12–15.

Cloïn, M., M. Schols, A. van den Broek, and M. Koutamanis (2010) *Tijd op orde? Een analyse van de tijdsorde vanuit het perspectief van de burger.* Den Haag: Sociaal Cultureel Planbureau.

ETUC (2005), *The Coordination of Collective Bargaining in 2006*, Resolution adopted by the ETUC Executive Committee in their meeting held in Brussels on 5–6 December 2005, Brussels. www.etuc.org.

EU (2010) *Comparative Analysis of Working Time in the European Union*. Dublin: European Foundation for the Improvement of Living and Working Conditions.

European Commission (2005) *Proposal for a Directive of the European Parliament and of the Council amending Directive 2003/88/EC concerning certain aspects of the organization of working time*, COM (2005) 246, Brussels, 31 May.

European Commission (2010), *Commission staff working paper: detailed report on the implementation by Member States of Directive 2003/88/EC concerning certain aspects of the organisation of working time* ('The Working Time Directive'), SEC (2010) 1611 final.

International Labour Organisation (2004) *Conditions of Work and Employment Programme Information Sheet WT-18. Working Time and Productivity.* Geneva: ILO.

Jacobs, A. and M. Schmidt (2001) 'The right to part-time work: The Netherlands and Germany compared', *International Journal of Comparative Labour Law and Industrial Relations*, 17 (3), 374.

Klaveren, M. van, K. Tijdens and N. Ramos Martín (2008) 'Working time', in M. van Klaveren and K. Tijdens (eds), *Bargaining Issues in Europe: Comparing Countries and Industries*. Brussels: ETUI, 25–60.

Knegt, R., J. A. de Groot, R. H. van het Kaar, G. J. Mulder, J. R. Popma and E. Verhulp (2011) *'Het Nieuwe Werken' en de arbeidsrechtelijke regelgeving*. Amsterdam: HSI.

Kodz, J. et al. (2003) *Working Long Hours: A Review of the Evidence. Volume 1 – Main Report*. London: Department of Trade and Industry.

Kuip, S. W. and E. Verhulp (2000) *De Wet Aanpassing Arbeidsduur* (WT Act). The Hague: SDU Juridisch & Fiscaal.

Lewis, J. (2002) 'Individualisation, assumptions about the existence of an adult worker model and the shift towards contractualism', in A. H. Carling, S. Duncan and R. Edwards (eds), *Analysing Families: Morality and Rationality in Policy and Practice*. London: Routledge, 51–6.

Ministry of OCW (2009) *Internationaal Onderzoek Tijdbeleid*. Door Dehora Consultancy Group iov min OCW. Zoetermeer: Ministerie van Onderwijs, Wetenschap en Cultuur.

Ministry of Social Affairs and Employment (2010) *The Working Hours Act*. Information for Employers and Employees. The Hague: Ministry of Social Affairs and Employment.

OECD (2009) *Employment Outlook: Tackling the Jobs Crisis*. Paris: OECD.

O'Reilly, J. and C. Fagan (1998) *Part-Time Prospects: An International Comparison of Part-Time Work in Europe, North America and the Pacific Rim*. London: Routledge.

SEOR (2010) *Maatschappelijke kosten-baten analyse van de tijdsordening van de Nederlandse samenleving*. In opdracht van het ministerie van OCW.

SER (2011) *Tijden van de samenleving. Slimmer organiseren van tijd en plaats van arbeid en dienstverlening*. Den Haag: SER.

Visser, J. (2002) 'The first part-time economy in the world: a model to be followed?', *Journal of European Social Policy*, 12 (1): 23–41.

Visser, J. and A. Hemerijck (1997) *A Dutch Miracle: Job Growth, Welfare Reform and Corporatism in the Netherlands*. Amsterdam: Amsterdam University Press.

Visser, J. and M. Yerkes (2008) 'Part-time work and the legacy of breadwinner welfare states: a panel study of women's employment patterns in Germany, the United Kingdom and the Netherlands, 1992–2002', in L. Kenworthy and A. Hicks (eds), *Methods and Substance*. New York: Palgrave Macmillan, 221–59.

Wattis, C., M. A. Yerkes, S. Lloyd, M. Hernandez-Sanchez, L. Dawson, K. Standing and M. Edwards (2006) *Combining Work and Family Life: Removing the Barriers to Women's Progression* (ESF report). Liverpool: Liverpool John Moores University.

Workgroup Het Nieuwe Werken en Arbeidsomstandigheden (2010) *Handreiking Het Nieuwe Werken: hoe blijf je er gezond bij?* Aandachtspunten bij een verantwoorde introductie. Utrecht: Kenniscentrum Werk & Vervoer.

Yerkes, M. (2009) 'Part-time work in the Dutch Welfare State: the ideal combination of work and care?', *Policy and Politics*, 37 (4): 535–52.

10. Implementation of the EU Working Time Directive in the United Kingdom[1]

Ralf Rogowski

The implementation of the EU Working Time Directive (WTD) in the United Kingdom has a chequered history. In fact it creates a unique case of stubborn resistance, half-hearted compliance and continuous attempts to opt out from parts or the whole of the Directive. This behaviour is, however, not unusual given the UK's general attitude towards implementation of EU law, in particular in the area of social and employment policy.

The chapter outlines both the British approach to implementing EU law and the concrete measure taken in implementing the WTD. It consists of five sections. The first section provides contextual information on the history of regulation of working time and Britain's relation to European social and employment policy. The second section analyses the UK approach towards implementing EU law, with a particular focus on the resistance to the WTD before its transposition in 1998. The third section introduces the Working Time Regulations (WTR) of 1998, the UK's legal measure of implementation of the WTD. The fourth section contains information on the impact of the WTD in British courts and specific industries in which implementation has caused problems, and the final fifth section comments on the unique political reactions in the UK to the Directive.

[1] I would like to thank Christian Mecklenburg-Guzman and Nutanesh Ramasawmy for research assistance and Mark Hall and Ania Zbyszewska for comments.

10.1 GENERAL HISTORICAL CONTEXT

One of the reasons for the difficulties British labour law has with European Union law relates to its history and in particular its reluctance throughout the 19th and 20th century to use legislation in regulating employment. The early attempts of legislation in the 19th century, the Factory Acts of the 1840s, were actually concerned with working time. They limited working hours for children and women. However, they did not lead to a comprehensive set of legislation. Britain opted instead for a system of collective laissez-faire based on the principles of voluntarism and state abstentionism that emerged in the second half of the 19th and the early 20th century. This approach dominated British labour law until the 1960s and meant that the regulation of working time was largely left to collective bargaining. For working time regulations this approach meant, on the one hand, incremental improvements of the early factory legislation and some reduction of working hours, but, on the other hand, prevented the emergence of proper 'general statutory regulation' and led instead to a 'pattern of selective and partial regulation' (Deakin and Morris 2009, 280).

Furthermore, the British approach to legislation is shaped by its common law focus that has characterised the legal system on the British Isles ever since it decided not to follow the Roman law path adopted on the European continent. The common law approach operates with precedents that result from case law; judicial decision-making is the main basis of common law and not legislation. Before employment protection legislation was introduced in the 1960s and 1970s, labour law was largely regulated by contract law governed by common law principles. Employment law was referred to as the law of master and servant and employment protection derived from expressive and implicit terms of the employment contract introduced and interpreted by common law courts.

Comprehensive labour legislation granting employment protection for all employees was introduced after the review of the industrial relations and the labour law system by the Donovan Commission in the mid-1960s. During the 1970s a number of employment protection measures, including equal pay, unfair dismissal and antidiscrimination laws, were enacted. This development was influenced by the two events of the accession of the UK to the European Economic Community in 1972 and the change of government from Conservative to Labour in 1974. During the short period mid to end of the 1970s, EU labour law was implemented relatively effectively. However, with the change of government in the UK back to the Conservatives under Thatcher in 1979, advancing employment protection through legislation came to a halt. The UK government adopted a hostile attitude towards workers' rights that also characterised its view towards European social and employment policies. Due to this opposition virtually no constructive influence on European social policy came from the UK during the conservative years and in only a few areas, in particular health and safety of workers and equal treatment, was European law followed.

During the 1980s the UK pursued a programme of deregulation of workers' rights which meant not only the removal of statutory protection, even though it had been in its extent very limited, but also undermining collective bargaining. At the European level the UK blocked initiatives of expanding employment protection proposed by the Delors Commission. The Thatcher government rejected on ideological grounds the Community Charter of Fundamental Social Rights of Workers, which was adopted in 1989 by all Member States with the exception of the UK.

Open confrontation occurred at the Maastricht Summit in 1992 at which the UK government refused to support the social policy proposals. It opted out of the so-called 'Social Chapter' (the Social Protocol and the Agreement on Social Policy) and adopted a minimum compliance approach. However, its insistence on prioritising labour market flexibility over workers' rights had some success later in the 1990s when European employment policies switched from focussing on employment protection to employment promotion while establishing the European Employment Strategy (Ashiagbor 2005; Rogowski 2008).

When Labour, under Blair, came into power in 1997, the British government abandoned its hostile attitude towards European social and employment policies. However, throughout the 13 years of Labour (1997 to 2010) the British government never engaged constructively with European social policies and remained passive (see also Bercusson 2009, ch. 2). Since the Conservatives' return to power in 2010 (in a coalition government with the Liberal Democrats), the familiar hostile tone has characterised official policy again. Indeed European social policy, and in particular the reform of the Working Time Directive, have been chosen as special targets by the Conservatives (further discussed in Section 10.5).

As far as regulation of working time is concerned, it has had little impact on actual hours worked in Britain. Britain is known for having an excessive working time culture. In a report commissioned by the Trade Union Congress (TUC) the following figures are documented for 2005: '3.6 million employees regularly work more than 48 hours per week, while nearly 5 million employees (4,759,000) worked on average an extra day a week in unpaid overtime (7 hours 24 minutes)' (Fagan et al. 2006, 8). It should be noted that this was the situation seven years after implementation of the WTD. According to figures released by the Chartered Institute of Personnel and Development, however, the average hours worked are falling and 'just under a fifth of people in employment work[ed] more than 45 hours a week' in 2011 (CIPD 2011).

10.2 THE UK APPROACH IN IMPLEMENTING THE WTD AND EU LAW IN GENERAL

Implementing EU law has been controversial in the UK since it joined the EU and this certainly holds true for the WTD. However, the political debate and attitudes have to be distinguished from actual legal implementation. In legal terms, the UK has in general not been a culprit when it comes to following legally binding EU law. Adopting Gerda Falkner and her team's classification of cultures of compliance with European law, Britain belongs to the 'world of domestic politics' in which countries transpose directives in time and in a correct manner; only in case of manifest conflict between EU legal requirements and domestic interest politics does non-compliance occur (Falkner et al. 2005, 2008).

Implementation research has introduced a number of hypotheses, some of which can be used for a discussion of the approach taken by the UK in implementing EU law. For example, the implementation process of EU directives can be divided into three stages: legal, practical and monitoring implementation (Lelieveldt and Princen 2011, ch. 11). Oliver Treib (2008) has called these three stages transposition, enforcement and application, which he claims are all monitored by the European Commission (Figure 10.1).

The advantage of differentiating implementation into three stages lies in the identification of different actors involved in the different stages of implementing EU law, in particular directives. The first stage, legal implementation or transposition, depends on the cooperation of government and administration as well as interest groups. However, after transposition the incorporation of EU law into the domestic legal and political culture depends on enforcement and on actual application, which requires the involvement of further actors.

Furthermore, at the levels of practical implementation or enforcement and application EU regulations can encounter resistance due to different traditions and cultures of labour market regulations or voluntarist traditions. A 'policy misfit' (on this concept see, in particular, Treib 2005) can occur when a high degree of change in domestic legislation and existing agreements and practices is required in order to fully implement the

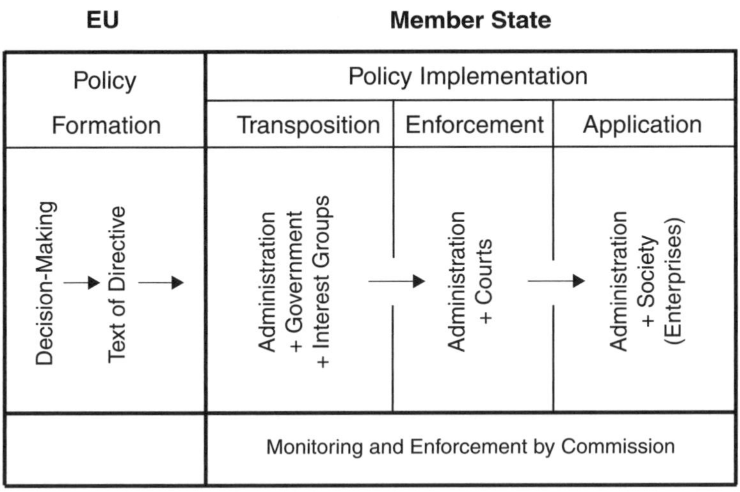

Source: Treib (2008), 6.

Figure 10.1 Stages of the implementation process of Directives

European regulation. Factors relevant for such an assessment are not only the number of legislative reforms but also administrative reforms, for example the reorganisation or attribution of new assignments to agencies, the formation of new bodies, the relationship between the state and interest groups, and economic cost implications.

Oliver Treib applied his misfit theory in analysing the UK's implementation of the WTD in the following way:

> the Tory government under John Major was firmly opposed to the European standards and refused to accept their implementation until it finally was voted out of office in May 1997. At first glance, this determined resistance by the UK government is in line with the expectations of the misfit hypothesis, since the Directive required significant reforms which involved enormous costs for private and public employers. The UK's tradition of voluntarism, together with the deregulation policies of Margaret Thatcher, meant that prior to the Directive, there were neither any statutory annual leave entitlements nor any legal provisions on working time limits or rest periods in the UK. This lack of state intervention in the area of working time was coupled with a pronounced 'long-hours culture'. (Treib 2003, 10)

Treib is certainly right to point out that the UK has comparatively few legal provisions in place for the regulation of working time. However, it can be disputed that the implementation of WTD led to 'enormous costs' for employers. In any case, not having proper working time regulations creates 'enormous costs' for employees.

It has been noted that failures of the UK in implementing directives found by the CJEU have created 'a dynamic tension between EC and UK labour law' (Bercusson 2009, 44–5). Although the Treaty of Rome's social policy provisions have been honoured in general, the Conservative governments of Thatcher and Major followed zealously a neo-liberal programme that perceives state intervention in the labour market as distortion and impediment to the flexibility of the alleged free labour market. These governments adopted the view that EU social policy hindered the UK's programme of deregulation of employment relations. The non-binding Recommendation on the 40-hour work week adopted in 1975 and a Draft Council Recommendation on reduction of working time in 1983 were both opposed by the UK, as well as all the other draft directives regulating working conditions, including the directives on part-time work and temporary work.

When the WTD was adopted in 1993 the UK government rejected the objectives of the Directive. It was opposed to setting ceilings to the daily, weekly and annual working time and limiting 'unsocial working hours', for example night shifts, and granting annual leave periods and free health check-ups. The UK government of the day was not even persuaded by the possibility that the WTD allows working in excess of WTD limits if the worker explicitly agrees (individual opt-out).

In fact the UK government went further and challenged the legality of the WTD. It sued the Council, arguing that the Working Time Directive had a defective legal basis.[2] The Directive should have been adopted on the basis of former Articles 100 or 235 EC Treaty, which required unanimity within the Council, rather than Article 118a EC Treaty, which allowed a health and safety measure to be adopted by majority vote in the Council. According to the UK, the connection of the areas regulated by the WTD, weekly working time, paid annual leave and rest periods, with the health and safety of workers was too tenuous and not supported by scientific evidence. In the UK's view, the WTD in reality represented an attempt to use the organisation of working time in the interests of job creation and reduced unemployment and to promote overall improvement

[2] *United Kingdom v Council of the European Union*, Case C-84/94 [1996] ECR I-5755 and Industrial Relations Law Reports (IRLR), Vol. 26, No. 1, January [1997] 32.

in living and working conditions of employees as part of the Community's social policy. The CJEU rejected the UK view and held that the principal objective of the WTD was the protection of the health and safety of workers by imposing 'minimum requirements for gradual implementation' within the meaning of Article 118a EC Treaty. 'It does not follow from the fact that the directive falls within the scope of Community social policy that it cannot properly be based on Article 118a, so long as it contributes to encouraging improvements as regards the health and safety of workers.'[3]

With the change of government in 1997 to Labour the resistance to the WTD was abandoned. It took a year to implement the WTD and the legal measure of implementation was secondary legislation in form of a Statutory Instrument (SI), called 'Regulation'. The official name was Working Time Regulations 1998, SI 1998/1833. The fact that the WTD was implemented by delegated (or secondary) legislation in accordance with the Statutory Instruments Act 1946 is not unusual. Most EU directives are implemented in this way in the UK and this practice reflects the frequent use of SIs in the UK in general, which outnumber the enactment of statutes.[4] Secondary legislation in the form of Statutory Instruments has equal effect in law although ministers can be legally challenged on the grounds that specific pieces of delegated legislation are not properly based on powers given by Acts.

The preferred or frequent usage of secondary over primary legislation can be assessed from a socio-political perspective. Using SIs saves time, since legislation can be introduced fairly quickly. Chances of meeting the implementation deadlines for EU directives are greater. And technical expertise and efficient use of resources are other advantages. However, there is also criticism of using delegated legislation. For many critics a main disadvantage is the removal of the issues regulated by directives from parliamentary debate. If the route of enacting the directive through a primary parliamentary act or statute is chosen, political scrutiny and an increase in accountability would be guaranteed. Furthermore, parliamentary deliberations would increase chances of EU regulations influencing reform processes of existing domestic policies in Britain.

---

[3] Ibid, IRLR at 36.

[4] Only 41 statutes in the form of General Public Acts in comparison to 2,969 SIs became law or were passed in 2010. Statistics proving data on statutes and SIs can be found at http://www.legislation.gov.uk/uksi/2010 and http://www.legislation.gov.uk/ukpga/2010. Accessed 15 December 2014.

10.3 THE UK'S LEGAL MEASURE OF IMPLEMENTATION: THE WORKING TIME REGULATIONS OF 1998

The process of transposing the WTD only began to take shape following the above-mentioned judgment of the CJEU in the Working Time Case,[5] which confirmed that the Directive had been validly adopted. Proposals put forward by the Conservative government in 1996 were subjected to further revision following the election of the Labour government in May 1997. In April 1998, the Department for Trade and Industry (DTI) published a consultation paper and draft regulations for bringing the WTD and relevant provisions of the Youth Working Time Directive 94/33 into force;[6] the WTR actually came into force on 1 October 1998 and have since been amended on a number of occasions.

The Labour government implemented the WTD in 1998 without great enthusiasm. Transposition was slow and an attempt was made to limit enforcement. However, one feature was outstanding and unique in comparison to implementation of WTD in other Member States. In Article 5(4) of the WTR a special reference was included to the possibility of granting workers the right to opt out of the 48-hour rule. According to the European Commission's 2003 Communication 'Concerning Certain Aspects of the Organization of Working Time' (European Commission 2003), the UK was at that time the only Member State since the enactment of the WTD in 1993 that made use of the Directive's blanket opt-out for workers to voluntarily decide on their working hours.[7]

In accordance with the WTD the WTR define in Article 2(1) WTR 'working time' as 'any period during which the worker is working, at the employer's disposal and carrying out his activity or duties, in accordance with national laws and/or practice' and a rest period as 'any period which is not working time'. It lays down limits on weekly working time, controls on night work and shift work, and minimum daily and weekly rest periods, but clarifies that this includes 'any period during which a worker is receiving relevant training' (Article 2(1) WTR). This is a

---

[5] *United Kingdom v Council of the European Union*, Case C-84/94 [1996] ECR I-5755.

[6] Measures to Implement Provisions of the EC Directives on the Organisation of Working Time and the Protection of Young People at Work, April 1998.

[7] Communication concerning certain aspects of the organization of working time COM(2003) 843 final, p. 8.

response to the *SiMAP* and *Jaeger* judgments,[8] in which the CJEU took the view that time spent on call by doctors could be 'working time' if they were required to be present at their place of work during this period, even if workers are allowed to sleep when their services are not required.

The WTR operate with a broad definition of the term 'worker' and include all those carrying out work for an employer, with the exception of those individuals whose work amounts to a business activity on their own account. Thus, agency workers, freelancers, casual workers and trainees are covered. The entitlements include the right to a minimum daily rest period of 11 consecutive hours between each working day, an uninterrupted rest period of not less than 24 hours in each 7-day period and an in-work rest break of at least 20 minutes where the working day is longer than 6 hours. It requires the employer to grant a minimum period of annual paid leave of 4 weeks. The original requirement that a new worker should complete 13 weeks of continuous employment before the right to paid holiday starts to accrue was removed with effect from 25 October 2001.

The limits of hours worked regulated in the WTR include a maximum weekly working time of 48 hours, including overtime, averaged over a 17-week reference period, and a maximum working period of 8 hours in any 24 hours, averaged over 17 weeks for night workers, while the same limit applies in the case of night workers whose jobs involve special hazards or heavy physical strain but without the possibility for averaging. Lastly, employers have the duty to provide free and confidential health checks for night workers and to transfer these workers, if they suffer from health problems connected with night work, to suitable day work where possible.

As mentioned, the UK took advantage of the individual opt-out permitted by Article 18(1)(b) WTD. It allows the employer to seek the worker's voluntary agreement that the 48-hour ceiling does not apply. However, the employee's opt-out does not relieve the employer from keeping records of the actual hours worked. The 1998 Regulations laid down detailed record-keeping rules but business complained that this 'gold-plated' the Directive (Barnard et al. 2003, 224). As a result of amendments made to the WTR in 1999, the record-keeping requirements were significantly watered down (Barnard 2000). The revised Section 4(2) WTR nowadays simply requires the employer to 'keep up-to-date

---

[8] Case C-303/98 *Sindicato de Medicos de Asistencia Publica (SiMAP) v Conselleria de Sanidad y Consumo de la Generalidad Valenciana.* [2000] ECR 1-7963 and Case C-151/02 *Landeshauptstadt Kiel v Norbert Jaeger* [2003] ECR I-8389.

records for all workers who carry out work to which it does not apply by reason of the fact that the employer has obtained the worker's agreement'.

10.4 THE WTD IN BRITISH COURTS AND PROBLEMS IN SPECIFIC INDUSTRIES, IN PARTICULAR NHS DOCTORS

If we look at the impact of the WTD in the UK, we can identify two areas where evidence exists of change of practices. These are the employment tribunals and the National Health Service (NHS).

At least statistically, the WTD plays a significant role in British employment tribunals. Working time claims have been consistently among the highest group of applications since 2005. According to the Employment Tribunal and Employment Appeal Tribunal (EAT) Statistics for 2010–2011, of the 382,400 jurisdictional claims received in 2010–2011, 114,100 (or 30 per cent) were working time claims[9] (see Table 10.1). Applications claiming breach of the WTR outnumbered all other areas of jurisdiction during this statistical period.[10]

In 2010–2011, about a fifth (18 per cent) of all working time cases were successful at the tribunal after a hearing. A little less than a third of the cases (29 per cent) were disposed through conciliation by the independent Advisory, Conciliation and Arbitration Service during the recorded period (1 April 2010 to 31 March 2011) and a quarter of all cases (26 per cent) were withdrawn; the remaining cases were either struck out, dismissed at a preliminary hearing, unsuccessful at the hearing or were disposed by a default judgment (Ministry of Justice 2011, Table 2, p. 8).

So far there has been no research interpreting the high number of WTD claims in the employment tribunal system. According to Alan Neal, the impact of the WTD has been limited because the complexities of the WTR provisions create barriers for UK workers (Neal 2004). However, in one area these barriers do not seem to exist. In looking closer at the WTD

---

[9] The statistics refer tellingly to Working Time Directive and not Working Time Regulations claims.

[10] A statistical note indicates a caveat for 2010–2011 insofar as a large proportion (although not specified) of working time claims consisted of multiple airline industry cases that were resubmitted every 3 months: Ministry of Justice (2011), p. 5 and Table 1, p. 7.

Table 10.1 Claims accepted by Employment Tribunals, 2008–2009 to 2010–2011

	2008–2009	2009–2010	April 2010 to March 2011
Total Claims Accepted	151,000	236,100	218,100
NATURE OF CLAIM			
Unfair dismissal	52,700	57,400	47,900
Unauthorised deductions (Formerly Wages Act)	33,800	75,500	71,300
Breach of contract	32,800	42,400	34,600
Sex discrimination	18,600	18,200	18,300
Working Time Directive	**24,000**	**95,200**	**114,100**
Redundancy pay	10,800	19,000	16,000
Disability discrimination	6,600	7,500	7,200
Redundancy – failure to inform and consult	11,400	7,500	7,400
Equal pay	45,700	37,400	34,600
Race discrimination	5,000	5,700	5,000
Written statement of terms and conditions	3,900	4,700	4,000
Written statement of reasons for dismissal	1,100	1,100	930
Written pay statement	1,100	1,400	1,300
Transfer of an undertaking – failure to inform and consult	1,300	1,800	1,900
Suffer a detriment/unfair dismissal – pregnancy	1,800	1,900	1,900
Part-Time Workers Regulations	660	530	1,600
National minimum wage	600	500	520
Discrimination on grounds of religion or belief	830	1,000	880
Discrimination on grounds of sexual orientation	600	710	640
Age discrimination	3,800	5,200	6,800
Others	9,300	8,100	5,500
Total	**266,500**	**392,800**	**382,400**

Source: Ministry of Justice, 2011, Table 1, p. 7.

claims it becomes apparent that the majority of cases concern entitlements to paid annual leave.[11] The high number of these claims seems to reflect a practice, at least among some British employers, of not observing leave periods. Employers seem to resist acknowledging paid leave entitlements, especially in relation to termination of employment. It could indeed be the case that a substantial number of annual leave claims originated from disputes over the termination of employment and serve as substitutes for full-blown unfair dismissal claims.

In addition to the impact the WTD had on the caseload of employment tribunals, there is at least one sector where the WTD and the WTR have led to major discussions (see Fernandez and Williams 2009; Davies 2010) and change of working practices. This is the medical sector, and in particular the problem of working hours of junior doctors employed by the NHS.

The above-mentioned judgments of the CJEU in *SiMAP* and *Jaeger*, requiring that the time doctors spend 'on call' should count as working time, had practical effects upon doctors, who have traditionally been required to be resident on site when on call, particularly junior doctors and care home workers. Implementation of the ECJ rulings was resisted by the UK for some time, with the result that doctors on call were not paid, unless they were on site. The reference in the 1993 Directive to 'doctors in training' excluded British junior hospital doctors from the scope of protection.[12] However, the Horizontal Amending Directive of

---

[11] It should be mentioned that there are hurdles for the employee claiming entitlements to annual paid leave. The Employment Act 2002 (Regulation 6(5)) provided that an employee claiming paid annual leave first had to begin statutory grievance procedures by submitting the grievance in writing to the employer (Employment Act 2002, Schedule 2, Part 2, implemented by the Employment Act 2002 (Dispute Resolution) Regulations 2004, SI 2004/752). This had to be done at least 28 days before submitting a claim to an employment tribunal and within 3 months of the date on which the employer is alleged to have refused to permit the worker to take annual leave or not paid the worker for leave taken (Employment Act 2002, ss. 32 (3) and 32(4)) (see Stothers and Porter 2011). However, the Employment Act 2008 repealed these requirements and replaced them with less stringent provisions that nevertheless allow tribunals to adjust awards in the event of non-compliance with a grievance procedure required by a Code of Conduct (Deakin and Morris 2009, 78). Given the procedural obstacles, it is remarkable how many claims of paid annual leave actually reach the employment tribunals.

[12] They could, however, sue with a claim of breach of the employer's common law duty to protect the safety and health of his employees: *Johnstone v Bloomsbury Health Authority* [1992] QB 333.

2000 and the Directive 2003/88/EC concerning certain aspects of the organisation of working time, which amended the 1993 WTD, introduced a gradual improvement of their position and the WTR was changed accordingly. WTD limits were transposed to doctors in training with effect from 1 August 2004 by the Working Time (Amendment) Regulations 2003 (SI 2003/1684). The transitional provisions were fully used up to 31 July 2009 as regards weekly working time, while the reference period was set at 6 months throughout, reflecting the working patterns of UK doctors in training. A new Article 25A WTR provided that a limit of 58 hours applied from 1 August 2004 to 31 July 2007, and one of 56 hours between August 2007 and 31 July 2009. The UK notified the Commission by 31 January 2009 that it wished to use the extended transitional provisions under Article 17.5 WTD until 31 July 2011 for specified posts in a number of defined specialties and hospitals. Accordingly, doctors in training in the UK in those specified posts could be asked to work up to 52 hours per week, averaged over not more than 6 months, until 31 July 2011 (European Commission 2010a, 32).

This change of law for junior doctors did meet considerable opposition (see, for example, Sim et al. 2004; Pounder 2008). The Association of Surgeons in Training (2009) complained that restrictions on working hours are damaging the training of doctors and putting patients' lives at risk. A 2009 report from the Royal College of Surgeons of England reported that there were not enough surgeons to fill rotas if they worked only 48 hours a week, that 90 per cent of trainee doctors were exceeding their timetabled hours on a weekly basis, that 55 per cent reported being pressured to falsely declare their actual hours worked, 68 per cent felt that their training and skills had deteriorated as a result of shift-working patterns introduced to meet the WTR, and 71 per cent felt the reduction in overall hours had not led to any improvement in their work–life balance.[13]

The current debate on the 'detrimental' impacts of the WTR on the training of junior doctors is characterised by some hysteria and is often based on erroneous statistics. A breath of fresh air was provided by the Temple Report (2010) that concluded that the transposition of the WTD is possible when training and service commitment are separated and reorganisations and restructuring of NHS structures are accepted. The

---

[13] The data and the report from the Royal College of Surgeons of England are cited by Grant (2009).

Report criticised the existing literature on the impact of the WTR for being biased, a fact that impedes on its validity and reliability.[14]

There seems to be evidence that the opposition to the WTR inside the NHS included acts of obstruction. In a Position Statement the Association of Surgeons in Training (2009) admits that young doctors are pressurised to violate WTR by falsifying documents (p. 9). The time for training of junior doctors is split by shifting their assignments to a series of different NHS trusts. Courts have intervened on a number of occasions. In one case the court required that a nurse who took two jobs and had to work 19 hours without a break is given rest periods and that her work needs to be interrupted in order to avoid risk to patients (*Havering Primary Care Trust v Miss F Bidwell* [2008] EAT). However, recently the courts and tribunals have been less lenient. When a nurse claimed longer breaks because she was 'on call' during breaks, the employment tribunal refused the claim since the *NHS Terms and Conditions of Service Handbook* laid down that breaks are only interrupted in exceptional cases and that there will be compensatory rest (*Martin v Southern Health and Social Care Trust* [2010] NICA 31). When a care worker employed in a residential home challenged a sleep-in payment, the employment tribunal decided that it did not constitute an allowance (S*mith v Oxfordshire Learning Disability Trust* [2009] ET).

10.5 POLITICAL OPPOSITION TO THE WTD AND IMPACT OF THE WTR

Although the WTR follow in legal terms relatively closely the text of the WTD, the fact that it expressly includes the possibility of individual opt-out somewhat contradicts and undermines the aim of the WTD. This fact also expresses the general hostile attitude towards regulation of

---

[14] The Temple Report criticised bodies conducting the research for often not being neutral because they are 'adversely' affected by the WTD. This criticism was directed in particular at the Royal College of Anaesthetists and the Royal College of Surgeons of England, which have long been concerned about the impact of shortened working hours under the WTD on patient safety, training and service delivery. Their qualitative research based on questionnaires and discussions was found to be biased in (i) content and purpose of question, (ii) wording and language, and (iii) types and form of questions. Furthermore, their collection of data through questionnaires or interviews is biased because of non-response error. Respondents that are not disadvantaged by the implementation of the WTR are less likely to contribute to the studies in contrast to people that want to object.

working time in British politics. The Conservative Party openly opposes this regulation, and this view is, although less vociferously, shared by the dominant market-friendly core of the Labour Party ('New Labour').

Critics of the working time regulations, for example the employers' association CBI, claim that the annual cost not only to the NHS is enormous, alleging that there are several billion pounds of loss to British industry as a result of implementing the WTD. The CBI's main target is the individual opt-out. It is feared that losing the opt-out would send the annual bill for this Directive through the roof[15] at a time when there is a pressing need to pay off public debts rather than spending tax money and business resources on complying with EU law.

The EU working time rules were a major issue during the UK general election at the beginning of 2010 as the Conservatives campaigned on a pledge to 'repatriate' social and employment policy back from the EU (Grant 2009). The government announced in November 2011 that it will propose further exemption from EU social and employment law as part of its overhaul of British employment laws,[16] although the liberal coalition partner was hesitant. In discussions before the disastrous summit on 8/9 December 2011, at which the UK marginalised itself by being the only Member State to veto treaty changes in order to solve the Eurozone crisis, the WTD was used openly as a bargaining tool and is frequently mentioned by Euro-sceptics as an area in which Britain should 'repatriate' EU powers.[17]

However, opposition to the WTD is not only coming from the Conservatives. New Labour is also defending the individual opt-out against attempts of the European Commission and the European Parliament to abandon this option. This includes opposition to socialist allies in

---

[15] A Eurosceptical think tank calculated in 2008: 'Open Europe has estimated that ending the opt-out could cost the UK economy between £47.74 billion and £66.45 billion by 2020, with a middle estimate of £57 billion. The calculations are based on the opt-out elapsing in 2011.' Press Release: 'Ending opt-out from EU working rules could cost UK £2,300 per household', Tuesday, 16 December 2008. Available at http://www.openeurope.org.uk/media-centre/pressrelease.aspx?pressreleaseid=94. Accessed 15 December 2014.

[16] *The Telegraph*, 'Coalition to relax employment laws', 23 November 2011.

[17] However, what 'repatriation' means is not clear. Vaughne Miller correctly comments in her House of Lords research paper (Repatriating EU powers to Member States, House of Lords Library Standard Note: SN/IA/6153, 7 December 2011, p. 3): 'The Government has not clarified which policy areas it would like to see repatriated or how it would achieve this, referring only to amending the "working time directive", which is not so much a matter of repatriation as of renegotiation.'

Europe. For example, in 2010 Spanish Socialist MEPs and European trade unions urged the Commission to scrap Britain's opt-out. John Monks, the General Secretary of the European Trades Union Confederation, called to the Commission to take on Britain over the opt-out. At least officially this was opposed by the Labour Party leadership at home.

The ideological background for this Labour opposition is a 'Third Way' philosophy. Hugh Collins has thoughtfully criticised the Third Way method in labour law as detrimental to individual employment rights. He demonstrates the negative impact in relation to the regulatory techniques in the UK Working Time Regulations of 1998 which permit derogations to be effected in various ways from the legal entitlements they contain.

> My explanation for this varied pattern in the legislation is that … it is believed that alienable rights are more likely to achieve efficient outcomes than fixed entitlements. The differentiation between rights that require collective negotiation for alienation or modification and those that permit individual alienation depends upon an assessment of whether individual employees will have the bargaining strength to achieve the optimal outcome. (Collins 2002, 467)

Indeed an alternative to individual opt-out would be opt-out through collective bargaining. However, this option was severely undermined during the period of Conservative governments (1979–1997) when in particular industrial relations in the mining industry were subjected to ferocious hostility. When miners refused to agree to opt out at the end of the 1990s, the court held in *Barber v RJB Mining (UK) Ltd* [1999] that they could refuse to work until the working time accords to the statutory limit. However, a problem that crystallised in the aftermath of the *Barber* case was the question of jurisdiction. Employment tribunals assume 'jurisdiction over contractual complaints only where they arise out of or are outstanding on termination of the employment relationship' (Collins et al. 2005, 380–81). Otherwise it is a question for the ordinary courts.

Insofar as impact of the WTD and WTR on actual working time in the UK is concerned, there is some evidence from empirical studies of incremental change. However, progress seems to be slow. Neathey and Arrowsmith (2001) found in their DTI study of the implementation of WTR that employers paid little attention to it beyond basic minimal compliance and used the individual opt-out that limited the impact of WTR. They also found widespread criticism by employers.

Linda Dickens and her colleagues report in their survey overview for the DTI that:

> a significant proportion of employees, especially men, continue to work over 48 hours each week. According to the Labour Force Survey (LFS), around 19 per cent of all full-time employees usually work in excess of 48 hours. This figure has, however, fallen by one-fifth since the Working Time Directive commenced in 1998. … In the CBI's Employment Trends Survey (2004), companies reported that 30 per cent of employees had signed an individual opt-out. … Similarly, in a survey for the DTI (BMRB Social Research, 2004), 34 per cent of workers who usually worked over 48 hours per week said they had agreed their long hours with their employer, and in most cases (75 per cent), this had involved a written agreement being signed. (Dickens et al. 2005, 17)

Catherine Barnard, Simon Deakin and Richard Hobbs (2003) found that WTR did not change the way working time is organised in British companies and that reliance on the individual opt-out has been the key route to flexibility. They comment that the absence of employee representation in the UK is likely to be the reason for an inflexible application of statutory working time standards by collective agreement, as permitted by the legislation (Barnard et al. 2005). Their conclusions, which they draw from their empirical study of opt-out practices, still seem as valid as they were in 2003 at the time of their research:

> We find that the individual opt-out is in widespread use and is regarded, in preference to other derogations, as the most convenient and effective mechanism for avoiding the 48-hour limit on weekly working time. In part because of the ease with which this limit can be avoided, the Directive has so far done little to change a long-hours culture, driven by employers' perceived needs for flexibility and workers' desire to supplement their earnings or status. (Barnard et al. 2003, 224–5)

This statement is also a powerful comment on the UK's attitude towards implementation of EU employment law in general and working time regulations specifically.

10.6 CONCLUDING REMARKS

Three aspects can be highlighted that have contributed to the exceptionalism of the UK in relation to the WTD. These are the politicisation of the issue, the attitude towards opt-out and instrumentalism in relation to changes of working time arrangements.

1. *Fundamental opposition.* Probably the most striking difference between the UK and other Member States of the EU is its

fundamental opposition to European employment law measures in general as means of regulating British industrial and employment relations. This attitude is even more pronounced in the case of the WTD. In fact the WTD issue is politicised to such an extent that it forms part of an almost daily political rhetoric used by the Euro-sceptic wing of the Conservative Party and the UK Independence Party. The National Health Service is used by the current government as the prime example of high costs incurred as a result of implementing an EU measure. Government figures have put the annual cost of implementing the WTD for junior doctors within the NHS at up to £3.9 billion a year, despite British exemptions from the legislation.

Given the one-sided rhetoric in the debate over the WTD it is somewhat astonishing that the mainstream Labour Party is also opposed to it, at least in relation to abolishing the individual opt-out.[18] It agrees with the Conservative/Liberal Democrat government that the opt-out is necessary in order 'to flexibilise' the application of the WTD in practice. This negative attitude towards a strict adherence to a health and safety measure speaks volumes about the relationship of the political elite in Britain towards the European Union in general.

2. *Individual opt-out.* Britain was the first country to introduce the individual opt-out in its implementing measure WTR. Individual agreements extending the maximum length of the working week beyond 48 hours are widely used in practice and limit the impact of the WTD.

   Abolishing the possibility of opt-out will encounter massive opposition in the UK, especially among employers. It can be predicted that it will be almost impossible to reach consensus with the current British government about reforming the WTD if the opt-out option is not kept. In fact the present Conservative–Liberal coalition under Cameron promises to fight the WTD and is determined to resist any attempt by the European Commission or the European Parliament to abolish the opt-out option.

3. *Incremental changes.* Despite the political opposition and the widespread use of the individual opt-out, WTD and WTR seem to have had at least some impact on actual working time. Evidence

---

[18] The TUC, the umbrella organisation of the trade unions in Britain, does not share this view. Research on working time published by the TUC recommends that 'the Working Time Directive needs to be properly enforced and the UK opt-out ended' (Fagan et al. 2006, 68).

exists that the overall number of employees working more than 48 hours during the working week has dropped. However, if this is an impact of WTD or result of other changes in employment is not clear. The WTD was most likely to have an impact on changing practices when accompanied by investments. The NHS provides examples that compliance with WTD was a result of increasing medical staff and/or rota redesign. Barriers to achieving compliance were mainly a combination of financial restrictions and staff reservations. The Temple Report could show that reservations were largely due to concerns about patient safety and medical training. It found that hospitals were compliant when senior management was actively engaged, for example within a WTD planning group. Where hospitals reported non-compliance it was clear that in many cases senior management staff were not engaged in the process.

A further impact can be observed in relation to the caseload of employment tribunals. WTD claims amounted to 30 per cent of all claims lodged with the employment tribunals in the period 2010–11. The most important issue listed under the rubric of WTD claims was paid annual leave. British employers seem notorious in neglecting this form of entitlement.

Incremental change of the working time culture in Britain is not only a result of the WTD and WTR. What should be analysed in a 'social impact study' that the European Commission promised as part of the reform of the WTD as basis for a revision of the WTD is an analysis of the link between hours of work and the type of working time arrangement. What is regulated by the WTR in the UK needs to be assessed in the wider context of cultural changes demanding new types of employment with accompanying arrangements of working time (Rogowski et al. 2011). In this way the UK opposition to WTD could be turned into something productive, leading to broader questions of adequate regulation of conditions of work that address both flexibility concerns of employers and demands for security and protection of employees.

BIBLIOGRAPHY

Ashiagbor, D. (2005), *The European Employment Strategy: Labour Market Regulation and New Governance*. Oxford: Oxford University Press.

Association of Surgeons in Training (2009), *Optimising Working Hours to Provide Quality in Training and Patient Safety: A Position Statement*. London: Association of Surgeons in Training.

Barnard, C. (2000), 'The Working Time Regulations 1999', *Industrial Law Journal*, **29** (2), 167–71.

Barnard, C., S. Deakin and R. Hobbs (2003), 'Opting Out of the 48-Hour Week – Employer Necessity or Individual Choice? An Empirical Study of the Operation of Article 18(1)(b) of the Working Time Directive in the UK', *Industrial Law Journal*, **33** (4), 223–52.

Barnard, C., S. Deakin and R. Hobbs (2005), 'Reflexive Law, Corporate Social Responsibility and the Evolution of Labour Standards: The Case of Working Time', in O. De Schutter and S. Deakin (eds), *Social Rights and Market Forces*. Brussels: Bruylant, pp. 207–44.

Bercusson, B. (2009), *European Labour Law*. Second edition. Cambridge: Cambridge University Press.

Better Regulation Task Force (2002), *Employment Regulation: Striking a Balance*, Cabinet Office, May.

CIPD (2011), *Working Hours and Time Off Work*. Available at http://www.cipd.co.uk/hr-resources/factsheets/working-hours-time-off-work.aspx#link_0. Last accessed 25 May 2014.

Collins, H. (2002), 'Is there a Third Way in Labour Law?', in J. Conaghan, R.M. Fischel and K. Klare (eds), *Labour Law in an Era of Globalisation: Transformative Practices and Possibilities*. Oxford: Oxford University Press, pp. 449–69.

Collins, H., K.D. Ewing and A. McColgan (2005), *Labour Law*. Second edition. Oxford: Hart.

Davies, M. (2010), 'The Demise of Professional Self-Regulation? Evidence from the "Ideal Type" Professions of Medicine and Law', *Professional Negligence*, **26** (1), 3–38.

Davies, P. and M. Freedland (1993), *Labour Legislation and Public Policy*. Oxford: Oxford University Press.

Davies, P. and M. Freedland (2007), *Towards a Flexible Labour Market: Labour Legislation and Regulation since the 1990s*. Oxford: Oxford University Press.

Deakin, S. and G. Morris (2009), *Labour Law*. Fifth edition. Oxford: Hart.

Dickens, L., M. Hall and S. Wood (2005), *Review of Research into the Impact of Employment Relations Legislation*. DTI Employment Relations Research Series No 45. London: Department of Trade and Industry.

European Commission (2003), Communication 'Concerning Certain Aspects of the Organization of Working Time', COM(2003) 843 final.

European Commission (2010a), *Detailed report on the implementation by Member States of Directive 2003/88/EC concerning certain aspects of the organisation of working time ('The Working Time Directive')*, Commission Staff Working Paper, SEC(2010) 1611 final.

European Commission (2010b), Communication 'Reviewing the Working Time Directive', COM(2010) 801.

Fagan, C., A. Hegewisch and J. Pillinger (2006), 'Out of Time: Why Britain Needs a New Approach to Working-Time Flexibility'. TUC Research Paper. University of Manchester.

Falkner, G., O. Treib and E. Holzleithner (2008), *Compliance in the Enlarged European Union: Living Rights or Dead Letters?* Aldershot: Ashgate.

Falkner, G., O. Treib, M. Hartlapp and S. Leiber (2005), *Complying with Europe: EU Harmonization and Soft Law in the Member States*. New York: Cambridge University Press.

Fernandez, E. and D.G. Williams (2009), 'Training and the European Working Time Directive: A 7 Year Review of Paediatric Anaesthetic Trainee Caseload Data', *British Journal of Anaesthesia*, **103**, 566–9.
Fitzpatrick, B. (1997), 'Straining the Definition of Health and Safety', *Industrial Law Journal*, **26**, 115–35.
Grant, C. (2009), *Can the Conservatives Achieve their EU Objectives?*. London: Centre for European Reform.
Hardy, S. (2006), 'Harmonisation of European Working Time in an Enlarged EU: A Case of Failed "Humanisation"?', *International Journal of Comparative Labour Law and Industrial Relations*, **22** (4), 563–601.
Hatzopoulos, V. (2005), 'Is it Healthy to have an EU Health Law?', *European Law Review*, **30** (5), 697–710.
Lelieveldt, H. and S. Princen (2011), *The Politics of the European Union*. Cambridge: Cambridge University Press.
Mestres, C.A., J.M. Revuelta and A.C. Yankah (2011), 'The European Working Time Directive: Quo Vadis? A Well-Planned and Organized Assassination of Surgery', *European Journal of Cardio-Thoracic Surgery*, **30**, 571–3.
Ministry of Justice (2011), *Employment Tribunal and EAT Statistics 2010–11*. London: Tribunals Service.
Neal, A.C. (2004), 'La reglementation du temps de travail au Royaume-Uni: "Des atouts" pour l'interface entre l'Union Europeenne et le Royaume-Uni?', in I. Daugareilh and P. Iriart (eds), *Leçons d'une Reduction de la Durée du Travail*. Pessac: Maison des Sciences de l'Homme d'Aquitaine, pp. 127–45.
Neathey, F. and J. Arrowsmith (2001), *Implementation of the Working Time Regulations*. DTI Employment Relations Research Series No.11. London: Department of Trade and Industry.
Pounder, R. (2008), 'Junior Doctors' Working Hours: Can 56 Go Into 48?', *Clinical Medicine*, **8**, 126–7.
Rogowski, R. (ed.) (2008), *The European Social Model and Transitional Labour Markets: Law and Policy*. Aldershot: Ashgate.
Rogowski, R., R. Salais and N. Whiteside (eds) (2011), *Transforming European Employment Policy: Labour Market Transitions and the Promotion of Capability*. Cheltenham and Northampton, MA: Edward Elgar.
Sim, D.J., S.R. Wrigley and S. Harris (2004), 'Effects of the European Working Time Directive on Anaesthetic Training in the United Kingdom', *Anaesthesia*, **59** (8), 781–4.
Stothers, S. and A. Porter (2011), 'Paid Annual Leave in the United Kingdom: The Problem of Holiday Pay'. Available at http://www.thomasmore.co.uk/Image Library/Holiday%20Pay%20Article.pdf. Last accessed 25 May 2014.
Temple Report (2010), *Time for Training; A Review of the Impact of the European Working Time Directive on the Quality of Training*. Report of the NHS Committee chaired by Prof. Sir J. Temple, May 2010. London: Medical Education England.
Treib, O. (2003), 'EU Governance, Misfit, and the Partisan Logic of Domestic Adaptation: An Actor-Centered Perspective on the Transposition of EU Directives', Paper presented at EUSA 8th International Biennial Conference, Nashville, Tennessee, 27–29 March. Available at http://aei.pitt.edu/6566/1/001317_1.PDF. Last accessed 25 May 2014.
Treib, O. (2005), *Die Bedeutung der nationalen Parteipolitik für die Umsetzung europäischer Sozialrichtlinien*. Frankfurt and New York: Campus.

Treib, O. (2008), 'Implementing and Complying with EU Governance Outputs', *Living Reviews in European Governance*, **3** (5). Available at http://www.livingreviews.org/lreg-2008-5. Last accessed 25 May 2014.

Cases

Barber v RJB Mining (UK) Ltd [1999] ICR 679 (HC).
Cotswold Developments Construction Ltd v Williams [2006] IRLR 181 (EAT).
Havering Primary Care Trust v Bidwell [2008] All ER (D) 297 (EAT).
Johnstone v Bloomsbury Health Authority [1992] QB 333 (CA).
Landeshauptstadt Kiel v Norbert Jaeger, Case C-151/02 [2003] ECR I-8389.
Pfeiffer v Deutsches Rotes Kreuz, Joined Cases C-397/01 to C-403/01 [2004] ECR I-8835.
Sindicato de Medicos de Asistencia Publica (SiMAP) v Conselleria de Sanidad y Consumo de la Generalidad Valenciana, Case C-303/98 [2000] ECR 1-7963.
Smith v Oxfordshire Learning Disability Trust [2009] ICR 1395 (ET).
United Kingdom v Council of the European Union, Case C-84/94 [1996] ECR I-5755 and Industrial Relations Law Reports (IRLR), Vol. 26, No. 1, January [1997] 32.

PART III

Social services of general (economic) interest in Europe

11. Legal uncertainty in social services: A threat to national social protection systems?

Jean-Claude Barbier

11.1 INTRODUCTION

'Social services of general (economic) interest' (SSG(E)Is) are but one among many possible instances where the influence of EU law and the interactions of the various legal orders can be explored empirically. Alongside labour law, this topic was chosen at the start of the GUSTO project to implement case studies in a cross-national manner.[1] (Incidentally, the range of cases chosen was never intended to be representative of European diversity; it however covers a very significant variety of situations that may credibly be generalized, as we will explain in our conclusion.) The overarching research question was whether the influence of EU law on social services was contributing to their 'sustainability' or rather to their 'uncertainty'. With this in mind, one could review legal literature and check it against the views of actors in the social services. The result yields the conclusion that the very concept of SSGI is apparently less clear than existing notions in national legal orders. As EU governance keeps extending its reach, more uncertainty is then presumed to happen in the future and engender fresh problems. These conclusions should be put in the wider context of the characteristics of EU law explored in this book as a key instrument of governance in a domain – social policy – where the EU has very few legal competences (see Hartlapp's and Barbier and Colomb's contributions in this book). The overall assumption at the start of the project was substantiated: in interaction with national law (and various forms of domestic regulation)

---

[1] The United Kingdom, France, the Czech Republic and the Netherlands are the countries where original inquiries were conducted by J.-C. Barbier, A. Koukiadaki, T. Sirovátka and E. Sol in 2010–2011.

EU law brings uncertainty with it, at least for certain groups of Europeans, and more explicitly in certain countries. This uncertainty is mainly of a legal nature. It does not mean, however, that this influence automatically translates into difficulties and threats to the existing domestic systems, for the essential reason that, between the making of EU law and its 'application' in practice, many complex processes happen, including the possibility of non-application (see Falkner et al. 2005; Hartlapp 2007; Falkner and Treib 2008). For this reason, consequences vary according to ideal-types of social protection, to countries, and also, within countries, to groups and individuals.

The chapter first stresses two essential dimensions of SSGIs as a distinct policy area: in many countries, under various names, SSGIs were in the past, and still often are, part of strategies of government (central and local) for *public provision*; partly because of a historically inherited diversity of production and delivery of such services (Moderne and Marcou 2001; Prosser 2005; Maucher 2011), and partly for other reasons, the EU has so far stuck to ambiguous definitions. On the other hand, at the early stages of the European Communities, social services were never supposed to come under the reach of EU law. Fifty years on, they have been affected by a process of spill-over which has brought threats with it. In a second section, we show how the very notion of 'subsidiarity' – an uncertain legal notion *par excellence* – goes hand in hand with the diversity of impact of EU law across member states. Thirdly, the situation of social services of general economic interest in the European Union may be characterized by two essential features that will probably command future developments: the prevalence of an unbalanced concept of economic activity in EU law; and the reluctance of the European Commission to move from the status quo, despite modest moves at the end of 2011. This opens up the identification of potential problems lying ahead.

11.2 UNCERTAINTY AND ITS CONSEQUENCES

11.2.1 The Vagueness of EU Law when Compared to National Legislations for 'Social Services'

The vague nature of EU law may be observed from three main points of view. The first is 'legal uncertainty': a common view among scholars has constantly substantiated this statement, again confirmed in 2011.[2] The uncertainty of definition is obvious in the legal literature (Krajewski et al. 2009). From a second, sociological and factual point of view, the basic policy concepts currently used demonstrate persistent lack of precision (see Box 11.1). At the same time, while no precise references existed in EU primary and secondary law, and the Court of Justice's case law remained scarce, the European Commission issued documents that were (essentially) *not legally binding*, on an *ad hoc* basis. It had to try and placate demands originating in many (but certainly not all) member states. This 'production' of texts of an uncertain nature pertains to a typical example of a 'spill-over' process from an initial article 90 of the Rome Treaty concerning 'public services' or 'utilities' (basically network services which in the past often were state monopolies). Hence, the gradual extension of the reach of the particular article (now article 106) and the growing stock of cases before the Court of Justice came to the following situation: 'traditional social services' will potentially be affected in three main ways: (a) traditional financial support provided to the providers of social services come under the suspicion of 'state aid' regulation, because of the principle of free competition; (b) because of the so-called 'fundamental freedoms',[3] free competition is deemed to exist for services, including the freedom of establishment of providers; the 2006 'Services Directives' covers this, and, depending on governments' choices,[4] partly applies to 'social services'; (c) finally, 'social services' are also affected by EU law dealing with 'public procurement'. All three legal provisions bring various forms of uncertainty to actors, stakeholders of the 'third sector' and citizens, or users of public services, but also 'consumers' of these. Some actors – notably private ones and many governments – support the extension of this uncertainty, whereas others do oppose it strongly (Barbier and Colomb, chapter 1 in this volume). Case studies conducted in the UK, the Czech Republic, the Netherlands and France, each with their specific focus on certain types of services, empirically confirm this uncertainty. Contrary to the regular claim articulated by officials in the Commission administration,[5] the vagueness of EU law and the uncertainty of its reach are observable in all

---

[2] At the Services of General Interest Conference, Copenhagen Law Faculty, 13 May 2011, where the main difficulties and ambiguities were exposed and discussed.

[3] Used by the Court of Justice, the expression does not feature in primary or secondary EU law.

[4] See later for the role of article 2.2.j in this respect.

[5] Interviews, EU Commission, 2010 and 2011.

the countries studied. Thus, it is not only for the 'continental' types of social protection system, as the Commission's officials would have it, that problems exist. The uncertainty has three dimensions: (i) the definition of legal notions; (ii) the extent to which social services are legally covered; and (iii) the insertion of foreign, autonomous, legal notions into the national legal frameworks.

BOX 11.1 A PERSISTENT PROBLEM OF 'DEFINITION'

Apart from the documents produced by the Commission, which one can see as a pragmatic and *ad hoc* mix of empirical material collected in member states and definitions drawn from EU case law, after more than 50 years of existence of the EC and the EU, no precise definition exists of what exactly a 'social service of general (economic) interest' is.

In current parlance, the very term SSGIs is contested by certain actors in the European public space: for instance, some of them deliberately use the term 'public services'[6] as an alternative. We will leave aside the question of the legal validity of the documents and simply note that, in matters of definition, neither legal sources in the Treaty (primary law) nor legal sources in secondary law (Directives or Regulations) are available. Apart from 'papers' issued by the Commission,[7] a growing body of texts is however essential to consider, for example decisions taken by the Commission and the Court of Justice of the European Union.[8]

Just as in its Green Paper (2003), in the Commission's White Paper (2004, p. 16) 'social and health services of general interest' were grouped together. But definitions changed over the years and the separate treatment of health services was confirmed by the 2006 Services Directive. It could seem that a 'definition' drawn from the 2006 Communication (177 final, p. 5) was now 'stabilized'[9] for the Commission, although it did not pertain to either primary or secondary law. However, the Commission kept issuing new documents where questions and

---

[6] This is the case of the European Trade Union Congress (see for instance its June (1–2) 2010 deliberation: 'Towards a new impetus for public services').

[7] We assume that such 'texts' are substantially different from decisions by the Commission and by the CJEU, with regard to their legal consequences (see Guinard 2009).

[8] Two such decisions were taken by the Commission about 'social housing' in the Netherlands. The first one dates from 2005 about housing cooperatives (*woningscorporaties*) (state aid E2/2005, ex-NN 93/02). The second decision is a letter to the Dutch government of 15 December 2009, C (2009) 9963 final. On 16 December 2011, the Tribunal dismissed a claim presented by Dutch housing corporations against the 2009 decision as 'inadmissible' (case T-202/10). The Court later annulled this decision (27-2-2014, case C-133/12P) and a new decision on the substance of the case is expected later.

[9] It is quoted in the 'biennial reports' of 2008 and 2010.

answers were addressed, including basic definitions.[10] For instance, in a document presented as a 'working paper', the question was again raised in December 2010 of 'What is an SSGI?' (European Commission, 2010b, Guide, p. 16).

The 2006 Communication said: 'What do we mean by social services in the European Union?' In addition to health services, which are not covered by this communication, 'we find two main categories of social services:

- Statutory and complementary social security schemes, organised in various ways (mutual or occupational organisations), covering the main risks of life, such as those linked to health, ageing, occupational accidents, unemployment, retirement and disability'.[11]
- And, the so-called 'definition' provided by Communication 177 (2006) moved on to a second category. This amounted to what one calls in French '*une liste à la Prévert*', an *ad hoc* list[12] of examples, which is not supposed to be exhaustive, and where certain types are explicitly excluded.[13]
- Other essential services provided directly to the person. These services that play a preventive and social cohesion role consist of customised assistance to facilitate social inclusion and safeguard fundamental rights. They comprise, first of all, assistance for persons faced by personal challenges or crises (such as debt, unemployment, drug addiction or family breakdown). Secondly, they include activities to ensure that the persons concerned are able to completely reintegrate into society (rehabilitation, language training for immigrants) and, in particular, the labour market (occupational training and reintegration). These services complement and support the role of families in caring for the youngest and oldest members of society in particular. Thirdly, these services include activities to integrate persons with long-term health or disability problems.

---

[10] The fact can be interpreted as a search for legitimating its position.

[11] These services are social and of general interest but deemed not to be 'economic': hence the principles of state aid rules, and competition, as well as the 2006 Directive do not apply to them. The main legal reference seems to be the *Poucet and Pistre* CJEU decisions (17.2.1993, C-159/91 and C-160/91).

[12] A similar approach is taken by the Study on Social and Health Services of General Interest (2008), quoted by the Biennial Report of the Commission (COM 2008 418 final). This report reads (p. 9): 'Ongoing discussions about the concept of "general interest" concern: the meaning and understanding of the term and its elements, what authority/institutions are competent to define missions of general interest and public service obligations, and the form in which these need to be explicitly and transparently defined. As far as the application of certain EU rules (competition rules and internal market rules) is concerned, concepts like "economic activity" or "undertaking" have become crucial.'

[13] Although 'they are services of general interest with a clear social function', education and training are not covered by this Communication. Health services are now also excluded and dealt with in other communications and legislation.

> Fourthly, they also include social housing, providing housing for disadvantaged citizens or socially less advantaged groups. Certain services can obviously include all four of these dimensions.

The 2010 Guide added a further element: 'SSGIs may be of an economic or non-economic nature, depending on the activity under consideration. The fact that the activity in question is termed "social" is not of itself enough for it to avoid being regarded as an "economic activity" within the meaning of the Court's case law. SSGIs that are economic in nature are SGEIs'[14] (2010b, p. 17). Consequently, it is not sure if full clarification will ever be achieved. It is not surprising that the definition produced by the Synthesis report commissioned by the EU Commission to experts (Huber et al. 2006) was also vague; it tested all sorts of definitions by approximation. Despite the probably good intentions of its authors, this document was essentially a piece of normative discussion about social services, as defined vaguely along the Commission's lines. However, this latter report enjoyed a certain support, because it was extensively used by the first 'biennial report' on SSGIs published by the Commission. The report's definitions were given according to the objectives the services were deemed to achieve, their role, the fact that they were 'a key element' of the so-called 'European social model' (but no one knew what the European social model was), by a list of characteristics these services were supposed to share, that other services did not possess.

In legal terms, Guinard (2009, pp. 450–60) has rightly noted that all the elements brought to the fore by the Commission's Communications and various documents only go so far as making a list of vague concepts.[15] Guinard concluded that SSGIs were '*une notion á géométrie variable dont la fixation du contenu dépend des décisions des autorités de concrétisation*' (ibid., p. 458), that is, a contingent concept the substance of which was dependent upon EU authorities' decisions. Approximation was the rule, as is also noted many times in Huber et al. (2006). Hence, the assumption of 'definition uncertainty' is amply documented (see also the contributions in Krajewski et al. (2009, p. 3), who qualify former article 86 of the Treaty as a 'messy provision').[16]

New legislation and draft documents were issued by the Commission in December 2011, in the context of the review of the 'Altmark package'. These documents are likely to alter the extent of uncertainty in the future when they are fully implemented, but it is too early to know for sure. They deal with state aid rules, public service compensation and the concept of *de minimis* aid granted to undertakings providing Services of General Economic Interest. As for the latest pieces of EU legislation being published in 2012, it is obviously too early to incorporate their full potential of influence in the present analysis. A limited

---

14 As Guinard (2009, p. 455) notes, SSGIs do not represent a category distinct from Services of General Interest (SGIs).

15 Such as, for instance, criteria proposed by the Communication 2006 (177) (pp. 4–5): 'comprehensive and personalised integrating the response to differing needs in order to guarantee fundamental human rights and protect the most vulnerable'; or 'strongly rooted in (local) cultural traditions', and so on.

16 This was also the mainstream conclusion presented in the seminar already mentioned (Copenhagen University, 12–13 May 2011) on SGIs.

number of interviews with actors in December 2011, however, showed that for the first time in ten years, the social sector's demands had been answered, at least for partial limitation of the reach of EU law and for increasing the thresholds of such applications.

11.2.2 Main Consequences Associated with the Implementation of the Notion of SSGIs

Let us sum up the main consequences of the legal uncertainty in the area of SSGIs. First, the process of EU integration has gradually spilled over in the area of social services: from an initially limited scope restricted to network services and monopolies, EU law now reaches far into the domain of legal definition; the spill-over process is typically at the same time an instance of 'negative integration', challenging national practices and introducing new rules by promoting the basic freedoms of movement (and the freedom of establishment), free competition and the common market. SSGIs exemplify the fact that the CJEU's power of decision hangs over the social services as a sword of Damocles. It remains within its power in last resort to define what sort of services fall in the 'economic' category, and what others fall in the complementary 'non-economic' one. Typically, the 'protection' from market rules that national social security regimes (pensions and healthcare, unemployment, etc.) enjoy today is effectively submitted to a radical uncertainty; no one can exclude the fact that the CJEU's case law might change.[17] In this respect, the possibility of fresh and unanticipated case law – that is, new legal interpretation – hangs over the actors of social services and provision as a sword of Damocles. Secondly, EU law has been undergoing a process of apparently inexorable economization. Thirdly, asymmetry (between economic and social rights) is closely intertwined with uncertainty for social rights, because the decisions of the Court of Justice bring with them the power of defining the conditions, and cannot be challenged before any other court (Barbier 2008). Among these powers, the defining power of what is 'economic' has led to a situation where social services have been more and more 'economized' (Neergaard 2009, pp. 42–7). Hence some interpret this as rampant 'economization' (Guinard 2009, pp. 463–7; Supiot 2009).

---

[17] This is what is assumed in a recent analysis by Driguez (2010), commenting on the decision *Commission v Germany*, C-271/08. The ETUC has denounced this decision as being on the same lines as the *Viking* and *Laval* decisions.

In theory at least this situation can be assumed to have manifold – albeit indirect – consequences for citizens. Confirmed in the case studies (chapters 12 to 15 in this volume), one of its main results is that the three EU concepts of services of general interest, services of general economic interest, and social services of general (economic) interest are not only alien to ordinary citizens, but also – when they are known at all by social actors – the source of confusion (Barbier and Colomb 2012). Another consequence lies in the larger problem of legitimating EU law among citizens. In all the countries surveyed, this question was noted during the surveys: with very different consequences across them, a growing politicization of the issues related to EU law in the domain of 'public' and 'social' services has been nevertheless observed from the first decade of the 2000s and since. In passing, one can note that this politicization was one defining characteristic of the European elections of 2014, even as SSGIs were seldom explicitly on the agenda of public debate in most member states.

11.3 WHEN CONSEQUENCES VARY ACROSS THE UNION

A generalized state of uncertainty – as defined above – does not however entail homogenous consequences across the Union. Although not representative, our survey is very significant and amply substantiates this conclusion.

11.3.1 The Exclusive Power of Naming

Applying across the board, one conclusion of the survey is that a fundamental ambiguity reigns in the EU with regard to the notion of 'subsidiarity', especially illustrated by the topic of 'social services'. Subsidiarity is often simplistically equated with the mere safeguarding of 'national competences' (sovereignty) in the area of social protection, labour law and social services. Even in matters deemed to be the preserve of member states, a more careful analysis shows that strategic and essential competence is the preserve of the Union: the complex Dutch legal conflict about social housing, which is the subject of the Dutch case study (see Els Sol and Mara van der Vos, chapter 12 in this volume), illustrates this clearly. In this case – and potentially in many other cases of social protection – EU authorities have acquired an asymmetric autonomous power of definition of legal notions that, because of the supremacy rule, prevail across the Union. With them (the Court of Justice and the Commission – mildly influenced by the European Parliament) rests the exclusive power of naming. This power of naming[18] what is economic, what is 'social', what is 'social housing', what are the 'right' target groups, what is 'solidarity', and so on has nevertheless been altogether ignored by the ordinary public, and even by the social actors and traditional stakeholders of social protection. They are now discovering it, as spill-over has already happened, and they were unaware of it.

11.3.2 Discussing Subsidiarity

SSGIs illustrate the multi-faceted ambiguity of EU law, which is linked to a number of EU legal concepts. 'Subsidiarity' is one of them. From a sociological point of view, one is surprised to learn that legal characteristics are attached to the notion that are completely unknown not only by the general public, but also by direct participants in EU forums and by social scientists in general. Few would contest that the notion finds its origin in the German Christian-Catholic tradition, which, *inter alia*, used to lead to the fact that in German political culture, independent associations (*Träger*) are privileged vis-à-vis other authorities (including state authorities) for organizing certain 'social' duties. Indeed, the German principle has lost a part of its meaning in Germany today (Sachße 2003, p. 209). However, the common interpretation of the European principle of subsidiarity is seen and communicated very often in the Commission's documents as being a legal confirmation of protection of member states' sovereignty (Protocol no. 26, initially no. 9, annexed to the Treaty). As we have seen, this very Protocol was imposed as a follow-up to a conflict over sovereignty between the EU authorities (the Commission) and the Dutch government (Sol and van der Vos, chapter 12 in this volume).

Interviewed in the context of the present study, legal specialists fall generally into two categories: those who contend that the subsidiarity principle is of a 'soft nature', meaning that it has, at the end of the day, little legal relevance in the application of EU law (some add that the CJEU case law on the issue is extremely rare, if not absent altogether).

---

[18] In the Dutch case, AEDES, one of the main lobbying organizations on behalf of the Dutch *woningcorporaties*, was apparently satisfied with a 'new' definition published in the Communication SEC (2011) 397 final (23/3/2011). However, this 'definition' (neither new nor really a 'definition') did not feature in the text of the final version of the Communication (COM (2011) 146 final) and, moreover it is different from the one present in the second biennial Report on services of general interest (2010). Such discrepancies only illustrate once more the *ad hoc* strategy implemented by the Commission.

To this group may be added scholars like, for instance, French Law Professor Pierre Rodière: his conclusion in his well-known and respected textbook almost amounted to the fact that, in matters of social and labour law, the boundary between competences does not really matter.[19] In a second category one finds experts who tend to see the principle as 'political', the adoption of which was necessary to placate 'political concerns' of member states as to the prospect of the EU extending its jurisdiction. These experts agree with the basic meaning of the principle, that is, that it deals with sovereignty, but they are sceptical as to its effective consequences in protecting the member states' sovereignty. This situation tends to contradict a widely shared view among social actors as to the principle's role as a protection against further forays of the EU into social matters. Few are the scholars who go so far as to argue that the principle is, *per se*, a vehicle for increasing the EU legal order's reach into national legal orders. Guinard (2009), however, convincingly argues in this direction. He notably stresses the essential point that, in the absence of any precise definitions of SGIs, SGEIs, and SSGIs, the ultimate defining test (what is deemed economic or non-economic) lies in the hands of EU legal authorities (the Commission and the CJEU). The very competence to define what an SGEI is, what is 'economic', now brings with it *de facto* extended EU competence, when one compares the situation for instance in the early 1990s when the EU legal order had not yet practically entered the debate, and national legal orders in member states were dealing with their public or social services – leaving aside an early application of article 86(2) for network and transport services. A 'large discretion' (as the Commission's expression goes) in the definition does not mean the monopoly of defining, which, in Guinard's terms, falls with the CJEU *in last resort, once services are deemed to be 'economic'*. Additionally, many legal circumstances[20] may be invoked by the EU jurisdiction to intervene in the matter: the important litigation about social housing in the Netherlands had at its heart the notion of 'manifest error' (Sol and van der Vos, chapter 12 in this volume). If one were to follow this (apparently paradoxical) interpretation, all claims made by

---

[19] The '*grande puissance d'expansion*' of EU law, writes the author, takes place '*en dehors même des domaines spéciaux dans lesquels les autorités communautaires ont une compétence pour agir*' (even in the absence of explicit competence) (Rodière 2008, p. 5).

[20] Also consider the notion of 'cross-border interest'. This notion is used in the Commission's guide concerning social services (see European Commission 2010b).

member states and various European actors for a stronger application of the subsidiarity principle would emerge as intrinsically contradictory.

11.3.3 Variety of Systems, Variety of Impact

Yet, the great variety of institutions, of social protection systems, of histories and of political cultures in Europe inevitably mitigates the consequences of the quasi-federalization of law – also happening even in the UK (Koukiadaki, chapter 13 in this volume) despite the consistent resistance of its governments. In two countries, namely the Netherlands (Sol and van der Vos, chapter 12 in this volume) and France (Barbier, chapter 15 in this volume), contradictions and difficulties are experienced that lead to overtly politicized conflicts, and to stronger and stronger challenges presented to the legitimizing of EU intervention in the domain. Yet, the dimensions and forms of these conflicts, happening in 'continental' systems,[21] vary greatly: from the 2005 opposition to the infamous 'Bolkestein' Directive within the general public in France, to the more limited conflict with the *woningcorporaties* (housing corporations) in the Dutch case, about which litigation has gone on, despite a first rejection of the case by the Tribunal of the EU in first instance.

In one country, the UK, the situation is extremely different, because of a legal tradition that does not treat public and private law separately, but also because of its long-term reform in the social protection and social services sector since the late 1970s (Koukiadaki, chapter 13 in this volume). Yet, questions arise in the healthcare and long-term care sectors which are more and more pressing. Given the overall and continuous hostility of the British public to European integration, fresh difficulties could become more bitter in a country that presently has one of the most Eurosceptic governments in its history.

The Czech Republic illustrates another type of difficulty. Certainly, the transformation from the previous 'socialist' system of provision to a largely deregulated and privatized provision of social services (in the context of general absence of application of labour law) cannot be linked to the intervention of EU law, in a world of 'dead letters' (Sirovátka, chapter 14 in this volume). However, problems lie in the general de-legitimizing of 'social policies', and of 'solidarity' among the Czech public, after the collapse of the former communist government. They also

---

[21] Although it used to be part of the continental cluster, the Netherlands has been undergoing reforms since the late 1980s that largely place it apart from the rest.

lie in widespread scepticism within the administration about the possibility to really address the demands of 'social investment' stemming from EU coordination of social policies. As Sirovátka notes, the Republic – as a typical example of Central Europe – is put into a catch-22 situation, made worse by the current crisis. At the same time, as will be seen in the second section of the chapter, the country is among the worse ranked for the affordability and quality of social services, if Eurobarometer no. 321 is to be taken as a relevant reference.[22]

All four country cases illustrate the fact that EU law is only one factor in accounting for developments in the 2000s. The observed phenomena reveal the existence of a gap between the *de-contextualized EU legal concepts* – mainly based on economic premises – and the national experiences. All harbour potential or already existing political conflicts. Whether or not this situation can be exactly attributed to any precise impact of EU legislation, in the old member states except the UK, EU law is seen as foreign and threatening by a significant part of the actors of social protection, but also by a significant proportion of citizens. Finally, the situation in the four countries surveyed illustrates the fact that a significant room for manoeuvre exists, with regard to governments' and actors' potential strategies of adapting to the often unexpected intervention of EU law. Moreover, in all countries, the consistency of government strategies in the area of social services has remained an essential factor.

11.4 CHALLENGES AHEAD

From our analysis, three main challenges emerge:

1. The overall rationale of the enactment, implementation and application of EU legislation is based almost exclusively on economic thought, as most of EU law actually is (Neergaard 2009; Supiot 2009; Barbier and Colomb 2012). This seems to ignore the limits economic imperialism should heed.[23] This begs the question of the quality and legitimacy of social services.
2. After the first debate in the European Parliament on services of general economic interest (Herzog 2003), the Commission

[22] EB 72.1 (2009) is commented upon in the next section.

[23] Ambiguity is, for instance, pervasively present in the present discussions about the notion of 'social enterprises' following the EU 2020 strategy. One of the names of the third sector, *économie solidaire*, seems not to be taken into account as a particular form among *many forms of economy*.

remained reluctant to address the problem and explicitly refused to envisage proposing new legislation. One must account for this 'stubbornness' and explain it.

3. Finally, the present findings should be placed in the wider perspective of a group of questions on which they shed light: Is it possible to deliver public services (universal services; SGIs, etc.) in a Union where economic freedoms are the overarching driving force? Can/should social services be seen as part of social protection, with special characteristics under a new regime, breaking with past traditions but still being protected from market rules?[24] Can such services be sustainable, continuous, of a good quality, and can they fit the expectations not only of 'consumers' but of citizens, whatever their providers' legal status. Can the prevailing influence of economic freedoms and free competition deliver efficiency and fairness in public services and social services in a better way, in comparison with traditional national regimes? Is there only one form of economy or do alternative economic forms coexist?

11.4.1 The Unbalanced Rationale of EU Legal Reform

In the area of social services as in all other areas, systematically upholding the legal philosophy of the EU, lies a rationale that directly contradicts the national traditions of public services (public utilities, *services publics*, *Dienstleistungen der Daseinsvorsorge*) (Moderne and Marcou 2001). This is not surprising: as a distinct legal order, the EU legal order is purposely constructed so as to be different from national traditions. This contradiction has been especially experienced in all the old member states, and particularly among those that are classically seen as 'continental'. Yet in the UK and, to a lesser extent, in the Scandinavian countries and in the Netherlands, the prevailing conception that 'public' services may be delivered by all sorts of providers, including the private sector, is now undeniably firmly established.[25] In Central and Eastern Europe, other traditions used to prevail but they seem – at least for the moment – to have been swept away after the demise of the communist order, by way of far-reaching privatization.

Hence the Court of Justice and the Commission, inasmuch as they act as decision makers of last resort, have been the supercilious and haughty

---

24 For instance because of the exception of 'solidarity'.

25 An interesting example is the German 'triangular' relation (*Dreiecksverhältnis*) between the provider, the customer and the funding authority, which, to a certain extent, contradicts the previous situation of traditional *Träger*.

guardians of a one-sided philosophy that contends that competition *per se* is the most efficient way of delivering any goods including services of whatever nature. As we have shown elsewhere (Barbier and Colomb 2012), this philosophy is often justified by the CJEU's Judges in terms of the heroic struggle they have been waging on behalf of individuals in the EU who have suffered discrimination.[26] Hence, collectively or hierarchically organized production of services should be reformed or even combated, in the spirit of negative integration. This unilateral ideology also contends that the legal framing of economic activities can be addressed with a unique corpus of law, resting on simple and uniform premises and universal concepts: there exist 'undertakings', the activity of which is 'economic' by nature, and they produce and deliver homogenous 'services'. This *inter alia* explains the rationale behind the 2004 failed Directive for Services, which, however seriously contained, remained at the core of the 2006 version of the Directive. Moreover, this ideology – sometimes seeming to verge on some form of 'fundamentalism' (Supiot 2009) – seems not to care about presenting facts and data that would substantiate the claim that the market is always the most efficient solution. Just as the process of spill-over displayed its first consequences in the social field, and until December 2011, this ideological stance translated in a dogged resistance of the Commission to open up new ways of thinking about social protection, social services and, by the way, labour law (see the chapters on labour law in this volume: Rogowski, Colomb, Sirovátka, and Sol and Ramos Martín). This position stood in obvious contradiction with what we have described as the 'Golden Age' of Social Europe (Barbier 2013).

However, the amount of knowledge and data about social services, their acceptance (legitimacy) by citizens (who are not only consumers), their quality and affordability, is far from satisfactory and universal. Until 2009, no cross-EU survey existed for social services, and Eurobarometer only surveyed individual economic services (like portable phones). In 2009, however, detailed inquiry was published about five sorts of social services of general economic interest (long-term care, care for children, public employment services, social housing and social assistance – questions QA 46, 47, 56, 57; see Eurobarometer, 322).[27] The main picture emerging from this survey can be summed up: (a) a negligible proportion of Europeans think that the private sector can be entrusted

---

[26] Judge Mancini is perhaps the most vivid example for the justification of this ideology and action of the Court.

[27] Updated figures in Eurobarometer 355 (December 2010) (74.1) are very similar.

primarily for the provision of child care and of long-term care; (b) overwhelmingly, between 80 and more than 90 per cent of people think that their provision is primarily the role of public authorities; and (c) at the same time, both in terms of quality and affordability, Europeans are not satisfied: the number of people who think that these services are of very good quality is minuscule, except in Belgium (12 per cent for long-term care); those who think that long-term care is very bad range from 5 per cent of the population (the UK) to 15 per cent in Poland and 26 per cent in Greece; for child care, satisfaction about affordability and quality seldom reaches a majority of respondents (with exceptionally high rates of non-respondents).

11.4.2 A Stubborn Commission

The topics of services of general interest, services of general economic interest, and social services/public services have been discussed for a long time now in the EU but it is only very recently that the debate *about social services* has started to expand (in some countries like France, Belgium and Germany, social actors were certainly aware earlier than in other countries – see Barbier, chapter 15 in this volume). However, our research shows that despite early awareness, these countries failed to organize alternative thinking in the face of the increasing pressure for liberalization, contracting out, and so on, brought about by the Commission: this failure had not only to do with dire linguistic difficulties, but also with traditions and institutions that were difficult to reconcile, and simply conflicting national interests. Because, at the same time, the Scandinavian countries, the UK and the Netherlands had already embarked on liberalizing strategies, the pressure to reform (negative integration) social services (in the three areas of public procurement, state aid and competition of providers) was lower in these countries. Meanwhile, Central and Eastern European countries that joined in 2004 and 2007 had already implemented major reforms after the collapse of communism (Sirovátka, chapter 14 in this volume): these countries have certainly never been candidates for promoting an alternative model to the market, at least so far (Sirovátka shows that the Czech Republic failed in promoting a more 'liberal' approach at the Vienna Summit in 2006). With no significant common counter-power, the only two countries left to promote an alternative model were Belgium and France.[28]

[28] This accounts for the fact that the most significant lobby in Brussels is French-dominated: www.sssig-fr.org (accessed 1 January 2015). It is only

When the Herzog report was discussed in the European Parliament in 2003, it strongly advocated the adoption of new legislation by the Commission. However, the Commission was unmoved. Instead of opening new fields for legislation, at a time when 'better legislation' was the motto, it preferred to embark on a series of 'non-binding' publications, the accumulation of which has resulted in the confusion described above. Sensing that the matter was however politically tricky, J.M.D. Barroso included a tactical mention of the problem of social services in his 2009 political manifesto.[29] In its communication strategy, happy to communicate that misunderstandings were marginal, the Commission stressed two things:[30] the great majority of contestations, and even questions raised in the various consultations, came from France, Belgium and Germany; and secondly, because of extreme institutional variety across the EU in the area of social services of general interest, the Commission was not expected by a majority of member states to move on a question that only troubled a minority of them, and, by the same token, European citizens. Blaming French and German actors,[31] and retreating behind a convenient formal respect for 'subsidiarity', documents issued by the Commission from 2004 onwards kept listing *ad hoc* answers repeating that opponents contravened CJEU case law.

This strategy, however, failed to mask the fact that, fundamentally, the Commission harboured hidden preferences which were closely linked to its legal and ideological approach to the nature of economics and the economy (Barbier 2008). Officials interviewed in DG Employment and Social Affairs explained to us, for instance, that the Commission's role was not to act as a defender of middle-class interests, but rather as the defender of the poorest: hence its active support for initiatives for homeless people, and the corresponding support for restraining special services in housing to a 'disadvantaged' target group, as is the case in the Commission's Decisions on social housing in the Netherlands (2005 and 2009). However, it would be misleading to ascribe the Commission a

---

apparently accidental that the Dutch lobby AEDES joined opposition to the Commission (as a member of the lobby CECODHAS, also linked to www.ssig-fr.org), in a country convinced in its majority of the necessary and beneficial privatization of public services.

[29] Note that this happened after the conflict with the Netherlands, sparked off by the 'housing' question, which resulted in the invention of a new Protocol (no. 9, now no. 26).

[30] Interviews, DG Employment, 2011 and 2012.

[31] Interviews in the Commission, DG Employment and DG Economy and Finance, 2011.

unilateral role in this situation.[32] Over the years from 2001, it has received much support, including recently from countries – like Germany – that used to ask for special legal treatment of social services because of their traditions and political culture.[33] Hence, the absence of a significant coalition of member states has allowed the Commission to privilege – if not always to explicitly promote – a conception of social services that differs from traditionally encompassing (sometimes, universal) public services as they have existed in many countries since World War II in Europe. This conception can be termed 'social services targeted at the most disadvantaged'. The on-going debates about 'social housing' are not the only area where this has happened, but they perhaps illustrate it the better. The definition quoted in the 2010 second biennial report published by the Commission explicitly said:

> social housing is defined as follows: the provision of housing at below market price to a target group of disadvantaged people or socially less advantaged groups as well as to certain categories of key workers. The target groups as well as the exact modalities of application of the system are defined by the public authorities. Social housing providers can also provide other related services to the target group. (European Commission 2010a, p. 47)

In the context of 'subsidiarity', one notes again that the 'large discretion' the member states are deemed to enjoy as to their 'definition' of 'target groups' remains under the firm control of a possible 'manifest error' made by a member state in its definition. What is more, the hidden preference for targeting has also met active support from many NGOs that are engaged in lobbying for 'fundamental rights' (Barbier and Colomb 2012).

Until December 2011, the Commission's refusal to engage in drafting new legislation about social (or public) services was based on a perception that crafting universal concepts was not possible. The case of SSGIs is a typical example of negative integration in the face of a difficult task to integrate 'positively'. However, in March 2011 new proposals were put

---

32 In the Dutch case, the government was indeed the main initial proponent for introducing income caps in social housing (Sol and van der Vos, chapter 12 in this volume).

33 Two elements are of great import here: the first was experienced in the early 1990s with the introduction of legislation on long-term care (*Pflegeversicherung*); the second was the success that prominent social actors achieved in securing a special treatment for social services delivered during the re-negotiation of the Services Directive (article 2.2.j) (see Barbier, chapter 15 in this volume).

forward by the Commission and certain constituencies in the European Parliament, and many lobbies asked the Commission to change its position as to the possibility of specific legislation. Drawing from the on-going process, in July 2011 at the European Parliament, Commissioner Almunia eventually announced a series of measures that were welcomed by many actors in the domain, and were published and adopted between December 2011 and April 2012 (European Commission 2012).

This evolution has to be interpreted in the context of the 2010 Monti report to the president of the Commission on 'A New Strategy for the Single Market', that was followed by a Communication of the Commission in 2011.[34] Indeed the Monti report had an important section acknowledging that the European publics were very reluctant towards the single market. It had 14 pages (out of 107) explaining this under the following title: 'less popular than ever, more needed than ever'. In this section, one learnt that 'there (was) a small core of strong and unwavering advocates of the single market'. However, a supposedly 'vast majority' of 'Member states, political groups and stakeholders' were 'conditional supporters' and the report mentioned that this group 'consider[ed] the single market to be insufficiently mindful of other objectives (for example, social or environmental)'. On this point, the report noted that 'a re-launch of the single market (was) likely to meet serious opposition' (European Commission 2011, p. 20). All in all, an influential section of high-level officials were pushing towards the adoption of a more flexible legal approach.

11.5 LIKELY DIFFICULTIES IN THE FUTURE

The cross-national analysis of significant case studies of the influence of EU governance and law on the provision of social services has shown that a long period of confusion and uncertainty has been on-going since serious case law and the application of state aid and public procurement regulations have gradually reached the social sector, a fact which was not at all envisaged at the beginning of the Communities. The 'foreignness' of EU law in general is in-built in the very process of EU law making (Barbier 2008), and misunderstandings and legal uncertainty have abounded across the Union; yet, this certainly did not translate into automatic and homogenous consequences.

---

[34] COM 2011 206 final 13.4.2011.

Three types of consequences were documented during our survey: difficulties, contestations and perceived threats to the existing systems of provision of social services (related to social protection systems). Even when a 'fit' could be expected (as in the UK) between the drive for negative integration in the area of social services (and the challenging of existing arrangements) and the already existing adoption of privatization, out-contracting and liberalization methods, the consequences of the EU legal reform of social services were not easy to monitor (see Koukiadaki's conclusion, chapter 13 in this volume). It was no easier in Central and Eastern Europe because altogether EU legislation was as weakly implemented as local legislation. The most explicit consequences, however, appeared in the 'continental' countries, which, for well-identified reasons (Barbier, chapter 15 in this volume) have never been able to formulate a consistent opposition to the Commission's doctrine, firmly underpinned by the Court of Justice's case law.

Sometimes, in a very subdued and indirect way, the topic of social services has however started to be politicized. Questions of legitimacy of EU legislation are increasingly raised in larger and larger parts of the public. To a certain extent, the eventual treatment of the Dutch and other 'social housing' questions could be an important landmark, after the legal changes introduced in 2011–2012. In a wider perspective, four main policy lessons should be stressed: (i) in the future, it is very unlikely that a homogenous single conception of economic activity should be able – as the current legal one pretends to do – to cover all forms of economies. Multiple economies, hybrid forms certainly call for adapted treatment in EU law; (ii) as the general trend for politicization of social questions with regard to the intervention of the EU has started to indicate, it is also highly unlikely that the European publics will accept without discussion and contestation the implementation of legal provisions that they see as threatening – not to mention the fact that national governments have kept trying to blame 'Brussels' and EU law for covering their own political decisions;[35] (iii) the Commission and the EU authorities cannot but deal with the main contradiction in EU governance in social matters: the growing tension between 'collective' rights (traditional social protection systems) and individual rights (fundamental rights). Even in economic terms, social protection, organized on a collective, national and occupational basis, is a key element of today's European economies. The

---

[35] See the example of the French transposition of the 2006 Services Directive in the areas of long term care, and childcare (chapter 15). See also the rampant and piecemeal examples of contestation of the principle of free movement of workers in many member states.

quasi-fundamentalist doctrine according to which the future social protection systems in Europe could be a mix of public-run safety nets targeted on the poor, the disabled, and so on, and a vast market providing for the middle and upper classes for all the risks traditionally dealt with by social insurance, has little chance to materialize, provided democratic processes are kept in Europe; (iv) finally, the orientations – legal and political – that the EU will take in the area of social protection and services ultimately depend on the mobilization of a number of social actors and national institutions in many member states.

REFERENCES

Barbier, J.-C. (2008), *La longue marche vers l'Europe sociale*, Paris: PUF.

Barbier, J.-C. (2013), *The Road to Social Europe: A Contemporary Approach to Political Cultures and Diversity in Europe*, Abingdon: Routledge.

Barbier, J.-C. and F. Colomb (2012), 'EU Law as *Janus bifrons*, a Sociological Approach to "Social Europe"', in Jean-Claude Barbier (ed.), EU Law, Governance and Social Policy, *European Integration online Papers (EIoP)*, Special Mini-Issue 1, Vol. 16, Article 2. Available at http://eiop.or.at/eiop/texte/2012-002a.htm. Accessed 29 May 2014.

Driguez, L. (2010), 'Les institutions de protection sociale face au droit de la concurrence: confirmations ou inflexions?', *Revue de droit sanitaire et social*, **6**, November–December, 1048–59.

Falkner, G. and O. Treib (2008), 'Three Worlds of Compliance or Four? The EU-15 Compared to New Member States', *Journal of Common Market Studies*, **46** (2), 293–313.

Falkner, G., O. Treib, M. Hartlapp and S. Leiber (2005), *Complying with Europe: EU Harmonization and Soft Law in the Member States*, Cambridge: Cambridge University Press.

Guinard, D. (2009), 'Réflexions sur la construction d'une notion juridique: l'exemple de la notion de Services d'intérêt général', PhD thesis, Université Paris-Sud XI, Faculté Jean Monnet.

Hartlapp, M. (2007), 'On Enforcement, Management and Persuasion: Different Logics of Implementation Policy in the EU and the ILO', *Journal of Common Market Studies*, **45** (3), 653–74.

Krajewski, M., U. Neergaard and J. van de Gronden (eds) (2009), *The Changing Legal Framework for Services of General Interest in Europe: Between Competition and Solidarity*, The Hague: TMC Asser Press.

Maucher, M. (2011), 'EU und soziale Dienstleistungen von allgemeinem Interesse – Politikentwicklung im Spannungsfeld zwischen Gemeinwohlorientierung und Wettbewerb', in A. Evers, T. Olk and R. Heinze (eds), *Handbuch Soziale Dienste*, Wiesbaden: VS Verlag für Sozialwissenschaften, pp. 515–35.

Moderne, F. and G. Marcou (eds) (2001), *L'idée de service public dans les Droits de l'Union européenne*, Paris: L'Harmattan.

Neergaard, U. (2009), 'Services of General Interest: The Nature of the Beast', in M. Krajewski, U. Neergaard and J. van de Gronden (eds), *The Changing Legal*

Framework for Services of General Interest in Europe: Between Competition and Solidarity, The Hague: TMC Asser Press, pp. 17–50.
Prosser, T. (2005), *The Limits of Competition Law*, Oxford: Oxford University Press.
Rodière, P. (2008), *Traité de Droit social de l'Union européenne*, Paris: LGDJ.
Sachße, C. (2003), 'Subsidiarität: Leitmaxime deutscher Wohlfahrtsstaatlichkeit', in S. Lessenich (ed.), *Wohlfahrtsstaatliche Grundbegriffe, Historische und aktuelle Diskurse*, Frankfurt: Campus, pp. 191–212.
Supiot, A. (2009), *L'esprit de Philadelphie, la justice sociale face au marché total*, Paris: Seuil.

Official Documents

European Commission (2003), *Green Paper on Services of General Interest*, COM (2003) 270, 21 May.
European Commission (2004), *White Paper of Services of General Interest*, COM (2004) 374, 12 May.
European Commission (2006), Communication from the Commission *Implementing the Community Lisbon programme: Social services of general interest in the European Union*, COM (2006) 177, 26 April.
European Commission (2008), *Biennial Report on social services of general interest*, SEC (2008) 2179, 2 July.
European Commission (2010a), *Second Biennial Report on social services of general interest*, SEC (2010) 1284 final, 22 October.
European Commission (2010b), *Guide to the application of the European Union rules on state aid, public procurement and the internal market to services of general economic interest, and in particular to social services of general interest*, SEC (2010) 1545 final, 7 December.
European Commission (2011), Report to the president of the Commission 'A New Strategy for the Single Market', COM (2011) 206, final 13 April (Monti Report).
European Commission (2012), Regulation (EU) No. 360/2012, 25 April (De minimis).
Herzog, P. (2003), Report on the Green Paper on Services of General Interest, European Parliament, COM (2003) 270 – 2003/2152(INI).
Huber, M., M. Maucher and B. Sak (2006), *Study on social and health services of general interest in the European Union*, Final Synthesis Report, report for DG Employment social affairs and equal opportunities.

12. Services of general interest, state aid and social housing in the Netherlands

Els Sol and Mara van der Vos

12.1 INTRODUCTION: SOCIAL SERVICES

Social services entail a broad range of activities, from the large network industries such as energy, telecommunications, transport, audio-visual broadcasting and postal services, to education, water supply, waste management and health, and go under the heading of 'services of general interest' (SGI). SGI are distinguished from ordinary economic services by the presence of public interests in quality, availability and affordability. Under EU law, social services of general interest (SSGI) are not a legally distinct category within services of general interest.[1] The term 'SSGI' is used only in policy documents of the Commission and not in primary and secondary EU law. Treaty provisions do not mention SSGI, and neither do EU harmonization measures such as the Services Directive pay attention to these services.[2]

The situation of social services has been the subject of discussion in recent years. Social services can be of an economic or non-economic nature depending on the activity under consideration. Although they are not defined, the 2006 Communication identified two broad types of social services:

1. statutory and complementary social security schemes, organized in various ways (mutual or occupational organizations), covering the main risks of life, such as those linked to health, ageing, occupational accidents, unemployment, retirement and disability;
2. other essential services 'provided directly to the person', such as

[1] Com (2006) 177 final, p. 4.
[2] Van de Gronden (2011), p. 125.

social assistance services, employment and training services, social housing and long-term care.[3]

These services are typically organized at a local level and are heavily dependent on public funding. Despite differences between EU countries, according to the Commission a general trend can be observed as regards the way in which modernization is taking place. Usually modernization is accompanied by decentralization, outsourcing and public–private partnerships.[4] This is also the case in the Netherlands.

In general, the case law of the Court of Justice of the European Union (CJEU) indicates that the EC Treaty gives Member States the freedom to define missions of general interest and to establish the organizational principles of the services intended to accomplish them. However, this freedom must be exercised transparently and without misusing the notion of general interest, and the Member States must take account of Community law when fixing the arrangements for implementing the objectives and principles they have laid down. Moreover, when it comes to services of an economic nature, the compatibility of their organizational arrangements with other areas of Community law must be ensured (in particular freedom to provide services and freedom of establishment, and competition law).[5] In the field of competition law, the ECJ[6] has established that any activity consisting of supplying goods and services in a given market by an undertaking constitutes an economic activity, regardless of the legal status of the undertaking and the way in which it is financed. With regard to the freedom to provide services and freedom of establishment, the CJEU has ruled that services provided generally for payment must be considered as economic activities within the meaning of the Treaty. It therefore follows that almost all services offered in the social field can be considered 'economic activities' within the meaning of Articles 43 and 49 of the EC Treaty. If a (social) service of general interest is regarded as economic, it is subject to internal market and competition rules. Hence, European institutions, especially the CJEU and the Commission, have the opportunity to influence the

---

[3] See *inter alia* Communication from the Commission. Implementing the Community Lisbon programme: Social services of general interest in the European Union, COM (2006) 177 final, p. 4.

[4] COM (2006) 177 final, para 1.2.

[5] COM (2006) 177 final, para 2.1.

[6] As part of the CJEU the European Court of Justice is tasked with interpreting EU law and ensuring its equal application across all EU member states.

provision of SSGI. Only in the case of economic activities has the (local) government to deal with state aid rules.

It is the Commission itself which notes that the interpretation of 'economic activity' within (S) and SGI will remain a source of uncertainty. In the words of the Commission:

> The public authorities and the operators in the field of social services of general interest perceive the constant evolution of CJEU jurisprudence, in particular for the notion of 'economic activity' as a source of uncertainty. Whilst the case law and Community legislation have endeavoured to reduce this uncertainty or clarify its impact, they cannot do away with it completely.[7]

Social housing is an example of a source whose economic activity has led to great uncertainty. The many cases in which the Commission had to make a decision whether or not state aid is involved speak for themselves:

- N209/2001 Ireland
- N42/2004 Germany
- E 2/2005 the Netherlands
- N798/2006 Sweden
- N358/2009 Hungary
- N642/2009 the Netherlands
- N725/2009 Ireland

The decision of the Commission on social housing in the Netherlands led to fierce disputes, partly due to the size and scope of this sector in the Netherlands. The decision of the Commission had far-reaching consequences for housing policy in the Netherlands. It created great uncertainty for the various actors who have to carry out the decision in the Netherlands, but the ruling also has potentially profound implications for many other housing markets in Europe.[8]

The structure of the chapter is organized as follows. In section 12.2, the case of Dutch social housing is highlighted. The relevant legal framework, typical characteristics of the Dutch social housing market and the effect of the EU ruling on Dutch social housing policy will be elaborated on. In section 12.3 some conclusions are drawn.

---

7 COM (2006) 177 final, p. 7.

8 See for example the following statement: 'If unchallenged [this kind of interference from the European Union] could have as profound an impact on social housing in this country as Tuesday's Budget' (Source: Inside Housing UK, 28 June 2010).

12.2 SOCIAL HOUSING IN THE NETHERLANDS

12.2.1 Introduction

In a letter dated 14 July 2005 on the financing of housing associations in the Netherlands (State Aid E 2/2005),[9] the European Commission expressed its doubts about whether the financing was compatible with European state aid rules. Despite the fact that this letter only contained a provisional standpoint, the message hit the Dutch social housing world like a bomb. The reason was that in a preliminary exemption Decision for the financing of services of general economic interest (SGEI) from early 2004, Dutch housing associations seemed to have been given considerable freedom to operate.[10] However, in line with the provisional standpoint, the final exemption Decision announced on 15 July 2009 confirmed the strict requirements the Commission places on this type of financing.[11] The Decision also impacted on a later report of the Netherlands to the Commission concerning special project support for the revival of declining urban regions to social housing associations (Case nr. N 642/2009).

The letter of 14 July 2005 was one of the pivotal points in a dispute that started in 2002 and is still ongoing.

12.2.2 Legal Framework

The decision whether an activity is to be considered of general interest lies with the (national or local) government in question. In this realm government has a large scope for discretion. In principle governments are entitled to decide for themselves what activities they consider to be of 'public interest', whether or not they will recognize a service as an SGEI and how a service is to be implemented.

However, their power is not unlimited: the European Commission (e.g. in the case of a state aid notification) and the CJEU (in the case of a conflict before the CJEU) can subsequently test whether or not the government has made a 'manifest error' in the identification of an (S)SGEI, and whether or not the allocation has been according to the

---

9 See state aid E 2/2005 (EX-NN 93/02) – Financiering van woningcorporaties – Nederland, 18 July 2005. The Dutch term is '*woningcorporaties*' (housing corporations). We prefer the more international term 'housing associations'.

10 White Paper 2004, p. 13.

11 N 642/2009.

procedural requirements. Only in retrospect does the Commission correct this definition for manifest errors.

In the Decision of 14 July 2005 the Commission reports an obvious problem in the definition of SGEI. The public service definition of the Dutch housing associations is regarded as being too broad. The housing activities of the associations are not restricted to a clearly defined target group of disadvantaged citizens or socially less advantaged groups. According to the Commission, the provision of social housing may qualify as services of general economic interest only if the provision is restricted to a target group of disadvantaged citizens or socially less advantaged groups.

Furthermore, any commercial activities by the housing associations should be carried out on market terms and should not benefit from state aid. There are four aid measures from which Dutch housing associations profit:

- subsidies from the Central Fund for Housing;
- guarantees from the Social Housing Guarantee Fund for the housing associations;
- the housing associations' exemption from corporation tax (until 2008);
- their right to borrow money from the Dutch Municipal Bank under favourable conditions.

The non-transparent division between public service tasks and commercial activities makes it difficult for the Commission to assess whether there is a question of overcompensation. In order to accomplish the aid of an SGEI being restricted to compensation, the CJEU has set four cumulative requirements, also known as the *Altmark* criteria. In July 2005, the Commission adopted the *Altmark* package, a Commission Decision (based on Article 86(3) of the EC Treaty) that specifies the conditions under which compensation to companies for the provision of public services is compatible with state aid rules.[12]

With the *Altmark* judgment the traditional state aid approach was replaced by the compensation approach. The CJEU held that a financial compensation by the government to an undertaking entrusted with an SGEI is not state aid within the meaning of Article 107(1) TFEU (ex Article 87), when the financing will be limited to compensation for the costs of an average, well-managed company. In that case there is no

[12] 2005/842/EC.

advantage for the company vis à vis its competitors, which places the company in a more favourable position in the common market.

The *Altmark* criteria are as follows:

1. the beneficiary must be charged with implementing clearly defined public service obligations;
2. the parameters for calculating compensation must be established in advance in an objective and transparent way;
3. the compensation must not exceed what is needed to cover the costs of providing the service including a proportionate profit;
4. if the company is not selected under a public procurement procedure, the level of compensation is set on the basis of an analysis of the costs of an average, well-managed company that is suitably equipped to provide the public service.[13]

On the positive side, since the *Altmark* judgment the compensation for SGEI no longer has to be notified. However, the government providing compensation must now itself apply the four cumulative criteria in order to comply with the conditions for non-notification, whereas in the traditional state aid approach, after notification, this was done by the Commission. In the case of social housing in the Netherlands the fourth criterion was not met and therefore in legal terms the compensation constituted (forbidden) state aid.

In the letter of 14 July 2005 the Commission asks the Member State the Netherlands to ensure that the activities of housing associations, which profit from state aid, have a direct relationship with socially disadvantaged households. Moreover, any commercial exploitation must take place under market conditions. Furthermore, the excessive structural overcapacity of social housing must be prevented. Summarizing, the Dutch government must ensure that state aid does not benefit activities that are performed in competition with the market.[14]

In December 2011 the European Commission updated its original SGEI package of 2005, which came into force on 31 January 2012 (with

---

[13] HvJ EG 24 July 2003, case C-280/00, *Altmark Trans GmbH and Regierungspräsidium Magdeburg v Nahverkehrsgesellschaft Altmark GmbH*, Jur. 2003, I-7747.

[14] European Commission, State Aid E 2/2005 (Ex-NN 93/02) – Financiering van woningcorporaties –Nederland, 18 July 2005.See also *Parliamentary Papers II* 2005/06, 29 453, no. 30; *Parliamentary Papers II* 2004/05, 29 846, 29 453, no. 7.

exception of a de minimis Regulation that was adopted in 2013).[15] The new package clarifies key state aid principles and introduces a diversified and proportionate approach with simpler rules for SGEI that are small, local in scope or pursue a social objective, while better taking account of competition considerations for large cases.[16] All social services have now become exempted from the obligation of notification to the Commission, regardless of the amount of compensation received. Previously only hospitals and social housing were exempted. The revised *Altmark* package seems to have no implications for social housing yet. The accord between the EC and Dutch government fits in with the new Decision according to Competition Commissioner Almunia. However, for Dutch housing policy, this accord does not provide a solution.

The substantial gap between the prices on the rental market and the market for owner-occupied dwellings has as a consequence that households with an income just above EUR 33,000 can have substantial difficulties in finding adequate and affordable housing. Since the Decision by the Commission, an increasing number of indications show that lower middle income groups are encountering problems, as they must rely on the more expensive private housing sector. The private sector housing market does not offer houses at prices a Dutch lower middle income household can afford.

The tremendous impact of the requirements of the SGEI package on the housing system in the Netherlands can best be explained by a closer examination of the Dutch housing market.

---

[15] Commission Decision of 20.12.2011 on the application of Article 106(2) of the Treaty on the Functioning of the European Union to State aid in the form of public service compensation granted to certain undertakings entrusted with the operation of services of general economic interest, OJ 2012, L7/3; Communication Commission European Union framework for State aid in the form of public service compensation, OJ 2012, C8/15; Communication from the Commission on the application of the European Union State aid rules to compensation granted for the provision of services of general economic interest, Brussels, OJ 2012, C8/4: De minimis Regulation 1407/2013.

[16] See also Sauter (2012) on the Commission's new SGEI package.

12.2.3 The Dutch Housing Market and the Role of Housing Associations

Housing markets in Europe differ from country to country. Anglo-Saxon countries tend to restrict social housing strictly to the poor, whereas Continental and Scandinavian countries also build for the lower middle class. These international differences in the characteristics and the segmentation of rental markets formed the basis for theoretical research by Jim Kemeny (1995, 2006).

Kemeny's thesis is that whereas in Anglo-Saxon countries the pursuit of a profit-driven private rental market has condemned social housing to a residual role, this is not the case in countries that have adopted a unitary rental housing strategy based on the social market approach. In the unitary market system social housing competes directly with a more regulated, and supported, private rental sector (Kemeny 1995). The Anglo-Saxon countries have chosen to promote an unhindered profit rental market, which, he argues, inevitably leads to growth in owner occupation and the need for a residual public rental sector (Kemeny 1995, p. 18).

At the heart of Kemeny's work is the contrast between the dual rental market and the unitary rental market. In a dual rental market quite different rent policies are adopted in the social and private, profit seeking, sectors. In contrast, most Continental European countries have adopted a unitary rental market, in which governments have, in various ways, sought to minimize differences in rents, quality and social attractiveness between the social and private parts of the rental sector. This entails forms of rent regulation but also a degree of subsidy for private landlords (Scanlon and Whitehead 2008, p. 21). The main features of the two housing rental market models are summarized in Table 12.1.

What differentiates the two ways of organizing the rental sector is the role given to the non-profit sector. In the integrated rental market, non-profit renting is accessible to the general public. In a dualist system, however, the non-profit sector is confined to the poor.

The provision of dwellings according to the non-profit principle has been excluded from the open rental market in English-speaking countries, in some Scandinavian countries – Norway, Finland and Iceland – and in a number of other countries. In stark contrast, in Germany, Sweden, Denmark, the Netherlands, Switzerland and Austria the economic strengths of non-profit enterprises have been cultivated and attempts made to combine/integrate them with the open rental market (Kemeny 2006). On the basis of the classification models in rental housing, the

Table 12.1 Features of dual and unitary rental markets

	Dual rental market	Unitary rental market
Objective of social housing policy	Separate non-profit from market: no direct competition between non-profit and for profit rental sector	Integrated rental market, with direct competition between profit and non-profit rental sectors
Function of non-profit rental sector	Safety net	Housing for broad layers of population
Development of non-profit rental sector	Financial resources are withdrawn from the non-profit sector when it reaches a certain level of maturation (by selling housing stock at a high discount)	Growth of non-profit sector is inhibited and financial resources are not withdrawn from the sector, but object subsidies are phased out as the sector becomes more mature
Brick and mortar subsidies	Non-profit rental sector strongly subsidized	Subsidies phased out as the non-profit sector becomes mature
Rent levels and differentiation	No market-dependent rent level and differentiation in non-profit rental sector: demand is by definition higher than supply	Market-dependent rent level, at a level that is lower than the market rent
Rent subsidy	Rent subsidy strongly dependent on income but independent of rent level and housing quality	Rent subsidy determined by market forces
Segmentation of the sector	Strong market segmentation. Owner occupation sector dominant. Profit rental sector is for those that do not want to buy. Non-profit sector is for those who are unable to buy (stigmatized)	Limited market segmentation. Owner occupation sector less dominant. Sectors compete for favours of households (tenure neutrality)
Households non-profit rental sector	Strong concentration of low income groups	Less strong concentration of low incomes, more medium and high incomes

Source: Derived from Kemeny (1995), in Elsinga et al. (2008), p. 23.

various European countries can be characterized according to their approach to social housing (see typology in Figure 12.1).

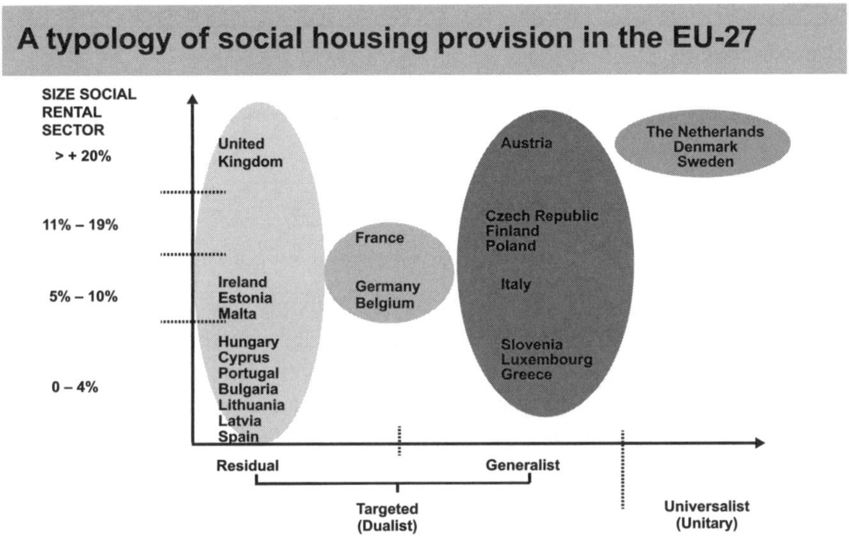

Source: CECODHAS Social Housing Observatory, http://www.ary.fi/aineisto/Kalervo_Haverinen_CECODHAS_ARY_HK_14122010.pdf (accessed 26 January 2015).

Figure 12.1 A typology of social housing provision in the EU-27

Continental countries with a corporatist regime have in the main opted for a unitary rental market (Kemeny 2006). The Netherlands is one of those countries. The country has the largest and most advanced of all integrated rental markets. Social rental housing in the Netherlands currently covers a little less than one-third of the total housing stock (Table 12.2). Despite the growth in home ownership during the latest decennia, the share of social housing has hardly decreased, until recently.

The social housing stock is managed by social housing associations. The first housing associations in the Netherlands were formed in 1850 by private initiatives. Amongst others churches, businesses and unions took the initiative to create better housing for the poor. In 1901, with the introduction of the Housing Act, the receipt of financial support for this task was explicitly allowed. Under the Housing Act a housing association is an authorized institution. As an authorized institution the housing association must meet with a number of housing rights and obligations in areas such as allocation and financing.

Table 12.2 Dutch housing stock by sector

Sector	1993	2001	2010	2013
Home ownership	47%	53%	57%	65%
Privately rented	15%	12%	10%	7%
Social rented	35%	35%	33%	28%
Total stock (mln)	6.0	6.7	7.1	7.3*

Note: *Estimation.
Source: Aedes.

After World War II until the 1990s public housing was controlled by the Dutch government in detail. In few other areas was the government as successful as in public housing. With a relatively free rental and owner occupied sector and a government funded and controlled social rented sector, a good and affordable housing stock was rapidly achieved.

In the early 1990s a turnaround began. The government had to cut back in favour of the free market: too much of the responsibility for living was said to be in government hands. In these years government policy largely became decentralized to the municipalities and further privatized with the objective of improving efficiency. The so-called 'grossing up action' of 1995 was a further cut in the direct relationship between public housing and government. With the introduction of the grossing law all outstanding loans and subsidies still to be received between the government and housing associations were crossed off. Since that moment the associations have been responsible for their own exploitation losses. Nevertheless associations are obliged to realize certain aims, as described in the *Decision on the Management of Social Housing* (BBSH). In return the Social Housing Guarantee Fund guarantees, under certain conditions, the associations' loans. Furthermore, associations can appeal for extra support from the *Centraal Fonds voor Volkshuisvesting* (CFV).[17]

The introduction of the BBSH meant a fundamental change in the regulation of housing associations: a switch from requirements in advance to remote monitoring and accountability afterwards.[18] As an elaboration of the Dutch Housing Act, the BBSH provides further rules,

[17] http://www.vrom.nl/pagina.html?id=19598#a30 (accessed 23 May 2013). The CFV is an independent administrative body whose main task is to financially supervise and restructure social housing associations in the Netherlands.

[18] http://www.wswonen.nl/Uploaded_Files/446_ce_BBSHAchtergronden2006.pdf (accessed 23 May 2013).

including on admission, on mergers and on pursuit of the business. Due to the public link which housing associations have as authorized institutions, they have some special rights and obligations. Thus, authorized housing associations are free to sell their assets but solely in the interests of public housing. The definition of their domain must be defined in the statutes. Making a profit is permitted but only when serving public housing. This provision is intended to compel associations to self-regulation. The strategy can be called a *slipstream strategy*: building social housing for the lower middle income group is done in the same neighbourhoods as the poor as part of a single housing project – so the whole neighbourhood's housing and living conditions will profit and thereby also the welfare of the broader society.

In 2010 there were 418 housing associations in the Netherlands and 14 per cent of the associations possessed more than 10,000 dwellings (Table 12.3). The average number of housing units per association was 5,600.

Table 12.3 Size of social housing associations (2010)

Number of dwellings	Housing associations	
	Number	Percentage
0–500	56	13%
500–5,000	228	55%
5,000–10,000	74	18%
10,000–20,000	38	9%
>20,000	22	5%
Total	418	100%

Source: Aedes.

Thirty-three per cent of housing stock in the Netherlands is owned by bodies that receive state funding. In 2005, the European Commission argued that having more than 30 per cent of homes belonging to the social housing sector seemed 'disproportionate'.

According to Scharpf (2009), interference in such a range of autonomous policy choices by a Member State tends to undermine the institutions and policy legacies of Continental and Scandinavian social market economies. He even suggested in an interview to 'refuse to comply with

CJEU rulings'[19] because they force all EU countries into the same neoliberal mould by increasing home ownership and marginalizing non-profit renting.[20] Although housing is not the concern of the EU, with the implicit encouragement of home ownership by the EU and the explicit support for home ownership in Member States, the rental sector will become a last resort. This policy can be seen as dismantling the unitary model by stealth.[21]

12.2.4 The Effect of the EU Ruling on Dutch Policy

12.2.4.1 Introduction

The reactions by Dutch associations to the EU ruling were in line with Scharpf's call. Their responses are described further below. First the Dutch government responded to the 2005 EC letter. It did not resist the provisional standpoint but decided to enter into negotiations with the Commission. In her 'Policy Vision' Minister Dekker addressed the letter from the Commission with its preliminary position (Dekker 2005). According to the Minister, the definition of the target group of social housing should be restricted to households with a maximum income of EUR 33,000. With this figure of EUR 33,000 the Minister expected to meet with the requirement of the Commission of a limited target group. Furthermore, she proposed a financial separation between the associations' social activities, funded by government, and their market activities.

Ever since the preliminary position by the Commission of 2005 there had been ongoing consultations between the Dutch government and the Commission about how to proceed. Simultaneously the Minister had been debating with the Parliament about a layout for the housing system in line with the requirements of European law.

12.2.4.2 The Commission Decision on state aid: Limitation of the social housing target group is needed

On 15 December 2009 the Dutch government received the Decision by the Commission on state aid, following negotiations between the Dutch

---

[19] Scharpf interview (2009) available at http://www.social-europe.eu/2009/04/interview-the-only-solution-is-to-refuse-to-comply-with-ecj-rulings (accessed 29 May 2013).

[20] See also Elsinga et al. (2008), p. 35.

[21] Ibid.

Minister and the EC.[22] In conformity with its preliminary position of 14 July 2005, the Commission indicated that in order to be qualified as a service of general economic interest, the social housing target group had to be limited.

In the negotiations the Dutch government promised to make several changes to the Dutch system in order to bring it in line with the European state aid rules. The most important compromise was that from 2009 90 per cent of the dwellings with a monthly rent under EUR 647 that became available annually had to be allocated by the housing associations to households with the set maximum income of EUR 33,000. The Dutch government and the Commission came to an agreement. By accepting these changes, the Commission believed that the Netherlands complied with its request and therefore with the definition of service of general economic interest. The Commission decided not to raise any objections to the newly notified measure on the ground that it constituted compatible aid under Article 106(2).[23] In the same Decision the Commission accepted project aid for the revival of declining urban regions to social housing associations (case nr. N 642/2009).

In the Netherlands the Decision based on an agreement between the Dutch government and the Committee received a negative response. Following the Decision, the Dutch Parliament urged the Minister to lobby amongst other Member States for allies in favour of the Dutch unified social housing system and against this ruling by the EC. Moreover, in a motion Parliament asked the Dutch government to ensure acceptance of Dutch housing associations serving a broader target group with state aid, in order to help citizens who were unable to find a house on the free market and to help associations fight segregation. Parliament feared the new narrow definition of social housing would have major consequences for the Dutch association sector, would harm national authority in determining a service as an SGEI (106 paragraph 2 EC) and would thereby undermine the whole Dutch tradition of social housing.[24]

After intensive lobbying by the housing associations, parliamentarians requested the Minister not to implement the Decision and to return to Brussels in order to reopen negotiations on the income limit.[25] However,

---

22 Commission Decision in cases No E 2/2005 and No 642/2009 (The Netherlands, Existing and special project aid to housing corporations) of 15 December 2009 by means of Directive C (2009) 9963.

23 Commission Decision, ibid., at point 109.

24 Motion by van Bochove et al., *Kamerstukken II* in, Parliamentary Papers, 2008/09, 29453, no. 125.

25 Motion by Karabulut et al., *Kamerstukken II* in, Parliamentary Papers, 2009/10, 29453, no. 173.

the motion to this effect did not get a majority vote. Because the motion on renegotiations with Brussels was not adopted, the Minister was able to implement the Decision on 1 April 2011.

12.2.4.3 Implementation of the Decision of the EC

Initially, the ministerial regulation implementing the Decision of the Commission was due to come into force on 1 October 2010. However, after a motion adopted by Parliament, the Minister postponed the date until 1 January 2011.

The transmission of the Decision of the European Commission into Dutch legislation eventually took place in two phases. First, on 1 April 2011, a ministerial order was introduced regulating (1) the activities for which state aid was allowed (including social property), (2) the housing allocation (the 90 per cent), and (3) the obligation to tender social property. The second stage concerned the administrative separation of activities of housing associations and the calculation and payment of any overcompensation that was regulated by law as part of a bill amending the Housing Act (Reform Act Authorized Institutions).

The ministerial regulation identified activities in the Netherlands for which activity or service state aid was allowed and regulated the social housing allocation as well as the procurement of real estate.[26] The Dutch government planned to amend the Housing Act so that the administrative separation of housing activities performed with and without state aid would be governed by law. As of 1 January 2011, the housing associations were obliged in each lease contract to take into account the income limit of EUR 33,614 and also to register the lease.[27] And since 1 January 2012 housing associations have been allowed to rent no more than a maximum of 10 per cent of their social houses to households with an income above EUR 33,614. In addition, the housing associations have to take into account that for certain activities there are no longer guarantees given by the Guarantee Fund for Social Housing.

Such is the case for example for the construction of apartments with a rent above the liberalization limit and for civil property that is not on the list, as described in the ministerial order.

As would be expected, the housing associations reacted predominantly negatively to the ministerial regulation. Thus, when a call came from one of the housing associations to let social housing targets prevail over the strict execution of the EC rules, nearly three-quarters of the directors of

---

[26] Government Gazette, 2010, no. 17515, p. 1.

[27] From 1 January 2012 the income limit is EUR 34,085.

the associations responded positively. Some housing associations continued to accommodate households with an income up to EUR 43,000 and took any penalties for granted.[28] This was the income limit, above which tenants could expect a yearly rent increase of inflation plus 5 per cent, as mentioned in the coalition agreement by the Christian Democrat–Liberal cabinet called 'Freedom and Responsibility' (October 2010). There were also housing associations which continued to rent housing to households with an income up to EUR 45,000 per year. Other housing associations, such as those in Amsterdam, used newspaper advertisements to show their dissatisfaction with the regime but did carry out the rules.[29] One housing association set its limit at EUR 43,000. This way it claimed to still meet the European rules, as for urgent cases it only needed to reserve a few homes a year. As a result, the allocation of households with incomes between EUR 33,614 and 43,000 fell within the allotted 10 per cent. The housing association monitored carefully so that action could be taken as 10 per cent space was fully utilized. Another solution used by another housing association was the provision of rental apartments above the limit of EUR 652.52 to households with an income above the EUR 33,614 limit while freezing the rent for five years.

On 30 April 2010 133 housing associations lodged a complaint against the Decision of the Commission of 15 December 2009 on two state aid Decisions at the CJEU regarding Decision N 642/2009.[30] According to the associations, many households had run into difficulties because they no longer qualified for a house from the social housing associations. In essence, the housing associations believed that the Commission was abusing its power, as it required a new definition of social housing from the Dutch government. According to the housing associations, the Commission did not have the power to impose a specific definition of the concept of services of general economic interest in the social housing sector.[31]

The Dutch umbrella organization Aedes, the European Liaison Committee for Social Housing Cecodhas, and the French (Union Sociale pour

---

[28] 'Corporaties spreken met gemeentes inkomensgrens af', http://www.aedesnet.nl (accessed 21 January 2011).

[29] http://www.dekey.nl/huurders/sociale-huur/hoe-kom-ik-in-aanmerking (accessed 21 January 2011).

[30] Case T/202/10 (Stichting Woonlinie and others/Commission), T/203/10 (Stichting Woonpunt and others/Commission).

[31] Press release, '133 corporaties in beroep bij Europees Gerecht', 3 May 2010, www.aedesnet.nl (accessed 20 May 2013); Appendix to the press release '133 corporaties in beroep bij Europees Gerecht, 3 May 2010: 'Samenvatting beroepsgronden tegen beschikking', www.aedesnet.nl (accessed 20 May 2013).

l'Habitat; USH) and Walloon (Société wallonne du logement) umbrella organizations supported the associations in their procedure. Already in 2008 the French USH had made public its belief that the perception of social housing as a service of general economic interest, developed by the Commission in its letter to the Dutch government on 14 July 2005, de facto reduced access to social housing to people who were socially underprivileged, reducing the classification of social housing as a service of general economic interest to the existence 'of a direct link with socially underprivileged people'. In other words, the Commission was accused of holding an exceptionally residual perception of social housing which created tension with the freedom of the Member States to define social housing missions, notably in terms of cohesion and social and housing diversity objectives.[32]

In the same week of 30 April 2010, when the housing associations lodged their complaint, the Association of Institutional Property Investors & Vesteda, a private housing association, also lodged an appeal against the Commission's Decision.[33] However, its argument was diametrically opposed to the argument of the social housing associations, as in its opinion the Decision would obstruct the *commercial* housing market. Dwellings owned by associations would be rented under the limit of EUR 647 per month, although these dwellings are partly commercial. Furthermore, in its opinion the limit of the social housing group to EUR 33,000 was set too high, because almost 43 per cent of Dutch households are covered by that category.[34]

In July 2011 a majority in the Dutch parliament once again urged the Minister to arrange for people with a lower middle income to be eligible for social rented housing on a more frequent basis.[35] But the Minister did not show any initiative. In October 2011 parliamentarians demanded the Minister provide information on the effects of the state aid ruling for the lower middle income group. The Minister refused; according to him it was too early days. As the Minister remained reluctant to commit to the cause, in November 2011 centre left Social Democrats in Parliament threatened a vote of no confidence if the Minister, against the wishes of the majority of Parliament, continued to refuse to make more social dwellings available for people with lower middle incomes. However,

---

32 L. Ghekiere (2008), p. 7.

33 T-201/10 (IVBN/Commission).

34 Press release, 'EU-beschikking blokkeert commerciële huurwoningmarkt. IVBN en Vesteda in beroep', http://www.ivbn.nl/persbericht/eu-beschikking-blokkeert-commerciele-huurwoningenmarkt (accessed 16 May 2013).

35 Dutch Parliament year of session 2010-2011, 29453, no. 200.

again the Minister refused and warned against the great risks of renegotiations with Brussels on the topic of state aid. According to the Christian Democrat Minister, all that had been won by the agreement and that had been gained could be jeopardized.

On 16 December 2011 the General Court treated the appeal submitted by the Dutch housing associations against the two state aid Decisions. The Court dismissed the complaint of the associations against the Decisions on technical grounds of inadmissibility; the Court made no statement in terms of content.[36] The Court in its judgment contested the admissibility of the application for annulment of the applicants on the grounds that the contested were not individually harmed within the meaning of Article 263 TFEU.

However, although Advocate-General Whatelet did agree with the argument of the General Court that the housing associations' lack interest in process – there was no relation between the Decision in state aid case N 642-2009 and state aid case E 2-2005 on the grounds of Article 263 fourth alinea of the TFEU – he contested the decision by the Court. According to the Advocate-General, Member States did have the capacity to intervene in the case without having to demonstrate any legal interests in bringing proceedings, unlike other stakeholders.

By the end of 2012 the Dutch social housing organizations had got support from an advisory committee of the European Parliament. According to the European Economic and Social Committee, access to decent housing was no longer affordable for many EU citizens, and not only in the Netherlands, due to the package. The Committee published an own initiative opinion on 'Issues with defining social housing as a service of general economic interest' in which it urged the Commission to reconsider its decision making practices for checking obvious mistakes: 'Member States should be given the discretion to set access conditions and prices for housing in a way that takes account of local needs and local preferences, as well as the real needs of disadvantaged or socially less advantaged groups, in accordance with the provisions of Protocol No 26 on services of general interest.'[37]

On 27 February 2014 the CJEU followed Whatelet's argument in its judgment and set the General Court ruling of 16 December 2011 aside.[38] According to the Court, in Case T-202/10 of Woonlinie and others against

---

[36] Case T-202/10 and T203/10.

[37] Opinion of the European Economic and Social Committee on 'Issues with defining social housing as a service of general economic interest' (own initiative opinion) 2013/C 44/09, section 7.2.

[38] Case C-132/12.

the European Commission, Member States had to be actively involved in the substantive proceedings on the definition of social SGEI. The Court of Justice declared the appeal of the corporations admissible and referred the case back to the General Court. The housing corporations were 'back in business' on technical grounds. The General Court of Justice would now judge the substance of the appeal, and answer the question whether Member States could file an application to intervene in proceedings, as in the case of Woonlinie and others against the European Commission, and thus exercise their full jurisdiction for defining SGEI, including social services of general interest. It was anticipated that the General Court would soon be ruling over the definition and scope of social housing in the domestic housing market, but the Court has not yet ruled.[39]

12.3 CONCLUSIVE REMARKS

In an international context, the Dutch social rental sector is often regarded as a solid system for providing affordable housing to those who need it, without the sector being marginalized and stigmatized. It is characteristic of the decentralization in the Netherlands that in the social rental sector individual social housing associations play a major active role. The EU appears to be hostile towards social housing associations, which should receive no public subsidies, unless and until they are restricted to the poor. Only then are subsidies acceptable to the EU. Yet, paradoxically, tax deductions for owner occupiers are not counted as subsidies.

The social service of social housing has always been the primary concern of national governments. But recent developments in the domain of state aid make clear that housing policy simply cannot be performed without taking European law into account. The EU ruling threatens to force all countries into the same uniform mould and to lead in a direction that will not tolerate divergent national social housing systems.

The case of social housing in the Netherlands discussed in this chapter has shown the asymmetry in the effect of EU legislation, which varies according to ideal types of social protection. EU legislation undermines the social markets of the northern welfare states (the Netherlands, Denmark, Sweden) to a point where their unitary housing market is forced to become a dualist market. (Legal) uncertainties over the definition and scope of social housing still exist. The question is, how far will the control of the EC go? Other European countries like France and

---

39 June 2014.

Sweden follow the discussion closely as they fear the EC will reduce their leeway in social housing as well. The battle is not yet over.

BIBLIOGRAPHY

Arnon, K.E. and Sluijs, J.J.M. (2008). 'Het arrest BUPA: publieke diensten en marktwerking', *Nederlands tijdschrift voor Europees recht*, (7/8), 206–213.

Centraal Fonds Volkshuisvesting (2009a). *Sectorbeeld realisaties woningcorporaties, verslagjaar 2008*. Naarden: CFV.

Centraal Fonds Volkshuisvesting (2009b). *Sectorbeeld realisaties woningcorporaties, verslagjaar 2008*, Naarden: CFV, new version.

Chalmers, D. (2006). *European Union Law: Text and Materials*. Cambridge: Cambridge University Press.

Craig, P.P. and Búrca, G. de (2008). *EU Law Text, Cases and Material*. Oxford: Oxford University Press.

Dekker, S.M. (2005). *Beleidsvisie toekomst van woningcorporaties*. Brief aan de Tweede Kamer. The Hague: Vergaderjaar 2005/2006, 29 453, no. 30.

Dekker, S.M. (2006). *Nota ruimte geven, bescherming bieden: Een visie op de woningmarkt*, The Hague: VROM.

Dol, K. and Haffner, M. (2010). *Housing Statistics in the European Union*. The Hague: Ministry of the Interior and Kingdom Relations.

Elsinga, M., Haffner, M. and Heijden, H. van der (2008). 'Threats to the Dutch unitary rental market', *European Journal of Housing Policy*, 8 (1), 21–37.

European Commission (2001). 'State aid, guarantee for borrowings of the Housing Finance Agency'. (2001/N209/EC), Brussels.

European Commission (2004). 'State aid, real estate transfer tax exemption for housing companies in the Neu Lander'. (2004/N42/EC), Brussels.

European Commission (2005a). 'On the application of Art. 86(2) of the EC Treaty to state aid in the form of public service compensation granted to certain undertakings entrusted with the operation of services of general economic interest'. (2005/842/EC), Brussels.

European Commission (2005b). *Better Off in Europe. How the EU's Single Market Benefits You*. Luxembourg: Office for Official Publications of the European Communities.

European Commission (2006). 'Implementing the Community Lisbon programme: social services of general interest in the European Union'. (COM/2006/0177final), Brussels.

European Commission (2009a). 'State aid, support scheme for housing loans'. (2009/N358/EC), Brussels.

European Commission (2009b). 'State aid, establishment of a National Asset Management Agency (NAMA): Asset relief scheme for banks in Ireland'. (2009/N725/EC), Brussels.

European Commission (2009c), 'State aid, existing and special project aid to housing corporations'. (2009/ N642/EC), Brussels.

European Commission (2010). 'Second biennial report on social services of general interest'. (SEC/2010/1284final), Brussels.

European Commission (2011a). 'The application of EU state aid rules on Services of General Economic Interest since 2005 and the outcome of the public consultation'. (SEC/2011/397), Brussels.

European Commission (2011b). 'The Communication from the Commission to the European Parliament, the Council, the European Economic and Social Committee and the Committee of the Regions'. (COM/2011/146final), Brussels.

Ghekiere, L. (2008). 'European perspectives 2009–2014. Issues of the French presidency', Union sociale pour l'habitat, September, Paris.

Gronden, J.W. van de (2011). 'Social Services of General Interest and EU law', in E. Szyszczak, J. Davies, M. Andenaes and T. Bekkedal (eds), *Developments in Services of General Interest*. The Hague: T.M.C. Asser Press/Springer, 123–53.

Hessel, B. (2010). 'Woningcorporaties en de Europese regels voor staatssteun', *Bouwrecht*, 10, 772–3.

Hessel, B. and Neven, A. (2001). *Staatsteun en EG-recht. Praktische handleiding and checklist. Deel 1*. Deventer: Kluwer.

Inside Housing UK, London. http://www.insidehousing.co.uk. Accessed 29 October 2014.

Jacobs, A.T.J.M. (2010). 'Sociaal recht en sociale politiek na de inwerkingtreding van het Verdrag van Lissabon', *Tijdschrift recht en arbeid*, 2 (11), 5–11.

Kaczorowsky, A. (2008). *European Union Law*. New York: Taylor and Francis.

Kemeny, J. (1995). *From Public Housing to the Social Market: Rental Policy Strategies in Comparative Perspective*. London: Routledge.

Kemeny, J. (2006). 'Corporatism and housing regimes'. *Housing, Theory and Society*, 23 (1), 1–18.

Kuypers, P.H.L.M. and Smallegange, S.G.J. (2008). 'Woningcorporaties en Brussel: een conflict? Het toenemende belang van de Europese regelgeving op de Nederlandse woningcorporaties nader beschouwd', *Tijdschrift voor Omgevingsrecht*, 2008 (2), 41–48.

Lavrijsen, S. and Vries, S. de (2009). 'Netherlands', in M. Krajewski, U. Neergaard and J. van de Gronden (eds), *The Changing Legal Framework for Services of General Interest in Europe: Between Competition and Solidarity*. The Hague: T.M.C. Asser Press, 383–423.

Neergaard, U. (2009). 'Services of general economic interest: the nature of the beast', in M. Krajewski, U. Neergaard and J. van de Gronden (eds), *The Changing Legal Framework for Services of General Interest in Europe: Between Competition and Solidarity*. The Hague: T.M.C. Asser Press, 17–51.

Sauter, W. (2012). *The Commission's New SGEI Package: The Rules for State Aid and the Compensation of Services of General Economic Interest*. DP 2012-018. Tilburg: Tilburg University.

Scanlon, K. and Whitehead, C. (2008). *Social Housing in Europe II: A Review of Policies and Outcomes*. London: London School of Economics and Political Science.

Scharpf, F.W. (2008). 'The only solution is to refuse to comply with ECJ rulings', *Magazin Mitbestimmung* 2008 (7/8), http://www.boeckler.de/36195_36456.htm. Accessed 29 October 2014.

Scharpf, F.W. (2009). 'The double asymmetry of European integration – or: why the EU cannot be a social market economy', *MPIfG Working Paper* 09/12.

Schlössels, R.J.N. and Zijlstra, S.E. (2010). *Bestuursrecht in de sociale rechtsstaat*. Deventer: Kluwer, 6th ed.

13. The impact of EU regulation on social services of general interest in the United Kingdom[1]

Aristea Koukiadaki

13.1 INTRODUCTION

The nature and provision of the so-called 'social services of general interest' (SSGIs) are tightly interlinked with the central question of the role that public authorities play in the market economy. In the UK, there is not a commonly agreed national definition of 'social services of general interest'.[2] In most cases, the generic term 'public services' is used to correspond with 'services of general economic interest' (SGEIs) as well as 'services of general interest' (SGIs) (Bauby and Similie 2010, p. 431). In this context, the UK model of social services usually includes 'the universal provision of health services, the diverse range of local authority services that encompass, inter alia, children's services, care in the community and long-term care for the old and disabled (and that may, or may not, be subject to means testing and/or contributions), through to the needs-based provision of social housing' (Davies 2013, pp. 518–19).

Before proceeding to consider how EU law and policy impact upon the provision of such services, it is useful to summarise briefly how health, social care and social housing are organised in the UK. Overall, the extent of devolution and decentralisation is significant in these cases.[3] In terms of healthcare, the responsibility for the UK National Health

[1] The author is grateful to all the interviewees for their time and assistance, as well as to the European Commission FP7 Programme and the Leverhulme Trust for financing the research.

[2] 'Social services' are limited to care for the elderly, the disabled and vulnerable children and do not include social housing, education or health (Bauby 2013, p. 38).

[3] As a result of devolution, the main part of the analysis is concerned with the English position only.

Service (NHS) is devolved to the component countries, with England, Scotland, Northern Ireland and Wales each responsible for administering the NHS in their respective countries. The model of health services has been traditionally constructed around the notion of a universal service for all based on clinical need, not ability to pay. It is important to recognise that the UK health system is financed out of general taxation, compared with those health insurance systems on which the Court of Justice of the European Union (CJEU) has issued rulings. But due to a number of far-reaching changes in recent years, which were largely motivated by the need to introduce different forms of competitive market and to augment patient choice, 'the system has moved from one organised on the basis of solidarity to one to which competition law applies' (Boeger and Prosser 2009, p. 367).

Social care, social housing, childcare services, care of the disabled and elderly care are regulated at the level of local self-government. Following the 1990 National Health Service and Community Care Act, local authorities started to contract out public services to private providers. However, the fact that services continued to be determined and financed by the public purse meant that only service provision has been 'market privatised' (Bahle 2008, p. 30), while financing, coordination and control remain in the hands of the local authorities. Partly drawing on the findings of the market study by the Office of Fair Trading in 2005, Prosser (2010, p. 123) suggests that 'the provision of social care operates in a highly market-based system, with an extensive role of private providers and privately funded provision subject to the ordinary competition authorities'.

Finally, social housing provision has been allocated traditionally according to need (the so-called residual model of social housing) (Scanlon 2008, p. 8). The role of local authorities was significant for the most part of the development of social housing in the UK. Until the 1970s, one-third of the British population lived in housing owned by the state. However, the Thatcher government introduced *Right to Buy* in the 1980s, which meant that qualifying tenants were given the right to buy the property in which they had been living at a discount of at least 33 per cent. Moreover, the state transferred their property to housing associations on a large scale. As a result of these changes, social housing has been provided through a mixed economy comprising the residual council stock, private landlords and housing associations (Cowan and McDermont 2008, p. 166).

Owing to the particularities of the political and regulatory regime in the UK, one would expect that the implementation of EU liberalisation plans in this area would be less controversial than in Continental Europe

(Boeger and Prosser 2009). Nonetheless, the regulation of a number of services continues to constitute a sensitive topic from a policy perspective. As we shall see, the increasing interest of the European Commission in this area of regulation has meant that EU law has grown in importance for the main actors involved in the definition and provision of SSGIs. Coupled with recent policy developments at domestic level that are oriented towards further marketisation in this area, it will be argued that the scope for interaction between EU law and UK services will increase substantially, with far-reaching implications for the definition of such services as SSGIs or SGEIs and the regulatory framework that will thus be applicable. In order to illustrate this, the analysis will focus on the interaction of UK regulation with EU law in three distinct areas: the Services Directive, public procurement and state aid.

13.2 INTERACTION OF UK REGULATION WITH EU LAW

13.2.1 The Services Directive

The Services Directive[4] was transposed into UK legislation by the Provisions of Services Regulations 2009.[5] In the guidance published by the Department for Business, Innovation and Skills (BIS) (2009), clarifications were provided with respect to the services that are not covered by the Regulations. According to the guidance, healthcare services are considered to be excluded from the Directive 'whether or not they are provided via healthcare facilities, and regardless of the ways in which they are organised and financed at national level, or whether they are public or private' (BIS 2009, p. 7). Social services relating to social housing, childcare and the support of families in need, where these are provided by the state, by providers mandated by the state or by charities recognised as such by the state, are also excluded from the scope of the Directive.[6] The BIS guidance went on to state that '[housing] services

---

[4] Directive 2006/123/EC of the European Parliament and of the Council of 12 December 2006 on services in the internal market, [2006] OJ L 376/36.

[5] SI 2009/2999.

[6] In the UK, there is no general legal prohibition on charities delivering public services, such as social housing and social care, under a funding agreement with a public authority or using their own funds to do so. Charities are a significant part of a wider sector in society known as the voluntary sector or voluntary and community sector. Not all voluntary and community organisations

provided on a commercial basis by registered charitable organisations or their trading subsidiaries are, however, in scope of the Directive' (BIS 2009, p. 7). Interestingly enough, the government's website BusinessLink,[7] which provides support services for organisations wishing to provide services in the UK, contained information concerning the authorisation of licences for a number of social services, healthcare services and social housing.

So far, there has been limited evidence that the Services Directive has impacted on the provision of welfare services in the UK. The introduction of the implementing Regulations has so far promoted a cultural change in the public sector as local authorities have begun to structure their services so as to address also issues related to foreign service providers (Local Government Association (LGA) interview notes).[8] However, the practical difficulties in delivering such services in the absence of a UK base/office may account partially for the lack of foreign services providers being active in this area. Still uncertainty exists, especially since there is absence of a clear-cut definition of social services in the UK legal context (Unison interview notes).[9] Notwithstanding the ambiguities concerning the scope of the Services Directive, the Commission came back to the question of the legal regime of social services with its Communication on services of general interest in 2006. In the latter, the Commission noted:

> In practice, apart from activities in relation to the exercise of public authority, to which internal market rules do not apply by virtue of Article 45 of the EC Treaty, it follows that the vast majority of services can be considered as 'economic activities' within the meaning of the EC Treaty rules of the internal market. (COM 2006, p. 5)

The response of the LGA to this was even-handed. In its LGA guide to EU legislation affecting local authority services, it was stated that:

> whilst welcoming competition in the social services sector, the LGIB [Local Government International Bureau] and its partners will work to send a clear message to the European institutions that it is primarily a matter for Member

are charities. The voluntary and community sector includes all organisations that are neither part of government (public or state sector) nor the private (for profit) sector.

[7] http://www.ukwelcomes.businesslink.gov.uk/bdotg/action/home?site=2000 (accessed 28 September 2011).

[8] The interview took place in 2010 in London.

[9] The interview took place in 2010 in London.

> States and their public authorities, rather than the EU, to decide how best to define, organise and finance their social services. (Rowles 2006, p. 5)

13.2.2 Public Procurement

The EU rules on public procurement do not require public authorities to outsource SSGIs. Instead, they apply only if a public authority decides to entrust the provision of a service to a third party in return for payment. In the UK, the use of procurement at the level of central and local government has been a characteristic feature of public services for a number of years.[10] The 1999 Local Government Act introduced a legal duty on councils to attain 'best value' for local public services, which, essentially, made it extremely difficult for councils not to tender contracts competitively, unless there are good reasons to the contrary; in practice, public authorities are thus unlikely to be able to demonstrate best value to the satisfaction of auditors and the Secretary of State by following just the 'traditional route' (Vincent-Jones 2006, p. 56). At central government level, the procurement policy is also founded on the 'value for money' principle.

The absence of a public law/private law distinction in conjunction with the lack of a special regime of public law contracts means that 'it is often difficult to translate European procurement concepts into domestic law; in theory we only have a single regime of private law for contracting, although in practice contracting is used as a means for the organisation of public services and for meeting public policy goals' (Boeger and Prosser 2009, p. 360). In response to the Commission's consultation on the modernisation of EU Public Procurement Directives 2004/18/EC and 2004/17/EC, the LGA called for the review to 'result in more coherent, consistent and above all significantly simplified legislation' (LGA 2011, point 6). In order to reduce the complexity of the procurement process, it was specifically suggested that EU procedural and administrative requirements, particularly detailed award procedures, should be reduced by simplifying the Directive and increasing flexibility for local authorities.[11]

---

[10] Directive 2004/18/EC has been implemented in the UK by the Public Contracts Regulations 2006, as amended.

[11] On Tuesday 11 February 2014, the General Affairs Council took the decision to adopt a new legislative package for the 'modernisation of public procurement in the EU' (Council of the European Union, Brussels, 11 February 2014, 6337/14). The decision of the Council relates to the adoption of new directives on: (i) public procurement, which replaces the 2004/18/EC Directive; (ii) procurement by entities operating in the utilities sectors (water, energy,

The impact of a number of CJEU decisions on the way local authorities can share services is an illustrative example of the implications of EU regulation for public procurement. Under Directives 2004/18/EC and 2004/17/EC, an EU-wide tendering exercise could be required if the financial amounts involved exceeded certain thresholds. This was because the local authority is effectively buying the service from another local authority, and private sector providers may want the opportunity to compete. In 2009, the CJEU decision on the *Hamburg* case[12] gave more freedom to public bodies and resulted in the dropping of a number of cases pending before the Court. A more recent decision, this time by the UK Supreme Court,[13] indicated that there is flexibility in local authority contracting arrangements. The case resulted from arrangements made by local authorities to establish a mutual insurance company (LAML) and to receive insurance services from the company. The arrangements were challenged on the basis that the local authorities had acted outside their powers in participating in the company and that it was in breach of public procurement legislation for the local authorities to arrange to receive services from the company without going through a procurement exercise. When the case reached the Supreme Court, the CJEU case law on the purpose and scope of the exemption was reviewed and it was held that Directive 2004/18/EC was not intended to protect the commercial sector by forcing public authorities to obtain the services which they need on the commercial market. Accordingly, the Directive did not apply where the authority obtained the services from its own resources; neither – following *Teckal*[14] – did it apply where the authority obtained services from a separate body, which was so closely connected it should be regarded as still obtaining the services in-house. The decision by the Supreme Court was particularly welcomed by the local authorities, as it was interpreted as paving the way for public sector bodies to join together and deliver shared services in a wider context.

---

transport and postal services), which replaces Directive 2004/17/EC; and (iii) the award of concession contracts. The new set of Directives that were adopted have to be implemented into national law within two years of their publication in the Official Journal of the European Union (OJEU) but the Cabinet Office has already undertaken work in an effort to introduce some of the reforms in autumn 2014. As the research was conducted before the adoption of the new Directives, the discussion in the chapter presents the situation under the 2004 Directive.

12 C-480/06, *Commission v Germany* [2009] ECR 2009 I-04747.

13 *Brent LBC (Harrow LBC appellant) v RISK Management Partners Limited* [2011] UKSC 7–9 February 2011.

14 Case C-107/98, *Teckal Srl v Comune di Viano and Azienda Gas-Acqua Consorziale (AGAC) di Reggio Emilia* [1999] ECR I-8121.

13.2.3 EU Competition

Under Articles 106 and 107 TFEU, the compensation granted by public authorities for the performance of an SGEI is subject to state aid scrutiny, unless the four cumulative conditions laid down by the Court of Justice in its *Altmark* judgment are fulfilled. SSGIs, which can be both economic and non-economic in nature, are only subject to EU competition law where they are indeed economic. According to Article 2 of Protocol 26: 'The provisions of the Treaties do not affect in any way the competence of Member States to provide, commission and organise non-economic services of general interest.' Providers of SGEIs are only subject to competition rules, in general, and to state aid rules in particular, insofar as the application of those rules does not obstruct the fulfilment of their tasks. For social SGEIs, the compatibility assessment is based on the package. No sector-specific EU rules exist. Under the SGEIs Decision, though, aid to social housing undertakings and hospitals is exempted from notification regardless of the amount of compensation involved, provided that the conditions of the SGEIs Decision are met.

In the UK, the Office of Fair Trading (OFT) is responsible for enforcing EU competition law. The Competition Act 1998 extended EU competition law prohibitions to cases that only affect trade within the UK. The BIS has lead responsibility within the UK government for the coordination and development of state aid policy. This includes providing advice and guidance on state aid rules, and coordinating and advising on complaint cases and formal investigations. The OFT guidelines state that the term 'undertaking' will be interpreted broadly to include any natural or legal persons capable of carrying on commercial or economic activities relating to goods or services. This approach reflects the 'functional' concept of an undertaking adopted by the CJEU, which has held that Articles 106 and 107 cover any activity directed at trade and goods or services irrespective of the legal form of the undertaking, and regardless of whether it is intended to earn profits.[15]

As Boeger and Prosser (2009, p. 363) suggest, little attention was paid by UK authorities to EU state aid law in the past. This changed following the 2003 *Altmark*[16] decision and the post-*Altmark* reform package, which was issued in 2005. Local and central government in the UK welcomed the post-*Altmark* reform package of 2005 'to the extent that it clarifies the application of the EU state aid regime' (Boeger and Prosser 2009,

---

[15] See, for instance, Case C-49/07, *MOTOE* [2008] ECR I-4863.

[16] Case C-280/00, *Altmark Trans GmbH and Regierungspräsidium Magdeburg v Nahverkehrsgesellschaft Altmark GmbH* [2003] ECR I-7747.

p. 364). All the same, the liberalisation in the provision of social care services in the UK may mean that competition law now applies to the activities of local authorities in the area. The official OFT position is that local authorities can qualify as 'undertakings'. The position of the LGA is different, and the association maintains that local authorities must not face a situation where competition law would undermine their flexibility as regards different commissioning and delivery models. It remains that the lack of guidance by the central state authorities concerning the impact of EU law has increased the costs for legal advice at local government level, as each individual authority has either to have in-house expertise or to contract legal advice in order to resolve any related issues.

Overall, the effects in the UK of the application of competition law-related EU rules have been relatively limited due to the extensive liberalisation already taking place as a matter of national policy. According to the OFT (2004a, point 1.12), 'due to the extent of deregulation and liberalisation of the economy that has occurred in the United Kingdom, it is unlikely that there will be a significant number of cases in which previous European Commission decisions will be directly relevant when considering whether the exclusion applies in the United Kingdom'. At a general level, Boeger and Prosser (2009, p. 360) comment that even though the EU case law 'has led to some anxiety, especially among local authorities, so far, there have been few areas where concrete legal conflicts have arisen'. In the context of the reform of EU state aid regulation, the Commission revisited the Monti-Kroes package of measures. In this context, the LGA lobbied for social services to be added to the state aid exemptions. Such an amendment, which would be in line with the procurement and legislation and Services Directive, would bring, according to the LGA, greater consistency (LGA interview notes). The new set of rules, named after Competition Commissioner Joaquin Almunia,[17] include now a Commission Decision that extends the *ex ante* compatibility with EU law to a larger range of social services than those covered in the previous package (which only included hospitals and social housing) and reduces and simplifies the threshold that, in general for other kinds of SGEIs, triggers the notification even if the conditions of the Decision are fulfilled (reduced up to a compensation of EUR 15 million per year).[18]

---

[17] See press release of the Commission of 20 December 2011: http://europa.eu/rapid/pressReleasesAction.do?reference=IP/11/1571&format=HTML&aged=0&language=EN&guiLanguage=en (accessed 8 May 2014).

[18] Commission Decision of 20 December on the application of Article 106(2) of the Treaty on the Functioning of the European Union to State aid in the form

13.3 SPECIFIC EXAMPLES

13.3.1 Social Housing

At the end of the 1990s and the beginning of 2000, certain Member States, including the UK, began reporting their systems of funding and state aid for social housing to the Commission. This activity was the result of growing uncertainty about the impact of EU law with respect to state aid and, by reporting, Member States aimed at obtaining the legal certainty required for the development and modernisation of the state aid systems for social housing (Ghékière 2008, p. 275). While there is no evidence of particular concerns about the application of state aid rules in the area of social housing, in its response to the Commission's Consultation on the functioning of the 2005 SGEIs State Aid Package, the UK government stated that case law can be helpful in this area and welcomed the Commission's decisions that send out a clear message that there must be a clear 'social objective'. In this respect, the government made specific reference to the statement made in the *Dutch Housing Associations* case[19] that 'the Commission feels that letting homes to households that are not socially deprived cannot be regarded as a public service'.[20] The UK agrees with this view as 'it balances the needs of Member States to support public services with the need to prevent abuse and maintain a level playing field for competition' (UK Representation to the EU Brussels 2010).

As a result of a move away of local authorities from being direct providers of social housing, new forms of provisions of social housing have emerged. Today, social housing can be provided by the so-called 'arm's-length management organisations' (ALMOs), in which the local authority retains the housing stock but the day-to-day management is transferred to a third party. For the purposes of EU procurement rules, the latter, that is, housing associations, are currently classed as 'bodies governed by public law'. This classification, which was based on a comparison with the French Habitats à Loyers Modérés (HLMs), is rejected by the UK National Housing Federation. Its members believe that this definition is not correct[21] and would like the UK government to

---

of public service compensation granted to certain undertakings entrusted with the operation of services of general economic interest [2012] OJ L7 p. 3.

19 NN 93/02, E 2/2005 and N/642/2009.

20 Paragraph 39 (NN 93/02).

21 The rejection of the classification is based on the argument that the regulator of social housing in England at the time of the Commission's opinion

reopen discussions with the Commission on the status of housing associations. According to the Federation, 'housing associations are more akin to Dutch corporations, private sector bodies which are not subject to EU procurement rules, and should therefore not be considered as public bodies'.

The implications of the implementation of EU Directive 2007/66/EC (the Remedies Directive)[22] have recently created some concern among housing providers as well. The Directive requires the courts to make a declaration of ineffectiveness for any public sector and utility contracts awarded in breach of certain fundamental EU public procurement rules. In contrast to the previous regime, contracting authorities or utilities that have acted in breach of those rules will also be liable to financial penalties. The National Housing Federation stressed that:

> since the implementation of the Remedies Directive last December, housing associations have reported receiving implied threats from suppliers during the tendering process and seen willingness from unsuccessful contractors to challenge the outcome. This has led to more money being spent on legal advice to ensure legal action is avoided. These funds could be better used and injected in improving local neighbourhoods. This could be addressed if there was a restriction on the reasons for challenge. (National Housing Federation, 2011: 11)

The repercussions of the Remedies Directive for social housing providers were also noted by CECODHAS (Comité Européen de Coordination de l'Habitat Social, now Housing Europe) in its 2011 response to the EU policy in public procurement. More particularly, the organisation noted that 'the fear of complaints (via the Remedies Directive) is so extreme in some countries, like in [the] UK, that it deters the production of social housing through more flexible tendering procedures such as the negotiated procedure' (CECODHAS-Housing Europe 2011, p. 3). The increase in challenges of procurement decisions by private companies also means additional costs and time for the local authorities that own the housing stock (Unison interview notes).

---

in 2002 (Housing Corporation) and the current regulator (Tenant Services Authority) did not exercise 'management supervision' as in the case of the French HLMs.

[22] Directive (EC) 2007/66 of the European Parliament and of the Council of 11 December 2007 amending Council Directives 89/665/EEC and 92/13/EEC with regard to improving the effectiveness of review procedures concerning the award of public contracts, [2007] OJ L335.

13.3.2 Social Care

The UK care market comprises local authorities and the voluntary and private sectors on the provider side, and local authorities (on behalf of individuals) and privately contracting consumers on the other. In the context of the previous regime of EU public procurement law, social care was called a Part B service and was in an annex excluded from most of the requirements applicable under the public procurement rules. This exclusion was considered helpful for the LGA as it granted the authority 'a greater degree of flexibility to interact with and form agreements with social service providers' (LGA interview notes). There was some evidence that because Part B services were still expected to comply with the Directive's principles of non-discrimination, equal treatment and transparency, a number of contracting authorities of social and health services used the OJEU process to avoid legal challenge. In response to the Commission's proposals in the *Green Paper on the Modernisation of Public Procurement* (Commission 2011) to abolish the distinction between Part A and Part B services and apply the full extent of the procedural rules to all services, the LGA emphasised the usefulness of the list of exclusions in protecting social care from the full operation of internal market law. The new Public Sector Directive removes the distinction between Part A services (subject to the full range of rules) and Part B services (subject to only limited procedural requirements) and provides a list of 'social and other specific services' in respect of which a 'light touch regime' will apply. Member States are free to choose the applicable national rules for running a 'light touch regime' as long as these ensure compliance with the principles of equal treatment and transparency.

Another area of EU law that influences social care is the rules on state aid. In 2002, the interaction between social services and competition law came to the fore with the case of *BetterCare Group v Director General of Fair Trading*.[23] In this case, Belfast Health and Social Services Trust, North and West ('the Trust'), purchased long-term residential care for the elderly from the private and voluntary sectors (such as BetterCare) on terms substantially lower than the costs it incurred in supplying similar care itself, in-house. No public procurement was undertaken by the Trust. The OFT rejected the complaint on the basis that the Trust was not an undertaking for the purpose of competition law. On appeal of the OFT's

---

[23] Case 1006/2/1/01, *BetterCare Group Limited v Director General of Fair Trading* [2002] CAT 6, [2002] Comp.A.R. 229.

decision in *BetterCare*, the Competition Appeal Tribunal (CAT) decided the Trust had acted as an undertaking, both in the purchasing of services from BetterCare and the direct provision of elderly care by its own statutory homes (in-house). The CAT remitted the complaint to the OFT for investigation and the latter found that the Trust's conduct did not constitute an abuse of a dominant market position as the Trust did not set the prices it paid for care of the elderly.

BetterCare was interpreted by some commentators as suggesting that the activity of purchasing in the market could be sufficient for a public sector body to qualify as an 'undertaking' (Munro 2006, p. 357). According to Pollock (2003, p. 237), private companies could challenge the purchasing power of the NHS and local authorities when using such power as bulk buyers to drive down prices; additional pressure would apply to increase user charges and top-up fees for users since the trusts could be forced to pay higher prices for nursing home care if it were found to be abusing their dominant position in a legal challenge to a public pricing policy; and commercial hospitals and foreign investors would be given a mechanism for challenging the prices paid for secondary and tertiary inpatient care. As Pollock (2003) also reported, private healthcare companies were planning to exploit the decision. For instance, the Federation of Independent Nursing Agencies stated: 'We've been waiting for this decision. The way is now open for the OFT to resolve our complaint that the NHS is unfairly discriminating against private nursing agencies by favouring NHS Professionals, which operate at uneconomic rates' (quoted in Pollock 2003, p. 237).

In a later case before the CJEU,[24] it was found that in examining whether an entity is engaging in economic activity there is no need to dissociate the purchasing activity from the subsequent use to which those purchases are put. Boeger and Prosser suggest that this decision does not overrule *BetterCare*, the reason being that it had not been established

---

[24] Case C-205/03 P (on appeal from Case T-319/99). FENIN is an association of undertakings involved in the marketing of medical goods used in Spanish hospitals. The European Commission (the Commission) had dismissed a complaint by FENIN that various public bodies which were responsible for the management of the Spanish health service (SNS) had abused their position as dominant purchasers of the goods produced by FENIN members. The Commission's grounds for dismissing the complaint were that the public bodies in question did not act as undertakings when they purchased goods from FENIN members.

whether the institutions in question did compete with private organisations, as this fact was not pleaded (Boeger and Prosser 2009, p. 374).[25] In August 2004, the OFT issued a policy note with the intention of clarifying its position. According to the note, the OFT was likely to close cases concerning public bodies that are engaged only in purchasing and not involved in the direct provision of goods or services in the market, on the grounds such bodies are not undertakings for the purpose of the Competition Act 1998. In addition, the OFT was unlikely to take forward cases concerning public bodies which are engaged in a mixture of purchasing and direct provision of goods and services for non-economic purposes (OFT 2004b).

13.4 HEALTHCARE

In the context of the government's intention to overhaul the provision of public services, significant developments have taken place recently that may alter significantly the provision of healthcare services in the future. In July 2010, the Department of Health published a White Paper, *Equity and Excellence: Liberating the NHS*, which set out radical proposals to reform the NHS. Following consultation, the Health and Social Care Bill was introduced in the House of Commons in January 2011. The Bill outlined a number of significant changes, including the creation of an independent NHS Board to allocate resources and provide commissioning guidance, the increase of General Practitioners' powers to commission services on behalf of their patients and the opening up of competition on the basis that care quality could be improved by offering patients more choice. The government proposals were met with strong criticism by a number of actors who concentrated, amongst others, on the risk that the measures may expand the influence of EU law. A contribution to the *British Medical Journal* suggested that 'the reforms further open up the NHS to EU competition law' (Dunbar-Rees and McGough 2011). In a similar vein, Unison argued that the NHS would become increasingly subject to European competition law, 'meaning that instead of devolving responsibility to the local level, government plans will permit the EU a greater say in the way the NHS is organised' (Unison 2011). While the Department of Health's impact assessment on the

---

[25] For a detailed analysis on whether the FENIN decision determines that competition law is not applicable to the NHS, see Cragg (2011) http://38degrees.3cdn.net/63442740413df6b835_clm6ib678.pdf (accessed 28 September 2011).

reforms did not consider the effect of EU competition law, such claims were not rejected by the government. The Health Minister, Simon Burns held that 'as national health service providers develop and begin to compete actively with other NHS providers and private and voluntary providers, UK and EU competition laws will increasingly become applicable'.[26]

In light of strong criticisms, the government set up an independent group, known as the NHS Future Forum, to review the Health and Social Care Bill. The group, which reported its findings to the government in June 2011, made a number of recommendations, including the removal of the provision in the Bill for Monitor (the new sector regulator for health) to 'promote competition' (NHS Future Forum 2011).[27] The Bill received the backing of the majority of the Members of Parliament in its third reading in September 2011 and it was passed by the Lords, with amendments, in March 2012. It finally received Royal Assent on 27 March 2012 and its main provisions came into effect in April 2013. Under the Act, Monitor has a duty only to address anti-competitive behaviour in the provision of healthcare services and not to promote competition, as originally proposed by the Department of Health. However, the introduction of 'any qualified provider' and private sector companies engaging in commercial activities in respect of healthcare services has the potential to make NHS bodies more likely to be considered 'undertakings', and as such subject to competition law. In addition, the Act makes provision for regulations relating to procurement to be made under it[28] and these are to operate alongside the existing procurement legislation, increasing further the risk for confusion in the area of procurement.

---

[26] House of Commons, written answers, 7 March 2011, Simon Burns MP response to Tom Blenkinsop MP.

[27] In response to further criticisms concerning the applicability of domestic and European competition law to the NHS (Cragg 2011), the Department of Health responded: 'We have consistently said that competition law would apply where it applies, with or without this Bill. However, we have also acknowledged that there is legal uncertainty as to when competition law would apply in the NHS due to the absence of relevant case law. We do, however, disagree with the conclusions drawn in the opinion from the *BetterCare* case, namely that it is more likely than not that a Court or Tribunal [...] would now conclude, as in *BetterCare*, that PCTs [Primary Care Trusts] are undertakings for the purposes of competition law' (Department of Health 2011, p. 5).

[28] S75.

13.5 CONCLUSION

The ambiguity surrounding basic concepts in this area of European social policy, such as 'public service', 'service of general interest', 'service of general economic interest' and 'social service of general interest', has been reflected in an increasing number of EU Acts, contributing to the legal uncertainty prevailing in the field. In the absence of a clear operating framework, the risk of recourse to judicial interpretation acts as a hindrance to the achievement of maximum legal certainty. While a number of actors agree on the need to clarify the concepts in question, significant divergence exists concerning the optimal means for doing so. Both the previous and the current UK governments have consistently opposed any attempts to introduce EU legislation in this area. When the 2003 Green Paper on Services of General Interest was issued by the Commission, the UK government stated that it did not believe that the Commission's analysis had established the case for a Community role that would provide greater clarity and greater benefit for Member States and their citizens in the area of SGIs. In the response to the questionnaire distributed by the Commission for its 2006 Communication on Social Services of General Interest, the UK government indicated its preference for 'a more targeted approach – looking at issues known to need addressing (primarily health care in the light of various CJEU judgments) and avoiding issues where the SSGIs dimension is not known to create any appreciable difficulties (e.g. in the UK context, at least, the provision of social housing, or public education services)' (HM Government 2006).[29]

On the other hand, Unison has called for the adoption of a Framework Directive. While the union recognises the limitations of such a measure, it has indicated that it would support such a proposal provided it recognises the need for public services obligations of the providers and respects the diversity existing in different Member States (Unison interview notes). Based on different grounds, LGA is in favour of more alignment between the different areas of EU law that interact with public services. The creation of a more common list of exemptions that apply in the cases of state aid, public procurement and free movement of services would ensure greater consistency and bring legal certainty for the local authorities that are responsible for managing the relevant contracts and grants (LGA interview notes). In contrast, any attempt to adopt a single

---

[29] http://ec.europa.eu/employment_social/social_protection/docs/replies/uk_en.pdf (accessed 28 September 2011).

Directive is considered by the LGA as ineffective on two accounts: first, the landscape of public services is constantly changing and as such it will be difficult for a single measure to be able to reflect such developments; and, secondly, the significant diversity in the definition of the social services in the Member States means that it will be very difficult to reach a conclusion on a single list of such services at EU level.

Any development at EU level will take place against a constantly evolving regulatory framework of SSGIs at domestic level. In the summer of 2011, the UK government published its *White Paper on Open Public Services* (HM Government 2011).[30] The White Paper is based on five principles: increased choice, decentralisation, diversity, fairness and accountability. With respect to diversity, the stated aim is to open up the majority of public services provision, moving away from public sector monopolies to a range of new and innovative providers of different sizes and sectors. It is argued that the delivery of public services can take place by institutions that are voluntary, community, private or new-style public service mutuals, which will all compete to offer a better service and raise standards. The UK government placed this initiative in the context of incentivising the voluntary sector but the proposals, if approved, have the potential to transform a significant part of public services, including SSGIs, and increase the scope for interaction between EU law and UK regulation. Unison is particularly concerned that private companies will move into the newly created markets and has argued for public bodies to deliver public services in-house (Unison interview notes). On a different note, the LGA has considered that diversification of service provision could be beneficial provided third sector groups could succeed in securing such contracts (LGA interview notes).

As a final note, the government's plans on public services were published on the day that private care home company Southern Cross announced it was closing down. The closure of Southern Cross, which was a care home provider, was attributed to the failure of its business model of leasing back homes from landlords. The crisis, which put at risk services for 31,000 residents, sparked concern across government and the social care sector about the risks to service users of private companies delivering care declaring bankruptcy. Aside from the impact of this failure on users, concerns were also voiced for the Southern Cross workforce, particularly after the provider announced 3,000 job losses and

30 The *Financial Times* reported that the White Paper, which was originally due for publication in January 2011, was delayed in the face of opposition from the Liberal Democrats and public concern over the privatisation of health and social care (Parker and Timmins 2011).

changes to working conditions, which unions said would damage the quality of care. The case points to a central issue underlying any discussion on the distribution of competence between the EU and Member States in the area of SSGIs. This is the question of how best to situate the concept of SSGIs in order to uphold citizens' fundamental rights and respect for human dignity. In the absence of such a discussion at EU level, any effort to bring greater legal certainty will be undermined by the discourse framing any initiative in the area.

BIBLIOGRAPHY

Bahle, T. (2008), 'The State and Social Services in Britain, France and Germany since the 1980s: Reform and Growth in a Period of Welfare State Crisis', *European Societies*, **10** (1), 25–47.

Bauby, P. (2013), 'Unity and Diversity of SSGIs in the European Union', in U. Neergaard, E. Szyszczak, J.W. van de Gronden and M. Krajewski (eds), *Social Services of General Interest in the UK*, The Hague: T.M.C. Asser, 25–52.

Bauby, P. and M.M. Similie (2010), *Public Services in the European Union and in the 27 Member States: Statistics, Organisation and Regulation*, Brussels: CEEP.

Boeger, N. (2009), 'Public Service, Autonomy and Community Law', in R. Nickel (ed.), *Patterns of Supranational and Transnational Juridification*, ARENA Report No. 1/09, Oslo: University of Oslo.

Boeger, N. and T. Prosser (2009), 'The Changing Framework of Public Services in Europe: the United Kingdom', in M. Krajewski, U. Neergaard and J. van de Gronden (eds), *The Changing Legal Framework for Services of General Interest in Europe – Between Competition and Solidarity*, The Hague: T.M.C. Asser, 357–382.

CECODHAS-Housing Europe (2011), *Public Procurement Consultation Contribution: Prepared by the Public Procurement Experts of CECODHAS Members*, available at http://www.housingeurope.eu/www.housingeurope.eu/uploads/file_/CECODHAS_publicprocurement.pdf, accessed 28 September 2011.

Commission (2006), *Implementing the Community Lisbon programme: Social services of general interest in the European Union*, COM (2006) 177 final, 26 April.

Commission (2011), *Green Paper on the Modernisation of Public Procurement*, COM (2011) 15 final, 27 January.

Cowan, D.S. and M.A. McDermont (2008), 'Obscuring the Public Function: A Social Housing Case Study', *Current Legal Problems*, **61** (1), 159–89.

Cragg, S. (2011), *Advice in the Matter of the Health and Social Care Bill and the Application of Procurement and Competition Law*, available at http://38degrees.3cdn.net/63442740413df6b835_clm6ib678.pdf, accessed 28 September 2011.

Davies, J. (2013), 'Changes and Challenges in UK Social Services: Social Services of General Interest or "Welfare" Services of General Economic Interest?', in U. Neergaard, E. Szyszczak, J.W. van de Gronden and M. Krajewski (eds), *Social Services of General Interest in the UK*, The Hague: T.M.C. Asser, 513–540.

Department for Business, Innovation and Skills (2009), *Guidance for Business on the Provision of Services Regulations*, London: BIS.

Department of Health (2010), *Equity and Excellence: Liberating the NHS*, London: The Stationery Office.

Department of Health (2011), *Response to Opinion of Stephen Cragg Published by 38 Degrees, on the Application of Procurement and Competition Law to the NHS*, available at http://www.dh.gov.uk/prod_consum_dh/groups/dh_digitalassets/documents/digitalasset/dh_129883.pdf, accessed 28 September 2011.

Dunbar-Rees, R. and R. McGough (2011), 'Challenges of EU Competition Law for General Practice Commissioning', *British Medical Journal*, 342:d2071, available at http://www.bmj.com/content/342/bmj.d2071?rss=1, accessed 8 May 2014.

Finn, D. (2005), '"Contracting-Out" and Contestability: Modernising the British Employment Service', in T. Bredgaard and F. Larsen (eds), *Employment Policy from Different Angles*, Copenhagen: DJOF Publishing, 233–249.

Ghékière, L. (2008), 'Social Housing as a Service of General Interest', in K. Scanlon and C. Whitehead (eds), *Social Housing in Europe II: A Review of Policies and Outcomes*, London: LSE, 271–86.

HM Government (2006), *Social Services of General Interest – UK Response to Questionnaire*, available at http://ec.europa.eu/employment_social/social_protection/docs/replies/uk_en.pdf, accessed 28 September 2011.

HM Government (2011), *Open Public Services: White Paper*, Cm 8145, London: The Stationery Office Limited.

House of Lords (2004), *Services of General Interest*, 29th Report of Session 2003-04, HL Paper 178, London: The Stationery Office Limited.

House of Lords (2005), *Completing the Internal Market in Services*, HL Paper 23, London: The Stationery Office Limited.

House of Lords (2006), *The Services Directive Revisited: Report with Evidence*, HL Paper 215, London: The Stationery Office Limited.

LGA (2011), *EU Green Paper: Modernisation of EU Public Procurement Policy, LG Group Response*, available at http://www.lga.gov.uk/lga/aio/18014039, accessed 28 September 2011.

Munro, C. (2006), 'Competition Law and Public Procurement: Two Sides of the Same Coin?', *Public Procurement Law Review*, **6**, 352–61.

National Housing Federation (2011), *Response to the Commission's Green Paper on the Modernisation of EU Public Procurement Policy towards a More Efficient European Procurement Market and to the Office of Government and Commerce's Policy Note 21/10*, London: National Housing Federation.

NHS Future Forum (2011), *Choice and Competition: Delivering Real Choice*, available at http://www.dh.gov.uk/prod_consum_dh/groups/dh_digitalassets/documents/digitalasset/dh_127541.pdf, accessed 28 September 2011.

OFT (2004a), *Services of General Interest Exclusion*, Competition Law Guideline, London: Office of Fair Trading.

OFT (2004b), *The Competition Act 1998 and Public Bodies*, Policy Note 1/2004, August, London: Office of Fair Trading.

Parker, G. and N. Timmins (2011), 'Public Service Reform Plan on Hold', *Financial Times*, 1 June, available at http://www.ft.com/cms/s/0/efb97dea-8c70-11e0-883f-00144feab49a.html#axzz1O5R1vISU, accessed 28 September 2011.

Penna, S. and M. O'Brien (2006), 'What Price Social and Health Care? Commodities, Competition and Consumers', *Social Work and Society*, **4** (2), 217–31.

Pollock, A. (2003), 'The BetterCare Judgment – A Challenge to Health Care', *British Medical Journal*, **326**, 236–7.

Prosser, T. (2005), *The Limits of Competition Law: Markets and Public Services*, Oxford: Oxford University Press.
Prosser, T. (2010), *The Regulatory Enterprise*, Oxford: Oxford University Press.
Rowles, D. (2006), *At Your Service: A Guide to EU Legislation Affecting Local Authority Services*, LGIB International Report no. 15, London: Local Government International Bureau.
Scanlon, K. (2008), 'Introduction', in K. Scanlon and C. Whitehead (eds), *Social Housing in Europe II: A Review of Policies and Outcomes*, London: LSE, 5–13.
UK Representation to the EU Brussels (2010), *UK Response to the Commission's Consultation on the Functioning of the 2005 SGEI State Aid Package*, available at http://ec.europa.eu/competition/consultations/2010_sgei/submissions/permanent_representation_of_the_united_kingdom_en.pdf, accessed 28 September 2011.
Unison (2011), *Department of Health: NHS Modernisation – Listening Exercise UNISON Response*, May, London: Unison.
Vincent-Jones, P. (2006), *The New Public Contracting: Regulation, Responsiveness, Relationality*, Oxford: Oxford University Press.

14. Social services of general interest in the Czech Republic: Towards poorly regulated markets[1]

Tomáš Sirovátka

In the area of social services, which represent an important pillar of the welfare state, EU governance has resulted in privatization and liberalization due to the impact of 'negative integration' (economic/common market integration), while 'positive integration' (social integration) has always been minimal (compare Barbier 2010, p. 10 and p. 14, or an earlier discussion in Scharpf 1999, 2009). With the accession of the new post-communist member states in 2004, this trend has become even more apparent: considering the more binding character of the economic agenda (Stability and Growth Pact), when compared with the 'social standards', this preference was perceived as a necessity due to the productivity lag behind the EU; for this reason the impact of economic integration has become more profound in these countries than in the other EU states.

The question with which we are dealing in this chapter is how the EU regulations concerning (social) services of general interest – (S)SGI – have influenced the performance of Czech employment services and what the consequences have been for legal and social (in)securities in the labour market. The chapter is divided into three sections. In the next section, we explain which aspects of the EU regulations and laws have been the most influential in the Czech Republic. In the second section, we discuss the developments of employment services and agency employment, and the social consequences in terms of labour market (in)securities. In the last section, we assess the Czech case in a broader European context.

[1] This chapter was written with the support of the Czech Grant Agency (Project no. P404/11/0086) Modernization of the Czech Social Policy.

14.1 THE CZECH REPUBLIC AND EU AGENDAS

The Czech Republic joined the EU in 2004. Before, during and after accession, its relationship to the EU has been ambivalent. One of the leading political parties (Civic Democrats) and the President (who was Prime Minister as the head of this party between 1993 and 1997) have always criticized the EU for intervening too much in national competences and for being 'socialist' and bureaucratic. They have preferred the EU to become a mere 'free market space' and have hoped to influence the future of the EU as such. On the other hand, during the pre-accession stage, and during the implementation of *acquis communautaire*, only pro-European parties were in government: the Social Democratic minority government was tolerated by the Civic Democratic opposition party during 1998–2002, as well as during the coalition of Social Democrats, Christian Democrats and Liberty Union from 2002–2006.

The attitudes of the Czech public are not without contradictions either: although rather pro-European, they are still very much reserved. From 1997 to 2002, the share of citizens supporting the idea of EU membership was between 54 per cent and 59 per cent, while the share of opponents was between 20 per cent and 29 per cent (Centre for Public Opinion Research, Sociological Institute, Czech Academy of Science (CVVM) 2002). In the referendum on membership in June 2003, the participation rate was 55 per cent, with 77 per cent positive votes. The Czech Republic ranked among the countries with lower participation in the referendum from the eight new member states in 2004 (lower turnout was only in Hungary and Slovakia); however, the result of voting was in fact average when compared to the other eight new member states in 2004 (Czech Statistical Office 2009a). On the other hand, the agenda of the 'national interest' raised by the Czech Euro-sceptics and echoed in the media strongly influenced the public as well as policy-makers: only 34 per cent of citizens in 2008 trusted that the decisions of the EU were in the interest of the Czech Republic; 41 per cent did not trust very much; and 17 per cent did not trust at all (CVVM 2008).

During the 1990s, the centre-right coalition strongly emphasized the principle of subsidiarity and protection of national competences against EU influence; sometimes they did not hesitate to compare certain EU regulations to the dictate of the Soviet regime. This position was also motivated by fears of solidaristic principles of the EU. On the other hand, they quickly borrowed the ideas of 'pure market' economy from Thatcher's UK. The economic dimension of integration was strongly supported, while the other aspects (social, ecological) were refused in principle. In contrast, the leading centre-left opposition party (Social Democrats), which were in power in 1998–2006, included in their election programme the ideas of 'The European Social Model' (regardless of the fact that in some respects they also preferred the economic dimension to the social dimension).

Thus the relationship of the key political actors to the EU has become strongly politicized: the actors have always been 'selective' in their approach and adopted those regulations which appeared to support their interests and preferences. This approach expanded the space for manoeuvring for these actors when implementing EU regulations.

Nevertheless, although different in their ideology and programmes concerning the attitude to the EU agendas, both the political right and left have prioritized the economic aspects of integration over the social aspects. The inconsistencies between the more binding EU economic criteria and less binding EU social policy agendas have implied in practice that the requirements placed on the new post-communist member states by the Stabilization and Growth Pact have from the beginning restricted their possibilities to implement the soft 'social agendas' (Ferge and Juhász 2004; Potůček 2004).

The findings by Falkner et al. (2005, 2008) on selected EU directives in labour law in the case of the Czech Republic and other Visegrad countries have documented the deficits regarding the enforcement and application of these directives. Similarly, Sirovátka and Rákoczyová (2009) have shown in their study on the implementation of the 'social OMC' in the Czech Republic that after the initial absorption of the 'European communicative discourse', in practice this agenda has been 'blocked' by the 'legitimacy gap', which has been larger than in any other post-communist Central–East European country. This legitimacy gap is underpinned by shared opinions/stereotypes on the causes of poverty and social exclusion which have been supported in neo-liberal policy discourse. According to the findings by Eurobarometer (2010), the Czech Republic is a country where, according to public opinion, the 'individual causes of poverty' are most emphasized[2] – specific individual causes: laziness 27 per cent (EU average 16 per cent) and being unlucky 19 per cent (EU average 13 per cent). The social causes are perceived to be much less important; specifically: injustice in society, 33 per cent (EU

[2] Indicated by the question: Why in your opinion are there people living in poverty? Options: they are unlucky, because of their laziness, there is injustice in society, or this is an inevitable part of progress.

average 47 per cent) and an inevitable part of progress, 18 per cent (EU average 16 per cent).

We may expect that the influence of the EU non-binding regulations which are promoting social objectives in the field of social services of general interest would be weak in these circumstances, while the spill-over of the economic/market principles through various agendas (including European Court of Justice (ECJ) case law) on social services would be more influential.

14.2 EMPLOYMENT SERVICES AND EMPLOYMENT REGULATIONS IN THE EU NATIONAL AGENDA

14.2.1 Social Services of General Interest as Contradictory EU Agenda

'Social services of general interest' in the EU agenda is full of contradictions: on the one hand, it promotes equal opportunities for all and underpins the principle of solidarity. On the other hand, the legal order of EU governance is essentially grounded in economic principles and 'fundamental freedoms' dating back to the Roma Treaty (Article 90-2) in the field of services of general economic interest ('negative integration'), as expressed in the Bolkenstein Directive from 2004, Directive 2006/123/EC (Directive on Services of the Internal Market) and by some related rulings of the ECJ. This contradiction between the economic and social agendas can be seen as the basis of the general legal uncertainty (Deacon and de Schuter in Barbier 2010). Similarly, legal and social uncertainties are produced in employment: although regulations exist which should guarantee social standards and fair conditions in employment relations, like the Directive on Posted Workers[3] and (more recently) the Directive on Temporary Agency Work,[4] the rulings by the ECJ bring legal uncertainty concerning their validity and diminish their impact.[5]

---

[3] Posting of workers Directive 96/71/EC (PWD).

[4] DIRECTIVE 2008/104/EC OF THE EUROPEAN PARLIAMENT AND OF THE COUNCIL of 19 November 2008 on temporary agency work.

[5] As seen in four recent ECJ cases – *Viking* C-438/05; *Laval* C-341/05; *Rüffert* C-346/06; *Commission in Luxembourg* C-319/06. The ECJ confirmed a hierarchy of norms, with market freedoms highest in the hierarchy, and the fundamental social rights of collective bargaining and action in second place.

14.2.2 Non-owned Notion of Services of General Interest

The definition of (social) services of general interest does not exist in the Czech Republic, nor is the notion of SSGI (or SGI) present in public and policy debate. Potůček et al. (2006) emphasize that the definition of 'social services' has become too narrow in the Czech Republic since the Act on Social Services (Act No. 108/2006 Coll.) defined social services as assistance services to people in dire social situations, typically institutional and non-institutional care for the elderly, handicapped and other disadvantaged groups like the homeless, socially excluded, and so on. This means that for the other types of services, more specific notions have to be used like employment services or childcare services. Thus the umbrella notion of '(social) services of general interest' is used only in communication between the Czech Republic and EU. This Czech understanding of social services corresponds well to the conception of social services termed 'targeted at the most disadvantaged' (see Barbier in chapter 11 of this volume).

One reason for the reluctance to use the notion of 'general interest' or 'public interest' is that this is perceived as inappropriate by the public: similar notions were very often misused by the communist political elites to force through and legalize many unpopular measures which harmed ordinary people. The notion of 'state interest' was used simultaneously with the notion of services of public interest and this made it difficult to distinguish oppression by totalitarian power from the interest of the public. Thus, the communist legacy provides legitimacy to the common neo-liberal arguments in the public debate which directly link 'general interests' to totalitarian state practices. More generally, the notions of solidarity and social justice have been discredited; instead the ideals of the individual freedom of citizens, which they had previously been denied, have been prioritized (e.g. Offe 1996; Ferge 1997; Saxonberg and Sirovátka 2009). However, it is still widely recognized that *some* of the 'social services' are definitely necessary and linked to the role of the state (although after 1989 its role has been diminishing), but rather targeted to the 'social poor'.[6]

---

[6] For example, data from the Eurobarometer 2010 clearly show that the Czech public strongly emphasize responsibility for social services by public (national or local) authorities, similar to the EU average.

14.2.3 Contradictory National Position towards the EU Directive on SGI

The low legitimacy of the notion 'general/public interest' implied the ambiguous position of the Czech Republic to the Directive on SGI. In 2004 the Czech government stressed the specific relevance of the category of services of general interest in the fields of social services and healthcare and that a separate framework was needed for these types of services (Ministry of Labour and Social Affairs (MLSA) Position 2004, in Potůček et al. 2006, p. 5). Furthermore, they stressed that a prevailing majority of social services are of a non-economic character and suggested that a substantive policy debate be carried out.

In contrast, a different official proposal of the service directive has also been the subject of the official view of the Czech government as formulated by the Ministry of Trade and Industry (responsible for this agenda); this was closer to the original EC proposal than to the EP proposal. This position preferred the broadest spectrum of services possible to be included in the Directive, thus easing cross-border provision of services and the administrative burden associated with the sending out of the labour force. In line with the above standpoint, the Czech Republic headed with the Netherlands at the Vienna Summit in March 2006 a meeting of 16 governments which did not see the EP declaration as inevitably final and tried to change the path of development. However, the attempt failed and Czech Prime Minister Jiri Paroubek (Social Democratic Party) endorsed the version of the EP. The inconsistency of the standpoints of the Czech political representatives may be assessed as an expression of the implicit controversy of the SGI agenda in the EU, as well as a legitimacy gap concerning the social agenda in the Czech Republic.

14.2.4 Developments in Employment Services after 2004

Employment services may serve as a good illustration of the influence of EU regulations and policies in social services of general interest for several reasons. First, due to the circumstances described in the previous sections, EU influence is not very visible at the level of implementation (a rather formal transposition took place, as explained by Falkner et al. 2008) in most areas of social services. Nevertheless, in the field of employment services, we have observed a stronger effect due to the synergy of several EU agendas: the European Employment Strategy and European Social Fund (ESF) resources available to various domestic actors; directives in labour law (Posted Workers Directive, Agency Work

Directive and other employment legislation); the Directive on SGI; and, lastly, the rulings of the ECJ with respect to all the directives mentioned above.

The impact of the EU Directive on social services of general interest itself in employment services is not easy to identify. Nevertheless, we have noticed an indirect influence through several channels: first, through the formal EU accession process and related transposition of the EU legislation (hard and soft law); secondly, through the cognitive effect and institutional learning of the policies in the other EU countries; and thirdly, through changing the overall policymaking environment due to the effects of the legislative and programme documents, their communication, transposition and implementation. This climate seems to have become more 'liberal' even in areas that traditionally had high responsibility of the welfare state accompanied with a strong trend towards marketization.

The Czech Republic is a low spender in the field of social services: expenditure on social benefits in kind (excluding healthcare) is among the lowest in the EU (0.8 per cent of GDP in 2010; see Eurostat 2012); as is expenditure on active labour market policies (0.23 per cent when Public Employment Service (PES) administration is included, it amounted to 0.39 per cent of GDP in 2010; Eurostat 2012).

District Employment Offices, which implement labour market policies, have always contracted out retraining programmes to educational institutions, including private ones. Due to accession to the EU (2004), the ESF resources available and the management rules of the ESF projects have led to the massive outsourcing/marketization of whole packages of active labour market policies, while, surprisingly, the scope of the programmes available has decreased. In 2009 the number of participants in the active labour market policy measures dropped below the 2008 level (from 26 per cent to 19 per cent of the unemployment stock). This trend continued in 2010–2012, when, in spite of the crisis, the national measures were cut to 22 per cent, 19 cent and finally 10 per cent, respectively.[7]

The marketized measures failed to bring better tailored services, better quality or better targeting. Instead, they have been assessed by leading staff of employment services as too expensive (the price of similar services provided by employment offices themselves when compared

---

[7] Source of the data is the web portal of the Czech Ministry of Labour and Social Affairs, http://portal.mpsv.cz/sz/politikazamest/trh_prace/ (accessed 15 September 2013), own computations.

with services by private providers is most often only half, sometimes even three to five times lower),[8] without better results due to typical market failures like the emergence of non-competitive markets and non-binding contracts due to the weak role of the public bodies responsible (for more details see Sirovátka and Winkler 2011). From 2011 'shared mediation' has been stipulated in legislation, that is, outsourcing of job-mediation from PES to private agencies. This measure, however, does not work in practice: the remuneration is 5,000 CZK (about 20 EUR) per person under the condition that 60 per cent of the clients obtain at least a temporary contract, plus remuneration for each permanent contract (1,250 CZK) and a further bonus (500 CZK) if the placement lasts longer than six months. From the perspective of private providers, such remuneration seems low and difficult to achieve considering the difficulties in finding job placements for these applicants in the open labour market.

14.2.5 Privatization in Job Mediation and Agency Work

Private job mediation (by employment agencies) was also allowed from the early 1990s (Employment Act of 1991). After the new Employment Act (2004) was adopted to harmonize national legislation with the EU, 'agency employment' was enabled (following the example of other EU countries), allowing the number of private agencies to rapidly increase. This precipitated, among other things, the import of cheaper labour from Slovakia, Poland and third countries (Ukraine, Russia, Vietnam, Mongolia, etc.).

In the Czech Republic many labour laws are not respected in practice, or are by-passed somehow (compare Falkner et al. 2008). Večerník (2009, pp. 33–4) refers to practices like informal payment (common in the catering sector), whereby the official low (minimum) wage is supplemented with 'pocket money'; subcontracting workers who have business licences in order to avoid payroll tax and labour contract requirements; and hiring foreigners (typically Ukrainians) for very low wages and in substandard working conditions (quite often on illegal contracts). Agency employment of foreigners (partly illegal, partly at non-standard working conditions) represents a specific form of the violation of labour laws. Data (Czech Statistical Office 2009b) show that between 2004 and mid-2008 (i.e. before the financial crisis), the official number of foreigners living (i.e. with at least a three-month residence

---

[8] Interviews by the author at Employment Offices (July 2010).

permit) in the country increased from 256,000 to 410,000 (about 4 per cent of the population); most of them come from Ukraine, Slovakia, Vietnam, Russia and Poland as cheap labour.[9] Moreover, many foreigners are working and/or living illegally in the country: expert estimates range from 40,000 to over 200,000 (Drbohlav and Lachmanová 2007, p. 14). Furthermore, Czech legislation is extremely liberal in approving self-employment or business licences for foreigners. For this reason many work agencies have been established which import labour forces from third countries but are not obliged to respect the domestic employment conditions (i.e. to the level of domestic workers). Lastly, foreign, and in some cases also domestic, employment agencies by-pass the legislation by establishing employment relationships on the grounds of 'co-operatives': the members of co-operatives are allowed to perform work which is not covered by labour contract or labour law.

The decisions of the ECJ certainly contribute to this poorly regulated market environment in which the employment practices of agency work have developed in the Czech Republic, at least with respect to those workers coming from EU countries (relevant for Slovak, Polish and other workers from new member states). Kavanová (2008) calls attention to the ETUC reaction to the ECJ judgment in the *Laval* case (C 341/05): 'the judgment confirms the ECJ's narrow interpretation of the Posting Directive in the Laval case and ignores the Public Procurement Directive 2004, which explicitly allows for social clauses'. She also points out that in 2007 the leading company in the automotive industry, Škoda Auto (owned by the VolksWagen group), employed workers from Poland under more disadvantaged conditions than those of Czech workers. Only after the Inspectorate of Labour and the Ombudsman's Office took an interest in this case did the company put things right. However, according to Kavanová, if the company had turned to the ECJ, the situation for Polish workers could have worsened, since the company would have been supported in its practice by the ECJ decision.

The number of foreign workers dropped during 2009 (the period of the main impact of the crisis) from 362,000 to 284,500 employees. Concerning the labour force from third countries, after the wave of dismissals in January 2010 there were still nearly 70,000 workers in the Czech Republic, mostly Ukrainians (44,000).[10] In 2011 there were 217,800

[9] See http://www.czso.cz/csu/cizinci.nsf/kapitola/ciz_pocet_cizincu (accessed 10 May 2012).

[10] See http://www.czso.cz/csu/cizinci.nsf/kapitola/ciz_zamestnanost (accessed 10 May 2012).

foreigners with work permits and 93,000 entrepreneurs (mainly from Ukraine, Slovakia, Poland and Vietnam) – their numbers seemed to have stabilized.

Consequently, the government was pushed in 2009 to launch a new programme of support for immigrants in order to enable them to return home (i.e. to provide them with an airline ticket plus a lump sum of 500 EUR, later 300 EUR). Nevertheless, returning to their home country was hardly possible, since many of the workers had had to corrupt the local mediators in their home country to make it possible for them to get the job in the Czech Republic; this got the workers into huge debt (and it was presupposed that the debt would be paid back from the expected earnings). In order to prevent the acceleration of such problems, the government adopted an amendment to the Employment Act in January 2011, which obliged the work agencies to be insured in case of bankruptcy.

14.2.6 Ineffective State Regulation

Incorrect approaches by employers and illegal practices in hiring foreign workers are not effectively countered by the state administration. The situation of non-EU migrants is complicated in several respects. During the 2008–2009 economic crisis, immigrants were the first to be laid off. According to a survey in the automobile industry, the number of agency workers dropped from 9,900 in June 2008 to about 5,800 in June 2009 (i.e. 60 per cent of the original number).[11]

From 2005 only Labour Inspectorates could check the working conditions of agency workers. Employment Offices could check whether the agency had received a permit to act and whether it fulfilled the obligations to provide information about its activities.[12] The Labour Inspectorates, which have the key responsibility, have proven to be ineffective. For example, the Ombudsman's Office criticized the Labour Inspectorate when it found that there were legal violations made by an employer of Mongolian workers; the Labour Inspectorate was satisfied with the formal announcement by the employer and did not adequately check to see that the actual state of things had improved (Veřejný ochránce práv 2009, pp. 39–40). Due to many similar findings, the

---

[11] See http://www.dnoviny.cz/dopravni-politika/prumysl-ocekava-do-cervna-propusteni-13-552-pracovniku-3909 (accessed 8 November 2009).

[12] This was changed in 2012 when Labour Inspectorates were made responsible for controlling agency work.

Ombudsman's Office initiated an examination of the Labour Inspectorates in 2008 concerning their checks on agency work which appeared as only formal and were ineffective.

The Report by the Government Office of the Labour Inspectorate (Státní úřad inspekce práce 2010) documents only 74 violations of the law in 2009 by employment agencies; interestingly the number of checked cases was evidently much lower than the number of law violations! For example, the report from the Central-Bohemian Region – Prague (the capital) refers to about eight checks and 24 violations; the report from the South-Moravian Region – Brno (the second largest city in the country) mentions 17 checks and 14 violations (own computations based on data in the report). This indicates that each of the scarce controls identified at least one violation of the law on average, or more. This fact did not, however, convince the responsible authorities to increase the intensity of the controls: the obstacle was the low personnel capacity of the responsible bodies and the lack of political commitment.

Similar to the Labour Inspectorates, the Labour/Employment Offices have been unable to eliminate the illegal and semi-legal practices of employment agencies. Although the agencies were obliged to provide statistical data on the number of placed workers to the MLSA (Employment Offices), about 400 agencies from a total of 2,150 (1,078 of them could employ foreigners) did not fulfil this elementary duty in 2008. The report by the MLSA for 2008 (MLSA 2009) said that the illegal employment of foreigners was the most frequent and most serious violation of the law identified in 346 cases/organizations. According to the report, this number represented only the 'tip of the iceberg': a substantial part of these violations were initiated by 'work agencies' in the form of temporary postings of workers to other legal or physical entities. According to the report, the battle against this phenomenon requires above all a sufficient number of staff-controllers capable of conducting the administrative proceedings.

From January 2009, it has been stipulated in the law that if agencies ignore their formal duties repeatedly, the MLSA is obliged to cancel their licence. The Employment Offices checked 674 agencies in 2009 and imposed 153 penalties (however, this amounted to a total of only some 22 million CZK/0.9 million EUR) (MLSA 2010a, 2010b). The most frequent violation of law was again the illegal employment of foreigners (MLSA 2010c): there were 1,898 checks of employers of agency workers performed and the findings showed that 401 of them employed foreign workers illegally (this is about 20 per cent!). Furthermore, in 68 per cent of cases of the checked employment agencies, other violations of the law were identified. In spite of this, the problem did not diminish in the following years so fast. In 2011 the Labour Inspectorate conducted 522 inspections of agency work in co-operation with the Employment Office, which showed 346 violations by 173 employers, that is, 33 per cent of employers controlled (Státní úřad inspekce práce 2012); however, only 13 sanctions were imposed. Similarly, in 2012 (Státní úřad inspekce práce 2013), 155 inspections were conducted which showed 236 violations of law by 76 employers (49 per cent) and only 17 sanctions were imposed. Since 2012, the control of illegal work in general has been prioritized by the government and harsher sanctions on employers applied.[13] In this year 25,392 controls were conducted which discovered 1,716 employers who employed 4,705 workers illegally, nearly two thousand of them foreigners. Thus only 7 per cent of employers (from the total number of those who were controlled) employed illegally, which is less than was formerly found in the case of the employment agencies: possibly it is the threat effect of the increased number of the controls and harsher sanctions. Nevertheless, a question remains about the effectiveness of the controls in discovering violations of law.

14.2.7 The Crisis and Aggravation of the Problems: Emerging Labour Market Insecurities

Illegal work or work in non-standard conditions of the foreign labour force brings about two negative effects in terms of labour market insecurities. First, the immigrant workforce is exposed to the risks of an insecure work contract, low and insecure pay, substandard working and living conditions, and lack of social and health protection.

The situation of agency workers has been researched in two qualitative studies on the case of Vietnamese agency workers (Hofírek and Nekorjak 2009; Krebs 2009). A common problem (described by more than 60 per cent of those interviewed) concerning wages was that most of the time, they did not get all the components of the wages that they were supposed to get, like bonuses for overtime work, different supplements to wages and sick pay (Krebs 2009). With respect to their working conditions (non-standard working time, often shift work), they are an isolated group. Often, because the workers themselves are highly flexible in accepting any wage and working conditions, it is impossible to identify when and where their rights are violated (Hofírek and Nekorjak 2009).

---

13 In particular, a minimum level of the penalty on employers who employ illegally has been set (at the level of about 10,000 EUR) and the controls of illegal work have intensified.

Secondly, the domestic labour force is threatened due to the social dumping of cheap labour from the third or other EU countries; they are more insecure in contract and pay as well. It is interesting that during the 2009–2010 crisis, Czech workers were open to proposals by employers to misuse the institute of 'non-colliding employment' in large numbers: in fact they were shifted in this way into the position of temporary, precarious workers who received unemployment benefits plus half the minimum wage from the employer, as well as some pocket money from the employer for some of them.[14]

14.3 CONCLUSIONS

The attitude of the Czech Republic to the EU agendas before, during and after accession has been in favour of economic integration, while social aspects of integration have been rather neglected. Irrespective of what the Directive on the provision of services on the internal market stipulates, the general trends in the Czech Republic are apparently towards the marketization of social services and the diminished role of public bodies.

In employment policy, massive outsourcing was made possible by the extensive use of ESF-financed projects in active labour market policies. Poor regulation implied market failures and inefficiency in the implementation of the measures. Another trend was the increasing role of private agencies in job mediation. Negative market externalities emerged in the form of widespread unregulated social dumping (agency work), which helps employers discipline the domestic labour force.

The Directive on SGI did not bring much factual change to these trends. Nevertheless, the key political actors are ready to purposefully use any arguments provided by EU regulations as strategic resources in order to improve their position: the EU regulations and policies are becoming highly politicized in the domestic arena.

To conclude, in the Czech case the role of the EU seems to be rather hidden; nevertheless, the lack of a clear definition of social services of general interest and regulations on their role as well as the decisions of the ECJ concerning the Directive on Posted Workers contribute to the uncertainties and negative externalities emerging from the poorly regulated performance of private actors in employment services, including agency work. Furthermore, the rulings of the ECJ in favour of the

---

[14] In 2009 about 130,000 unemployed (i.e. more than two per cent of the labour force) participated in this form of employment (analysis on primary data by Public Employment Offices).

liberalization and marketization of social services could become more influential in the future (as well as the Directive on SGI) at a later stage of development, if the social services and protection standards become more effectively enforced. This has not, however, been the case so far.

REFERENCES

Barbier, J.-C. (2010), 'Stratégie de Lisbon: les promesses socials non tenues', Paris, *Documents de Travail du Centre d'Économie de la Sorbonne/CES working papers*, No. 18.

CVVM (2002), *Actual Attitudes of the Public to the Accession to the EU*, Prague: CVVM, press release. Available at http://www.cvvm.cas.cz/upl/zpravy/100017s_PM20402.doc (accessed 18 June 2012).

CVVM (2008), *The Czechs on Membership of the Czech Republic in the EU*, Prague: CVVM, press release. Available at http://www.cvvm.cas.cz/upl/zpravy/100017s_PM20402.doc (accessed 18 June 2012).

Czech Statistical Office (2009a), *Referenda on Accession to the EU and Statistics*. Available at http://www.czso.cz/csu/redakce.nsf/i/vysledky_referend_a_statistika/$File/referenda.pdf (accessed 18 June 2012).

Czech Statistical Office (2009b), *Cizinci v České republice 2008*, Praha: ČSÚ.

Drbohlav, D. and L. Lachmanová (2007), *Irregular Economic Activities of Migrants in the Czech Republic (a Delphi Study about Adaptations in a Globalising Economy)*. Available at http://www. natur.cuni.cz/ksgrrsek/illegal.htm (accessed 12 December 2011).

Eurobarometer (2010), *Poverty and Social Exclusion: Special Eurobarometer.* EB 72.1. Brussels: Eurobarometer TNS Opinion & Social. Available at http://www.bing.com/search?q=Eurobarometer%20(2010)%2c%20Special%20Eurobarometer%20on%20Poverty%20and%20social%20exclusion%2c%20EB%2072.1&FORM=LEMBLB&PC=MALC&QS=n (accessed 28 December 2013).

Eurostat (2012), *Statistical Database*. Available at http://epp.eurostat.ec.europa.eu/portal/page/portal/statistics/themes (accessed 28 November 2012).

Falkner, G., O. Treib, M. Hartlapp and S. Leiber (2005), *Complying with Europe: EU Harmonization and Soft Law in the Member States*. New York: Cambridge University Press.

Falkner, G., O. Treib and E. Holzleithner (2008), *Compliance in the Enlarged European Union: Living Rights or Dead Letters?* Aldershot, Burlington: Ashgate.

Ferge, Z. (1997), 'The Changed Welfare Paradigm: The Individualization of the Social', *Social Policy and Administration*, **31** (1), 20–44.

Ferge, Z. and G. Juhász (2004), 'Accession and Social Policy: The Case of Hungary', *Journal of European Social Policy*, **14** (3), 233–52.

Hofírek. O. and M. Nekorjak (2009), *Vietnamští imigranti v českých velkoměstech – Integrace přistěhovalců z Vietnamu*. Research report. Brno: Masarykova universita.

Kavanová, K. (2008), *Kontroverzní rozhodnutí Evropského soudního dvora týkající se minimálních mezd zahraničních pracovníků*. Prague: Multikulturní centrum.

Krebs, M. (2009), *Analýza procesu agenturního zaměstnávání Vietnamců a Vietnamek v ČR*. Prague: La Strada, O.P.S.

MLSA (2009), *Informace o výsledcích kontrolní činnosti úřadů práce v roce 2008.* Prague: MLSA.

MLSA (2010a), 'More than 230 Thousand Foreigners are Working Legally in the Czech Republic', press release. Available at http://www.mpsv.cz/cs/8228 (accessed 15 July 2012).

MLSA (2010b), 'The Most Frequent Violation of Law was Illegal Employment of Foreigners', press release. Available at http://www.mpsv.cz/cs/8228 (accessed 15 July 2012).

MLSA (2010c), 'Nearly One From Four Work Agencies has Violated Law in 2009', press release. Available at http://www.mpsv.cz/cs/8228 (accessed 15 July 2012).

Offe, C. (1996), *Modernity and the State: East, West*. Cambridge: Polity Press.

Potůček, M. (2004), 'Accession and Social Policy: The Case of the Czech Republic', *Journal of European Social Policy*, **14** (3), 253–66.

Potůček, M., P. Hanulová and P. Kopecká (2006), *Study on Social and Health Services of General Interest in the Czech Republic*. Unpublished country report prepared for the Study on Social and Health Services of General Interest in the European Union, by M. Huber, M. Maucher and B. Sak, prepared for DG Employment, Social Affairs and Equal Opportunities, DG EMPL/E/4, VC/2006/0131.

Saxonberg, S. and T. Sirovátka (2009), 'Neo-liberalism by Decay? The Evolution of the Czech Welfare State', *Social Policy and Administration*, **43** (2), 186–203.

Scharpf, F.W. (1999), *Governing in Europe: Effective and Democratic?* Oxford: Oxford University Press.

Scharpf, F.W. (2009), 'Legitimacy in the Multilevel European Polity', *MPIfG Working Paper 09/1*.

Sirovátka, T. and M. Rákoczyová (2009), 'The Impact of the EU Social Inclusion Strategy: the Czech Case', in A. Cerami and P. Vanhuysse (eds), *Post-Communist Welfare Pathways: Theorizing Social Policy Transformations in Central and Eastern Europe*. Basingstoke: Palgrave Macmillan, pp. 240–59.

Sirovátka, T. and J. Winkler (2011), 'Governance of Activation Policies in the Czech Republic', in R. van Berkel, W. de Graaf and T. Sirovátka (eds), *The Governance of Welfare States in Europe*. Houndmills, Basingstoke: Palgrave Macmillan, pp. 173–94.

Státní úřad inspekce práce (2010), *Zpráva o činnosti Státního úřadu bezpečnosti práce za rok 2009*. Opava: SÚIP. Available at http://www.suip.cz/rocni-zpravy/ (accessed 12 June 2012).

Státní úřad inspekce práce (2012), *Zpráva o činnosti Státního úřadu bezpečnosti práce za rok 2011*. Opava: SÚIP. Available at http://www.suip.cz/rocni-zpravy/ (accessed 12 September 2012).

Státní úřad inspekce práce (2013), *Zpráva o činnosti Státního úřadu bezpečnosti práce za rok 2012*. Opava: SÚIP. Available at http://www.suip.cz/rocni-zpravy/ (accessed 9 July 2013).

Večerník, J. (2009), *Czech Society in the 2000s: A Report on Socio-economic Policies and Structures*. Prague: Academia.

Veřejný ochránce práv (2009), *Souhrnná zpráva o činnosti veřejného ochránce práv za rok 2008*. Brno: Veřejný ochránce práv/Ombudsman. Available at http://www.ochrance.cz/zpravy-o-cinnosti/zpravy-pro-poslaneckou-snemovnu (accessed 8 February 2012).

Veřejný ochránce práv (2010), *Souhrnná zpráva o činnosti veřejného ochránce práv za rok 2009*. Brno: Veřejný ochránce práv/Ombudsman. Available at http://www.ochrance.cz/zpravy-o-cinnosti/zpravy-pro-poslaneckou-snemovnu (accessed 8 February 2012).

15. Social services of general interest in France: The uncertain impact of the increasing reach of EU law

Jean-Claude Barbier

15.1 INTRODUCTION

'Social services of general (economic) interest' (SSGIs) provide an interesting case for studying the influence of EU law on social protection systems (see chapters 11 to 14 in this volume). A sociological inquiry into this matter discovers a situation of uncertainty among actors in France.[1] This uncertainty is legal, not in the strict sense legal scholars attach to the concept, but in the sense of a perception by social actors of the uncertain legal context to which they have to adapt to continue to manage and provide social services they had been traditionally delivering until the beginning of the 2000s. Traditional actors – mainly associations in relation to public funders – are destabilized, whereas some private newcomers appreciate the avenues opened to them by what they see as opportunities (Barbier and Colomb 2012). In this chapter, we proceed in four steps. The next section sets the situation of what one can call the 'social services sector' (SSS) in France. These services are funded by public resources, either central state or the local authorities to a large extent. In the key sectors, such as home care, long-term care, childcare, social housing and employment services, the *mouvement associatif* has long been the key provider. The situation started to change from the 1990s, however, but unequally according to types of service. In section

[1] The methodology of the study has involved a long-term round of interviews; dating back before the start of the GUSTO project some pertain to participant observation conducted in the 1990s that prepared the ground for 2006–2011 interviews with social actors (around 25 interviews). Material was also collected during two seminars, one with French actors of social services policies, and one with legal scholars.

15.3 we address the problem of an uneasy cohabitation of concepts, namely the historic *services publics* and SSGIs. In section 15.4, we describe the gradual transformation of the sector and its partial 'economization', which dates much further back than the 'arrival' of EU law; this leads to stressing the factors of transformation that make it relatively autonomous in a multilevel governance context. The next section is devoted to a rapid focus on two key sub-sectors of the SSS: childcare and long-term care for elderly persons. The uncertain influence of EU law on social services is finally assessed in the conclusion of the chapter.

15.2 FRENCH ASSOCIATIONS AS KEY ACTORS FOR SOCIAL SERVICES

In the French SSS, the role of *associations* is essential (not very dissimilarly to their German counterparts, despite very different modes of organization and regulation). Associations are private not-for-profit organizations that engage in an immense variety of activities. Their common legal basis is the 1901 Act (for non-lucrative/non-profit legal persons). In the last 20 years an on-going debate has been active within the world of associations with regard to what are their genuine and relevant 'specificities'. A former president of UNIOPSS,[2] François Bloch-Lainé, inquired about what he called their *specific merits* (*spécificités méritoires*), their special *raison d'être*, in the view of their members, with comparison with alternative providers of services.[3] The question was raised in particular because in their majority associations have mostly become 'delegates' of the state as providers of services upon its commission. In the social sector, their economic role and their contribution as employers are very significant. Their share of the economy is generally placed under the label *économie sociale* (or third sector,[4] now often referred to as *économie sociale et solidaire*). An international debate about the identification of various forms of economy has been going on for a long time now, and it has a strong echo in France (Laville 2010). As the present debates about what is a 'social enterprise' or a 'social business' illustrate at the EU level, one of the key problems

---

[2] UNIOPSS is the big umbrella organization of the social and healthcare sector.

[3] His article '*Perfectionner le pacte associatif*' was published in *RECMA*, 1996.

[4] See the concept used in *Insee Première*, March 2011, 'Le tiers secteur', from which the figures quoted are drawn.

of the 'social economy' envisaged as a functional cross-national concept is the immense variation of organization it takes across member states. In France, it is generally estimated that *économie sociale* accounts for 6 to 7 per cent of the GDP (including *mutuelles*[5] and cooperatives), of which 3 per cent from associations only. Ten per cent of the French workforce is employed in the social economy (associations, *mutuelles* and cooperatives). A double uncertainty follows from European diversity: it pertains both to the boundaries of the sector, heterogeneous across national frontiers, and the list of social services involved. From many points of view, this uncertainty is fundamental in the European Union, as we will see, and it explains at least part of the legal uncertainty that social actors experience. While welcomed by many actors, the Commission's new decision in December 2011 concerning state aid rules did not solve this uncertainty.[6]

Excluding *mutuelles* (chiefly active in the healthcare sector) the not-for-profit sector employed 1.45 million persons in 2008, before the financial crisis. Accounting for about 2.9 per cent of GDP, its essential part is in the social and so-called *médico-social* sector (60 per cent of the entire share of associations). This sector is the central potential target for EU regulation of SSGIs. Focussing on '*économie sociale*', the French statistical institute (INSEE) calculated (December 2008) that in health and social services (*santé humaine* and *action sociale*) *économie sociale* accounted for 16 per cent of employment in the sector. For the provision of care for young children and services for the elderly, we will give further information in section 15.5, as these two types of service have been at the forefront of the discussion in France (Thierry 2009). In *services à la personne* ('personal services'), cross-cutting important new legislation was enacted from 2005 (Borloo Act, see later), which boosted the development of the private sector's share. Statistics, however, are often tricky to analyse. The ministry for employment calculates the

---

5 *Mutuelles* are voluntary associations (not very different from mutual (or friendly societies) that have managed social insurance funds since the 19th century). After the Second World War, they mainly became entities managing complementary social insurance, on a professional/occupational basis. Insurance *mutuelles* are also important. The new *Code de la mutualité* (1992, 2001) has integrated EU law rules. For a number of years a project for a special European statute for *mutuelles* has been discussed (*mutual insurance*). *Cooperatives* are especially active in France in the banking industry.

6 A list of services is provided by the Commission decision of 20 December 2011, under its recital 11.

number of hours of work in the sector:[7] provision by private firms amounted to about 30 million hours in 2008, out of a total amount of 800 million hours (DARES 2010). The area where the increase of the commercial share has been the highest is *aide à domicile* (home/domiciliary care): there, the share of associations has decreased from 93 per cent to 65 per cent for the number of institutions from 2001 to 2010, and from 96 to 77 per cent of employees (CNAR 2011). With respect to employment, training and 'insertion'[8] services, the role of associations is also very important and caters for many recipients of services (Balmary 2004). In social housing, the situation has tended to be treated separately because of the specific organization of housing societies. France's share of 'social housing', as usually defined by professional housing organizations, is at a medium level in the European Union, according to the profession's international statistics used by Huber et al. (2006). These statistics, however, provide only a first-aid comparison.[9]

The range of social services potentially concerned by EU legislation is ill defined, in the official texts of the Commission. It is thus difficult to provide a picture fully comparable with other member states. In the context of the French official transposition of the 2006 Services Directive, the – apparently exhaustive – scope of social services affected in France was listed in Thierry (2009, pp. 7–8) on the basis of the legal source that determined the way such services were authorized, managed and funded.[10] While no clear definitions exist in EU law, it is all the more difficult to implement cross-country comparisons: this methodological

---

[7] The sector does not exactly fit the definition of 'social services' by the Commission in its 2007 Communication.

[8] '*Insertion*' is generally translated as similar to 'integration'; this is however an oversimplification. Insertion policies cannot only be considered as catering for 'excluded persons' (it is different from, for instance, the 'integration of disadvantaged people', a term used in Huber et al. 2006).

[9] The share of 'social housing' in France, as defined by CECODHAS Housing Europe, was at 19 per cent in 2005 (cf. 35 per cent in the Netherlands; 20 per cent in the Czech Republic and 21 per cent in the UK). However, figures published are to be taken with much precaution, especially with regard to new member states. Figures updated in 2011 give 17 per cent for France (2010) and 17 per cent 'municipal flats' in the Czech Republic. See www.housingeurope.eu (accessed 1 January 2015).

[10] This approach basically encompasses six different legal regimes, among which the most important concern '*services sociaux et médico-sociaux*', where the mainstream text is the 2 January 2002 Act; legal regimes for crèches and institutions dealing with young children and childcare services, including preschool services; and housing and employment services.

hurdle could not be entirely circumvented by Huber et al. (2006). The French report corresponding to their project was written by Petrella and her colleagues (2006) and was focussed on childcare, 'social integration and reintegration' and long-term care. All in all, despite a number of reforms implemented from the early 2000s, associations have remained a key player in the delivery of social services and their views can be seen as capturing essential representations of the 'public' side of the world of social services. On the other hand, the share of the for-profit sector is increasing at a quick rate.

15.3 SSGIS AND THE LONG-TERM TRADITION OF *SERVICES PUBLICS* IN FRANCE

In France, as polls keep showing, opinion is largely biased in favour of strong public services. Although not strictly in a causal manner, this situation may be linked to the existence of a strong legal tradition in France (Moderne and Marcou 2001; Guinard 2009, p. 73; Denoix de St Marc 1996),[11] a tradition which is not only symbolic. However, a 'clash' of legislation (national and European) with respect to public services is certainly not specific to France. In recent surveys the question was asked about the negative EU influence on public services[12] (EB Flash 230, May 2009). Only 93 per cent expressed an opinion, and those who strongly disagreed were 24 per cent. Those who disagreed somewhat were 26 per cent and those who agreed were 43 per cent (14 per cent strongly). In national surveys, the popular support for '*services publics*' has been explicit for decades. One such recent survey (TNS Sofres, September 2008) found that 80 per cent of the French public were satisfied (9 per cent very satisfied, 71 per cent somewhat satisfied) with the quality of

---

[11] '*Service public: les mêmes mots désignent, en France, des missions très diverses. Ils s'appliquent tant au cœur de l'action de l'État, justice ou sécurité, qu'à l'éducation nationale, à la protection sociale ou aux services publics industriels et commerciaux. Bien plus que d'autres pays, la France prête à cet ensemble d'activités une grande cohérence, au point de les rassembler sous un concept unique. Plus que d'autres, les Français associent service public et secteur public, alors même qu'une partie des activités dont il s'agit, comme la distribution d'eau ou la propreté, sont assurées par des entreprises privées. Les Français sont profondément attachés à l'idée de service public, et lui accordent une place centrale dans leurs représentations collectives*' (Denoix de St Marc 1996, p. 13).

[12] The question was: '*La construction européenne représente-t-elle une menace pour nos services publics*?'.

services publics in the country. This went up to 88 per cent for employees in the public sector. Figures had increased compared with a similar survey in September 2006. In the same survey, interviewees were puzzled to answer a question about the influence of the EU on '*le processus de modernisation de l'État français*': one-third said that there was no influence; 41 per cent thought that it increased 'modernization' and 22 per cent that it slowed it. Moreover, despite interpretations according to which the notion of SSGI is likely to be equivalent to the former domestic denomination of social services, especially in the 'old' member states, the preference of voters and citizens for trusting some services to the public remains.[13] Important actors in the EU policy keep on using the term 'public service' symbolically: this is the case for the European Parliament 'intergroup' but also for the ETUC.[14] Some francophone quarters also actively mobilize in favour of their support.[15]

15.4 THE DIVERSIFICATION AND ECONOMIZATION OF SOCIAL SERVICES

It would certainly be wrong to ascribe EU law the only role in triggering profound changes in the provision of social services across the EU over the last 30 years. The French case shows that a much more complex set of factors have played their role.

15.4.1 Failed Attempts at Forming an Advocacy Coalition in Favour of Positive Integration

According to P. Herzog, a former French MEP who was *rapporteur* for the European Parliament in 2003, French high-level officials were aware from 1993 on of the importance of potential legal difficulties for France. Nevertheless, even at this rather late stage in EU integration, the topic of 'social services' remained marginal. Some in the French associations sector reflected over the matter early but their awareness did not translate

---

[13] EB 355 (December 2010) (74.1) confirms the previous 2009 figures, where more than 80 per cent think these services should be provided by the public (at national or regional level).

[14] See for instance its 'social progress Protocol' at http://www.etuc.org/a/5175; and its resolution on public services in 2010: http://www.etuc.org/speeches/workers%E2%80%99-rights-and-economic-freedoms#.VKV3JXtc4_M (accessed 1 January 2015).

[15] See www.ssig-fr.org website (accessed 1 January 2015).

into much mobilization, information and understanding of issues until 2009, when the process of transposition of the 2006 Services Directive was eventually completed in France. Originating in the cooperative banking sector[16] and the associative movement, a group of experts had met from the early 1990s to the early 2000s and endeavoured to enlighten the elites of the time in the non-profit sector.[17] At the time, these activities were cross-national although they failed to achieve sufficiently common conceptions to organize significant cross-national and EU-level lobbying. Because associations are organized on the basis of their national political institutions, legislation and cultures, like unions, they are confronted with similar obstacles on the way to cross-border cooperation, contrary to business organizations.

As we documented more precisely in our interviews with German and French social actors, easy cooperation is hindered by many factors, especially language. While Belgium is close to France, Germany and France occupy an especially important position in the area of 'social services' but have very different political cultures and institutions in this area. Apart from these three countries, other 'old' member states have changed their traditional approaches over the last years.[18] When the first discussions about the influence of EU legislation upon the way social services were delivered and managed in member states started, France and Germany would have been 'natural candidates' for the promotion of a special legal status, special political attention, and so on, to be ascribed to social services. This accounted for why bottom-up cooperation was effectively started in the late 1990s. Working groups were formed, including UNIOPSS, the umbrella organization of the French, and its counterpart in the German BAGFW, the influential federation of *Wohlfahrt* associations. CEDAG[19] (*Comité européen des associations d'intérêt général*) was formed in 1989 and fought for a broader recognition of the specificity of associations. A 'roundtable' of associations (European roundtable of charitable welfare associations) was later formed, which was to be dissolved only in 2006, according to our

---

16 The sector controls a considerable amount of deposits in France (estimated at 60 per cent of French deposits).

17 *Cahiers de l'UNIOPSS*, no. 5, 1993 established that associations were subject to EU law in matters of competition for their economic activities. It explicitly discussed the consequences of public procurement rules.

18 See the case of Scandinavia with increased privatization and outsourcing in the name of 'choice' of users/consumers; and the case of the UK (Koukiadaki, chapter 13 in this volume).

19 Now called the European Council for Non-Profit Organizations.

interviewees. The roundtable, which grouped representatives from Germany, France, Portugal and Finland, participated in the 2002 European Convention. These people at the time wished social services not to be considered under the scope of social services of general economic interest and the future Directive on services. CEDAG and the roundtable also fought especially to limit the scope of the future 2006 Service Directive.[20] When the roundtable was later dissolved, actors involved in it became active in the 'Social Platform', an umbrella group promoted by the European Commission. So, why did this long-term endeavour never achieve its common goals? The explanation pertains to the diversity of institutions and political cultures and the uneven paths of reform that member states experienced across time. As our interviews demonstrate, the introduction of *Pflegeversicherung* in Germany in 1995 changed the ways of funding associations and opened up the possibility of competition, especially through the introduction of the 'triangular' model (state/provider/customer or user) which allowed providers, including from the private sector, to compete with one another. At the particular time, views and doctrines were very different in France, which prevented further agreement between the two federations of associations. From our interviews, we also learn that in the run-up to the adoption of the 2006 Services Directive, the German lobbies were especially active in order to secure a special legal status for members of the BAGFW[21] (the exemption of charitable associations in article 2.2.j (*von allgemeinem Interesse*) of the Services Directive). As no corresponding situation existed in France, cooperation eventually failed. One can see this failed attempt at building an advocacy coalition with common goals as another illustration of the asymmetry between negative and positive integration. Language questions are also precisely linked to the institutions of each country and have been another obstacle to working together. French and German

[20] A common declaration was signed by CEDAG and the roundtable on 12 January 2006. This said, inter alia, 'Therefore, as non-profit service provider associations, we believe that the current proposals do not do justice to our demands and concerns. The proposals do not take into account the specific features of these services which refer to their missions (i.e. taking care of the common good; implementation of fundamental rights; be a part of social protection systems; ensuring social cohesion; taking care of vulnerable people for social services), but instead inappropriately mainstreams them – while putting in place some exemptions – including them with broad commercial services.'

[21] BAGFW (*Bundesarbeitsgemeinschaft der Freien Wohlfahrtspflege*).

actors have a different approach, for instance, with regard to subsidiarity and the strategic uses of it.[22]

15.4.2 A Long-Term Economization Trend

In France as elsewhere, over a long period since the early 1980s, more and more activities performed by associations have been qualified as 'economic'. This process of '*economization*' can in no way be related only to the influence of EU law.[23] It has a much longer history and this should not come as a surprise. In the second half of the 1980s, the French administration started to implement new accounting practices and obligations both in the public and the non-profit sector. For a long time associations performed *activités économiques* that were taxed.[24] On the basis of this trend, actors in the association movement became gradually aware that refusing the label 'economic' was certainly not going to be considered legitimate in the future. Such a refusal was even less credible after some actors in the associative movement elected the label '*économie sociale*' (or '*économie sociale et solidaire*') as their own. Today, this leaves open the possibility of distinguishing between various forms of 'economy' (Laville 2010). Market economy is but one of these forms. 'Social economy', as a rough equivalent, has long been used by certain groups of actors in the social sector and beyond. Recently, the Commission has started to use this concept as part of its EU 2020 strategy.[25] As a consequence, actors interviewed in the associative sector now tend to consider that fighting over the refusal of the label '*activités économiques*' would be a rearguard move. However, although they are fully accepting of the economic character of their activity, they claim (1) that such activity cannot be assimilated to mainstream economic activity (i.e. market), and (2) that this specificity is denied by EU legislation. Actors especially challenge the idea that as economic actors they should be

---

[22] There are of course many conceptions of *Subsidiarität* but its original meaning lies in the German Catholic doctrine.

[23] The characters of an economic activity have since been defined precisely by EU case law. Any activity consisting in offering goods and/or services on a given market is an economic activity. In this context, the fact that the activity concerned may be qualified as 'social' is not relevant.

[24] One reason for extending such rules and specifications to associations was also the government's legitimate suspicion that many associations were not genuine non-profit associations.

[25] This is part of the EU 2020 'platform against poverty and social exclusion': 'Working in partnership and harnessing the potential of the social economy'.

treated in a similar manner as mainstream 'undertakings', for example operators of large-scale public transport or post office networks, in all three domains where EU legislation applies (state aid, competition and public procurement).

15.4.3 Autonomy of National Reform: The 2002 and 2005 Acts

Interviews show that the main drivers for change in the area of social services in France are national-specific. Despite minority initiatives, awareness among the (non-profit and public) stakeholders of social services remained very limited until very recently. Interviews lead us to note the lack of a proper encompassing and explicit political strategy on the part of successive governments. These important challenges tended to be treated on an ad hoc basis (as, for instance, the employment services regulation).[26] Without such a strategy, French governments tended to see the growing influence of EU law as an opportunity to foster reforms, and especially to promote the fresh supply of services (by way of incentives to users, easing regulations and promoting private provision). In the world of associations, on the other hand, awareness was still limited in 2010 as to the possible consequences of an increasing reach of EU law. Two important legal milestones in the evolution of social services in France were the 2002 and 2005 Acts. The former[27] reformed the functioning of *établissements* (institutions for children or for the old and the disabled) and introduced new procedures for authorization and evaluation. Hence, more than with changes happening at the time in EU legislation, French stakeholders were affected by these domestic transformations. The Act reformed the rights of users and also saw the first reform of funding by the *Caisse nationale des allocations familiales* for childcare, which favoured the funding of private units, and was to be generalized in 2005 (Petrella et al. 2006, p. 24). As Petrella and her colleagues (2006, p. 76) have shown, the 2005 Borloo Act was also a key

[26] Two interviews in 2011 with former high-level managers in the employment service (two different organizations) show that the behaviour of the top levels in these organizations was often opportunistic. Another interview in 2012 showed that top-level officials went so far as dismissing the possibility of application of EU law to their area of policy. This observation is consistent with Gerda Falkner and colleagues' (2005) assessment of 'limited compliance' in France.

[27] Loi no. 2002-2 of 2 January 2002 reforming the principal pillar of the French legislation on institutions in the social and healthcare system (loi no. 75-535 of 30 June 1975).

change. A National Agency (*Agence nationale des services à la personne*) was created and was put in charge of promoting the development of personal services. Aimed at supporting the creation of service enterprises, platforms of services were opened in order to foster partnerships between the non-profit and for-profit sectors. A voucher, CESU (*Chèque Emploi Service Universel*) was introduced, thus contributing to a new increase in employment in the sector, by relaxing administrative obligations for employers. Finally, in January 2010 the government enacted a new regulation (*Circulaire du 18 janvier 2010 relative aux conventions d'objectifs et simplification des démarches relatives aux procédures d'agrément*). Given the debate about the transposition of the Service Directive during the previous six months of 2009, this decision appeased some of the worries of associations as to the durability of their state commissioning, because it formalized new 'pluri-annual' conventions. Indeed, the main official justification for the regulation was the 'security of partnerships between associations and the state administration, especially in the context of the changing European legislation'.

15.4.4 Uncertainty and the Government's Strategic Choices for the Transposition

When transposition came on the agenda, the French government was anxious not to start an open public debate about social services. It had learnt from the disastrous campaign about the project for the Constitutional Treaty. As noted above, its main objective was fostering additional private supply for childcare and long-term care for the elderly. Hence it chose to proceed by identifying the social services concerned in French law in a piecemeal way (Thierry 2009). On the other hand, no specific French legal category was exactly relevant to the notion of '*association caritative reconnue*'.[28] Neither did the government pick up the possibility of exempting all long-term care for the elderly and childcare from the reach of the Directive. It reviewed all sectors potentially covered by the Directive bar social housing.[29] At the last moment in 2009, the opposition (Socialist Party) presented an alternative '*proposition de loi*' in Parliament that was defeated. When transposition was completed, uncertainty was thus significantly increased for associations with regard to two

---

28 There was no legal category known as '*association caritative reconnue*' corresponding to that mentioned in the Services Directive (article 2.2.j).

29 Social housing, even before the 20 December 2011 Commission decision had, like hospitals, a special status (see Koukiadaki, chapter 13, and Sol and van der Vos, chapter 12 in this volume).

topics: the quality and security of the services delivered, and their sustainability, because of the legal provisions to which childcare and personal services were now more explicitly submitted. What was also remarked by many stakeholders was that the government refused to adopt specific regulations with regard to the rules applying to local authorities, especially concerning the procedure of 'mandating' in the sense of article 2.2.j. This led to pending problems on the side of the funding of services and to various initiatives taken by the lobby SSIG-FR (www.ssig-fr.org) (promoting template documents for inviting local authorities to decide about mandating providers). Yet, bar citizens, the two main actors concerned in France by the question of SSGI are associations and local authorities. As for associations, three main areas of uncertainty remain: the implementation of the Services Directive and the promotion of the free establishment of service providers; the implementation of public procurement rules; and the implementation of 'state aid' rules.

On the first count, uncertainty is especially alleged about the level of quality and the continuity of the provision of services. Interviewees admitted that there were certainly examples of low-quality provision under the previous legal rules, but they doubted that free competition would automatically lead to better effectiveness and efficiency, in areas where personal links were essential in the service relationship and where persons could not be seen as only consumers (or perhaps not consumers at all). On the second count, sensibility to threats exercised by the systematic implementation of tenders is high. Levels for thresholds were recently modified in 2011–2012 (see Koukiadaki, chapter 13 in this volume). Nevertheless, associations tend to think that funding authorities use tendering as a device to destabilize the sector and they fear for the sustainable provision of services.[30] On the third count, which probably raises the more important short-term problems, associations did not understand why rules similar to those applied to big monopolies or network industries like the post office should apply to them. Secondly, in the sector, state aid may appear under many guises. Moreover, many think that this will be impossible to implement. It will be a long time before changes in the legislation introduced from December 2011, when this chapter was being written, can be assessed: traditional actors, however, aired their satisfaction at seeing that at least some of their long-standing legal demands had been heeded.

---

[30] This assessment was made notably in the light of the conclusions of the GUSTO October 2010 Dissemination seminar. See www.gusto-project.eu/index.php?option=com_content&view=article&id=241:seminar-141010-synthesis&catid=44:wp5&Itemid=61 (accessed 1 January 2015).

15.5 CHILDCARE AND LONG-TERM CARE FOR THE ELDERLY IN INCREASED COMPETITION

Our study has further explored two sub-sectors: childcare and long-term care for the elderly. Both are mainly provided by associations and funded by different levels of government and social security funds (branches of *sécurité sociale*, jointly administered by social partners). Both are mentioned in article 2.2.j of the Services Directive. After mentioning data related to an earlier French report (Petrella et al. 2006), we will conclude with the main trends in both sectors.

15.5.1 Childcare

Whereas childcare services are largely regulated at state level, *départements* (*Conseils Généraux*) and municipalities are the central players for the development and monitoring of the supply of places for children. The provision of services was opened up to private providers, including for-profit enterprises from 2003 onwards. Tax credits were introduced for enterprises in 2004 and even, for a short time, privileged subsidies for private childcare firms. Globally, the share of places controlled by private enterprises has nevertheless remained rather limited; but, according to our interviewees, this share is rapidly growing. Statistics[31] published by the ministry of social affairs showed that 63 per cent of children were cared for during the week by their parents (67 per cent of the time by their mothers and 33 per cent by both parents or their father). Only a minority of children had access to collective or individual care. Eighteen per cent were cared for by *assistantes maternelles agréées* (individual childminders, an equivalent of 769,000 places), and 10 per cent were in 'collective' care (essentially *crèches*). Four per cent were cared for by their grandparents. Although the number of childminders grew rapidly in the 1990s, the share of collective and individual childcare has not changed significantly since 2004. The number of places offered in the various types of crèche (and similar institutions) grew from 309,000 (2004) to 343,000 in 2008. These figures explain why governments have been so anxious to foster the supply of new places in crèches and the services offered by *assistantes maternelles*. One expert interviewed estimated the shortage of places in 2011 at between 200,000 and 400,000 places. In a situation where traditional arrangements still prevailed, EU

[31] For 2008, see *Études et Résultats* no. 678 (February 2009) and no. 715 (February 2010), DREES, ministry of social affairs.

law as such potentially applied to a minority of childcare provision. According to our interviews, there were 5,800 places in commercial crèches at the end of 2008 but 14,000 at the beginning of 2010, as private actors aimed for an objective of 17,500 places. If 14,000 was the actual figure in 2010, this accounted for less than 5 per cent of the supply of collective childcare.[32] 'Collective' crèches are organized mainly by public and non-profit organizations and public organizations remain the main providers of crèches. In 2003, 80 per cent of crèches were provided by a public organization (68 per cent of them by a municipality and 12 per cent by a *département* authority). In 2008, the corresponding figures were 62 per cent and 11 per cent, as 19 per cent of collective crèches were administered by associations and 8 per cent by other institutions. A major structural reform of funding, the *Prestation de Service Unique*, was generalized in January 2005. The first element of the reform concerned the nature of services. Crèches could now provide both full-time and part-time care, and were called *multi-accueil* structures. Services were supposed to fill their crèches with occasional care as soon as hours of vacancy were available. The second element of the reform was a modification of the funding mechanism by the *Caisses d'allocations familiales*.

Collective services have to meet the quality requirements stipulated in the decree of August 2000 and are controlled by the *protection maternelle et infantile* administration. Once childcare services meet these, they are eligible to public subsidies of different forms. After accreditation, each institution is supposed to be monitored on a regular basis by the local authority (*département*). Quality requirements are much lower for childminders, however. The lack of adequate control was a major issue for their development at the time of the Huber report (Petrella et al. 2006), a fact confirmed by our interviewees. Their question was, what exactly is a 'quality supply' of childcare services? The gradual introduction of market mechanisms began in the early 2000s, as municipalities started to implement tendering procedures systematically. This is certainly one of the major issues of concern, we learn from our interviewees in the non-profit sector, and the indirect influence of EU law has certainly been at work in this matter. The tax credit for private firms and the voucher system are also market mechanisms.

---

[32] One of our interviewees explained that three big firms control three-quarters of the total commercial supply (from 45 crèches in 2006 to more than ten times that in 2011).

15.5.2 Old Age Long-term Care

In the area of old age long-term care, the diversification of services has also been very significant over the 2000s. For the early 2000s, Petrella and her colleagues reported statistics showing that the non-profit sector controlled 51 per cent of the capacity, the public 42 per cent and the commercial sector 7 per cent, and noted that these proportions were stable.[33] Since then, figures have changed significantly:[34] in 2008, corresponding shares were, respectively, 54 per cent, 28 per cent and 17 per cent. Four years later, our interviewees in the ministry estimated that the private share was more than 20 per cent in 2011. Hence, given the prospect of increasing needs with population ageing, a considerable market for private for-profit services was building up. From 2003 to 2007, comparative rates of increase in the number of places show a maximum +17 per cent for commercial *maisons de retraite*, while corresponding rates for the public (+6 per cent) and the non-profit (+7 per cent) sector were much lower. On the other hand, the number of places – which was small in commercial *logements-foyers* – had considerably decreased over the same period (–38 per cent) as against a mean –7 per cent overall. As comparable statistics in other countries show, it is probably in the elderly care sector that the main issues of application of EU law are to be met in the future (see also Koukiadaki, chapter 13 in this volume). Commercial services for home care in France are still at relatively low shares. It is not surprising, then, to listen to interviewees in the non-profit sector who are concerned about issues of quality. The question directly links up to issues of staff training, wages and human resources practices, as well as interpersonal relationships established by the carers with the elderly persons. Because our inquiry was incomplete, we did not have time to explore data concerning the evolution of quality: while evaluation procedures were deemed to be the rule since the application of the 2002 Act already mentioned, our correspondents in the ministry of social affairs reported that they were actually missing significant comparative data, even after the creation in 2007 of ANESM (*Agence nationale de l'évaluation et de la qualité des établissements sociaux et medico-sociaux*). At the same time, new legislation was

---

[33] Petrella et al. (2006), p. 78, for the two main types of institutions, called in French *maisons de retraite* and *logements-foyers*.

[34] Figures are taken from *Études et Résultats* no. 689 (May 2009) and no. 699 (August 2009), ministry of social affairs.

introduced in 2005 with the Borloo Act which made agreement/authorization procedures more flexible for home care only (Petrella et al. 2006).

15.6 CONCLUSIONS

As we have seen in this case study, three guiding challenges remain in the French SSS: the link between service supply and employment creation, a sector where jobs are generally of lower quality; uncertainty about the monitoring of the quality of services; and, thirdly, the diversification of actors in the sector. A fourth, the impact of the introduction of market mechanisms, was our central concern in the present case study. Because of its modest scope, it is however difficult to draw decisive conclusions from our study as to the *direct links* between the increased reach of EU law (public procurement, free movement of services and state aid) and the evolution in the sector, even for those sub-sectors we were able to look at more closely. One can easily assume that, through the spread of new public management techniques in the social economy or third sector (as is documented elsewhere), new practices have gradually and increasingly affected the provision of social services. Interviewees are unanimous in reporting that local authorities are using public procurement techniques more and more, in order to protect themselves against legal uncertainty; their rationale is also driven by the reduction of costs, bearing on collective wage agreements, and their wish to develop supply, a situation especially reinforced in the context of the crisis that started in 2008. What our survey mainly documents, then, is the present link between (1) the legal uncertainty of concepts used in EU law and, to a large extent, their 'foreignness' (Barbier and Colomb, chapter 1 in this volume) and (2) a destabilization of previous references and traditions that is spreading among the majority of actors. Commercial actors are still marginal in childcare services but we are told that they are eagerly adapting to a varying scope of services, more flexible and more linked to flexible family practices, gaining an edge in terms of costs. Commercial actors in the long-term care sector are thriving in the *maisons de retraites* area: important financial groups with cross-national links[35] are emerging. Employment (its quality, the amount of training, the sustainability of

[35] The group Korian was mentioned to us by interviewees in the French ministry of social affairs, who pointed out that high-level civil servants formerly in the French administration of social services were now the main executive officers of a successful cross-border corporation.

collective agreements) is a key aspect of the quality of the service. Overall, CJEU case-law has not been especially favourable to employment quality in the years since the *Viking*, *Rüffert* and *Laval* cases, not to mention the case *Commission versus Germany* (2009).

The very quality of the service delivered to old or disabled people and to children, not to mention vulnerable people looking for employment or for housing, is at the core of anxious interrogations by our interviewees. On one side, we have the radical legal doctrine implemented by the judges in Luxembourg, whereby more competition is deemed to automatically yield more efficient and better services. On the other hand, whether in childcare or in long-term care provision, the actors we meet have very little evaluative evidence about this quality. The anxiety about the future of service quality, as well as the sustainability and continuity of services, is perhaps overstated by those stakeholders who are directly challenged in their traditional practices: in this, we witness the typical consequences of negative integration. As two German interviewees, we may assume that more competition will provide better availability of services in France, especially in long-term care, as is apparently already the case in Germany after the 1995 reforms. But this is certainly not the common view of the stakeholders we met in France. Additionally, reforms and changes are still probably too recent in the country for researchers to fully document this crucial question of the *quality of services*. Attention to the concerns of non-profit actors was central in the preparation of the 2013 Bill organizing a new framework for what is called in France *Économie sociale et solidaire* (*ESS*). As the present chapter is being revised, this Bill is being finally approved by the French parliament. The final 2014 Act (*Loi sur l'économie sociale et solidaire*) tries at the same time to support the legitimacy and the specificity of the social economy, thus responding to many of the uncertainties reviewed here, and to consolidate the emerging participation of 'social enterprises'. The latter are actively promoted by the recent initiatives of the EU Commission but future developments in this regard are difficult to predict.

REFERENCES

Balmary, D. (2004), *Politique de l'emploi et recours aux opérateurs externes*, Paris: Conseil national de l'évaluation et Commissariat général du Plan (rapporteurs C. Chevrier-Fatôme et B. Simonin), La Documentation française.

Barbier, J.-C. (2008), *La longue marche vers l'Europe sociale*, Paris: PUF.

Barbier, J.-C. and F. Colomb (2012), 'EU law as *Janus bifrons*: A sociological approach to "Social Europe"', in Jean-Claude Barbier (ed.), EU Law, Governance and Social Policy, *European Integration online Papers (EIoP)*, Special Mini-Issue 1, Vol. 16, Article 2. Available at http://eiop.or.at/eiop/texte/2012-002a.htm. Accessed 29 May 2014.

Bloch-Lainé, F. (1996), 'Perfectionner le pacte associative', *RECMA: Revue internationale de l'économie sociale*, no. 262.

CNAR Uniopss (2011), 'La place des associations du secteur privé sanitaire et social', December.

DARES (2010), *Analyses, Les services à la personne*, April 2010, no. 020 and no. 089, December, Ministry of Social Affairs.

Denoix de St Marc, R. (1996), *Rapport au Premier ministre, Le service public*, Paris: La documentation française.

Driguez, L. (2010), 'Les institutions de protection sociale face au droit de la concurrence: confirmations ou inflexions?', *Revue de droit sanitaire et social*, 6, November–December, 1048–59.

Falkner, G., O. Treib, M. Hartlapp and S. Leiber (2005), *Complying with Europe: EU Harmonization and Soft Law in the Member States*, Cambridge: Cambridge University Press.

Guinard, D. (2009), 'Réflexions sur la construction d'une notion juridique: l'exemple de la notion de Services d'intérêt général', PhD thesis, Université Paris-Sud XI, Faculté Jean Monnet.

Huber, M., M. Maucher and B. Sak (2006), *Study on Social and Health Services of General Interest in the European Union*, Final Synthesis Report, report for DG Employment Social Affairs and Equal Opportunities.

Laville, J.-L. (2010), *Politique de l'association*, Paris: Seuil, Économie humaine.

Moderne, F. and G. Marcou (eds) (2001), *L'idée de service public dans les Droits de l'Union européenne*, Paris: L'Harmattan.

Petrella, F., J. Priou and N. Richez-Battesti (2006), *France, Country Study* (for Huber et al. 2006), 103 pages, mimeo.

Thierry, M. (2009), *Mission relative à la prise en compte des spécificités des services d'intérêt général dans la transposition de la Directive 'services' et dans l'application de la législation européenne sur les aides d'État*, Paris: Documentation française.

Index